Managing Indirect Spend

Managing Indirect Spend

Enhancing Profitability through Strategic Sourcing

JOE PAYNE AND WILLIAM R. DORN, Jr.

WILEY

John Wiley & Sons, Inc.

Published by John Wiley & Sons, Inc., Hoboken, New Jersey.
Published simultaneously in Canada.

For general information on our other products and services or for technical support, please contact our Customer Care Department within the United States at (800) 762-2974, outside the United States at (317) 572-3993 or fax (317) 572-4002.

Wiley also publishes its books in a variety of electronic formats. Some content that appears in print may not be available in electronic books. For more information about Wiley products, visit our web site at www.wiley.com.

Library of Congress Cataloging-in-Publication Data:

Payne, Joseph.
  Managing indirect spend : enhancing profitability through strategic sourcing / Joseph Payne and William R. Dorn.
    p. cm. — (Wiley corporate F & A series)
  Includes index.
  ISBN 978-0-470-88688-5 (cloth); ISBN 978-1-118-13145-9 (ebk);
  ISBN 978-1-118-13146-6 (ebk); ISBN 978-1-118-13154-1 (ebk)
  1. Industrial procurement--Management. 2. Business logistics. 3. Strategic planning.
  4. Purchasing. I. Dorn, William R. II. Title.
  HD39.5.P39 2012
   658.7′2—dc23

                                                                    2011016569

Printed in the United States of America

10 9 8 7 6 5 4 3 2 1

This book is dedicated to Abraham Podolak and Steven Belli. Without your perseverance, vision, and enthusiasm, these pages would surely not have been written. Your joint leadership, guidance, and compassion have built a unique company that stands apart, and we are excited to see what is in store for us next as we all continue to grow our professional and personal relationships.

Contents

Preface

MANY LARGE ORGANIZATIONS, whether publicly traded services companies with no procurement department, large industrial manufacturers that allow each plant to purchase independently without leveraging volumes, or healthcare providers that have relied on their group purchasing organization to effectively manage budgets for them, still do not know how to achieve substantial cost savings on all of the "stuff" they buy. The people burdened with these tasks often do not know where to begin. It is for these beleaguered souls that this book has been written.

In our experience, resources for these types of companies are sorely lacking. Many consulting firms and analysts pitch sourcing optimization and a variety of other buzzwords with which they seek to replace the term *strategic sourcing*. For some reason, people have begun to associate strategic sourcing with the standard three-bids-and-award process that most companies have been using for decades. They all believe they are sourcing strategically, therefore management does not see the need to provide the proper people, technology, time, and training to effectively manage spend and look for cost-reduction opportunities. Industry analysts and other experts are already looking to identify the next big thing—calling strategic sourcing irrelevant, outdated, or ineffective—while their customers continue to struggle with getting their arms around the basics of what it means to source strategically.

WHAT THIS BOOK WILL DO FOR YOU

Whether you are an executive, procurement professional, or any individual concerned with reducing spend and strengthening your supply chain, this book will provide you with the knowledge and necessary tools to successfully reduce costs in the area of indirect spend. The processes and real-world examples in this book are based on more than 20 years of consulting experience and successful implementation of cost reduction strategies for clients of all sizes, in just about every industry and in hundreds of spend categories.

Specifically, this book provides you with:

- An overview of the challenges faced when sourcing indirect spend categories
- An overview of the strategic sourcing process
- Tools that can help drive savings
- Examples based on real-world experience
- A how-to guide that will walk you through specific sourcing engagements and provide the information needed to source effectively

This book focuses on specifics instead of theory and will detail how to actually get started, run through the process, and implement cost savings across a wide variety of indirect spend categories. It also details the most important aspects of strategic sourcing that many other books overlook: the use of creativity when performing research; how to identify leverage points during negotiations; and, most importantly, effectively dealing with people, both externally and within your own organization.

 ## WHO WE ARE

Recently, the procurement profession and supply chain industry as a whole have received more focus than ever before. In fact, procurement and supply chain professionals are now regularly covered in mainstream media publications and are even quoted on cable news channels. Because of this sudden new awareness of our profession, there is no shortage of consulting firms jumping on the bandwagon and offering strategic sourcing services. However, these firms typically employ the same standard tactics that companies have been using for years, while trying to rebrand their services under the labels of optimization, next practices, and a variety of other buzzwords to make their organizations sound more impressive.

We—the primary authors of this book—were utilizing strategic sourcing techniques long before they were well known. Our team consists of experienced supply chain consultants from Source One Management Services who have led and managed thousands of strategic sourcing initiatives for mid-market and Fortune 500 customers. We are successful in producing savings in over 97 percent of all of the initiatives we have tackled. Over the course of our work we have seen what companies do right, and more importantly, what companies do wrong, and in many cases, fail to do at all.

Both of us are hands-on practice managers who work day to day to provide oversight in every project area, develop sourcing strategies, perform negotiations, and assist in the development and implementation of best practices. Together, we have produced an average 18 percent savings in every category we have sourced, in areas ranging from the chemicals used to clean power transmission plants to satellite Internet service for rural state parks.

We also pulled in some key members of our practice to assist in writing specific commodity content for this book. David Pastore, Kathleen Daly, Jennifer Ulrich, and Scott Decker are project managers at Source One, overseeing the day-to-day activities on projects such as telecommunications, office supplies, facilities services, and shipping, to name a few.

Source One was founded in 1992, predating the current trends and making it one of the oldest providers in the industry. Source One is not just another one of the many consulting firms out there that decided to capitalize on a hot market. In fact, unlike most other firms that offer strategic sourcing consulting services as one of many offerings, strategic sourcing is the only thing that Source One does. Our entire staff is dedicated to one purpose—strategic sourcing.

Source One gained industry notoriety in 2005 when it released the WhyAbe.com website. WhyAbe.com shook up the marketplace, as it was at the time, and still is, the only completely free electronic sourcing toolset available in the world. Other providers charge hundreds or even thousands of dollars for basic RFP and reverse auction tools. Source One decided to give them away for free. In 2008, the WhyAbe.com tools were recognized by Gartner, Inc. as a "Cool Vendor in Procurement and Finance," and finally gained acceptance from the naysayers who criticized the tools for not being sustainable without charging buyers or suppliers. Ultimately, this free service forced other vendors to lower pricing, change their revenue models, and rush to join the software-as-a-service provider marketplace.

In January of 2008, Source One launched its own blog, the Strategic Sourceror (www.StrategicSourceror.com). "Sourceror" is a play on the words sourcing and sorcerer, because the savings we produce are often referred to as magic by our customers. The blog was originally developed to fill a gap in the industry, as most blogs in the space mainly talk about software or provide reviews of vendors. The Strategic Sourceror provides an outlet for the Source One staff to demonstrate their knowledge of particular spend categories, discuss industry best practices, and even provide the occasional rant or commentary on a hot news item. In mid-2010, the Strategic Sourceror added supply chain and procurement news to its lineup and has rapidly become one of the most-read publications in the industry. All of the contributors to this book are also contributors to the Strategic Sourceror.

 HOW THIS BOOK IS ORGANIZED

The book is broken into four sections: Process, Tools, Examples from the Field, and How to Do It.

Part One: The Process

Part One of this book provides you with a detailed, step-by-step account of the typical sourcing process, outlining the steps with which most sourcing professionals are already familiar, including: data collection and spend analysis, research, the RFx process, negotiations, contracting, implementation, and continuous improvement. Each step of the process is covered as a separate chapter in this section, providing an explanation of the goal of that step in the process, a high level overview of the tools needed to reach the goal, and the people involved. Each chapter also provides an in-depth account of how to work with people, both inside and outside your organization, to achieve results.

Part One concludes with a chapter on "What Not to Do," specifically focusing on our years of hands-on experience seeing the mistakes other procurement professionals have made in the past (and continue to make), and offering lessons to help you avoid similar pitfalls. Some of the lessons learned we discuss include sending spam RFPs, creating overly complicated sourcing documents, allowing a supplier to write the RFP for you, and not engaging the right stakeholders within an organization.

Part Two: The Tools

Part Two of this book provides an overview and analysis of the resources and technologies that can help the professional source more effectively. The first chapter in this section defines market intelligence (MI) and its importance as a primary tool in the strategic sourcing process, while also providing a distinction between static and dynamic MI, and how to use each. It continues by describing types of static and dynamic market intelligence, including industry publications and commodity reports, group purchasing organizations, online tools, and consultants.

The second chapter in this section focuses on the technologies and software tools that are available in the marketplace. It explains the advantages and disadvantages of using software tools and sheds light on some of the best-kept secrets of procurement tools and little-known free technologies that are available on the web.

The last chapter in this section discusses using stakeholder engagement as a tool to motivate suppliers and implement change within the organization, outlining how critical it is to your organization to have a team of committed stakeholders to ensure the success of your sourcing project.

Part Three: Examples from the Field

Part Three provides a detailed account of some firsthand experiences we have had helping customers reduce costs through the strategic sourcing process, including some of the most creative solutions we have developed, as well as some of the most challenging sourcing engagements we have come across. Each chapter in Part Three offers you an example of each experience and covers different sourcing strategies.

The first chapter defines some of the creative methods you can use to get your incumbent supplier, or potential supply base, to assist you in strengthening a relationship and reaching your own company goals. We discuss tactics that can be used to help get your suppliers on board with your goals and help them help you drive savings.

The second chapter discusses tactics that help you become the ideal customer in the eyes of your supplier. Typically, gaining this status leads to improved supplier relationships and even larger savings opportunities. We then conclude with specific examples in which customers have leveraged supplier feedback to gain improvements in their supply chain.

To summarize, we also discuss uncovering savings through data analysis. The last chapter in Part Three focuses on ways to achieve savings without negotiations by purchasing more efficiently and utilizing easy-to-manage tracking tools and scorecarding tools.

Part Four: How to Do It

In Part Four we provide insight and sourcing strategies for specific indirect spend areas, focusing on office supplies, telecommunications, cell phones, small parcel shipments, MRO, freight, and services. Each spend area is detailed in its own chapter and provides an industry overview with sourcing strategies you and your company can use to produce the optimal result.

BEGINNING YOUR JOURNEY

As you read through the book, keep in mind that the methods and processes we discuss are not rigid instructions that you should apply to your organization. Just as markets are ever-changing and flexible, so should be your sourcing strategy. Start thinking about how to apply these concepts in the most effective way based on the objectives, constraints, and culture of your own organization. Only by customizing your sourcing strategy based on internal considerations and restrictions will you successfully transition from process to profit.

Acknowledgments

WE THANK OUR EXCELLENT TEAM for taking time out of their lives to help us develop content for this book. David Pastore, Kathleen Daly, Jennifer Ulrich (who was Jennifer Puvel when we started this initiative), and Scott Decker are a group of professionals that anyone would be fortunate to have the pleasure to work with at some point in their careers. We apologize for making them rewrite their sections multiple times.

We thank Alex Howerton, who provided some great suggestions and made our words look more good.

Last but not least, we thank our wives, Jill and Jennifer, who feigned interest when we discussed our project over the last year and a half.

What Is Indirect Spend, and How Does One Manage It?

"WE PAY HOW MUCH?!"

The story is the same at most companies. Chief executive officers (CEOs), chief financial officers, and other C-suite executives decide that it is time to take a closer look at what they pay for the goods and services required to keep their businesses running, and are often shocked at the excessive costs they are paying. Mostly these costs are in areas that have not been closely managed in the past, ranging across categories such as office supplies, telecommunications, insurance, and marketing materials. Indirect spend—spend not tied directly to the creation of a finished product or service—can make up 40 percent or more of an organization's total expenses.

 ## THE TYPICAL SCENARIOS

All too often, oversight of most expenses is left to the group that owns the budget: finance, human resources (HR), administration, or marketing. The problem is, the stakeholders who manage the spend category or signed the original agreements were probably not hired based on their ability to manage costs or budgets and have little or no formal training in procurement or strategic sourcing.

1

As management comes to this realization, a knee-jerk reaction soon follows. Regardless of the product or service category, their immediate gut reaction is that the cost is too high. The executive team issues a mandate: Reduce costs, in any way possible. To complicate the matter, the executive team usually issues a goal that has no basis or reasoning behind it, such as "save 10 percent in the next 12 months."

Once challenged, stakeholders and end users immediately go on the defensive to justify why the prices paid for the last several years are fair. They start to point to rare instances when the incumbent supplier did something beyond the normal course of business for them. They put together a myriad of reasons why no other supplier can do what the current supplier does. They present market information used in the last bid, which might have taken place years ago (while, in reality, over time, the stakeholder and the sales rep have worked closely together as a team, even becoming friends, thus compromising the objectivity of the data). With the original objective of the selection process long forgotten and the market untested in recent years, the reasons for using a certain supplier become increasingly subjective.

Stakeholders come up with a lot of reasons their initial decision was the right one: the supplier has the best service, the supplier is the only one that can provide a certain type of report, the supplier comes in each week and brings donuts for the administrative staff (usually unstated), the cost to leave the supplier is too high. The team tasked with reducing costs is inundated with information that the stakeholders have amassed after years of managing the category. Pushback comes from the most unlikely of places—even from the people that originally called for the formation of the team. As it turns out, even indirect spend categories have political ramifications within an organization. The reason is simple: Purchasing is a sensitive subject. Think about it—in your personal life, you want your friends and neighbors to know what a great deal you got on that car, TV, or even on a dinner tab. But in reality, have you ever met a person that told you that he or she got a poor deal on a new car? Everyone thinks that he or she is the best possible negotiator, and is not afraid to tell you so. Corporate purchasing operates with the same dynamic, and challenging someone else's ability to get a good deal can result in bruised egos and the digging-in of heels.

In the end, one or two suppliers get changed out, the team disbands, and the can is kicked down the road for another year. What starts out as a simple premise, reducing costs for noncritical items, ends in failure or lackluster results.

The inherent problem is that even though indirect spend typically makes up about 40 percent of the overall costs of an organization's operations, these expenditures are often viewed as a group of one-off purchases, or tangential to the main focus of the business, and are generally not targeted as savings categories. The product or service that is purchased is necessary for the business to operate, but it is not a raw material, a major capital expenditure, or payroll. Somewhere along the line, the responsibility of managing these costs fell to someone with no training in strategic sourcing or negotiations, and spend management migrated to the bottom of their to-do list. By the time management realizes that the opportunity for savings exists, territory has already been marked. The biggest hurdles to overcome have not been erected where you would expect them to be—getting suppliers to provide lower prices. Instead, you find internal challenges, such as collecting meaningful spend data, understanding the scope of work and specifications, and dealing with egos and internal political issues, to be the biggest barriers to success. In this chapter we examine each of these challenges and explain why they exist within most organizations.

COLLECTING MEANINGFUL SPEND DATA

Indirect spend represents the cost of all products and services needed to run your organization that are not directly tied to the creation of a finished product or service. Many companies believe indirect expenditures are synonymous with administrative expenses, but the idea encompasses much more. Any type of product or service that is required by most companies in order to function on a day-to-day basis should be considered indirect spend. A sampling of common indirect spend categories includes:

- *Administrative expense*: office equipment/copiers, office supplies, furniture, postage, small package/expedited shipping services
- *Facilities expense*: HVAC services, elevator maintenance services, plumbing/electrical services, maintenance supplies (lightbulbs, etc), cleaning/janitorial services, security services, electricity
- *Finance and HR*: payroll processing, corporate checking, merchant accounts, benefits, property/casualty insurance, outsourced collections
- *Sales and marketing*: promotional items, printing, market research, advertising
- *Information technology/telecommunications*: software, hardware, voice and data networks, cell phones, local and long-distance services

Taking a look at the different types of spend on this list, it is probably easy to recognize why meaningful spend data is hard to find. First, the management of most of these categories can be highly decentralized, particularly if your organization has multiple locations. Along with multiple spend owners there are many different suppliers, requirements, and types of products being purchased. Gathering this information across all locations or spend owners often becomes rather burdensome.

Second, it is often difficult to determine where this information resides within your organization. Many of these categories might not have purchase orders (POs), and even if they do, the PO probably does not have the level of detail you need to truly understand what is being purchased. While you might have a great inventory or enterprise resource planning (ERP) system able to capture line-item detail of spend for direct materials (products and services necessary to build your finished product or service), many times these systems are not used effectively, or not used at all, for indirect materials. Unfortunately, in many companies, the only way to find internal data and information that helps clarify what you are getting from your supplier is a mountain of paper invoices and some old contracts, if you are lucky enough to find them.

 ## CLARIFYING THE SCOPE OF WORK

Once you get over the first hurdle of understanding what you buy from your suppliers, you will run into the second challenge: understanding exactly what the supplier does for you (beyond what shows up on an invoice). By simply looking at an invoice, you might see that an office supplies vendor sells you pens and paper, but to the person or group of people the supplier works with on a day-to-day basis within your organization, the company might do a lot more. In the office supplies example, the supplier might manage the stockroom, provide preferred payment terms, or maintain an online ordering site that makes it very simple to place orders. There could be other factors that may have benefits to your organization beyond just the buying group. For instance, the supplier may have developed a green initiative within your organization or provide consignment inventory, which may have impact on your marketing teams or tax filings.

You will gain an understanding of this scope of work by talking to the spend owners or end users that work with the supplier on a daily basis. While some of the services and value-adds are very clear, such as those discussed previously, others may not be. End users might say they need a supplier that "is strategic," "understands our requirements," and can "adapt quickly to changes." We call these the intangible specifications. Of course, everyone wants a supplier that understands the unique requirements of an organization and adapts quickly to change, but the question becomes how those requirements are defined in order to compare a certain supplier's offering to other suppliers in the marketplace. Translating these intangible specifications into objective requirements, and factoring in which requirements are actually needed (versus merely desired), is key to a successful engagement.

IMPLEMENTING CHANGE DESPITE OFFICE POLITICS

Throughout Part One of this book we offer ways you can complete the first two challenges of managing indirect spend: collecting meaningful data and identifying a clear scope of work. Once you have cleared these two hurdles, you can develop a sourcing strategy and use various tactics to uncover cost savings opportunities. The last hurdle you will face is the internal issue of change management, which typically occurs during sourcing and the subsequent implementation process.

Indirect spend categories can be one of the most politically sensitive subjects in your organization. This is particularly true when senior management has historically taken a hands-off approach in managing indirect categories, and the end users that work day to day with suppliers feel that it is *their right* to control the spend. Many times they also believe that, over the course of time, they have optimized their choice of suppliers, and that a better price at the required service levels is not available in the marketplace.

Challenging and changing the status quo can be very difficult. Even if senior management supports the sourcing initiative, you may find that they initially developed some of the supplier relationships you are tasked with reviewing, and getting them to agree to change suppliers can be a daunting task, even when the numbers support your decision.

Ultimately, you will probably discover that identifying suppliers willing to provide better services at lower prices is the easy part of managing indirect spend. Getting internal support and aligning efforts to effectively execute the cost-reduction strategies you uncover, in the face of political considerations and end-user misconceptions, becomes the primary challenge. Unfortunately, many people entering into this type of supply chain review do not realize these challenges until it is too late to change course and avoid the pitfalls.

***

Chapter 1, "An Introduction to Strategic Sourcing," provides insight into how strategic sourcing can be used as a powerful tool to manage indirect spend. As we take you through the necessary steps of managing indirect spend in Parts One through Four of this book, we discuss ways to help offset the common misconceptions and political restrictions that exist within many organizations. We include advice on how to build sponsorship internally to ensure the end result is sustainable for you and your team and how to demonstrate value so that the project is perceived as a success by and for the entire organization.

PART ONE

The Process

CHAPTER ONE

An Introduction to Strategic Sourcing

MANY BOOKS HAVE ALREADY BEEN WRITTEN on the subjects of strategic sourcing and supply chain management. Each describes a sourcing process that generally includes five to seven steps, and overall the primary differences between these books are the ways those steps are defined and segmented. The process we describe in this book does include six steps, starting with the inception of the initiative (project kickoff) and concluding with final monitoring of the implemented program (continuous improvement). However, our process applies strategic sourcing techniques specifically to indirect spend categories and offers insights and strategies that have been used successfully in real-world practice. Our process is not based on theory; the techniques described have been refined based on years of experience working with many types of companies to reduce their costs for indirect goods and services. As you will discover as you progress through the book, the process itself serves primarily as a project management tool. The use of creative strategies and the ability to adapt to ever-changing conditions are the key elements that make your sourcing initiative truly strategic.

Many companies still do not apply strategic sourcing techniques to indirect spend categories. Instead, indirect spend is treated as a series of one-off purchases, or is sourced with a simple three-bid strategy with no efforts beyond reviewing the supplier price responses. Typically, with indirect spend, per-item prices are relatively low, the product or service is not crucial to the business, and the overall costs are rarely examined because of the difficulty entailed in gathering meaningful spend and market data. Strategic sourcing allows companies to shift away from thinking about indirect spend in this ad hoc manner, and provides spend visibility, objective decision making, and a project management tool to ensure efficient use of the sourcing team's time and efforts.

 VISIBILITY

Strategic sourcing provides visibility into business processes, operational issues, and spend details that may not have been clearly available to management and stakeholders in the past. The process of strategic sourcing provides a road map for collecting and analyzing this information to determine how the purchase of a particular product or service truly fits into the overall business operations of an organization, from the identification of the need to the use of the product or service and (if necessary) its disposal. This includes identifying:

- Who buys the product
- How it is ordered
- How it is received
- How it is paid for
- Where the payment information resides in your systems
- What the payment reconciliation processes are
- Where the product is stored
- When it is used
- Why it is needed
- Who the suppliers are
- What value-adds or services are provided
- What happens to the product after its useful life is over

As we discuss throughout the book, all of this information is necessary to properly perform strategic sourcing, to ensure the most efficient processes and tools are utilized, and ultimately to implement and maintain the final program developed as a result of the process.

OBJECTIVITY

Strategic sourcing allows companies to shift the management of indirect spend from a series of one-off purchases to a more coordinated effort with checks, balances, and objectivity that justifies costs and requirements. Historically, indirect purchases and spend for most companies were managed by one or many individuals, with little oversight from management and no requirement to justify their selection of suppliers. Strategic sourcing provides a process to identify the true requirements of the organization (rather than those of the individual managing the spend) and to identify suppliers and price points that appropriately meet those requirements. The process is performed in such a way that requirements are identified well ahead of supplier identification, and stakeholders agree to those requirements before alternatives to the existing arrangement are presented.

 ## PROJECT MANAGEMENT TOOL

Finally, a well-designed strategic sourcing process becomes a project management tool that ensures the engagement will not end in failure due to scope creep or lack of a clear path forward, and that those working on the project make the most efficient use of their time. Attempting to reduce costs without a formalized strategic sourcing process can easily end in frustration, as roles are not clearly laid out between team members, steps are not identified, and timelines are not set. As we discuss throughout the book, the strategic sourcing process includes many challenges, and teams can easily get bogged down in noncritical details or fail to come to consensus on next steps. The process in itself includes steps that can be integrated into a comprehensive project plan that avoids convoluted outcomes.

The six basic steps of the strategic sourcing process are:

1. Data collection and spend analysis
2. Research
3. The RFx process (requesting information, quotes, and proposals from suppliers)
4. Negotiations
5. Contracting
6. Implementation and continuous improvement

Our goal is to help you navigate through specific activities that most sourcing books fail to cover—dealing with and effectively utilizing internal constituents, motivating the supplier marketplace, and gathering the information required to make informed decisions during each step of the process.

Data Collection and Spend Analysis

Once you identify the need for strategic sourcing, the next step is collecting and analyzing spend data. The purpose is twofold. First, the data is needed to determine where you should focus your efforts. Your resources are more than likely limited, and it will not be possible to immediately reduce costs across all areas where your company spends money. Areas of opportunity need to be identified and a project road map created to provide context and timelines for your efforts.

Second, data is needed to determine both quantitative and qualitative requirements associated with a spend category. When we discuss the quantitative aspects, we are referring to current price points, discounts, payment and freight terms, and other costs associated with a particular area of spend or supplier. Qualitative requirements refer to the quality and services tied to these costs. The current suppliers were more than likely chosen based not just on price, but other value-added considerations as well, and these factors need to be understood and considered. The quantitative baseline and qualitative requirements become the launching pad for the rest of the engagement, which makes it critical not just to identify them, but also to make sure they are agreed on by other interested parties within your organization before moving to the next step.

Research

The research phase provides context to the categories you are sourcing. The purpose of research is to develop or refine your sourcing strategy by determining what competition exists in the marketplace; what alternative products, services, or processes are available; and whether or not current market conditions make it a good or bad time to go to market. We will define market intelligence in greater detail and discuss its importance as it relates to your ability to drive savings in a spend category.

The RFx Process (Requesting Information, Quotes, and Proposals from Suppliers)

During the RFx phase you will execute the sourcing strategy developed during the data collection and research phases. In all likelihood this will include requesting proposals or quotes from alternate suppliers or performing a reverse auction. However, depending on market conditions, the competitive landscape, and how the product or service purchased fits into your overall business strategy, it could also mean focusing on other cost reduction strategies that do not involve bidding out the business. We outline some of these strategies and point to a couple of case studies where bypassing the request for proposal (RFP) was a successful strategy. During the RFx stage of strategic sourcing you will also evaluate the proposals and other information submitted by suppliers to determine both the quantitative (cost savings) and the qualitative (service/value-add) benefits through the objective process of scorecarding or grading.

Negotiations

Once initial proposals are received, refined, and analyzed, you will move into the negotiation phase of strategic sourcing. At this stage you will develop target price points for the products or services you buy, identify preferred suppliers (incumbents or alternates), and request that suppliers meet the established targets in order to win your business. Chapter 6 provides strategies to help you identify how to come to your price targets and how you can leverage multiple bids against each other.

As we discuss in detail in Chapter 6, considering negotiations as a separate step in the sourcing process is slightly misleading, and separating it from the rest of the process can be detrimental to the overall results of the project. Some form of negotiation should be taking place with the supplier community throughout the strategic sourcing process.

Contracting

Once the final supplier or suppliers are selected, your next step is to award the business. The contracting phase converts the business terms agreed to during the sourcing phase into a legally binding document detailing the rules of engagement between the customer and supplier. The contracting phase does not necessarily end in a signed contract between two organizations; it could result in a pricing agreement with agreed-to terms or a simple purchase order.

Implementation and Continuous Improvement

Often overlooked or considered outside the scope of strategic sourcing, implementation and continuous improvement ensure that the work performed during the sourcing process is properly utilized and taken advantage of by your organization for years to come. Simply entering into an agreement with a preferred vendor does not result in cost savings. End users and stakeholders need to make purchases under the terms of the agreement, as maverick buying is often the primary reason savings are not achieved. Savings need to be tracked to ensure that the supplier is upholding its end of the bargain (price) and your organization is holding up your end (volume). This means rolling the agreement out internally, reviewing invoiced pricing as well as other internal documentation to ensure internal customers are not buying off-contract, and requesting credits for improper billings.

IN SUMMARY

Part One of this book covers each of the steps in the strategic sourcing process in great detail. While some of the challenges discussed may not apply to your organization, we have taken care to use examples we find in many of the companies we work with, regardless of size, industry, or type of project.

While the strategic sourcing process on its own can produce cost savings, working to optimize your results requires you to think about the steps in the process and determine the best way to customize those steps for your organization. Developing cost-savings strategies, delving into market research, and negotiating with internal stakeholders and external suppliers requires a highly creative approach—it is not all analytics. Applying strategic sourcing techniques to indirect spend categories can be a challenging endeavor; however, for companies looking to cut costs or enhance profitability, these spend areas can provide a wealth of untapped savings opportunities.

CHAPTER TWO

2

Data Collection and Analysis

YOU CANNOT JUDGE HOW FAR you have journeyed unless you know where you have come from. Data collection is the starting point for any strategic sourcing project and it lays the foundation for the engagement. The information you gather during this step is used to quantify results later on, but data collection is much more than just the process of gathering and analyzing data. This stage is a launching pad that sets the tone for the entire initiative. Approaching it with care can help build sponsorship within your organization, inspire collaboration, and create the required momentum to complete projects and get results.

In this chapter we start from the beginning, by looking at pulling data out of internal accounting systems and analyzing it in order to develop a list of potential strategic sourcing projects, also called a project road map. We then examine how to gather data for specific projects and kick off the initiative.

 ## WHAT IS DATA COLLECTION?

On the most basic level, engaging in data collection and spend analysis enables you to identify your starting point. Having a detailed understanding of where you are right now in terms of price, as well as what you are getting for that price (service, quality, etc.), provides the context for analyzing offers from alternate suppliers in a much more meaningful way. In addition, establishing an accurate starting point helps justify your position when decisions come under scrutiny from your peers.

Understanding the data is not just helpful for making and justifying decisions internally. Providing alternate suppliers with a complete and accurate picture of current requirements allows them to take the guesswork out of their proposals and eliminates additional costs that can get factored in when the scope of work is unclear. Before digging in to the most effective ways to collect data, let us first identify the types of data you need to get started on any sourcing engagement.

On the surface, quantity and price seem to be the two pieces of raw information you need to get started. However, once you begin to dig, you will discover that there can be some tricky complexity hidden within these data points. For example, a logical first question is, how much does the company buy (total units) and how much does it cost (price per unit)? As you explore the answer, the notion of price quickly grows in complexity when you realize that unit cost is not the only component you need to consider; other factors come into play. Are there quantity price breaks? Is freight included or are there additional charges? What are the payment terms, and is there a discount for early payment?

Sometimes net cost per unit is not the only way to evaluate price. Consider a project that includes a basket of items, some purchased regularly and others rather infrequently, such as office supplies. In this scenario, high-volume items might be identified as having a fixed unit price, but what about items for which a fixed price wasn't negotiated? It is not likely that you will have negotiated a fixed unit price for everything in a supplier's catalog. Still, controlling the costs of the less-frequent purchases is also important. For these items, you likely have a discount structure based on a list price. For instance, pens and pencils that are not listed as contract items might receive a 20 percent discount off of list price. In this example, price is a combination of net costs, list prices, and discounts. Collecting pricing information may appear to be a simple concept but, as you can see, there are many factors that must be considered to understand the total cost.

Usage, or volume—how much you buy of a particular product or service—is the other basic component in the data collection process. In most cases, companies consider the last 12 months of usage to be reflective of future purchases; however, this may not always be the case. If business has shrunk or increased dramatically, volume may have shifted, and those changes should be documented before engaging in the RFx process. In some cases, consolidating volumes across locations (if you have multiple sites buying the same products) might make sense; in other cases the data should stay separated. Order size may also make a big difference, so line-item detail of purchases across locations becomes critical. As we discuss later in this chapter, getting this level of detail out of your own internal systems can be a challenge, if not impossible.

Price and usage are the foundation of a spend analysis, but there are many other factors that should be considered during the data collection and assessment process. Understanding existing contractual commitments, contract terms and conditions, quality levels, and scope of work are also important. Business concerns such as the order-to-payment process, the shipping and receiving process, and a detailed understanding of the historical relationships with current suppliers should all be reviewed and evaluated during this stage. With all this data to collect, getting started can prove to be a daunting task. In reality it is not that difficult, as long as you have a clear idea of what you are looking to accomplish.

 WHERE TO START?

So where to begin? For the purpose of this book, we assume you are starting from scratch—you are about to engage in a strategic sourcing initiative and your goal is to maximize the amount of dollars your organization can save. You need to identify categories or projects and develop a plan to source those categories. You want to build momentum for your engagement with a few quick wins and you do not want to squander limited resources on projects unless the payback is significant. To do this, you need to identify the low-hanging fruit— categories that can be sourced quickly and where the savings opportunity is substantial.

To get to that point, you must identify your supply base and categorize the suppliers into buckets based on the products or services they provide. From there, projects can be identified and additional data can be collected.

The next few pages detail the manual way to collect data and perform spend analysis. Before we go into detail on that process, it is important to note that there are tools that can make the spend analysis process easier. Spend analysis tools have many advantages, which we discuss later in this chapter. Most also require an investment of time and money to implement properly. If you are or your organization is new to strategic sourcing, you should consider the investment as a phase two initiative that brings efficiency to the strategic sourcing process after you have shown that it works. Regardless, the process we outline over the next few pages should only be considered if you do not have access to spend analysis tools.

The best place to start is in the general ledger or accounts payable ledger. The general ledger provides a list of all financial transactions, normally classified into groups used by the accounting department. However, using these categories as a basis for a sourcing engagement is a mistake, as purchasing requirements are typically not considered during the categorization process. For example, most general ledgers include a category for supplies, which can include anything from coffee filters to paint. Since you will probably want two different suppliers (and therefore will want to perform two distinct sourcing initiatives) for these items, classifying them the same way isn't helpful. While general ledger classification requires refinement, the ledger points you in the direction of what categories, from an accounting standpoint, have the highest levels of spend and therefore the biggest impact on the organization, which is the goal of this phase of data collection.

Typically each line item in the general ledger includes a description or comment field, and if that transaction represents the purchase of a good or service, the supplier used will most likely be included in the description. The problem is that this description data, which is pulled from an accounts payable (AP) or purchase order (PO) database, will not be consistent for each transaction and requires additional manipulation of data.

Table 2.1 provides an example of general ledger data that provides supplier name, but the name is not consistent enough to properly utilize the data as is.

In this case, our supplier, Widget Providers, is listed in the comments field; however, the comments also include other information, such as the PO

TABLE 2.1 General Ledger Information

GL Account Code	Period	Date	Journal	Comments	Debit
5162600-02	03	3/26/2009	AP-002926	40WIDG000 WIDGET PROV 22809 PO 6361	$12,472.20
5162600-02	04	4/23/2009	AP-003106	40WIDG000 WIDGET PROV 33109 PO 7258	$15,145.00
5162600-02	05	5/31/2009	AP-003336	40WIDG000 WIDGET PROV 43009 PO 7412	$17,595.00

number. In order to get a good understanding of how much is spent over the course of a year with Widget Providers, an analyst might create a spreadsheet that includes all the information above, and include an additional field called *Cleansed Supplier Name*, as demonstrated in Table 2.2.

Now that the data is standardized, it becomes much easier to analyze spend by supplier. Taking it a step further, we might also add a column called *Category* and identify Widget Providers as a provider of office supplies. Categorizing Widget Providers under this general category, along with other office supplies vendors, provides a good basis for identifying spend areas to be considered as part of a sourcing engagement. We will cover categorization in greater detail later in this chapter.

Depending on your enterprise resource planning (ERP) system, an accounts payable report may also be a useful tool to help give focus to sourcing opportunities. The accounts payable report has several advantages over a general ledger. First, while the general ledger includes every financial transaction (debit or credit) made by the organization, an accounts payable report only shows money paid to vendors. Second, because the report is vendor specific, supplier names will likely be standardized to a higher degree than the general ledger, making the cleansing process much easier. A potential disadvantage to using an accounts payable report instead of a rolled-up general ledger report is that, depending on how your financial reporting is structured, each business unit or location within your company may be operating under its own accounts

TABLE 2.2   General Ledger Information with Cleansed Supplier Name

GL Account Code	Period	Date	Journal	Comments	Debit	Cleansed Supplier Name
5162600-02	03	3/26/2009	AP-002926	40WIDG000 WIDGET PROV 22809 PO 6361	$12,472.20	Widget Providers
5162600-02	04	4/23/2009	AP-003106	40WIDG000 WIDGET PROV 33109 PO 7258	$15,145.00	Widget Providers
5162600-02	05	5/31/2009	AP-003336	40WIDG000 WIDGET PROV 43009 PO 7412	$17,595.00	Widget Providers

payable journal, which means you need to run a report for each location, then consolidate files (if you are sourcing across multiple locations).

 ## DEALING WITH DECENTRALIZED DATA SETS

This leads us into the next challenge, which is how to deal with decentralized spend. When considering strategic sourcing for a category, decentralized spend typically means that a supplier relationship (and subsequent payment to that supplier) does not flow through a single point of contact or group, such as a centralized accounts payable team and payment process. Instead, employees out in the field or at satellite locations are able to place, pay for, and process orders for goods and services without oversight from a centralized entity.

This ties into spend analysis in several ways. First, if your company has grown by acquisition, it is possible that different sites utilize different ERP systems. These systems may or may not roll into a single financial system.

Second, when the responsibility of ordering and paying for goods and services falls to multiple people (or groups of people), it usually results in a variety of procedures being used to actually pay for goods. For example, some locations might run all purchases through a purchase order system and pay via check, while others may pay via a purchasing (credit) card, and others may receive invoices and pay via electronic funds transfer.

Depending on your situation, it may be a good idea to enlist the support of the finance department, the IT department, or both. If you are dealing with a situation in which multiple ERPs are used, finance can give you a good indication of how those systems interact with each other. Finance can also shed light on the types of payment options that are used within the organization and how those options are reflected in various ledgers and reports.

IT should also be able to help run the reports you need. In addition, IT may be able to provide assistance in standardizing and consolidating data sets coming from different sources.

If some payments are going to vendors through a procurement card (p-card), the transactions you pull out of your ERP are only going to reflect payments to your p-card company, not the vendors you were actually paying. However, most providers of p-cards can give you reports that detail whom you have paid with their cards. These reports can be as simple as a list of suppliers and total amounts, or as detailed as a line-by-line account of particular items purchased and quantities.

If you do not already have access to this data, finance should be able to provide you with the appropriate reports.

When working with IT or finance, remember that during this first pass of data collection you are simply trying to identify total spend by supplier over a period of time, normally a year. Two to three years might also make sense if one of your goals is to identify trends over time.

 ## SPEND ANALYSIS

Now that you have collected data sets representing at least one year's worth of spend across all operating units within the company, the next step is to consolidate and standardize the information. It is important to note that at this point, the goal is to identify project areas. Capturing line-item details such as product purchased, quantity, and price comes later.

If you are consolidating data yourself, review each data set to determine which columns of information are important. Transaction Date, Supplier Name, and Spend are the three most critical pieces of information; however, you may want to capture other data as well. Pull this information out of each individual data set and add it to a new consolidated spreadsheet file that includes a column indicating which data set the information came from. For instance, if you pull data for a particular location (let us say location X) out of an AP report for that location, add a column called *Location* and indicate location X, then add a column called *Source Data* and indicate AP report.

Once the data is consolidated, it is time to standardize and categorize the information. Sort the data by the supplier field and create a new column called *Cleansed Supplier Name*. As discussed previously in this chapter, you may find that each data set, and even data within the same set, has multiple names for a particular supplier. Let us use FedEx as an example. If your company makes payments to FedEx, you will probably see this supplier listed as FedEx, Federal Express, FedEx Corp, and so on. In the cleansed supplier name field, standardize all these different options to a single name. Repeat the process for all lines of data.

At this stage it may not make sense to standardize supplier names across 100 percent of the data. If you are dealing with hundreds of thousands of records, this could be a very tedious task. If that is the case, utilize the 80/20 rule. Run a pivot table on the data by supplier, then total up the spend. Identify which suppliers make up 80 percent of the total spend and focus your efforts on standardizing those supplier names. Ignoring 20 percent of the spend may seem troublesome, but keep in mind that within this data there are likely to be repeat entries for the same supplier (for example, FedX instead of FedEx). At this point, we are simply identifying target areas. Once we identify worthwhile projects we then focus on collecting more detailed information; at that point we will look more closely at the FedX data.

Once you have cleansed and standardized supplier names, it is time to group the data into *sourcing categories*. Sourcing categories are essentially high-level identifiers that indicate suppliers that provide the same or similar services. Grouping them together allows you to identify project areas and, eventually, leverage opportunities.

Creating your category list is the first real step in the spend analysis process—turning data into information. Spend analysis is not an exact science; there is no right or wrong way to do it, although there are some best practices that are worth considering.

First, be general in your initial classification. Start at the highest level of categorization you can identify, knowing that you may want to drill down later in the process. For example, you may know that Staples is used for pens and pencils and Xerox is used for paper products, but categorizing them in different buckets is not appropriate at this time. At its base, the initial spend classification is looking to identify which suppliers provide the same or similar services. Right now, you may use Staples for some items and Xerox for others, but a potential sourcing strategy might be to consolidate all of this spend with a single supplier. So for now, classify both suppliers under the category *Administrative Supplies*.

Many suppliers provide a wide range of goods and services, making classification difficult. If you have managed to capture any line-item usage details in your initial data collection, this information can be used to classify the supplier. If a single supplier performs two different services or provides two very different types of goods, it is important to provide only one high-level classification for the supplier at this time. The final stage of spend analysis is an overall opportunity assessment, and understanding the full impact of a supplier relationship is critical to identifying these opportunities. This high-level classification will aid that analysis.

Another way to develop the initial list of supplier categories is through the use of industry standard categorization tools, such as NAICS (North American Industry Classification System) or UNSPSC (United Nations Standard Products and Services Code). NAICS is used predominately in the United States, Mexico, and Canada, and classifies suppliers based on the most general category of products or goods they provide. UNSPSC is recognized globally and classifies products and services down to the line-item detail. Both coding systems are used regularly in the United States. As we discuss in a later chapter, classifying your supply base using these codes comes in handy when researching alternate suppliers.

Once you have completed the initial classification, it is time to start ranking categories for further analysis. Run a pivot table that shows spend by category, then sort the data by spend. You can now see which categories contain the highest spend and therefore have the greatest impact on the organization.

Now add the supplier column to the pivot table. You can now see how many suppliers make up each category of spend. Table 2.3 provides an example of an analysis of spend by category and supplier.

TABLE 2.3 Pivot Table with Category and Supplier

	Sum of Total Spend	
Category	**Supplier Name**	**Total**
Facilities maintenance	Safi Elevator Company	$ 1,421,000
	Waste Services Incorporated	$ 908,312
	Steven's HVAC	$ 532,127
	Complete Maintenance Solutions	$ 444,893
	Heating and Cooling Supply Company	$ 364,459
	Universal Plumbing Associates	$ 320,276
	Jan-Tastic Cleaning Services	$ 200,555
	Maintenance Supplies Unlimited	$ 143,264
Facilities maintenance total		*$ 4,334,886*
Marketing	Franklin Advertising Agency	$ 2,170,000
	Budget Print Services	$ 989,767
	Color True Graphic Design	$ 270,312
	National Printing	$ 95,000
	Standard Market Research of New York	$ 62,123
Marketing total		*$ 3,587,202*
Administrative expense	Office Max Incorp.	$ 750,309
	Federal Express Corporation	$ 546,999
	Warehouse Direct	$ 506,380
	U.S. Postal Service	$ 413,075
	Xerox	$ 311,189
	United Parcel Service	$ 281,406
Administration total		*$ 2,809,358*
Grand total		$10,731,446

When ranking categories, you are essentially determining the order in which you plan to drill down further into the data. Factors to consider when developing your ranking include how much spend is in a category, how many suppliers are in a category, which categories have not been sourced recently, and which categories can be sourced most quickly (and with the least resistance). Understanding your company culture is important for properly managing this step. For example, depending on the industry you serve, the category of marketing will probably be very high up your list in terms of spend and supplier utilized. However, many marketing departments maintain tight control over their supplier selection and are typically very reluctant to work with people outside the marketing department on supplier selection or supplier negotiations. If you are unfamiliar with strategic sourcing, or you get the impression that there is high resistance from marketing, you may not want to identify this area as a starting point. Instead, focus on areas of the company that are more open to change or are less politically sensitive.

This is not to say that marketing spend should not be examined. The purpose of a strategic sourcing initiative is to reduce costs and hopefully create significant savings opportunities in the area of marketing. However, building sponsorship and buy-in to the process is critical, and sometimes the best way to do that is by showing some positive results from a strategic sourcing engagement. Starting with a department that is reluctant to engage will not help you build that business case.

Now that you have ranked the categories, it is time to subcategorize the information into projects. During this stage you are identifying what you consider to be distinct strategic sourcing initiatives, each with its own project plan, timeline, and sourcing strategy. In doing this, you are developing a preliminary sourcing strategy based on leverage points—grouping the spend in a way that provides the best opportunity for a supplier to reduce price, improve service levels, or provide additional incentives.

At this stage you probably will not have a clear concept of price points, a full understanding of the supply base (capacity issues, regional variances, service differentiators, etc.), or other aspects that could create leverage; all you know is spend by supplier and category.

Start with the categories that you have ranked the highest. Review the suppliers in the category and determine the types of products they supply. Ask yourself the following questions:

- Are there other suppliers in the category that provide the same or similar products or services?

- Is there overlap between the products in this category and the products purchased in another category?
- Can I include spend from two different suppliers in the same bid?

The easiest way to answer these questions is to think about the suppliers you would want to participate in the bid process. When thinking about administrative supplies, you may want to invite Staples to a bid for paper, but you probably would not invite Xerox to a bid for other office supplies. So your subcategory now becomes office supplies. Down the road you might find it necessary to segment paper into its own bid, or you might decide to allow Xerox to participate in the paper portion of the office supplies bid, but it is not necessary to make that decision at this time. Conversely, you might know that Konica Minolta sells your company copiers and printers, which Staples or most other suppliers of office supplies (or paper products) do not. Therefore, your subcategory for Konica Minolta would be either copiers or office equipment.

It is at this point that the question comes up: How do you handle a supplier that provides a very diverse set of products or services a diverse set of markets? For example, Xerox sells copiers as well as paper. While there may be leverage in combining these two spends when working with Xerox, Konica Minolta would have no interest in providing the paper products, and a paper supplier such as Staples would have no interest in providing the copiers.

Down the line, consider either possibility—the optimal solution may be to keep both the paper and copiers with Xerox, or it might make more sense to split it up. Until further research is done and negotiations are performed, ascertaining the best result is difficult.

There are a few options for subcategorizing suppliers that have these characteristics. First, in some cases the supplier may go by two different (although similar) names in each of the markets it services. For example, FedEx is typically known as Federal Express in the Small Parcel Ground/Expedited shipments world and FedEx Freight for less-than-truckload (LTL) services. If this is the case, the data is probably already classified in different subcategories, perhaps even into different categories. Still, you should add a column or a flag in your data in a way that allows you to identify the potential category overlap for these suppliers once you are ready to begin sourcing.

Unfortunately, the more likely scenario is that your multiservice supplier is not labeled as such in the data. If this is the case, add a new column to your spreadsheet called *Secondary Subcategory*. Identify the primary subcategory as where you believe most of the spend is. Using this example, let's say that your organization uses Federal Express Small Parcel Services much more than their

TABLE 2.4   Project Road Map

Project	Total Spend	Total Suppliers	Ranking
Elevator maintenance	$1,421,000	1	1
Office supplies	$1,256,689	2	1
Shipping and postage	$1,241,480	3	1
Maintenance supplies	$ 588,157	2	1
Copiers and paper	$ 311,189	1	1
Printing	$1,084,767	2	2
Garbage disposal	$ 908,312	1	2
HVAC services	$ 896,586	2	2
Advertising	$2,170,000	1	3
Plumbing services	$ 320,276	1	3
Janitorial services	$ 200,555	1	3
Graphic design	$ 270,312	1	4
Market research	$ 62,123	1	4

LTL services. In the subcategory field, identify FedEx as small parcel. In the secondary subcategory field, indicate LTL. This safeguards against overlooking potential sourcing engagements or leverage points as you move to the next step in the process.

Now that your subcategories are laid out, run a new pivot table to determine which subcategories have the greatest spend, number of suppliers, and so on, similar to when you initially categorized the data. Now rank your subcategories, or projects, based on the order in which you want to source them, remembering that you want to tackle quick-win projects first to demonstrate the success of your engagement. You now have a preliminary sourcing road map with a list of potential projects. An example project road map is provided in Table 2.4.

 SPEND ANALYSIS TOOLS

Previously in this chapter we briefly mentioned toolsets that assist companies in the spend analysis process. There are many toolsets to choose from (Iasta, Zycus, and Emportis, to name a few), but a detailed discussion of the merits and differences of each is beyond our current scope. Websites such as Spend

Matters or Sourcing Innovation, and research firms such as Gartner, AMR, and Forrester can provide detailed insights into the toolset best suited to your organization.

On their simplest level, spend analysis tools automate the process detailed earlier in this chapter. Data is uploaded into the tool and information is cleansed and categorized based on criteria developed by the toolset provider, along with customized rules you develop based on your industry, the types of data being entered, and what type of analysis you want to see.

Besides saving a lot of time that would have been spent manually cleansing and categorizing data, these toolsets provide several other advantages.

First, spend analysis tools can be used over and over again on new data as purchases continue to be made. Once you have established that a supplier should be named and categorized a certain way, you can rerun reports with real-time data. The manual process is based on data from a specific time and, subsequently, can become stagnant or outdated.

Another key advantage to spend analysis is the types of reporting you can get from the data at the beginning of the initiative, as well as during and after the completion of the initiative. In Chapter 8 we discuss monitoring implemented programs and methodologies to track success. Spend analysis tools can provide these tracking activities and even help report savings produced through the program.

Depending on the amount of information that requires cleansing and classification and the overall goals and objectives you have for your sourcing initiatives, you may want to consider utilizing a toolset during the spend analysis phase of the project.

 ## KICKING OFF THE PROJECTS

One stage of the strategic sourcing process that is often overlooked is the project kickoff. Regardless of your role within the organization, it is important to make sure that you are not operating in an isolated bubble. Others should develop an understanding of the goals and objectives of your initiative, from the executive team to end users and many in between.

The executive team should be made aware of the initiative and support it. The reason is simple: change does not always come easy. Over time, you will find that the biggest roadblock to achieving savings is not the supply base; rarely has a supplier offered the absolute best price or the most efficient process, thus creating many opportunities to discover savings. In many cases, the greatest impediment turns out to be implementing change within the organization. All too often, purchasing or finance teams uncover an opportunity to reduce costs substantially and, naturally, believe that letting the facts speak for themselves is all it takes to make the necessary changes. Change, however, does not come easily, and even with the best business case you will find that having the support of the executive team or other higher-ups within the organization pays off.

While you probably will not get the attention of the executive team on a weekly basis, try to establish a monthly meeting to report status and present findings. At the very least, you should be providing a written status update to the team on a regular basis. This way, if you run into a roadblock that requires their attention, they will already be aware of progress to date.

End users and other interested parties should be made aware of the initiative as well. As we discuss later, end users have a stake in the project, as they are dealing with the day-to-day realities of working with the supply base. Try to form a cross-functional team that includes members of several different departments: finance, purchasing, operations, and other affected parties. Having a cross-functional team allows you to get the perspective of a diverse group within the organization and aids in consensus building as projects move through the sourcing process.

Depending on the scope and breadth of the initiative, you will likely assign other resources to help collect data and perform research. These resources could include members of the cross-functional team, end users, or others within your organization, and they should meet at least biweekly. During these meetings, members of the team can report status, troubleshoot issues, and solicit advice on current initiatives.

END-USER INTERVIEWS

You have now identified project categories, developed a project road map, identified end users and other interested parties, and introduced your plans to the executive team. Other than supplier name and spend, you still do not have a clear concept of the specific products purchased, nor do you know the details of that particular supplier relationship. The next step is to add some context to the data you have analyzed. The best way to do this is through end-user interviews.

End users can take many forms. They could be the people that currently interact with a particular supplier or group of suppliers, or the people that receive or use the product. The end user could even be the person who initially established the relationship with that supplier, even if that person has long since moved into a different position within your organization.

In most cases, there are multiple end users within the organization for a particular project, from buyers to finance to engineering and beyond. Depending on your history with the supplier and the category being sourced, one or all of these types of end users could provide important information. It is critical to get feedback from anyone who has a stake with the supply base, directly or indirectly. Otherwise you may overlook some aspect of servicing, or a unique attribute of the current supplier, that could cause a lot of anguish during an implementation phase if it were absent.

Initial end-user discussions should seek to accomplish several things. First, they should build buy-in and sponsorship for the initiative you are undertaking. Second, they should provide you with a detailed understanding of the current relationships with suppliers, including a history of the relationship, the reason that particular supplier is used, and the quality and service requirements that are required if an alternate is to be considered. Third, ground rules should be set regarding the roles and responsibilities of the end user during the sourcing and negotiations phase. Let's discuss each of these points in detail.

Building Sponsorship

People have a tendency to fear the unknown. Poking your head into an area that someone else manages can cause that person discomfort. An end user that is reluctant to engage has the ability to negatively impact the project by providing incomplete information, talking to suppliers without your knowledge, providing the incumbent supplier with details that should not be disclosed to them, and so on. An end user could even tell his or her favorite supplier, "Do not worry about this initiative. We will never change vendors." Such a response could upset negotiations with the incumbent further down the road.

Most times, a brief introduction to the project and an explanation of what you are trying to accomplish is all the prompting an end user needs to buy in to the process. However, if you sense that end users are still reluctant to participate, there are several steps you can take to ensure they are on board.

First, let them know that they are not being singled out. It is important for them to understand that there is an effort to reduce costs and improve bottom-line profitability across the organization. Their participation is critical to the process.

Second, let them know that the success or failure of the project is tied directly to their engagement and collaboration. Be direct and make sure they know you recognize that they have the power to upset the applecart, but also that you are not going to allow it.

Third, tie the project to the end user's list of objectives for the year. If there are some end users who do not report to you, work with their direct supervisors to include this project in the next performance review.

If it is not clear that you have end-user support after initial discussions, it is critical to engage senior level management to enlist the support you need. Otherwise, all the work you do after this step could go to waste.

Understanding the Project Category

Now that you have end users engaged, it is time to mine them for information. It is likely that for a given project category, the end user is working with the incumbent supply base on a regular basis, fielding offers and sales pitches from alternate vendors, and probably has at least a basic understanding of the marketplace. This base knowledge has advantages and disadvantages. The key advantages are that the end user can give you a detailed picture of how suppliers work with your organization; what is important in terms of servicing, quality, terms, and so on; and what the critical components of supplier relationships are. They can also give you a good historical perspective on supplier relationships, why any particular supplier is used, why others are not, what suppliers do best, and where they can improve.

What end users probably cannot give you, but may think they can, is an objective perspective of the marketplace as a whole. After years of managing a category the same way, many people stop exploring alternatives and become closely tied into existing processes. Changing suppliers at a substantial cost savings may be possible, but end users could be reluctant because it would mean they would have to work with the supplier a different way. Even if the new process is more efficient or would mean less work for end users, there could be reluctance if they perceive that they would need to change their internal processes.

It is important to note that not all end users are subjective thinkers that care only about maintaining the status quo. Many are objective, have done their homework, and have a great understanding of the marketplace and the opportunities available. Others may not have as much detailed knowledge but are not happy with current suppliers and are ready for change. Regardless, the critical consideration here is that you, as the project lead, remain objective and do not become tied into old ways of thinking about supplier relationships specifically or the marketplace in general.

As detailed earlier in the chapter, there are several types of end users. Some could be buyers, others could be finance people, and still others could be members of the engineering or operations team. Based on the category and the role of the end user, the types of questions you will want to ask can be very diverse. In Part Four of this book, we detail specific project examples and provide a recommended list of end-user questions for those examples. In general, there are eight categories you should review with your end users.

1. *Business relationship*—Understand the initiation, selection criteria used, progression, value, and the short- and long-term direction of the business partnership with the supplier.
2. *Product or service*—Understand your company's need, use, and application of the product or service being purchased.
3. *Locations*—Obtain a list of all locations that use this product or service and understand how the supplier's product or service is used in each location, particularly regarding similarities and differences and their ensuing impact.
4. *Financial*—Understand all costs related to the product or service: history of price changes, reasons for discounts, payment terms, who negotiates and when, annual volume, and current and future volume usage.
5. *Contractual*—Understand the contract terms and language, reason for existence or non-existence, history, changes since signing, and reasons for such changes.
6. *Reports*—View and understand the various reports produced (by the supplier as well as internally) to track costs and performance.
7. *Service*—Understand service standards, expectations and measurement used, service process, level of customer satisfaction, and company satisfaction.
8. *Supplier ranking*—Ask the end user to rank the supplier according to commitment to the quality of the product or service, value of the partnership, accuracy, creativity, responsiveness, and assistance.

Defining Roles and Responsibilities

The last component to focus on when engaging end users is defining roles and responsibilities during the sourcing process. Providing a consistent message to the supply base, both incumbents and alternate suppliers, is critical to ensuring a positive end result. A supplier that hears different things from different members of your team either disengages from the process or provides a proposal that factors in uncertainty. For this reason, it is essential to assign a project lead. This person, who may be an end user, should be the primary point person that suppliers go to when asking questions, requesting clarification, or providing input. This primary point of contact is also responsible for collecting information and providing your requirements to suppliers throughout a sourcing engagement.

This arrangement does not imply that the rest of the team should be disengaged from the process. By all means, the team should work together to develop the strategy, build requirements, identify alternates, create documents, review proposals, and develop responses to supplier questions. But to ensure consistent messaging, all that information should be provided to the supplier base through a primary point person.

As you move to later stages of the sourcing process (such as finalist presentations, negotiations, award, and implementation), more members of the team become engaged, at which point it makes sense to have members of your team work directly with members of the supplier's team. But as a starting point, designating a primary point person to provide your requirements to the supplier community helps to avoid a large amount of confusion and miscommunication.

 ## LINE-ITEM DETAIL AND GETTING THE MOST FROM YOUR SUPPLY BASE

End users can provide you with a good understanding of supplier relationships and history, service levels, and other critical aspects of the requirements of the product or service being purchased. You may have even collected some information you did not have before, including contracts or purchasing agreements, specifications and forecasts, or other reports that end users have available. This information is a necessary part of the analysis process, but the most critical piece is most likely still missing—line-item detail of purchases. Looking at your AP or PO data probably does not help; the descriptions in that data are likely to be as inconsistent as the supplier name and transactions at the invoice level. If you have a good inventory requisition system or have implemented a software system like Ariba, you are starting off in a better position than most, but the system may not include all the data you need beyond unit price, such as freight, terms, additional charges, and so on.

You can collect the data that does reside within your company by pulling invoices and manually entering the information into a spreadsheet. Depending on the category and the level of centralization within your organization, this can be a very tedious process and, without an army of interns at your disposal, could extend the sourcing timeline substantially.

The most efficient way to gather the requisite line-item detail is to approach your supply base directly. While most companies do not keep good records of the items they buy, particularly for nonproduction purchases, all organizations keep excellent records of what was sold.

Almost all of your suppliers have line-item details for everything they have sold you and can provide reports in spreadsheet format detailing those purchases; however, some are naturally reluctant to do so. Suppliers understand that a customer looking for data of this nature is typically seeking to reduce prices, either through a one-off negotiation or as part of a bidding and sourcing process. With that in mind, you should consider this request for information as the first step in negotiations with your incumbent supplier, and be prepared for one of three responses to your request: acceptance, avoidance, or pushback.

Response 1: Acceptance

Depending on the category you are sourcing and the sophistication of the supplier sales rep, often a request for historical sales information is perceived as business as usual. The supplier gladly gives you the information you need and even follows up to make sure you understand the data. This is the ideal response.

Response 2: Avoidance

It is often possible to confuse the avoidance response with the acceptance response. A supplier may initially appear agreeable to meeting your request; however, weeks later you still may have not received the data. Once the data does eventually arrive, it could be incomplete or not comply with the level of detail you requested. If the sales rep seems to be saying all the right things but ultimately can't deliver what you are asking for, the supplier is using the avoidance response. There are several steps you can take at this point.

First, when making the request for data, provide a template that shows the level of detail you are looking for. Review the template with the supplier and make sure the rep understands what the template means. Then set a due date for completion.

As the due date gets closer, follow up with the supplier and ask for a status update on the reports. If your sales rep appears unsure of the status, or does not appear optimistic about the outcome, request to speak directly to the IT contact responsible for creating the report. This demonstrates that you are serious about your request, and it can often overcome the supplier's stall tactics.

Response 3: Pushback

At times, a supplier flat-out refuses to provide a line-item detail report. This is typically the exception and not the rule, but when this issue does arise it is important to understand why.

First, the sales rep might not know how to get the reports you need. An inexperienced rep may decide to tell you the reports are not available rather than try to find out how to get them, or try, fail, then give up.

Second, the report may truly be unavailable. While this is highly unlikely in most industries, small businesses often do not have access to the same reporting capabilities or sales tracking systems as do larger organizations. The pushback may be due to the great deal of time and effort necessary to create a custom report or to have someone enter data into a spreadsheet for you.

Third, the relationship between your company and the supplier may not be very good. A supplier that has not been paid on time, has experienced numerous account management issues, or simply does not value your account may decide that a request for reports is the last straw, and may even decide to terminate the relationship.

The last reason a supplier may not provide line-item detail is the most obvious and the most common. The supplier knows it is not competitive and it wants to prevent you from discovering that. In an industry with a limited supply base (one or two predominant suppliers), this is the most common type of response.

The pushback response is the most difficult to overcome, but as you can see, there are many different reasons why the supplier might take this position. It is important to understand your supplier's rationale before formulating your response. If a supplier truly does not have access to the requisite reporting, you may need to look for other ways to collect the data. If a supplier has decided the request is too much of a burden on an already tumultuous relationship, you can look for ways to improve the relationship first and get the data you need later.

If you find the supplier is taking an aggressive posture to protect high margin, you may need to take one yourself to get the supplier to honor your request. There are several tactics you can employ, including going around your primary sales representative and requesting a meeting with someone two or three levels higher within the supplier organization, working with your own internal end users to find a better contact within the supplier organization to get the data you need, requesting a new primary sales representative, letting the supplier know that competitors would be willing to provide the data, or suggesting that an agreement might not be renewed if the request is not met.

These aggressive tactics should be used only as a last resort and with a supplier that you are confident has access to the data you need.

It is also important to note that many contracts already include language stating that a supplier agrees to provide reports or to be audited, yet many times these contractual obligations are overlooked when requests for reports are made. If you are experiencing pushback, the first thing to do is determine whether or not these legal obligations exist.

Handling the Responses

As you can see, there are several approaches you can take to handle each type of response (acceptance, avoidance, and pushback) to a request for line-item detail. However, there are also things you can do when making the initial request of suppliers to ensure more suppliers comply with your request and less counter it with pushback.

First, you should never make an initial request for line-item detail via e-mail. An e-mail request is often perceived as informal and therefore not as important as requests made face-to-face or over the phone. This will be the first of many requests you make of your supply base over the course of the project, and kicking it off in an informal manner sets a tone that will not be acceptable later on.

Even if an e-mailed request is given the appropriate amount of attention, it is much easier to avoid: ("Oh, I must not have gotten that e-mail.") Or it is often simply forwarded to IT, with little thought given to the data being requested or a timeline for getting the information back to you.

Making a request either over the phone or face-to-face is the preferred method for the request and gets a better result than an e-mail. As a best practice, requesting the information as part of an overall account review (rather than as a one-off request) can get a supplier not just to comply with your request, but also to see it as a positive step in the relationship. The account review can also be a good platform for the next step in the data collection process, the supplier interview.

 ## SUPPLIER INTERVIEWS

The rationale for interviewing incumbent suppliers is the same as that for interviewing end users. The purpose is to get a contextual understanding of the category beyond the data derived from spend analysis—learning the background or history of the relationship, finding out what the supplier provides in terms of service, determining critical aspects of the relationship, and understanding what contractual obligations exist. In some cases you may find that this is a repetitive step, and that the information provided by the supplier is similar to or exactly the same as that provided by end users. Often though, suppliers provide insight into the relationship that end users are not aware of, or can shed light on market conditions, new processes and technologies, and additional products and services that could be advantageous to your organization.

Overall, the supplier interview should be viewed as a collaborative brainstorming session. You should not invite the supplier in only to formally request information about the relationship. Instead, use the meeting as a platform to find out the supplier's pain points and motivation. What can your organization do better to help the supplier? What does a perfect customer look like? What additional business would the supplier like that it does not currently have? As we discuss in Chapter 6, understanding supplier motivation and leverage points is a vital part of the sourcing and negotiation process, and the supplier interview is the optimal time to get this information.

As part of the agenda for the meeting, ask the supplier to bring sales reports that you can review, along with any relevant paperwork, such as contracts or pricing agreements. In addition, you will find it useful to request that the supervisor of the primary sales rep attend the meeting, which helps you better get to know who to go to if you are not getting what you need from your rep. This also gives you a good indication of how your primary rep works within the company, and how aware the supervisor is of your account. If the supervisor is well up to speed, your account is probably important to your supplier, and your primary rep is doing a good job communicating your needs within his or her organization.

As described earlier in this section, during the meeting you will want to uncover more details about what the supplier does for your organization and, if possible, learn more about the marketplace. A list of questions to consider asking during the supplier interview includes:

- How long have you been a supplier for our company?
- In terms of account size, is our company a top 5 customer, top 10, or other?
- How would you rate us as a customer?
- What could we do better as a customer?
- What issues (quality, service, delivery, payment, other) have you encountered while working with our company? How have issues been resolved?
- What services do you provide our company that might not be in the contract or on an invoice?

- How would you distinguish yourself from each of your competitors?
- Why do your competitors win business that you do not?
- What measures do you take to ensure the quality of your product or service?
- What is the process by which quality problems are resolved and corrected?
- Do you provide any indemnification or insurance for your customers to protect against risk of loss due to product failure?
- What are your standard payment terms? What are the terms for our company?
- Does our company take advantage of discounted terms?
- How do you receive payment (check, ACH, etc.)? Do you have a preference?
- What market changes and innovations are on the horizon for your industry? How does your company intend to address those changes?
- What are your goals and expectations for our account?

Of course, depending on the market and the supplier relationship, other questions should be considered, including questions concerning price changes, freight terms (if applicable), and services, but these questions are a good start.

After going through the interview questions, review the reports that the supplier brought in. Do they include line-item detail? If not, make the line-item usage detail request an action item to be completed once the meeting is over. As discussed earlier in the chapter, follow up the request by providing the supplier with a template indicating the type and detail of data you need and provide a deadline for completion of the request.

The last agenda item for a supplier interview is to inform the supplier of the process you are about to engage in. You should be open and honest about the initiative. Let the supplier know this is a company-wide initiative and it is not being singled out. Keep in mind that at this point you do not know much about the competitiveness of the supplier's current pricing—you may already have a very good deal. Let the rep know that that just because your company is looking to reduce costs, this does not mean that there will be a bid). Make sure the supplier understands that all the critical aspects of the relationship and the supplier's service offering will be considered as you engage in this process.

 ## ANALYZING CONTRACTS AND PRICING AGREEMENTS

By the time the end-user and supplier interviews are complete, you will have collected any contracts or pricing agreements that are in place with your suppliers. At this stage in the process, your goal is not to rewrite agreements, but rather to identify current contractual commitments and requirements. There are several key components to contracts and pricing agreements that need to be analyzed, including general terms, conditions and pricing information, service level information, and liability. This section of the book reviews the types of contractual commitments; Chapter 7 covers what types of commitments you need to consider when entering into a new agreement.

General Terms

General terms include items like contract start and expiration dates, renewal clauses, and termination clauses. It is important to understand contract start and end dates and termination clauses for several reasons. First, if a contract was executed recently and does not have a termination clause beyond default (essentially allowing the customer or supplier to cancel the agreement if terms of the agreement are not met), then you will not be able to change suppliers until the contract end date.

Renewal clauses (also known as autorenew or evergreen clauses) are also important, because they may require that a termination notice be given a certain amount of time prior to contract expiration. For instance, a contract may expire in February of next year. However, the renewal clause states that the contract automatically renews for a one-year term unless written notice is provided no less than 60 days before agreement expiration. This means you need to give notice that you do not intend on renewing the contract by November of this year.

Pricing Information

Of course, pricing information is another important aspect of a contract or pricing agreement. While unit pricing is the most obvious pricing factor, contracts often include many other types of pricing, including:

- Mechanisms for changing price. These could include an index-based formulation linked directly to supplier raw material costs or a stipulation that prices will not exceed a certain percentage over a certain period of time.
- Notification for price changes and guidelines for accepting or rejecting changes.
- Miscellaneous charges, such as freight or other servicing fees.
- Payment terms, including early payment discount and late payment fees.

- Discount or markup structures for goods and services not specifically unit-priced in the agreement (such as non-core items for office supplies, or a tariff discount with AT&T or FedEx).
- Taxes and surcharges, including how they are applied.

There are many other types of pricing information that could be included in a contract or agreement, depending on the category. For example, a contract for print services might include tiered levels of pricing depending on the amount of items printed in one order. We cover some of the other pricing information you can expect to see for specific categories in Chapter 7, "Get It in Writing: The Contracting Phase."

As you can see, it is important to understand all aspects of pricing, beyond just the unit price. When the time comes to evaluate proposals from alternate suppliers, this information is critical to developing an apples-to-apples comparison.

Liability and Other Specific Terms

Most contracts also have clauses dealing with liability, insurance, indemnification, confidentiality, and so on. Some of these terms are fairly generic; others include information critical to the definition of the relationship between your organization and that of your supplier. Unfortunately, many end users hand this information over to their lawyers without fully understanding the business terms inherent within them.

A full evaluation of the types of clauses that could (or should) exist in a commercial agreement for products or services is beyond the scope and intent of this book. Many books and online resources are available that can help provide additional insight into contract law and the legal obligations of commercial relationships. However, it is important to note that when reading through these clauses you should understand not just what they are saying, but why they exist in the agreement. Is there mutual liability and confidentiality? Should there be? Is the supplier insured and is this insurance adequate if the product fails? All terms need to be understood before they are executed in an agreement.

Service Level Requirements, Specifications, and Scope of Work

Some service level requirements and specifications will be detailed in the contract or pricing agreement and others may not. Regardless of where the information resides (within the terms of agreement or outside), this is the last piece of information to gather as part of the data collection process.

Service Levels and Scope of Work

Customers and suppliers often negotiate minimum service levels into agreements, particularly agreements that provide a service (rather than the purchase of a product).

Many defined service levels are generic and often are included in an agreement regardless of the product or service being provided. Examples include an agreement to provide sales or usage reporting on a regular basis, quarterly account reviews, or a dedicated sales rep or customer service phone number.

Other service levels are more specific to the product or service provided; these are often referred to as the scope of work. Examples include a minimum amount of cleaning per week for a janitorial agreement, or the maximum number of service calls accepted for a software maintenance agreement. Understanding the scope-of-work details is important when introducing your requirements to alternate vendors and for validating an apples-to-apples comparison of proposals.

For example, if you are about to engage in a sourcing effort for janitorial services, your real requirement is keeping your building clean. However, this requirement is fairly subjective and most lawyers will not allow that type of guarantee into an agreement. On the other hand, outlining a schedule for the frequency of the cleaning (three days a week) and listing the types of cleaning services (dusting, vacuuming, bathrooms, windows, etc.) can give some assurances that the building will be satisfactorily cleaned. If, later on, you find that the building is not properly cleaned, you can refer back to the scope of work and verify that the supplier is performing the list of services specified in the contract.

Specifications

Specifications, which define specific criteria regarding attributes, quality, or performance, are typically included in a purchasing agreement for products. Specifications are often defined in raw materials agreements, but can be overlooked when dealing with indirect spend categories. However, understanding specifications for indirect spend categories can be just as important. Let's use office supplies as an example. In your organization, you might have some employees that use standard blue pens and others that require felt-tipped pens. Some pens may have a special type of grip. And the executive or sales team might have specially made pens with a logo or other features. In this scenario, asking a supplier to price out pens results in receiving a very diverse set of quotes.

In areas like office supplies you might find it nearly impossible to get a good idea of specifications for every potential purchase. You probably buy many different types of pens, staplers, and paper clips, among other items. How can you be expected to sit down with everyone within your organization who purchases office supplies to understand what it is they purchase? That process is time consuming at best and, in many cases, just infeasible.

Rather than interviewing each end user about the specifications of hundreds of different products, you can collect this information from the current supplier by requesting the manufacturer name and part number to be provided in a line-item usage report. Particularly if the goods are purchased through a distribution model (in which the manufacturer sells the goods to the distributor and the distributor sells the goods to you), the manufacturer part number provides competing suppliers with a good indication of the exact product being purchased and ensures an apples-to-apples comparison.

While requesting the manufacturer part number works well in a distributor model, or a model in which the products purchased are standardized, it will not help if the product you are purchasing is customized (or semicustomized) for your organization.

Examples of customized products might include corrugated boxes or printed marketing materials. In these cases, asking for the manufacturer part number will not give you the information you need to understand what is being purchased, nor will it provide alternate suppliers with a clear understanding of your requirements. If you are not already familiar with the products being purchased, there are several steps you can take to quickly get up to speed on important specifications.

First, during the supplier interview, ask suppliers to detail the factors that affect the cost of the product—specifically those related to the construction of the product. For a corrugated box, ask them to provide specifications such as box dimensions, box strength, color, and other relevant factors.

Second, take a look at similar products being purchased online. What do suppliers indicate as important specifications when selling their products? In some cases, suppliers might even put a quote form on their website. What information are they asking for in order to provide quotes?

Lastly, ask the supplier for a spec sheet, which can give you a precise list of all the important specifications tied to a particular product. A word of caution—if you are purchasing a product that is proprietary to your current supplier (i.e., this is the only supplier in the market that sells it), the supplier may ask you to sign a nondisclosure agreement before providing you with specifications. In this case, you are obligated not to share the specifications with others outside your organization, including competing suppliers.

 ## THE FINAL ANALYSIS: BUILDING A BASELINE

By now you have collected a wealth of information—line-item pricing reports, contracts and pricing agreements, and scope-of-work and specification documents. You have interviewed end users and suppliers to better understand some of the more subjective aspects of the relationship. It is now time to build your baseline document.

The baseline document is a summary of everything you have learned during the data collection process. This document comes in handy when reporting back to end users, developing RFPs or other bid documentation, and comparing proposals later on during the process. It is also used to calculate any savings achieved during the initiative.

The baseline document converts your data into four types of information:

1. Pricing information (including an analysis of line-item detail)
2. Service level information
3. Contractual requirements
4. Move-forward strategy

Pricing Information

When dealing with pricing information, start from the highest summary level you can and then break the data down from there. The baseline price analysis should start with a recap of total spend by supplier for the category. If you have multiple suppliers, demonstrate the spend by each supplier separately and then provide a total.

Then review the spend and see if it can be categorized by product or service type. For example, in a services baseline such as maintenance for your HVAC systems, break out the spend to show how much represents scheduled maintenance and how much represents service calls. If your organization has multiple facilities, you may want to break out the spend by location as well.

The pricing analysis also includes a summary of ancillary or other incurred fees, such as minimum order penalties, fuel surcharges, overtime charges, and so on. It is important to note not just what these charges are, but also how often they are incurred and the reasons why they are incurred.

Next, summarize the current cost structure. Are you paying a discount from a list price? Are you getting net prices across the board, specific to certain volumes or ordering patterns? Is pricing based on a markup structure by category?

Finally, provide a spreadsheet showing usage history and price point paid. Analyze the data to demonstrate ordering patterns, high volume items, and which products or services represent the most spend. All of this information will be used later on to develop a sourcing strategy, as well as to relay requirements to alternate vendors.

Service Level Details

The service level section of the baseline should provide a clear recap of service level requirements, including requirements that are listed in a contract or pricing agreement as well as those identified by end users. Review these service levels to determine which are true necessities for your organization (needs) versus value-adds that may not be necessary (wants). If it appears that you are paying for more service than is required, your assessment should make a clear distinction between minimum requirements and options that are nice to have but not required.

Contractual Requirements

The baseline report should also summarize any contractual considerations related to the spend category. This section should detail existing obligations, provide insight into the current agreement termination date, and identify clauses dealing with termination before that date. It should also provide an assessment of specific requirements regarding the scope of work, insurance, liability, and other important contract clauses. Finally, this section of the report should provide some context for how these obligations will be addressed during the sourcing process.

Move-Forward Strategy

By now you have developed a full analysis of your current supplier's cost structure, service levels, and contractual requirements, thereby turning your data into useful information that you can now use to develop a preliminary sourcing strategy.

A preliminary sourcing strategy describes the course of action to take after completing the data collection process. It defines the type of research to perform, the types of suppliers to contact, and the rationale for these decisions. Some factors to consider include:

- How many suppliers do we currently utilize?
- Are there other suppliers in the marketplace that provide this product or service?
- Do we have a contractual obligation with our current supplier? What happens if that obligation is not fulfilled?
- When was the last time we negotiated this contract?
- How integrated are we with the current supplier(s)? Will there be a high cost of change?
- Does it make sense to aggregate all the spend in this category together or to look at components of it separately?

It is important to note that at this point in the process you have probably developed a basic understanding of the marketplace, but you are by no means an expert. As you move into the research phase, you might find that your preliminary sourcing strategy was missing steps, or you might find that a different approach altogether is more appropriate. This is okay—the preliminary strategy is essentially a draft concept. The research process further refines and develops the strategy.

Presenting the Baseline

Now that you have created the baseline report, it is time to present this information to your team. As discussed earlier in the chapter, your team includes both stakeholders (those with direct involvement in managing the spend or working with the suppliers) and the executive(s) sponsoring the project. Many times supplier relationships are subjective, especially to those who work closest with the suppliers. Providing an objective assessment of the current supply situation and having stakeholders agree with it is the first step in the consensus-building process, critical to future assessments. If the stakeholders do not agree on your starting point, it will be more difficult for them to accept change later on.

Executives also need to be briefed on your baseline, but for a different reason. For the executive team and other sponsors, understanding the process undertaken to collect data and build the initial baseline assessment provides context for the project scope and a basic knowledge of your starting point. This makes bringing them up to speed much easier if their assistance is needed later on in the process, and also demonstrates credibility, in that you started the project in an objective way that they could agree with.

 ## IN SUMMARY

Remember, at this stage in the process it is not clear if changing suppliers or altering processes will be necessary, but in a strategic sourcing initiative, those events should always be considered as possibilities. Change management is not always easy, but a project that is done inside a bubble with no involvement from others will typically fail if change becomes necessary. Reviewing and agreeing to a baseline with those involved often seems like an unnecessary step; why present to them what they already know? But this initial step creates an easy win by demonstrating that you understand the category and that the process you are about to undertake will be an objective one.

Once you have obtained team agreement on a starting point, the research phase of the project can begin.

CHAPTER THREE

Conducting Research

O NE OF THE MOST CRITICAL, YET OFTEN OVERLOOKED, steps in any strategic sourcing initiative is conducting research. However, most people think the biggest challenge of research is knowing *what* to look for, while it is actually equally important to know *where* to look for information. The research phase of a strategic sourcing initiative requires both creative, out-of-the-box thinking and business acumen. Its purpose is to use the information analyzed during the data collection phase to begin developing market intelligence, which means identifying potential opportunities for cost reduction.

TYPES OF COST-SAVINGS OPPORTUNITIES

Cost-savings opportunities come in three forms—leveraging opportunities, process improvements, and product or service changes.

The most common type of cost-savings opportunity is the leveraging opportunity. Leveraging opportunities are created by using information to achieve a lower net price for the product or service being purchased; either through a negotiation with the current supplier or a transition to a new supplier. Often this includes gathering intelligence that relates to the price of a product or service by identifying alternate suppliers and soliciting pricing proposals. The goal is to leverage the information you have acquired in the data collection phase in order to drive the supply base to provide a better price, product, or level of service than would normally be offered to an uninformed client.

It is important to remember that strategic sourcing is not just a process to lower unit hard costs. It also includes investigating and implementing efficiencies that could result in decreased processing time, lower transaction costs, or enhanced support for your organization. Process improvements and product or service changes are often overlooked during a strategic sourcing engagement; however, these factors have the potential to reduce overall spend much more than unit cost negotiations, as they remove costs all together. Just because you currently order a certain way or use one type of technology to support a requirement does not necessarily mean that those are the best or most efficient methods. During the research phase you begin to explore the alternatives as they relate to technology, processes, products, and services.

In this chapter, we review the components of the research phase of a sourcing project. More important, we help to identify what to look for in your research. We then discuss the predominant method used to collect this information—the request for information, or RFI.

 ## UNDERSTANDING THE CATEGORY

During the research phase of your sourcing initiative, you are taking your preliminary sourcing ideas, adding context to them, and converting them into a final sourcing strategy. To accomplish this, you need to gain a broad understanding of the category being sourced. This sounds like a simple concept, but many times professionals engaging in a strategic sourcing initiative do not take the time to properly understand the category they are about to source. Instead, those procurement professionals rely solely on processes and documentation developed by their predecessors.

Relying on previous work alone is a mistake for several reasons. First, suppliers can easily pick up on your lack of understanding and insight into the category. If they perceive that you do not have a firm understanding of the market, they often quote higher prices in the hope that you will not realize their price is high.

Second, without some market insight brought about by independent research, you may not identify all the suppliers in the marketplace, or you may overlook the right type of supplier. We review types of suppliers in greater detail later in the chapter, but for now, a simple example would be a manufacturer versus a distributor. Currently you may buy all your copy paper through a distributor, such as Staples. However, if the volume of paper you consume is substantial enough, and you have inventorying capabilities, it may make better financial sense to contract directly with a paper manufacturer and purchase paper in truckload quantities. Without a firm understanding of the market, you may overlook this type of opportunity.

Third, a lack of market insight inclines you toward mimicking the methods and obtaining the results of the person or group of people who sourced the category before you. Without independent research, a sourcing professional has the tendency to use documentation, formats, and requirements already developed and available to them. However, markets are fluid and change constantly. New technologies, new products, or new ideas that could be beneficial to your organization may have come into existence since the last time the product was sourced. Alternative processes, sourcing tools, or services may be available that have not been considered before. Without market research, these opportunities can easily be overlooked.

Each spend category can have a vastly different type of research associated with it. However, there are some general elements common among all products or services that should be explored during the research phase of any strategic sourcing engagement. Those elements include:

- Identifying suppliers
- Understanding supply chains
- Understanding market conditions
- Understanding the factors of *cost*
- Review of technologies available
- Review of alternative processes
- Review of alternative products and services
- Performing a want-versus-need assessment

IDENTIFYING SUPPLIERS

Perhaps the most obvious step in the research process is supplier identification. It simply would not be possible to engage in a strategic sourcing effort without a supply base to source from. However, many times this step is not given the level of attention required. Identifying suppliers can be a tedious task—there is a wealth of information available on the Internet, but often this information is overwhelming and difficult to sort through. In an effort to save time (and sanity), many sourcing professionals adhere to the three-bid rule, meaning they only ask three suppliers to provide a quote. The three-bid concept normally ensures you are not getting completely gouged with poor pricing, but it by no means ensures you are getting the best price or service.

Others identify more than three suppliers, but may choose to arbitrarily exclude suppliers from their list. For instance, if an end user expressed that a certain supplier used to have the business but the relationship ended due to a dispute, you may have the tendency to avoid this supplier in the sourcing process. However, former suppliers often already have good insight into the needs of your organization, and over time they may have taken efforts to correct the issues that resulted in their termination. If nothing else, they may be able to provide some previously unrealized insights into the markets in question.

Another common problem is that procurement teams prepare an RFI or RFP and send it to dozens of suppliers, but they never communicate properly with those suppliers. The suppliers, who receive an unsolicited bid document with no further communication from the prospective buyer, perceive the document as a "phishing" attempt to discover the pricing range for a product or service with no serious desire to actually acquire what is being requested, and do not bother providing a proper response.

Overall, the goal of supplier identification is to create a rather comprehensive list of supplier names, contact information, and other relevant information. During the bid phase of the project you begin to narrow this down to a short list. There are many tools that can be used to help identify suppliers, and many of these tools are discussed in Part Two.

UNDERSTANDING THE SUPPLY CHAIN

The question that comes up most often when talking about supply chains is "Who is the supplier of my supplier?" Often these discussions revolve around the concept of risk and determining how reliable the supplier's supply base is to obtain what is necessary to be able to supply you with what you need to operate your business.

Particularly when sourcing raw materials, it is critical to understand who your suppliers get their material from. Generally, in the case of indirect spend, the risk of outage is somewhat reduced—while it may result in inefficiencies in your business, it probably will not stop your business from running. However, there are several reasons beyond just risk as to why you need a firm understanding of the entire supply chain. Your research period is the best time to ask the question, "What type of supplier should we be buying from?"

Each basket of goods or services or individual spend category has its own unique characteristics, and therefore each has unique types of suppliers that serve the market. The three most common types of suppliers that span most categories of indirect spend are local, regional, and national suppliers; manufacturers and distributors; and brokers, group purchasing organizations (GPOs), and other third-party suppliers.

Local, Regional, and National Suppliers

Typically, during a strategic sourcing initiative, large companies with multiple locations seek to consolidate their purchasing, particularly for indirect spend categories. If the company has locations across the country, this means that it is ideal to identify suppliers that can provide nationwide service. If the company has multiple locations that are all general in the same general region, this might entail looking for national and regional suppliers. If a company only has one or two locations, and both locations are in the same region, local suppliers might also be considered.

While overall, the consolidation of suppliers in less-strategic spend categories makes sense, in certain markets it might also result in paying a substantially higher per-unit price, particularly for products for which freight is a major component of cost, such as corrugated boxes, wooden pallets, or light bulbs. Spend categories in which services are somewhat unique to particular locations or regions may also contravene a single-supplier strategy. A good example is janitorial services, for which onsite presence is required daily by the cleaning crews.

In order to determine the type of supplier that makes the most sense for your sourcing initiative, look at how the products or services are currently being purchased. Are you currently buying from multiple suppliers across multiple locations? If so, why? It might be because different locations have different requirements, or because freight costs make a local source of supply the better option. Of course, it might also mean that there is an opportunity for cost savings through supplier consolidation.

Remember that during the research phase you are looking to develop a long list of suppliers that will be refined as you move into the bid phase. At this stage, including local, regional, and national suppliers on your list is better than limiting it to only one type of supplier, but it is important to understand the differences and distinguish between these supplier types when going to market.

Manufacturers and Distributors

The difference between manufacturers and distributors becomes a consideration when purchasing products (rather than services). A manufacturer is the company that actually produces the good you are utilizing. A distributor purchases the goods, normally in large quantities, warehouses them, and then ships them to you, typically in smaller quantities. In the office supplies example used earlier, Staples is a distributor of paper products; however, Staples does not have any facilities that actually produce paper. Instead, the company buys product from a manufacturer and warehouses it across the country.

The question of sourcing and purchasing from a manufacturer versus a distributor comes down to three primary factors: cost, quantity, and service level. Most manufacturers prefer to sell product in quantities of a truckload at a time; however, some may accept half-truckload or even pallet-load orders, depending on the market. If you believe the quantities you purchase of a particular product are a motivating factor to the manufacturing community, then you may want to consider including manufacturers in your supplier long list.

Conversely, if your quantities are low, or if you believe you require specific service levels, such as dedicated account management, same-day deliveries, and so on, along with the product being purchased, then you may want to focus your supplier list on distributors only.

As a side note, many sourcing strategies include engaging with both distributors and manufacturers, even if the end result turns out to be purchasing through a distributor. For example, in the area of maintenance, repair, and operations (MRO) supplies, working with manufacturers to standardize the types of products being purchased and committing to a certain volume with those specific manufacturers results in obtaining special pricing for your organization above and beyond what a distributor can offer. The distributor still delivers the product, with their markup on top of it, but the base price will be lower.

Another example is enterprise software acquisition, such as Microsoft licensing, or maintenance programs with hardware manufacturers, like Cisco. In both cases, it is common to actually negotiate directly with the manufacturer, and then have the manufacturer require your selected supplier to pass on the negotiated prices. We discuss manufacturer and distributor collaborative strategies in greater detail in Chapter 20.

GPOs, Brokers, and Other Third Parties

Often overlooked as part of a sourcing strategy, GPOs, brokers, and other third parties provide a wealth of market intelligence and can give you access to pricing or services that are not normally accessible. The basic concept behind these types of organizations is that they receive a small markup, normally paid by the supplier, to bring that supplier new accounts or additional sales.

GPOs normally aggregate volume from several members in order to get lower pricing from suppliers, and often provide account management and other enhanced services to members across multiple categories of spend. Most GPOs are tied to one specific supplier for a particular category of spend, although some have multiple suppliers for certain categories.

Brokers are experts in a particular market and help identify the right supplier for you based on your specific requirements. Brokers typically have relationships with multiple manufacturers and distributors, and some even warehouse product and might get involved in distribution.

Other third parties, such as manufacturer representatives, are paid to bring sales into an organization that does not have its own dedicated sales team, or desires to supplement its internal sales team with additional resources. These third parties work with one or multiple manufacturers and across one or many types of products or services.

You should consider looking at third party options when developing a supplier long list, particularly if you are unfamiliar with the category in question, lack resources, or if you feel the category adds little value to your organization and your eventual goal is to outsource management of it.

 ## UNDERSTANDING CURRENT MARKET CONDITIONS

Market conditions are comprised of the current trends or recent events going on in the marketplace, such as capacity issues, supplier consolidation or deconsolidation, new regulatory changes, natural disasters, and political or socioeconomic changes. Often, these conditions can play a major role in the results of a sourcing initiative.

Having a firm understanding of ongoing market conditions ensures that you go to market at the most advantageous time for your organization. For example, if markets are currently unstable or fluctuating dramatically, it is probably not the best time to request a price decrease from a current supplier. In addition, if product is scarce and capacity is unavailable, alternate suppliers are going to be less likely to provide you with a low price. Instead they focus on ensuring supply for existing customers. For example, you would not want to approach your suppliers for discounts for oil-based products during hurricane season, because that is when oil prices typically peak, due to speculation. You also would not want to go to market for electricity during the summer, when electricity consumption is normally at its highest, keeping prices high.

Conversely, periods of excess supply are optimal for reaching out to your suppliers and signing long-term pricing contracts.

UNDERSTANDING THE FACTORS OF COST

Understanding the factors of cost can be the most difficult piece of the research process, particularly for a category with which you are unfamiliar. Cost factors include the materials that make up the product being purchased (plastic, copper, oil, etc.) as well as the other components of cost besides materials (labor, freight, processing, etc.). Identifying the components that go into the cost of a product or service can help identify the right types of suppliers. For example, if a product has a rather high cost for freight, you may want to consider a local source of supply in order to minimize that freight cost. Knowing that copper is a major component of raw material costs in a certain product may help you decide to put off sourcing that product until a copper shortage is rectified.

REVIEW OF TECHNOLOGIES, PROCESSES, PRODUCTS, AND SERVICES

Most strategic sourcing engagements tend to focus on a strict apples-to-apples comparison of products or services, meaning that the only options researched or considered are those that match the current requirement. If alternatives are considered, they are often reviewed as second-stage initiatives once a supplier is selected, or in lieu of a strategic sourcing process altogether. The pitfall to these approaches is that an alternate supplier may be better suited to fill your future requirements, but you sourced to a specification that only identified your current requirement.

Alternative Technologies

Technology means a lot of different things to different people—from the systems put in place to help you integrate with current suppliers, through the telecommunications used to connect you to the outside world, to the software used to manage your business. The one common element across all these technology platforms is that they become dated very quickly.

If there is a technical component to implementing the requirement you are sourcing (for example, your current supplier transmits reports concerning a certain product or service that integrate directly into your enterprise resource planning [ERP] system), there is most likely a cost associated with that implementation, and many times that already amortized cost is used as a reason not to look at alternative sources of supply. However, it could be that the requirement is outdated and difficult for the supplier to maintain, which results in them adding additional markup to your pricing. It could also be that a different technology may produce efficiencies that would result in less need for management oversight.

Do not let a desire to achieve the sourcing project quickly or to minimize the effort involved by performing only a strict apples-to-apples comparison lead you to inadvertently exclude competing or alternative technologies from consideration. Exploring these options and performing a thorough total cost analysis (including the cost of change) could provide for cost savings opportunities well beyond what could be gained from a unit-cost perspective alone.

Alternative Processes, Products, and Services

It is common to discover during initial discussions with end users in your organization that stakeholders tend to define their requirements based on the way they have always done things. End users usually develop a mind-set that they need to order supplies in a certain way, they need specific reports provided on specific days of the week, and they need suppliers that are certified (to the end user's satisfaction) in specific processes, software, or quality control methodologies, among other personal requirements.

Sometimes there are good reasons for these requirements. Many end users have worked hard to figure out what they believe to be the best and most efficient processes, and perceive that having a supplier who matches those requirements makes their jobs easier, freeing them to do other things that add more value to the organization. In other cases these requirements were developed based on what was most familiar to the end user or due to an unwillingness to go through the learning curve associated with mastering a new process. In some cases, the requirements were actually developed by the existing supplier, carefully and intentionally implemented in the guise of free training.

What end users often fail to realize is that mandating specific processes or other servicing requirements onto the supply base without considering alternatives can add costs that exceed any efficiencies the current processes provide. First, stringent servicing requirements can add to the unit cost of the product or service being purchased. You may not get charged extra for those additional customized reports you receive from your current supplier, but the likelihood is the supplier factored the cost to produce the reports into the unit cost of the item being purchased.

Second, developing specific requirements that only a small number of suppliers can meet limits competition and eliminates alternative processes or enhancements that may be more beneficial to your organization. An example of this might be requiring that your supplier have x number of years servicing companies in the identical market that your organization is in. Some end users do this on purpose to intentionally limit the number of respondents to a sourcing initiative, to make the selection process easier, as they see it.

Another common example is requiring a particular software certification from a supplier as it relates to the company's reporting or transaction management functions in the ERP system. Often end users require that any alternate supplier have the same level and type of certification that their current supplier has. Many suppliers can integrate into the major ERP systems or other common software programs used by most businesses. However, not all suppliers expend the time and energy to go through the process of becoming certified with a particular software vendor. There are many reasons for this, the primary being that software vendors charge to certify—and these costs can be substantial. Companies go through the certification process to distinguish themselves as partners of a particular software vendor and use that certification in their own marketing materials, but certification in itself does not prove that one company is more qualified than another to integrate with a particular system. Ultimately, the only real difference you can confirm (without further research) between a company with a certification and one without is that the certified company paid for the certification.

In this example, if you require some level of integration between your systems and those of your supplier, the real requirement is that the supplier is capable of achieving that integration, not that it is certified. This might mean it has experience with your particular software or similar software programs. It could even mean that the company partners with a third party that is certified with the right software. To achieve proper supplier integration, you need to work with your IT team to determine the types of information being shared, the formats of that information, and other relevant technical details. Having a certified supplier does assure you that a company has integration experience, but it does not mean you have the supplier that can provide the most value to your organization.

End users argue that looking at alternatives or changing processes requires an investment in time, and that "time is money." Yet without performing a total cost analysis to determine whether process changes actually cost more than the associated unit cost reductions or other enhanced efficiencies, this argument is not valid.

It is important to note, particularly when considering alternate processes and products, that the current supplier may have helped design the current requirement. This is especially true when long-term suppliers are involved or when it appears that only one or two suppliers can appropriately serve your needs. Suppliers usually have a very detailed knowledge of the marketplace and understand the differences between their service offerings and those of their competitors. They often customize their products or services to ensure that no other supplier in the marketplace favorably compares during an apples-to-apples assessment. This makes understanding the history of a supplier relationship and who was involved in developing the initial requirement all the more important.

Performing a Want-Versus-Need Assessment

During the data collection phase of your sourcing initiative, you determined the current requirement or scope of work, meaning you identified not just the costs associated with a particular spend category, but what you are getting for that money. Hand-in-hand with a review of alternative technologies, processes, products, and services, it is worthwhile to determine what the current requirement *should be.* Many companies tend to develop a certain level of inertia in their procurement processes—if your organization has purchased a certain item in the past, it tends to continue to be purchased that way in the present and future. This is especially true if the reason for the purchase is no longer clear, if multiple end users purchase the same or similar products and services, or if the original purchaser has moved into a new role or has left the company. Part of the reason for identifying current costs is to determine which of those costs can be factored out entirely.

A particularly striking example of the value of performing a want-versus-need assessment can be found in the area of corporate banking—particularly corporate cash management (corporate checking accounts). If you are familiar with this category, then you know that the statement you get every month could detail hundreds of charges. Many of these charges come with unclear descriptions that are difficult to understand, such as "CD CK Fine Sort" or "ACH NOCS." In one sourcing engagement, the authors, along with a Source One team, assisted a client in sourcing banking and treasury services. After collecting recent invoices, we sat down with representatives of the client's bank and reviewed each and every charge on their invoices. We asked them to explain charges that were unclear. In the end, we found that many of the charges were based on services that were no longer required or were redundant. In one case, the customer was paying for the same reports to be sent to them electronically, on a CD-ROM, and faxed—each of these services incurred its own charges! This happened primarily because as new technologies became available, end users were reluctant to retire the old methods, for fear of making mistakes or not getting all the information they needed. This concern drove the decision to continue the duplicate services; however, neither the fax nor the CD-ROM tools had been used for years. Those services were eliminated as part of the sourcing project.

If a want-versus-need assessment had not been performed before sourcing and negotiations on this project, it is possible that the customer could have obtained a lower price for each of these report formats. However, removing these costs altogether produced a much greater savings than reducing unit prices ever could. As you can see from this example, a want-versus-need assessment is an integral part of a complete spend analysis.

 ## COLLECTING MARKET INTELLIGENCE THROUGH THE RFI PROCESS

There are many tools you can use to help gather market intelligence and uncover cost savings opportunities, such as trade publications, online directories, and e-sourcing tools. In Chapter 11 we discuss these tools and distinguish between standard and real-time market intelligence. In this section we discuss the predominant method companies use to collect information about the supply base once suppliers have been identified: the request for information, or RFI. An RFI is one of three functions of the RFx (request for x; either information, a quote, or a proposal) process. The other two functions, the request for a quote (RFQ) and the request for a proposal (RFP) serve different functions later in the sourcing process, and are discussed in detail in Chapter 4.

RFIs are typically used by companies as fact-finding tools to learn more about the supply base and help narrow down the long list of suppliers to a shorter list that should be considered to be invited to respond to an RFP or RFQ. RFIs can be configured in many ways, from a simple list of questions in an e-mail to a formal document or online questionnaire with specific instructions and formats for responses. Typically, the questions in an RFI revolve around company financials, quality controls, account management, customer service, technical capabilities, locations, and other general information.

Developing and submitting an RFI to alternate suppliers may be your first exposure to the supply base. This introduction is critical, as it sets the tone for your future relationship with them and begins the process of transitioning the project from the research to the sourcing phase. As such, there are some basic concepts to consider when developing the RFI to help you build a motivated supply base.

Do Not Rely Solely on the RFI

The first common mistake is to rely solely on the RFI to gain market intelligence. An RFI should be used to supplement independent research and fill in gaps where information is not available. In fact, the questions you include in your RFI document should be developed based on your understanding of the market after independent research has been completed. Many people make their RFI generic and all-encompassing. This merely gets you a wealth of generic and all-encompassing responses, or data dumps, which contain a lot of information extraneous to your sourcing project and do not necessarily help you develop strategies or aid in the decision-making process.

Consider Your Format

The second common mistake is assuming that an RFI must be a written, formalized document. Rather, asking a few informal questions in an e-mail or over the phone might make more sense at this stage. In some cases, having suppliers come in to present their service offerings and asking key questions at that time might be the best approach. We discuss this strategy in greater detail in Chapter 4.

The format of your RFI depends largely on two factors—how suppliers prefer to go to market, and current market conditions and timing factors. If a product or service is in high demand and suppliers have many requests from existing and new customers, taking the time to provide you with a thorough written response can cause delays in acquiring the information you need. Conversely, it is rare that a supplier would decline an invitation to meet face-to-face to discuss their offering.

Always Start with a Phone Call

If you have decided on a written format, do not initiate the RFI by sending it via e-mail. Once suppliers are identified, make voice contact with them before sending the document. Explain what you are trying to accomplish and get a feel for the way they would approach engaging in further discussions. If most of the suppliers you speak with recommend delivering a presentation, you may want to include that as a next step.

In Chapter 9, "What Not To Do," we outline in more detail why it is critical to reach out to suppliers via the phone, and why sending e-mails to "info@xyzsupplier.com" or "sales@abccompany.net" typically does not yield positive results.

Important Considerations for Properly Designing an RFI

While the main purpose of an RFI is to fill in the gaps in your independent research, you can also use the process to begin establishing a working rapport with potential suppliers. Important considerations in this regard include:

- The first interaction with each potential supplier should take place over the phone. Engaging in casual conversations with the supply base opens the lines of communication, as suppliers will be pleased to have some personal interaction with a prospective customer. During these phone calls, make suppliers aware of the upcoming issuance of an RFI, then inquire as to the approach they wish to take in responding to this request.
- Giving suppliers the option to respond to the RFI in their chosen format allows them to feel most comfortable and, in turn, deliver the best results. A few points to remember:
  - Consistency is not needed in the RFI format, just in the questions being asked.
  - When initial contact is made with a supplier's representative, he or she may wish to address requests at that time; therefore, be prepared with your questions.
  - Expect the format chosen by a supplier during the RFI process to be similar to the one it wishes to use in the RFP and RFQ phases.
  - Some suppliers may be willing to pay you a visit to present their offerings face-to-face and have open dialogues concerning the goals of the sourcing process.
- Ask specific questions in the RFI. In earlier phases, you have already developed an understanding of the spend category being sourced, and the RFI

should be designed to expand that understanding, not just legitimize it. Therefore, the questions asked in the RFI should be geared toward discovering this new information. Questions that are too general usually only produce information that has already been gathered.

▪ RFI results and independent research are not interchangeable. The purpose of an RFI is to fill in the missing pieces of your research. If the results only validate the results of the already-gathered research, keep in mind that the RFI may not be a necessary step in future initiatives.

In some cases an informal conversation over the phone may be the best method to get the message across about your company's needs. The supplier may give some insight into its ability to compete for the business. This could save both of you some time if you determine it is not a good fit. Alternatively, the conversation may help you drive better savings later on if the impression received is that the company very badly wants to win your business. An effective way to prequalify this situation is to ask suppliers three key questions:

1. What do you need from us in order to succeed in a mutual, long-lasting engagement?
2. What would be the ideal result of forming a relationship with my organization?
3. How can you help us distinguish ourselves from our competition?

Through asking these questions, buyers can get a sense as to whether they should continue discussions with a supplier.

Bypassing the RFI

In some instances, buyers may be confident that they have captured enough market intelligence on the spend category being sourced without the use of an RFI. They have thoroughly analyzed their research and it appears complete. As long as an exhaustive, in-depth research effort has been performed, an RFI can often be bypassed.

Most importantly, try to avoid developing this mind-set: "It wouldn't hurt to issue an RFI." Issuing an unneeded RFI adds inefficiency to the sourcing process and does not help you find the quickest path to savings. In addition, it is important to be considerate and respectful of a potential supplier's time and effort. Suppliers may have a sincere interest in working with you, but overwhelming them with unnecessary requests may cause them to lose that interest. Remember to use the RFI process to begin establishing a good working rapport with potential suppliers.

 IN SUMMARY

Depending on the types of products or services you purchase, you may find suppliers' offerings to be fairly generic, without many differentiating factors. Additionally, independent research may have uncovered everything you need to know about the suppliers. If this is the case, an RFI may not be necessary. Regardless of how you have collected your market intelligence, once you have acquired it, you are ready to develop your final sourcing strategy.

The final sourcing strategy identifies the cost savings opportunities you believe are available in the marketplace and details the steps to exploit those opportunities. This might include requesting quotes from a group of suppliers, asking for full proposals that detail alternative technologies or processes, or bypassing alternatives altogether and requesting unit-cost concessions from your incumbent supplier.

Not all markets lend themselves well to an RFP process, and not all suppliers respond favorably to a direct negotiation, but your research should determine which approach or approaches have the most merit. Regardless of the final strategy, the likelihood is that you are now ready to engage in the next phase of the strategic sourcing process—the bid phase, which uses all three functions of the RFx process.

CHAPTER FOUR

4

The RFx Process

THE MAJORITY OF THE WORK performed thus far has taken place within the boundaries of your organization. The only outside party you have consistently interacted with at this point is the incumbent supplier. The bid phase, often referred to in industry jargon as the RFx process (request for *x*; either information, a quote, or a proposal), is the step in which discussions begin with other outside parties—competitors of the incumbent. In this phase of the sourcing initiative, buyers utilize the research gathered in earlier phases and the list of suppliers, which has been whittled down from long to short in the previous phase, to begin requesting proposals and pricing from the supplier community. While continuing to communicate with the incumbent, buyers are also ready to present current and future business needs to the marketplace.

The RFx process is considered by many to be the most important step of a strategic sourcing initiative, as it is the phase where crucial information is exchanged between buyers and suppliers. RFx branches off into three primary functions—request for information (RFI), request for proposal (RFP), and request for quotation (RFQ). The previous chapter defined the purpose of an RFI and the role it plays within the research phase of a sourcing process. This chapter further expands on this method, but concerns itself primarily with the additional methods companies utilize to collect information from potential suppliers: the RFP and RFQ. The techniques used during the RFx phase will have a direct correlation to the results produced. This chapter details the key strategies to consider when developing a go-to-market approach. Furthermore, guidelines for drafting and executing the RFP and RFQ are discussed, as well as caveats to be mindful of as the chosen sourcing strategy is carried out.

USING THE RFI TO BEGIN THE SOURCING PHASE

The previous chapter detailed how to properly execute an RFI and the purpose it serves in filling the knowledge gaps in your research. The execution of a properly-designed RFI process delivers the added benefit of transitioning the buyer from the research phase to the sourcing phase. The results of the RFI, along with independent research, serve as a guideline to determining the best route in working with the potential supply base. This is the first step in developing an effective sourcing strategy.

A major component of developing this strategy is determining how you plan to keep suppliers engaged throughout the sourcing initiative. The responses to the RFI (if one is conducted) give you the first indications of how suppliers will respond to requests and wish to communicate throughout the sourcing engagement. It sets the tone for all future correspondence with the supply base and acts as a stepping-stone to the actual sourcing process.

As a step in your analysis of research and RFI responses, regroup with your team and review the supplier list that has been developed. It is quite possible that some team members may have insight into a certain supplier on the list that can either disqualify it or keep it in the running. Also, you may have done business with some of the selected suppliers in the past. If so, find out which individuals within your company communicated directly with these suppliers and inquire about their performance. This will help you refine your target list for the RFP and RFQ steps.

The results of the analysis of your research and RFI responses, if administered, will help determine if an RFP or RFQ is the next best step in the sourcing process. Additionally, the way suppliers are approached from here on out and the information being asked of them are determined by the product or service being sourced, the requirements for that specific commodity, and the current market conditions.

DEVELOPING YOUR SOURCING STRATEGY

The primary goal of any sourcing initiative is to achieve sustainable savings through a best-in-class agreement. Your research may deliver enough leverage to negotiate with the incumbent supplier, rather than necessitating a full sourcing initiative. On the other hand, your research may suggest that conducting a full RFx will most likely unveil additional savings opportunities and a better snapshot of the competitive landscape. Regardless of what the research indicates, the sourcing strategy will dictate the outcome of the entire initiative, and research and RFI results are the main input for its development.

With these inputs in mind, the next step is to sort products or services being sourced into one of four classifications: tactical, leveraged, critical, or strategic. Figure 4.1 details how these four classifications relate to each other and how to place a particular spend category into the appropriate classification.

Products and services are bucketed into these four groups by analyzing their risk of supply loss and actual value within an organization. Each spend classification is marked low to high in terms of its impact on these two factors.

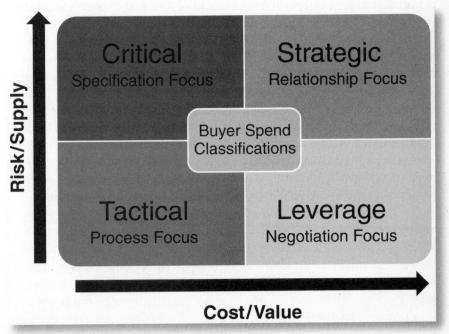

FIGURE 4.1 Buyer Spend Classifications

Furthermore, each classification is associated with a specific sourcing strategy. Once a product or service category is classified, it is easy to determine which sourcing strategy is most appropriate. Depending on how the product or service is viewed in the marketplace and used within your company, the corresponding strategy focuses on lowering the risk of supply loss and the cost of the product or service while maintaining value in the eyes of the final consumer. This system will help your company implement a standardized process for developing sourcing strategies related to the items that fall into each of the four classifications, enabling consistent results in sourcing efforts.

Let us now define each spend classification and the sourcing strategy paired with each one.

Tactical—Low Risk of Supply Loss, Low Cost/Value

Products and services that are purchased at very low costs and are widely available among suppliers are normally considered tactical purchases. A purchase is also considered tactical if the company's internal process cost to acquire a certain product or service is equal to, or more than, the actual cost of that product or service. For example, if more than $2 of time and resources is required to purchase a $2 box of pens, that product is a prime candidate for the tactical category. Therefore, the focus of your efforts should include eliminating as much time as possible in acquiring these products and services. When sourcing a tactical spend category, significant hard-dollar savings may not be realized due to the already low costs for these products and services; however, soft-dollar savings are normally achieved through improved ordering and payment processes, vendor and invoice consolidation, enhanced technologies, and so on. If an RFP is released for a tactical spend category, make sure to include an inquiry about a supplier's ability to help your organization reduce supply chain costs. Online purchasing capabilities via the supplier's website or other automated ordering processes should be included in the set of criteria for selecting a supplier.

Two spend categories normally classified as tactical are maintenance, repair, and operations (MRO) products and administrative expenses, such as office supplies. Many MRO suppliers offer vendor-managed programs in which the supplier tracks a customer's stockroom inventory and refreshes it when needed. Therefore, the supplier does the ordering for the customer. If this type of program is implemented, be sure to specify the quality of products you wish your supplier to pull from their inventory when refreshing yours. For example, some suppliers may provide a product that has a higher grade of stainless steel or other specification that is of higher quality than needed. For office supplies, work with the supplier to automate the ordering process and mandate low-cost generic products over name brands. Setting up this type of program allows for centralized control over products purchased and makes it as easy as possible for employees to gain access to the supplies they need.

Sourcing strategies for the MRO and office supplies spend categories are discussed later, in chapters designated for each spend category. Typically, an RFP is issued for tactical spend categories in order to evaluate suppliers' capabilities in regard to streamlining a company's acquisition processes.

Leveraged—Low Risk of Supply Loss, High Cost/Value

A product or service is classified in the leveraged category if the risk of supply loss is low and the cost associated with the product or service is high. Negotiation is the key to sourcing leveraged categories. There are not many differentiating factors among the suppliers that offer leveraged products and services. Service levels and pricing are generally consistent across the supply base. Potential strategies include negotiating discounts in the form of volume pricing agreements or long-term contracts in exchange for price concessions. Leveraged categories sometimes do not lend themselves well to an RFP process since you already generally know what the results will be. However, an RFQ may be necessary to make sure current pricing is in line with the market.

Uniforms are a good example of a leveraged spend category. This commodity could be a good or a service (depending on whether the uniforms are purchased or rented). In this category, there are many players in the marketplace with very similar offerings, which creates a great opportunity to negotiate. The introduction of competition is an excellent fulcrum from which to leverage improved price points and enhanced service levels.

Critical—High Risk of Supply Loss, Low Cost/Value

Critical purchases are those essential to the buyer's end product or operation. Therefore, the sourcing strategy should focus on making a product's specifications as generic as possible in order to expand the supply base and eliminate dependence on a single source of supply. There are several ways to accomplish this goal.

One method is to include suppliers in the sourcing initiative that are able to provide substitutes for specialized equipment or parts. These products are normally less expensive, but also may come with quality or reliability issues. To counter this during the RFP process, make sure information is gathered pertaining to the supplier's warranty policy and ensure that all liabilities are covered.

The equipment currently utilized to create an end product may require expensive replacement parts, regardless of whether they are purchased from the original manufacturer or an alternate. A good sourcing strategy for the critical classification is to explore similar equipment that has more options with regard to replacement parts. Investing in new equipment or supplies may be worthwhile if it allows for more flexibility in specifications. For example, an end product may involve the use of a polypropylene film with tight specifications dictated by the machine on which the film is run. You may decide that you need to source new machinery, but also be open to suppliers that offer alternative film specifications that could be compatible with existing machinery. In the long term, the savings available through a transition to a different specification may be greater than the investment required for the new piece of equipment compatible with the new film specification.

Furthermore, it is quite possible that the incumbent supplier only made you aware of one certain specification compatible with your equipment. Film with slightly different specifications may run seamlessly with the equipment as well. Information gathered during the baseline phase will help you understand why a certain product is being purchased over another. The best sourcing approach for critical purchases is to issue an RFP with an associated RFQ exhibit that provides precise specifications for the current products being purchased. In the RFP portion, present these specifications as the current state and encourage suppliers to present alternative options that will produce the same or similar end results. Such recommendations for process changes or improvements should always be considered and welcomed during the RFP process. The objective for sourcing critical products and services is to develop a procurement process that eventually allows them to be categorized as tactical purchases.

Strategic—High Risk of Supply Loss, High Cost/Value

For items that are strategic to a business, the main focus is on developing quality relationships with suppliers. In the other three purchasing categories, buyers generally should maintain a commercial relationship with their supply base. For strategic categories, the emphasis is on developing a mutually beneficial relationship or partnership. Buyers should establish agreements with their suppliers to share information and closely integrate systems to obtain operational efficiencies. The goal is to reduce costs and maximize benefits for both parties. The supplier's willingness and ability to collaborate and develop a long-lasting partnership mind-set should be closely evaluated during the vendor selection process.

For example, a higher learning institution should consider the student information system software used to manage each student's relationship with the university, from applicants to alumni, as falling within the strategic spend category. The cost for this software is significant but, based on its role in the organization, it is worth the investment. It is essential to make sure that the software provider realizes that its customer is highly dependent on its products and services. Therefore, such a provider should be prepared to deliver value-added services as part of the package, including training when new members join the customer's organization, high-quality customer service to effectively address any implementation or operational problems with the software, competitive pricing, and reasonable annual maintenance charges and support fees, which need to be monitored closely.

A strategic item is a product or service that allows your business to separate itself from the competition. Therefore, if a supplier does not effectively deliver quality products or services in this classification, this will disrupt your business operations and eventually impact the final consumer, and ultimately your bottom line.

 ## GOING TO MARKET

Once you have assigned your spend category to a classification, it is time to go to market. Be prepared to fully engage the RFP process. The release of the RFP and gathering of responses will be followed by individual face-to-face meetings between a cross-functional team from your organization and the supplier finalists. A significant portion of the RFP should be designated to discovering the service offerings of alternate vendors and how they would integrate into your organization. The implementation process also needs to be carefully evaluated, as a seamless transition is a necessity.

For purchases falling into the strategic classification, detailed conversations exploring partnership possibilities also need to be held between the buyer and RFP respondents. If a supplier is not able to invest the human resources necessary to address the buyer's needs and concerns during the RFP process, it will most likely not be able or willing to do so during the relationship.

Your approach to the RFP process will vary depending on the classification of the spend. As a buyer, you need to understand how valuable the product or service being sourced is to your overall company's operations. To accomplish this, imagine your current supplier of that product or service suddenly going bankrupt. Will your business operations come to a screeching halt? If the answer is yes, and the change will eventually impact the final consumer, a strategic-supplier approach needs to be implemented. Playing out certain scenarios will help you determine which classification best applies to the spend category in question. All buyers are continuously focused on attaining the best total value for their procurement dollar with the least amount of time and money invested. It stands to reason that more effort and time is needed to source spend categories that are considered an integral part of the overall business. It is best to invest time in sourcing initiatives that offer the greatest opportunities for realizing savings or added value. Classifying spend categories will allow for proper resource allocation and an easy determination of the sourcing strategies to execute, pinpointing those spend categories that have the greatest need for improvement and those that require less attention along the way.

A common mistake during sourcing initiatives is to lock in to the strategy suggested by your initial classification, regardless of how complex or volatile a market is. After a sourcing strategy has been designated to the product or service being sourced, regroup with your team to assess the strategy further. Markets continually change, delivering a constant stream of new information. Therefore, always be prepared to revisit the initial strategy and adapt to new market intelligence. Constant fine-tuning will encourage suppliers to provide outside-the-box ideas, and help ensure that an optimal solution is identified and implemented.

 ## GENERATING THE RFP AND RFQ

The RFx process delivers a great deal of information. However, such information does not always translate into the *correct and relevant* information needed to select the most qualified supplier for current and future business needs. This phase of the sourcing process is highly dependent on the internal baseline established during the data collection stage, which objectively defined what was done in the past, both qualitatively and quantitatively. The baseline helps you identify what is being sourced and from whom, the current pricing structure and service level requirements, and future considerations for the spend category. Essentially, the baseline becomes the foundation for the RFP and RFQ documents.

At this stage of the process, a short list of suppliers will be fully engaged and ready to receive an RFP or RFQ. This section details the elements necessary to include in the RFP and RFQ documentation in order to produce the right results to use for scoring suppliers and beginning negotiations.

Buyers often make many mistakes during this stage of the process. These mistakes are normally a result of strict internal policies within an organization for drafting and issuing RFPs. The following list briefly discusses some of the more common errors in the RFx creation and release process. Each will be addressed in greater detail in Chapter 9, which is devoted to avoiding these problems, but it is worthwhile at this point to provide a general overview of the potential pitfalls, due to their essential nature in delivering the best responses.

- The RFP document should be supplier-friendly and not overly convoluted in its design. One of the most common complaints of suppliers is that complex, static RFPs do not permit them to address the benefits, ideas, opportunities, and competitive advantages that they offer, and only allow them to submit a financial response. A straightforward and uncomplicated document will encourage suppliers to participate and allow them to present their most competitive offer.
- Keep the RFP open-ended. This gives suppliers the freedom to present more creative solutions and introduce fresh ideas into the process.
- "Sell" your RFP to suppliers by representing the reasons why your company's business is attractive and valuable. Provide the suppliers' salespeople a business case that they can take to their management to drive steeper discounts and more value-added services. The more potential business there is at stake, the more aggressive the suppliers will be in trying to win it.

Open communication is crucial. Suppliers often have questions about the RFP document and its content. These questions need to be addressed in a timely, organized, and straightforward manner so that suppliers can appropriately respond to the RFP. Schedule time with each supplier to review the document and ensure that they completely understand the requirements and expectations.

Be prepared to *not* receive responses to RFx or reverse auction (discussed later in this chapter) requests. As the suppliers review the requests, they may realize that they cannot meet the requirements. It is quite possible that they do not have adequate human resources to submit a proposal, and will therefore not be able to handle the business if they win it. Keep in mind that for those suppliers that are tight on time and resources, there are alternative options for gathering information on their overall offering and how they can provide value to your organization as a potential business partner. Your acceptance of flexibility and creativity as a buyer should be made known among the potential supply base. Overburdening formalities of an RFx or reverse auction process may contradict this message. You want to ensure that the best results are achieved in the strategic sourcing initiative, and sometimes information is gathered better through means other than an RFx or reverse auction. Always be willing to consider other options in gaining information from suppliers, as detailed later in this chapter.

The Differences between an RFP and an RFQ

Sometimes buyers consider an RFP and an RFQ to be interchangeable. However, differences exist between the two sourcing methods. An RFP is a more formal document utilized in sourcing a spend category that plays a significant role in a company's operations. It is more sophisticated than an RFQ and focuses on more service-related offerings. An RFP also involves more technical-related aspects of a spend category and how they relate to your company's overall operations. An RFQ is typically used when the majority of participating suppliers have similar, or the same, levels of service. The servicing aspect is, of course, a critical piece, but pricing is the main driving factor in the evaluation process.

The Elements of a Typical RFP

By including the following typical elements in a well-designed RFP, you will capture the most comprehensive and targeted responses from the supply base.

Cover Page

The cover page should clearly indicate who you are and what you are seeking to source. Elements include:

- The words "Request for Proposal."
- Buyer's company name and logo.
- The name of the product or service being sourced. This may be accompanied by an RFP identification number, if desired.
- The month and year the RFP is released.

Header and Footer

A header or footer, or both, are usually included on all pages of the document except the cover page.

- The footer usually displays the page number.
- The header typically contains the buyer's company name and the month and year the RFP is released.

Table of Contents

This is not a necessary page to include, but it helps keep the RFP supplier-friendly by providing a quick snapshot of the RFP's contents. As final changes are made to your document, be sure the pages correspond correctly. Reference all exhibits and appendixes that are attached to the RFP. The table of contents provides suppliers with a checklist as they complete the RFP.

Business Description

The heart of the document includes:

- *Company abstract:* Provide an overview of your company (100–150 words). Include products or services provided, current operations, and location(s). Other possible elements to present include:
  - Business objectives
  - Technology
  - Record of sales
  - Achievements and recognition
- *Program goals and purpose of the RFP:* Present the objective(s) of the RFP. Include any projects or services the contract affects. Discuss your company's current status and why you are requesting a proposal. Include any areas of the company that this proposal would affect.
  - Example: The primary goals of this initiative are to reduce the overall cost of <Insert Spend Category> paid by <Insert Your Company Name>, develop a best-in-class agreement, and improve service levels and reporting capabilities. To this end, participating suppliers will be evaluated based on a combination of cost improvements, account management and value-added services, and billing and reporting features.

RFP Details

This section details the steps necessary for a supplier to respond to the RFP.

- *Contact information:* Provide the point of contact for your company's main interface during the RFP process. Include the following information:
  - Name
  - Company
  - Phone

- Fax number
- E-mail address
- *Specific submission requirements (e.g., electronic submission):* Specify how you wish to receive responses.
- *Dates of submission:* Provide a date for suppliers to submit their finished proposals. Specify whether different portions of the RFP (e.g., Notice of Intent to Respond) need to be submitted prior to the final due date. Table 4.1 details a sample project timeline, helpful for keeping suppliers on track.

Scope of Work

Provide in detail the requirements and duties to be executed under this proposal. Include any information needed for creating a proposal (a specific format, tables, charts). Insert a high-level breakdown of the types of products or services required, as well as any other relevant high-level information, such as volumes.

RFP Evaluation Process

It is important to clearly indicate to suppliers how to get questions answered, and how the responses will be evaluated.

- *RFP questions:* Specify that all questions must be submitted in writing via e-mail, or the method of choice being used to administer the RFP. Notify suppliers that each response must reference the applicable section and subsection number from the RFP. Also emphasize the deadline in stating that questions must be received no later than the deadline defined in the Request for Proposal Details section (allowing for reasonable response time).

TABLE 4.1 Sample Request for Proposal Milestones

Activity Description	Date
Issue RFP to vendor finalists	April 9th
Conduct vendor teleconferences to review RFP	April 11th
All supplier questions submitted	April 14th
Response to questions released to all suppliers	April 17th
Receive RFP responses	April 23rd
Conduct vendor reference checks	April 23rd–April 26th

TABLE 4.2 Sample Table of RFP Requirements

Response Section # or Title	Requirement	Reference #
Executive summary	Respond within RFP document	5.1
Company information	Respond within RFP document and also complete Appendix A directly	6.1
Pricing	Respond within RFP document	5.2
Quality and service	Respond within RFP document	5.3
Appendix B	Respond within RFP document	6.2

■ *Response submission:* Detail to suppliers that the proposal response and all supporting documentation should be submitted to a designated e-mail address. If an e-sourcing tool is being used, provide specifics for access and use in this section. The RFP should not be the first time the suppliers are being introduced to the e-sourcing platform being used. Repeat the deadline date and state that each supplier's proposal response must be received by the deadline.

Table 4.2 provides a reference for each supplier to make sure all items in the RFP are addressed.

■ *RFP evaluation process*
  ■ Evaluation: Describe any criteria that will affect the bidders' qualifications. Note and describe all elements of the RFP that will be evaluated and its impact on the final decision.
  ■ Award criteria: Describe the criteria used to determine the award to the qualified bidder. Describe all stipulations regarding the confidentiality between the company requesting the RFP and the bidder.

RFP Response

It is important to give clear guidance to potential suppliers on the type, format, and scope of the information you would like them to return in their responses. The elements below outline the structure of an RFP response, and may change depending on the type of RFP.

■ *Executive summary or profile:* Ask suppliers to include contact information for the person submitting the proposal and a brief company background. This section may also include references from the bidder submitting the RFP and contact information for other departments of the bidder. Also request an overview of the product or service capabilities and why the company is best suited to meet requirements.

- *Product or service capabilities and pricing:* Reference an attached RFQ document containing full line-item detail of annual purchases and usage. Be as specific as possible in this section. Ask suppliers to include information on payment methods (pricing, additional charges, fees, pricing policies, etc.). Some sample questions are:
  - Do you agree to hold quoted prices for <*x* amount of time>?
  - Do you agree to provide <insert your company name> with documentation that justifies price changes?
  - Detail all ancillary fees including delivery charges, minimum order fees, and so on.
- *Quality and service:* Ask suppliers to describe any currently available programs and discounts that could pertain to the proposal. Request information on any insurance or protection plans. Inquire about lead times, inventory management, account management capabilities, and other value-added services. Also ask suppliers to outline their customer service programs.
- *Technology:* Inquire about any available online management tools, software, technological improvements, and reporting capabilities.
- *Payment:* Ask suppliers to describe the payment process in detail, including terms, methods, and so on. Gather information on suppliers' invoicing and billing methods. Inquire whether they offer consolidated invoices.
- *Implementation:* Require suppliers to outline an implementation plan and address how they will manage compliance across your organization through the proposed program. Be sure to ask what resources will be assigned to the implementation process.
- *Additional information:* Request information about any available additional value-added services.

Appendix

Create an appendix for additional information that pertains to the RFP and for a standardized format.

- *Appendix A—Sample*
  - Company information
    - Annual sales. (Please break down by company and product.)
    - Are you a public or private company?
    - Is your company recognized as a diversity supplier?
    - Please list your company's warehouses.

Company's Warehouses

#	City	State	Country
1.			
2.			
3.			

Manufacturing Locations

#	City	State	Country	# of Employees	Total Warehouse Size (Sq. Feet)
1.					
2.					
3.					

- *Appendix B*—Sample
  - Create an appendix for contact information and references.

Company Contacts

Name:

Department:

Phone number:

E-mail:

Date and time available by telephone:

References for Bidder

Client Company Name:

Address:

Contact:

Title:

Telephone:

Availability:

Disclosure

Proprietary agreement: Describe all stipulations regarding the confidentiality between your company and the bidders. For example: "This request for proposal contains information proprietary to <insert your company name>. Each recipient is expected to maintain its confidentiality. This document should be disclosed only to those employees involved in preparing a response. This RFP may not be duplicated."

Liability Clause

Advise suppliers that your company will not be liable for, or required to pay, any expenses or losses that are incurred by suppliers as it relates to the preparation and submission of the RFP response.

It may also be beneficial to clearly state that inclusion in the RFP process is not equivalent to a contract offer. This may be obvious, but it is always best to spell this out as suppliers eager to win business may look for less-than-ethical ways to exert pressure on you and other decision makers within the organization. Also, be sure to thank all suppliers for their participation in the RFP process.

Customize the RFP Design as Needed

Overall, the format outlined can serve as a template for any RFP regardless of the spend category. While the foregoing example gives a good template structure for a typical RFP design, as you build your own, make sure the questions are geared toward your specific needs and expectations, and structure the RFP to foster more of an open dialogue, rather than just eliciting responses to a yes-or-no questionnaire. For example, rather than asking suppliers *whether* they provide training to end users, ask *how* they provide initial and continuous training services to end users.

The Elements of a Typical RFQ

Be sure to include the following information in an RFQ so that suppliers can present an accurate pricing model and service-related offerings:

- Price request.
- Cost per unit on contract items and/or pricing schedule with discount structure and margins. The pricing structure will be based on your baseline and the spend category being sourced.

- Annual quantities required.
- If product-related, provide drawings and specifications.
- If service-related, provide description of services.
- Warranty information.
- Manufacturer part numbers. Specify a willingness to switch manufacturers if suppliers match specifications.
- Delivery and lead times.
- Freight charges.
- Payment terms.
- Minimum order quantities or spend amount.
- Account management information.
- Contract terms and conditions, sample agreement.
- Date due.

In many cases, the RFQ is a section of the RFP and is included as an exhibit to an RFP. For example, the packaging supplies spend category requires a great deal of service, but pricing is also an important factor. Therefore, it is often advantageous to release an RFP with an attached spreadsheet that specifies the RFQ provisions which provide detailed spend information and line-item usage. A summary page of the spend information, such as that illustrated in Table 4.3, can be included in the RFP document.

This table should also be included in the exhibit to the RFP. Additional information can be included in the remaining tabs of the spreadsheet that show line-item detail, actual usage, and specifications. This exhibit serves as the template for evaluating all supplier pricing compared to the baseline price.

The fields included in this exhibit are:

- Customer reference number (could be a number or a letter), to allow for data manipulation

TABLE 4.3 Summary Page of Volume Information

Product Category	Total Volume	Unit of Measure
Corrugated boxes	9,500,000	Box
Tape	76,800	Roll
Stretch film	150,250	Roll
Air pillows	4,200	Roll
Miscellaneous paper and poly products	268,100	Various

- Product category
- Specifications (color, gauge, width, length, package quantity, current manufacturer, and so on)
- Volume and current units of measurement (UOM)
- Any relevant notes
- Delivered price (to be completed by bidder)
- UOM (to be completed by bidder)
- Manufacturer (to be completed by bidder)
- Notes (to be completed by bidder)

Whether an RFP or RFQ process is being conducted, the supplier-friendly aspect of the format should always be a design consideration, which should also be incorporated into how the RFP and RFQ are administered.

Deadlines

One component that should be strongly emphasized when releasing an RFx is the due date, and late submittals either will not be accepted or will be accepted at the sole discretion of your company. As mentioned before, you are trying to find the fastest path to savings and a best-in-class agreement. Therefore, you do not want this process to be delayed by any participating suppliers. The deadline of the RFx should be clearly indicated and referenced in multiple instances, so there is no confusion on this topic.

A deadline in an RFx is always a necessity; however, depending on the scope and complexity of the RFx and the nature of the project, if multiple participating suppliers request a deadline extension, it may be best to grant one. It is possible that without an extension, the most promising suppliers might be excluded from further participation. Enough time should be given in order for suppliers to clearly identify specifications for all items in the market basket, develop innovative solutions, and provide pricing. All participating suppliers should still be made aware that the RFx is a time-sensitive process and that their timely responses will be a component of the final evaluation criteria. If you provide suppliers leniency with regard to submitting an RFx response, the process will drag on unnecessarily. It is beneficial to relay a sense of urgency in making a decision. Buyers should always retain the upper hand, but be sure to be considerate of the suppliers' time and effort, and give them a reasonable time frame to submit a quality response. As the deadline approaches, a friendly reminder to each supplier via e-mail is recommended.

SUPPLIER SELECTION AND SCORECARD CRITERIA

As noted previously, a section of the RFP should include an overview of how you will score and evaluate all the supplier submissions. The evaluation, scorecarding process, and final decision will incorporate multiple elements and should include, but not be limited to, the following (in no particular order):

- Product and service capabilities
- Pricing structure
- Quality and service
- Technology
- Customer references
- Supplier financials
- Implementation plan

Make it clear that you reserve the right to adjust the evaluation criteria at any time or reject any or all responses as you see appropriate without explanation and without any liability. The scorecard criteria are discussed further in Chapter 5, which details the guidelines for evaluating supplier RFP responses. A scorecard is typically not needed when conducting an RFQ because the focus is on supplier pricing.

ADMINISTERING THE RFx PROCESS

The three primary methods used for releasing RFx documents to potential suppliers are traditional ("snail") mail, e-mail, and e-sourcing tools. The best method for going to market depends on the tools buyers currently employ or are willing to invest in, and how they wish to store the bids received from suppliers. Buyers should also take into account any input suppliers may have regarding the distribution of the documentation.

The RFx process is the step in the sourcing phase in which many buyers are required by existing company policies to follow traditional methods. Many companies have yet to adopt innovative technical advances, and continue to cling to old ways of doing things. Some buyers are required to obtain hard copies of proposal responses. However, the purpose of a sourcing process is to implement improvements and increased efficiencies. A one-stop shop for all RFx responses and supplier contact information can eliminate headaches and allow for quick access to the documentation needed to adequately respond to an

RFx. This resource not only serves as the main interface for all communication with the potential supply base, but also allows for better management of all bid documents. An e-sourcing tool fulfills this function well by serving as a central repository for suppliers, RFxs, and supplier bids. If a certain spend category is revisited in a few years, this resource allows a buyer to access all the files used and supplier information gathered in the previous initiative.

A variety of E-procurement tools are accessible all over the Web. Contract management solutions and RFx and reverse auction capabilities are the most commonly used tools. In order to optimize the sourcing process, it is worth looking into utilizing a free toolset. It may seem hard to believe that free tools are available in the marketplace, but it is true. Certain providers offer free, viable e-sourcing tools and if you find they fit your needs, you may be able to avoid all costs associated with this type of resource.

Regardless of which solution is adopted, be careful to properly use the tools in your organization. Purchasing and e-sourcing software solutions should not be used as replacements for your due diligence and thoroughness in conducting your research and analyzing your data. No tool provider has the exact solution for any given vertical market. Find a solution that best fits your organization's requirements; do not allow a technology to dictate how you do business. Tools can facilitate project communications, shrink project timelines, and retain templates and analysis for future use, but you, as the chief architect of the strategic sourcing project, should always remain in control. Keep in mind that overreliance on purchasing technology tools and processes may only automate and cement in place the inherent problems in the sourcing strategy. Before investing in new technology, be sure to thoroughly analyze existing processes to identify opportunities for improvement. And whatever you do, be sure that your organization does not become an RFx spammer. Sending unannounced RFxs to a collection of e-mail addresses (gathered from trade shows and other venues) without properly communicating with those suppliers beforehand will not produce any positive results. Worse, it will give you skewed information, based on the supplier's interpretation of the RFx and assumptions about your true intentions (for example, "phishing" for quotes to use as a basis for negotiations with your incumbent supplier), so the information returned will essentially be garbage.

Many people assume that the e-sourcing tool will do the work for them. Frequent mistakes buyers make while utilizing an e-sourcing tool to administer an RFx include:

- Neglecting to individually invite suppliers
- Not contacting suppliers before sending an RFx invitation

- Not inviting the right suppliers or the right person within the supplier's organization
- Including poor specifications
- Not making sure the suppliers are familiar with and comfortable using the tool

E-sourcing tools provide efficiency and organization and can help expedite the sourcing process. However, they will not replace the necessary human element of supplier identification, specification preparation, and supplier engagement.

The method for distributing an RFx may also depend on the number of suppliers involved. If proposals have been requested from just two or three suppliers, e-mail may make more sense, as there is a limited amount of information to manage. After the RFP is released to the supply base, confirm receipt of the bid and the supplier's intention to participate. Be available to field initial questions from the supply base and welcome any feedback.

 ## REVERSE AUCTIONS

If the product or service being sourced can be clearly defined and standardized across vendors, a reverse auction may be the most appropriate sourcing strategy to implement. A reverse auction is a type of request for information from suppliers in which you allow them to offer increasingly lower (hence, reverse) auction-style bids to win the business (imagine Ebay turned upside-down). A product or service can only be considered for a reverse auction if buyers can easily evaluate the pricing submitted by participating suppliers by applying standardized metrics. If conversions need to be made to gathered information in order to perform apples-to-apples bid comparisons, then a reverse auction will not deliver the best results. This sourcing event allows for a quick exchange of pricing information; therefore, the spend category in question should have no more than a handful of items that need to be quoted. Buyers need to be particularly aware of their supply base's constraints when carrying out a reverse auction. Requiring suppliers to quote too many items more than once in a short amount of time may discourage supplier participation.

It is worth considering employing a reverse auction if the commodity being sourced has the following attributes:

- An adequate number of suppliers are willing to participate in the auction. If the incumbent supplier does not agree to take part in the sourcing event, this should not stop a buyer from conducting the auction. The buyer should inquire about the incumbent's wish to not participate and address any concerns. It is quite possible that the incumbent supplier is aware of who the competition is and knows it is unable to meet the pricing demands that may be requested. After all, the incumbent's pricing is the baseline and they would essentially be competing against themselves.

▪ Specifications are clearly defined and easily understood across the supplier community.

▪ The annual budget for the product or service being sourced should be relatively significant to motivate suppliers. Sometimes, depending on the tool being utilized, costs are incurred for holding an auction. Therefore, buyers should be confident, based on their research, that the savings achieved will be greater than the fees paid for carrying out the auction. Keep in mind that free reverse auction tools are available in the marketplace.

Suppliers are often hesitant to participate in reverse auctions. If you have difficulty getting buy-in from the supply base, point out the following advantages reverse auctions present for suppliers:

▪ *They are money savers and time savers.* Suppliers are always on the lookout for more business. That is, if they can handle it. Buyers should make suppliers aware of the fact that once they register for one reverse auction they are logged in the auction site's database. Therefore, if future sourcing events arise, suppliers may receive invitations to participate in these events. Buyers can then engage suppliers without requiring those suppliers to invest additional resources beyond registering for the initial reverse auction in which they participated. A supplier's involvement in a single reverse auction can then serve as a conduit to additional business opportunities. This advantage could, in turn, decrease the supplier's sales and marketing costs. During a reverse auction, very little time is expected of suppliers. Resources are only needed to submit pricing and respond to questions they are typically used to answering. An RFx process often requires more supplier involvement and additional efforts if a negotiation phase is carried out for a long period of time. Overall, reverse auctions cut timelines and costs, and also serve as a marketing tool for suppliers.

▪ *They make the market more transparent.* During a reverse auction, all participants—the buyer and engaged suppliers—are able to see the pricing information exchanged (to some extent). Therefore, all parties are able to gain a better knowledge of pricing levels and where the market floor is for a particular product or service. When information is exchanged, only the buyer is able to see which supplier submitted the most recent pricing. However, suppliers are still able to view their competition as a whole. If a particular supplier wins an auction but has still maintained a decent margin, this solidifies their case to buyers that they are competitive among other suppliers. If a supplier loses an auction and several others thereafter, they may need to reevaluate their cost structure in order to gain ground on the competition. If an RFx is utilized, buyers may not provide constructive feedback to suppliers or indicate why suppliers were not selected or lost the account. Overall, reverse auctions provide suppliers with instant feedback on their pricing structures and reveal what is available through competitors.

Out of fear of publicly revealing too much information, or unfamiliarity with the tools or process, many suppliers are hesitant to participate in a reverse auction, so buyers should encourage them to participate based on the aforementioned advantages. Point out that their willingness is no different than their willingness to participate in an RFx process. Make suppliers aware that price is not the only deciding factor. If a competitive advantage exists through a process improvement or other alternative options, indicate that they will also be evaluated based on this aspect of their offering. A supplier does not need to be the lowest bidder in order to win the business. A buyer's intention through their utilization of a reverse auction is not to dictate how a supplier sells their product or service. The purpose of a reverse auction is to emphasize the importance of price, but also note that this sourcing method will include the same evaluation process that would take place in any other bidding event.

Much of the time, suppliers choose not to participate in reverse auctions out of fear. They are unfamiliar with this type of sourcing event and are not very tech-savvy. Communication with the supply base is crucial regardless of the sourcing event being used. Just as you would with an RFP or RFQ, work with suppliers to address their concerns and educate them on your sourcing goals, as well as the methods being used to achieve them.

Reverse auctions deliver pricing information in a quick, easy format. However, both the buyer and supply base require significant preparation before the reverse auction begins. It is quite possible that you will need to educate the supplier pool on the tool being used to administer the auction process. Suppliers may request a test run or the ability to set up a testing environment prior to the auction. Be willing to accommodate these types of requests. Also be sure to provide any contact information in case a supplier runs into technical issues during the auction process. Most of the time, an individual within your IT department is the most appropriate person to address these issues. Make sure suppliers understand the auction rules as well. The start and end times should be clearly defined before the auction begins. For example, some auctions add three minutes to the end time after each bid is placed. This makes it impossible for a supplier to make a low bid at the last second of an event.

ALTERNATIVES TO THE RFx—THE IMPORTANCE OF FLEXIBILITY AND CREATIVITY IN THE SOURCING PROCESS

It is important to treat the RFx process as a fully integrated component of a sourcing strategy; give it and the participating suppliers the full attention they deserve. When suppliers perceive that they are engaged in an arm's-length RFP process, buyers receive arm's-length results. Rather than formally requiring suppliers to demonstrate their capabilities and pricing through an elaborate RFx response in cases that don't require the full range on information outlined above, offer some alternatives. The most important message to relay to a potential supplier is that the sourcing initiative in question is going to be a collaborative effort with open communication.

For a particular spend category, some suppliers may not be willing to commit to a full written proposal. Resource-constrained sales teams that do not have enough bandwidth to pursue every opportunity will focus efforts on customers where they believe they have the best chance of winning significant business. Do not allow the sourcing initiative to die through the application of overly formal procedures if these are the circumstances. The quickest path to savings may lie in a shift away from an RFx. A good alternative that often motivates suppliers is conducting face-to-face presentations and capabilities reviews.

If you do decide to bypass the RFx process and hold such meetings, there are several things to keep in mind. First, be sure to ask specific questions during these meetings. Suppliers' responses will give a good indication of whether they understand the complexities of your requirements. Some ways to ascertain whether suppliers are aware of predisclosed requirements include paying close attention to their sales pitches. If they have been provided with a detailed outline of requirements, and are asked to customize their sales presentations based on those needs, and they still come in with their standard sales pitches, this can be a clear indicator that they have no intention of trying to meet those requirements or do not offer the flexibility to customize their solutions.

References are also a good indicator of whether or not the supplier understands what you are looking for. Always ask for references with similar requirements to your own. When interviewing those references during the scorecarding phase, explore how similar they really are. If they do not match, the likelihood is that the supplier still does not understand what you are looking for. It is also beneficial to speak with the supervisor of the main sales contact. If the requirements are customized, the boss should be relatively up to speed on your account. If that person is not familiar with the account, chances are the main contact still is not clear what you are looking for, or is hoping he or she can sell a simpler solution.

Suppliers are often much more motivated and engaged when buyers take an alternative approach to the traditional RFx process. In some cases, a written response may still be required and a formal quote will definitely be needed, but overall this process works well when determining supplier finalists. A supplier may appear to meet all of your needs on paper, but a presentation may reveal otherwise. A creative and flexible approach will allow you to avoid setting arbitrary limits on the results received from the supply base. It is important to be open to suppliers offering value-added solutions in addition to the needs expressed in a typical RFx. We go into greater detail on how and when to bypass an RFx in Chapter 14, "Leveraging Supplier Feedback."

 ## IN SUMMARY

Buyers have many strategies from which to choose in implementing this step of the sourcing process. The challenge is pinpointing the strategy that will deliver the optimum solution. At the end of the sourcing process, buyers want to hold a best-in-class agreement in their hands. Choosing the right sourcing strategy, based on the considerations outlined in this chapter, makes that outcome more likely. The common message to deliver across all sourcing initiatives is that the buyer desires open communications with the supply base. Respect for suppliers is also a key ingredient for a successful RFx process implementation. Remain flexible and be sure to develop an awareness of the supply base's needs and wants just as much as your own. Doing so will motivate the supply base to invest far more time and effort in winning your business.

The RFx process should not be used as a substitute for understanding the market and engaging with suppliers. The previously conducted market research and preliminary supplier discussions often drive the information sought in an RFx, and generate meaningful metrics by which to evaluate suppliers. The RFx responses provide objective data to justify decisions made by your team. Once all proposals have been submitted, it is time to objectively evaluate each supplier's offering through the use of independent research, supplier interviews, and RFx responses.

Now that you are a step closer to determining which suppliers will be considered and which ones are not a good fit to fulfill the requirement of the spend category in question, Chapter 5, "Supplier Scorecarding," details how to analyze the information collected up to this point.

CHAPTER FIVE

Scorecarding Suppliers

F ROM DATA COLLECTION THROUGH THE RFx (request for x: information, proposal, or quote) stage of the strategic sourcing process, most of
a buyer's time is spent analyzing current and future requirements for the
spend category, conducting independent research, and developing and executing the RFx process. The scorecarding phase ties together the analysis and
research already performed and the RFx responses received from the potential
supply base. Scorecarding allows buyers to fully understand the availability of
their requirements among the suppliers they are considering. Through this
process, buyers are able to grasp how each supplier can provide specific value
to their businesses. As supplier proposals are evaluated, buyers inch closer to
decisions that will have real impacts on their organizations. Supplier scorecarding is a thorough and objective methodology for choosing the optimal supplier.
It helps ensure that you make the right decisions in the selection of your future
business partner.

The supplier scorecard should include both a quantitative and qualitative component in order to measure every aspect of each supplier's offering.
From a quantitative perspective, scorecarding provides a bid evaluation phase
that compares pricing proposals and identifies areas in which suppliers have a
competitive advantage. It also allows a buyer to easily pinpoint incorrect bids

and errors made during the quoting process. On the qualitative side, the scorecarding process includes the utilization of an RFP matrix and preestablished decision criteria to objectively evaluate responses based on the actual needs of an organization.

The scorecarding process is more than an evaluation tool. For example, checking suppliers' references delivers additional insight into the market that a buyer is not able to gather during the research process. Through conversations with actual customers of the potential supply base, direct feedback is received from individuals who actually went through the sourcing process before you. Furthermore, scorecarding can be used as a team-building exercise. Using a team approach to evaluate proposals ensures that an adequate variety of viewpoints are considered so that the best supplier is selected for the spend category being sourced. It also helps build organizational consensus around the chosen supplier, which serves as a benefit during the implementation process.

This chapter details the steps to take in order to properly evaluate supplier proposals against one another. It also discusses how to get the most out of reference checks, and how to use teams to develop buy-in from end users on the strategic sourcing process as a whole, as well as from the supplier ultimately selected. The end result is a supplier that provides clear value to your organization and an organization that understands and supports that value.

MEASURING VALUE: DEVELOPING SELECTION CRITERIA

Value is a subjective term. How buyers measure value depends on their organizations' needs and expectations. Value is perceived to exist if needs and expectations are met or exceeded. A supplier offering next-day delivery at no extra cost can be viewed as business-as-usual for one customer but an added perk for another. A dedicated account representative available 24/7 might be a must-have for some, while regular working hours suffice for others. To understand how a supplier can provide value to your business, you need to already know how your incumbent supplier does so. This is the starting point for building the supplier selection criteria. These criteria serve as the groundwork for the RFP matrix that measures the qualitative aspects of each supplier's offering.

The selection criteria were roughly established during the baseline phase and refined as the RFx processes were developed. The incumbent supplier's pricing, service levels, and overall offering are the initial inputs for the criteria. As a wide net was cast into the marketplace to build the potential supply base, you had already determined minimum standards, which were then validated or nullified through initial conversations with each supplier before releasing an RFx. Therefore, be confident that the remaining suppliers are all capable of being a good fit for your organization. The scorecarding phase allows you to identify the supplier that will be the *best* fit. The questions in the RFx clearly indicate how each supplier is going to be measured. The only element of the scorecarding phase that the suppliers are not aware of is how each question's response will be weighed. This portion of the scorecard will be expanded upon in the development of the RFP matrix.

It is never too late to add more selection criteria to the RFx process. In fact, buyers should constantly consider adding more criteria. The market research and RFx results may reveal a servicing aspect that several suppliers offer except for the incumbent. Selection criteria should be reviewed internally before and after evaluating supplier proposals. If certain criteria are added, be sure to make all potential suppliers aware of this change. Once a buyer begins to inquire about capabilities not mentioned in the RFx, suppliers realize that they are being measured according to additional factors. Therefore, as a reminder to all suppliers, point out this informal addition to the RFx. Questions that were overlooked when the RFx was developed can be responded to via e-mail in order to obtain suppliers' responses in writing.

Establishing the correct selection criteria dictates the results of the sourcing process. The goal of the sourcing process is to identify a supplier that is able to deliver the following:

- High quality
- Adequate quantity
- Competitive pricing
- Easy-to-use technology
- Responsive flexibility
- Quick delivery
- Superior service

It may be challenging to identify a supplier that can meet all of these requirements. However, these capabilities are key indicators of a supplier that is able to meet your organization's current and future business needs. Most companies consider pricing to be the most important aspect of a supplier's proposal, and some buyers are willing to sacrifice quality for significant savings. Other buyers, however, may want to give greater weight to other requirements. The bid evaluation phase or quantitative component of the scorecard process is the starting point for identifying which suppliers have a competitive advantage, according to the important criteria to your organization. It also allows for an easy comparison between current pricing and other opportunities available in the market.

 THE QUANTITATIVE ANALYSIS: EVALUATING THE BID PORTION OF SUPPLIER PROPOSALS

When evaluating supplier proposals, most buyers consider price to be the most important factor. This is particularly true if a request for quotation (RFQ) is released rather than a request for proposal (RFP). The pricing established during the baseline stage is the point of reference during this step of the scorecarding process. There are two strategies buyers can use to compare other suppliers' pricing to the baseline price—the Best Alternative to Negotiated Agreement (BATNA) approach and the Best Single Offer approach. These two methods are explained further in Chapter 6, "Negotiations," as targets are built for the supplier finalists.

Chapter 4 outlined the information requests to be included in the bid portion of an RFx. This exhibit serves as the template for the pricing analysis and is usually in the form of a spreadsheet, which includes line-item detail with projected annual quantities and specifications. In their responses, suppliers complete this spreadsheet by providing the requested information outlined in Chapter 4. Be sure that your internal reference number is included with each line item on the spreadsheet so that any necessary v-lookups can be performed to pull data in where needed. Once you have checked that all the requested information has been obtained, you are ready to take a closer look at the numbers.

Best Alternative to Negotiated Agreement

This analytical approach consolidates the best elements of each supplier's proposal into a single offer. In order to perform this analysis, use the baseline pricing and the internal reference number to pull in all the bids. In your evaluation spreadsheet, create a column for each supplier and pull in the proposed pricing through v-lookup functions. Using the minimum function, pull the minimum for each line item and extend these price points out by multiplying by the projected annual quantities set forth in the baseline. Compare this extended amount to the baseline extended amount and calculate the savings and savings percentage. The savings percentage is the ratio between the baseline extended amount and the minimum bid extended amount over the baseline extended amount. These numbers give a quick snapshot of how the baseline pricing compares to the available pricing across all suppliers. These numbers will be refined as you pinpoint errors made in quotes and begin the first and second rounds of negotiations. Chapter 6 provides additional guidance on how to use these numbers to request revised pricing proposals from the supply base.

Best Single Offer

This approach compares all aspects of each proposal and identifies the single best offer. The best way to perform these calculations is to begin by creating a spreadsheet with a worksheet designated for each supplier. Include a summary worksheet that allows you to view how each supplier compares against the others and the baseline at a high level. Pull the baseline price into each worksheet using the internal reference number. Extend each line-item bid by its projected annual quantity and do the same for the baseline. Calculate the savings and savings percentage per line item and overall. As mentioned earlier, the savings percentage is a quick indicator of where each supplier falls within the competition.

As you analyze pricing further, be sure that all comparisons are made on an apples-to-apples basis. If you discover a savings percentage of 80 percent, a bid unit of measurement may not have been properly converted to the baseline unit of measurement. Pay close attention to the details in this step of the process. Be sure to focus more on the high-volume items, as they will skew the overall calculations the most.

These steps comprise most of the analysis necessary to identify the finalists in an RFQ process; in most cases, a scorecard is not necessary. Additional useful information may include references, as well as details regarding:

- Warranty information
- Delivery time and lead time
- Freight
- Payment terms
- Minimum order quantities
- Account management information
- Contract terms and conditions, sample agreement

For evaluating RFP submissions, the pricing analysis is just the beginning of the process.

THE QUALITATIVE APPROACH: DEVELOPING THE RFP MATRIX

Price is not the only factor in analyzing RFP responses. Quality, service, and other supplier attributes are also important to understand and evaluate. It is important to note that as you move from the quantitative (price) analysis to the qualitative analysis, you should not eliminate any suppliers. Some suppliers may have bid high, planning to be flexible in lowering their prices during negotiations. Furthermore, even if a supplier cannot provide a competitive price, its proposal may provide some market insight or other relevant information that you were not aware of prior to analyzing the response.

An RFP matrix is synonymous with the term *scorecard*. A scorecard is only really necessary when a great deal of qualitative aspects exist for a spend category. The RFP matrix, manipulated in a spreadsheet file, includes the finalized decision criteria. Its main purpose is to objectively evaluate responses based on the actual needs of your organization. Each supplier will be measured based on the selection criteria and each criterion is weighted according to its importance. Table 5.1 is an example of a portion of a scorecard. It is helpful to track the section of the RFP to which each question refers.

In this scorecard, the weights are based on the buyer's need for the supplier to meet that request, or the importance of that requirement to the organization. The maximum score any single criterion can receive is 10 and the added total of the weight percentages must equal 100 percent. Therefore, the maximum score a supplier can receive is 100. If a formal RFP has been issued for a product or service, it is likely that quality and service will be weighted significantly. This, again, depends on your company's needs.

The goal of strategic sourcing is to develop a consistent and responsive supply base that is capable of meeting current and future business needs. The seven qualities that are universally evaluated in any scorecarding process are:

1. Quality
    - Can the supplier provide a quality product or service?
    - Is a supplier willing to offer extended warranties, thereby expressing confidence in the quality of its products?
2. Quantity
    - Can the supplier meet demands for a product?
    - Will product ever have to be backordered?
    - What are the lead times?

TABLE 5.1 Quality and Service

Question	Score (Max 10)	Weight	Weighted Score	Scoring Rationale	Notes
1. Outline your sales support and customer service programs (Section 5.2 Q 2).	10	3%	0.3	Weak = 0 Dedicated sales rep = 5 Sales = 10	A business manager, program coordinator, industry specialist, and customer service rep will be assigned to account.
2. Are you able to supply all products listed in the attached market basket? (Section 5.3 Q 1).	10	5%	0.5	No = 0 Yes = 10	
3. Please detail the discounts and markups you will provide for items not listed in the market basket (Section 5.3 Q 5).	10	5%	0.5	None = 0 Unfavorable discount factor = 5 Favorable discount structure = 10	Margin offered for items not in RFP.

3. Delivery
   - What logistics are involved to obtain a product?
   - Is the delivery process seamless?
   - What is the turnaround time on placed orders?
4. Technology
   - Does the supplier offer a fast, easy method for placing orders?
   - Is the ordering process easy to learn?
   - Is free training offered to employees for the supplier's online ordering tool (if it exists)?
   - Can the supplier integrate with the current ordering system?

5. Flexibility
    ■ Is the supplier willing to adjust payment terms?
    ■ Is the supplier willing to make other adjustments to its normal business process based on your needs?
6. Service
    ■ Will your account be assigned a dedicated service representative?
    ■ What backups are in place if the dedicated representative is not available?
7. Cost
    ■ Is pricing competitive?
    ■ How often does pricing change?
    ■ Are any rebates or incentives available?

When scoring a proposal, be sure to account for all the gray areas. For example, if the proposal asked whether the supplier has certain software, the answer is typically yes or no. However, the supplier may be going live soon with the requested software. If this is the case, a score of 0 may not be warranted. If the new system is up and running by the time you are ready to implement, this question may warrant a response of 10, or perhaps somewhere in the middle, to reflect issues that might arise when working with new software for the first time.

In the RFP matrix, it is best to have a master spreadsheet and a worksheet designated for each supplier, similar to the pricing scorecard. Once a scorecard has been completed for each supplier, include a summary worksheet that links to each supplier worksheet to retrieve the total points of each supplier. (See Table 5.2.) This will allow for an easy high-level comparison across all suppliers. Keep in mind that pricing has not been factored into these rankings.

TABLE 5.2 RFP Scorecard Summaries

Category	Supplier 1	Supplier 2	Supplier 3	Supplier 4	Supplier 5
Quality and service	44.3	41.2	38.6	37.4	41.2
Lead times and inventory	16.8	17.5	15.3	16.4	16.0
Technology	10.0	8.5	10.0	9.5	7.5
Implementation and relationship	19.2	19.4	19.3	18.7	18.2
Additional information	6.0	6.0	5.5	4.5	4.5
Total score	96.3	92.6	88.7	86.5	87.4

The total scores, ordered from highest to lowest, reveal the final supplier rankings.

Keep in mind that this is a qualitative analysis, with some subjective components to it. Even though Supplier 1 received the highest total score, you do not want to assume that you have now discovered the best choice. There are still many other aspects to consider, the most important one being price. If price shows that Supplier 1 and Supplier 2 both deliver a great deal of savings, take a closer look at where the savings are distributed. It is possible that one supplier offers significant savings on a certain product category and the other supplier is competitive in another one. If so, consider the option of awarding both suppliers a portion of the business. However, there is still some more analysis to be done before this option is seriously considered. It is quite possible that one supplier can meet targets developed based on the other supplier's pricing. Also, reference checks will provide a great deal of insight into each supplier's overall offering.

REFERENCES

References provide additional perspectives and excellent insight into conditions in the supplier evaluation process that are not adequately reflected in written responses, and supply you with concrete feedback from actual end users.

Conversations with references should be held over the phone and questions should be prepared beforehand. The objective of the interview is to discover how similar the reference's business conditions are to your own. If they do not correspond, it is likely that the supplier does not fully understand your company's needs and what you are seeking in your sourcing initiative. Therefore, keep the wording of the questions as objective as possible. Questions to references are often modified depending on the category being sourced, but some questions are consistent across all categories, and include:

- How long have you been a customer of <Supplier X>?
- How would you rate that company as a supplier?
- What product or service do you receive from <Supplier X>?
- What could the company do better as a supplier?
- How did you choose <Supplier X> (e.g., a similar sourcing initiative or an alternative approach)?
- Who were some other potential suppliers you considered in the process?
- Which company did you use prior to <Supplier X>?
- Why did your company choose to switch?

- Overall, how would you rate the transition to <Supplier X>? What could the company have done better?
- How did the implementation plan work?
- How many locations do you have across the country? Were all of your locations that were included in the project adequately accommodated during the implementation?
- Are you satisfied with the pricing and ordering process?
- Have you encountered any issues while working with <Supplier X> (related to quality, service, delivery, payment, etc.)? How have issues been resolved?
- How would you rate <Supplier X's> account management?
  - Do you typically work with the same account representative?
  - If so, what is the level of responsiveness from the rep? If not, how responsive were the company's reps with whom you worked?
- What aspect of <Supplier X> would you say is most beneficial to your company?
- Is there anything else we should know that we have not yet discussed?

Do not be swayed by a glowing reference. Suppliers will, as a rule, provide references that will shine the best light on them. Rarely if ever will they give you references to less-than-satisfied or disgruntled clients. That is why it is important to ask detailed questions and get a full history of the relationship.

The results of these conversations should be factored into the scorecard results. They add value to the evaluation process and give you a better idea of the competitive landscape. Share the results with team members so you can accommodate the widest possible range of viewpoints, giving you an adequate basis to judge the impact of a potential change in the supply base.

 ## TEAMWORK AND OBJECTIVITY

The scorecarding process is a great opportunity to build team morale and make team members aware that their input is valued. Several areas of a company are usually impacted by an organizational change. Therefore, make sure approval is received from each department and stakeholder in regard to the supplier finalists.

Picking a team to assist in the strategic sourcing process can be a rather challenging task. It can make or break the whole project, as biased views can alter results and lead to arguments over the final decision. This is often why third-party providers are engaged to conduct strategic sourcing processes.

They tend to be more objective than individuals who are directly impacted by a change or who currently manage the spend category.

Objectivity during the scorecarding process is critical. Some team members may be biased with regard to the companies with whom they prefer to do business. However, every supplier that submitted an RFP did so because it believes itself to be a potential good fit. Therefore, it is important to acknowledge the sources of bias while also recruiting team members who have objective viewpoints on the supply base and the needs of the company. If you do not acknowledge and compensate for biases in the sourcing initiative, then team members who would be negatively impacted by a change in the current process might influence the process so that those suppliers that would require more work receive lower rankings than those they prefer.

Get your team involved throughout the decision-making process by having them work on:

▪ Reviewing submitted proposals and identifying additional criteria to add to the scorecard
▪ Completing RFP matrices (for example, if eight proposals are submitted, get four members involved and assign proposals randomly to each team member)
▪ Developing reference questions
▪ Interviewing references

Do not allow members of your team to view other members' scorecards. If they were to do so, they might be inclined to try to validate some of their responses based on others' evaluations, and this may skew the objectivity of the results. Choose some team members that have participated in a scorecarding process before so that you do not spend an inordinate amount of time training team members.

Many organizations have blinders on at times and become focused strictly on the pricing structure offered by each supplier. This often leads to suppliers creating ways to recapture shortfalls in revenue due to those low prices in the form of ancillary charges. For this sole reason, several team members need to be included in the evaluation process in order to properly focus on all aspects that a supplier is proposing. This limits the blinders that often exist when only one stakeholder is managing a spend category.

In general, the most objective scorecarding methodology includes developing selection and scoring criteria prior to receiving bids. Preestablished criteria ensure that questions are not weighed solely in terms of supplier preferences or unneeded services, but rather on true business requirements.

Furthermore, while it is not always possible to achieve, the most objective supplier scorecarding also entails the suppliers' identities remaining unknown to the scorers. If possible, remove any references to suppliers' names in responses before assigning proposals for grading. Keeping the responses anonymous ensures that you and other end users are as objective as possible in your analyses and do not give higher scores (intentionally or not) to suppliers you are familiar with or have had positive experiences with in the past.

 ## TECHNOLOGY'S ROLE

The scorecarding process is not as complex as some e-sourcing systems make it out to be. A simple toolset like Microsoft Excel allows a buyer to easily share scorecards with team members and retain templates for future use. However, sophisticated tools can prove to be useful depending on the category being sourced.

E-sourcing systems have become rather sophisticated, and many provide advanced features to help buyers in their decision-making process. Various technologies exist that can help a buying organization quantify certain aspects of a supplier's offering and the value of doing business with suppliers beyond just price. First, these tools can help a buyer model costs based on more variables than straight unit cost. For example, for a small parcel sourcing event, many smaller companies just take their previous-year contracts with their suppliers and draft a formal RFP. These buyers then merely monitor the percentage discount offered by each carrier (UPS, USPS, FedEx, and others) and often award the business to the carrier that offers the greatest discount. However, this is a poorly designed tactic that will likely result in mediocre savings. The proper use of an e-sourcing tool can help companies develop a more comprehensive approach and capture more information than just price points.

Optimization through the use of e-sourcing tools allows a buyer to dive much deeper into the project and responses from suppliers. For instance, in telecommunications sourcing, a good first step that e-sourcing tools can help with is to normalize tariff rates between suppliers, as each supplier usually quotes a certain discount off of their own tariff rates, which are not the same as other carrier base rates.

Secondly, the buyer needs to be responsible for understanding the characteristics of their shipping habits, which can be easily tracked in an e-sourcing tool. Carriers know how to carefully craft an RFP response with apparently excellent rates by offering rather high discounts on shipment types that your business uses the least. Optimization tools can help buyers decide which service types they should be focused on and which will help in negotiations. For example, being willing to give up a large discount on a product or service type that you use infrequently in exchange for a larger discount on a frequent shipment type can generate an extremely large savings opportunity. Besides a strict price point comparison, other aspects can be factored into the decision process, such as the financial viability of the supplier.

Continuing with the small parcel example, other important aspects to consider include guarantees for on-time shipments, pickup and drop-off times that work best for your shipping departments, and flexibility in nonscheduled shipping events. If an emergency shipment needs to go out the door on the last day of the month, it would be good to know whether your carrier can accommodate that event, and whether there would be extra charges for such a service.

There are plenty of technologies available to aid in the decision-making process. Keep in mind, however, that many of these technologies, tools, and processes can also be developed in-house or acquired temporarily through a consulting firm. It is not always necessary to purchase an expensive e-sourcing system that features a myriad of advanced tools when you may only ever need them every three years or so, during a contract renewal process. As with any technology, the tools are only as valuable as the data entered and the ability to use those systems properly, so be extremely careful not to rely too heavily on the decisions resulting from using the tools. Be sure to audit the decision outputs of any system you use; this becomes a worthwhile check to the whole sourcing process and keeps you in charge of the project. The human element should always be paramount.

 ## IN SUMMARY

At this stage in the process you have qualified supplier finalists based on an internal team review of the scorecard findings. Process improvements and value-added services can save costs in the long run, as well as time for you and your staff. It is essential not just to select a supplier who offers the lowest price. Some suppliers are merely concerned with the rate at which they produce goods and the amount of orders they take in and nothing else, and this in turn can affect the quality of their output, which may ultimately cost you far more in the long term than the amount you will have saved by choosing that lowest-cost supplier. Sometimes, for example, a slightly higher price for your spend category from a supplier in your state or region will benefit your company more in the long run than a lower price from an overseas vendor. For this reason, it is best not to immediately notify suppliers that are not selected as finalists. You are not yet sure how the initially chosen finalists will respond to negotiations, and the suppliers that received lower rankings in your analysis may end up having the most room to be flexible on price and value-adds.

Regardless of which suppliers are selected, you have arrived at your decision through a fact-based analysis and can objectively narrow the field to two or three finalist suppliers. At this stage of the process, it is still worthwhile to consider all the opportunities presented by your finalists and find value in each one of their offerings. This becomes the basis for developing a negotiation strategy.

CHAPTER SIX

Negotiations

H UNDREDS OF BOOKS, websites, training sessions, and seminars are available that go into great detail about negotiation tactics. While you can use those resources to hone your negotiating skills, this chapter reviews the role negotiations play in the strategic sourcing process and provides general guidelines for a negotiation strategy that allows you to get what you want from your suppliers.

Suppliers often maintain a distinct advantage over customers during the negotiation process, especially in the case of indirect spend. The reason is simple—suppliers negotiate over their product or service every single day. Suppliers operate in a single market in which they understand their margins and those of the competition. They meet with customers every day and talk about their products. They have done their homework and the likelihood is that they figured out how much they could make on a particular account the day they were introduced to it. The sourcing team in a company, on the other hand, has to deal with day-to-day operational issues that span multiple project areas. Also, they may be sourcing multiple categories at any given time. Sourcing and negotiations may be part of their jobs, but it is probably not the main focus.

To put this in perspective, while the supplier is 100 percent focused on selling its product, the sourcing team focuses 5 percent of their time (or less) on buying that same product. Or the buyer may dedicate much more time, but only once every year or three, when a contract is up for renewal. Much like walking into a used car lot on a whim one Saturday morning, the odds of getting a good deal under these circumstances are low.

To counter this advantage on the part of suppliers, many sourcing professionals adhere to a strict process—identify suppliers, solicit proposals, pick the top two or three, request a best and final offer, and finally sit down for a formal negotiation. This strategy provides a framework for negotiations; however the process still strongly favors a supplier that knows its market and is experienced in negotiating deals. It also gives the supplier clarity on the process—the supplier understands when the formal meeting occurs that it probably has a 50 percent shot at winning the business (if it is one of two finalists).

When a supplier has all these advantages, it can become very difficult for a customer to get the best price. However, you can shift the paradigm by incorporating some level of negotiation throughout the entire strategic sourcing process—without the supplier knowing negotiations are taking place. Formal negotiations may still be necessary at some point, but using the techniques described in this chapter provides you with a much lower starting point in price as well as a much higher expected level of service before the formal discussions begin.

 ## KNOWING WHAT TO NEGOTIATE

You cannot negotiate over that which you do not know. Often people judge the results of their negotiations on what they have successfully obtained from the opposing party without causing that party to say no. For instance, a purchasing manager might brag that he or she asked the company's office supply vendor for a 10 percent discount, and the vendor agreed to give it to the company. While 10 percent is surely better than nothing, this purchasing manager did not realize that 20 percent might have been available had it merely been requested.

This fairly simplistic example begs the question, "How can I determine what the optimal amount is?" In the field of strategic sourcing, the goal of any negotiation is to obtain the absolute best price available—when factoring in required service levels, quality standards, and contractual obligations. The strategic sourcing process that has been detailed up to this point provides clarity as to what that price is.

During the data collection phase and throughout the research phase, you develop a clear scope of work and outline the requirements associated with a particular spend category. During the sourcing phase you relay these requirements to incumbent and alternate suppliers and solicit proposals. During the scorecarding phase you and your team analyze the submitted proposals, comparing not just cost, but suppliers' ability to meet predetermined requirements. This allows you to identify the best overall single bid, as well as the best price points for individual services.

Of course, using these price points as the target for negotiations assumes all suppliers have provided you with their best and final offers. If the prices you are using for comparison are based on RFx responses alone, the likelihood is this is not the case. Suppliers rarely come in with their best offers during the first round of a bid. There are many reasons for this, including:

- Some part of the RFx document was unclear to a supplier, so it factored the unknown component into the offered price to offset perceived risk.
- The supplier is concerned that the bid process might be a "phishing" expedition and does not want its pricing used merely to leverage an incumbent.
- The supplier perceives that it is the preferred vendor and it is hoping to make a windfall profit.
- The supplier believes further rounds of negotiations will occur and does not want to come in with too low a starting price.

Keeping these dynamics in mind, using first round bids as the basis for final negotiations might not result in achieving the best price available in the marketplace.

There are ways to ensure suppliers do not add in extra margin during their first-round bid, thereby putting you in a better starting point for final negotiations. The key is incorporating your negotiation strategy into the entire strategic sourcing process. Every interaction with a supplier, from the first introduction through the implementation phase, is an opportunity for negotiation. The negotiation may not be a formal request for the supplier to lower price or provide additional services, but rather an opportunity for you to present a business case to suppliers on why this business is something they cannot afford to lose, and will profit much by gaining. There are several techniques that can be used at various stages of the strategic sourcing process to ensure your final pricing is the best price that supplier can offer, including:

- Motivating the supply base
- Creating a team environment
- Identifying leverage points

Motivating the Supply Base

Most salespeople (particularly those in an outside sales role) manage their work by employing a *sales pipeline*. As salespeople identify opportunities to make sales, they feed them into their pipelines, with notes on the account, the scope, and how hot the opportunity is. Salespeople periodically review their pipelines with management to review the status of various leads and identify and target the most preferred opportunities.

Your goal in the sourcing process is to get the salesperson to move your account toward the front of this pipeline list, becoming one of the targeted opportunities. Once you are there, the management of your supplier will become much more aware of your account and will ask for more frequent follow-ups from your primary sales representative. The more visibility an account has with a supplier's senior management, the more invested the salesperson becomes in winning the business, thereby making him or her more willing to reduce price and make other concessions in order to win the account. So how do you go about getting a potential supplier's salesperson to move your account to the front of the sales pipeline? The key is through motivating the supplier.

Most salespeople are accustomed to hunting for business, chasing down accounts, presenting proposals, and getting deals done, altogether known as *prospecting*, all with limited access to information relating to the true requirements of an organization. If you can make their prospecting tasks easier, it often translates into motivating them to present an offering you would not otherwise have access to. There are several commonsense steps you can take that will go a long way in motivating your suppliers, including:

- Providing a clear scope of work and requirements
- Becoming the perfect (potential) customer
- Backing up promises with action

Providing a Clear Scope of Work

As has already been established, providing a clear scope of work during the sourcing phase helps eliminate guesswork for suppliers. The less guesswork (and associated risk) salespeople have to accommodate, the lower the price they can quote. However, providing a clear scope of work does more than minimize the risk factor in a quoted price. Taking the time to properly identify your requirements demonstrates to suppliers that you have carefully planned the sourcing project and that you have taken the time to develop the details of the requirements of the category.

This may sound obvious, but as we discuss in Chapter 9, many customers provide suppliers with very little information during the bid process. They do this for several reasons. Some are "time-bankrupt," and do not have the mental bandwidth to do the necessary research. Others feel that providing suppliers with too much information backfires on them in the long run if requirements change or implementation problems lead to suppliers not getting the level of volume they expected. Some simply do not have access to the information, due to their existing suppliers having too much control of the spend category. And, quite frankly, others are simply too lazy to gather the information, which almost always leads to a contract renewal with incumbent suppliers.

Providing limited or unclear scopes of work and requirements can still produce results, but these will not be optimized. A supplier that has a clear scope of work can devote more time to developing a proposal tailored to your needs and less time asking you follow-up questions and trying to determine how to handle unknown components. This shift in the supplier mind-set often opens up conversations you normally would not have with a supplier, and can lead to market intelligence that becomes useful later on in the negotiation process.

Becoming the Perfect (Potential) Customer

Most buyers think that the only motivator they can offer to get a good price from their supply base is volume. However, suppliers often care much more about intangible aspects of the account than they do about volume commitments. As a customer, you should take the time to find out what are the requirements, wants, and needs of your supply base. Rarely is a supplier asked by a buyer, "What can I do to be a better customer?" but the question alone can show willingness to work with the supplier community and begin to develop a partner mentality in a potential supplier.

During the initial stage of the project, try to learn who the suppliers' best customers are and why. In the supplier interviews, ask what makes the perfect customer, and listen closely to the responses. Then, as you build your bid documents, include information that demonstrates you can become one of those customers. Building a business case that demonstrates this helps your supplier build an internal business case as to why you should be offered a lower price and closer cooperation.

In Part Three of this book, we discuss some real-world examples of how to leverage supplier feedback. We also dive a bit more deeply into the concept of becoming the perfect customer.

Backing up Promises

Even more critical than saying you will become the perfect customer is taking concrete action to demonstrate that you will actually do it. There are many traits suppliers look for in a perfect customer, including a reference-able account, consistent early payment, or competent electronic-order submission. They may want a certain inventory commitment, technology integration, or the ability to provide additional goods and services.

Buyers often discover the wants and needs of their supply base during the sourcing stage but choose to take no action. After all, they are the customers—why should they change? Others hear the suppliers loud and clear, but choose to put off taking any action until after they make an award and move into the contracting phase. However, waiting until after a supplier is selected to become the perfect customer loses the effect of motivating the supplier, because at that point the working relationship already will have been set, and neither side will want to make any further changes that are now perceived as unnecessary.

You should begin going through the process of learning what it would take to become the perfect customer during the sourcing phase. If a supplier would like to receive payment in 20 days and your normal terms are 60, start speaking to your finance team early about the possibility and explore what they would need from you to justify the change. If some level of technology integration would help the supplier, bring your IT team into the discussions to learn what that integration would entail. Providing potential suppliers with visibility into these conversations gives them a higher comfort level that you are not just paying lip service, but instead intend to act on their requests if they are awarded the business.

Creating a Team Environment

The typical approach customers take to negotiations is an adversarial one. Many books on negotiations talk about the use of body language and tone in negotiations, even suggesting that keeping your chair slightly higher than that of your opponent gives you an advantage during the discussions.

Posture, tone, and even seating arrangements may give a perceived advantage during formal negotiations, but creating a collaborative working relationship with your supply base can ultimately be far more effective in lowering unit prices. Establish a team within your organization, formed with people from different divisions, all working on the same issue, toward the same common goal. Everyone on that team is able to share information freely and learn about each other's perspectives on the sourcing project, often causing team members to become invested in the result. They see progress and want to make sure the project is a successful one.

Working with suppliers is not very different. You need product, and your supplier wants to sell you that product. Both parties are working toward the same common goal, yet somewhere along the line the supplier ends up at the other side of the table, in an adversarial relationship. Negotiations tend to proceed with a zero-sum-game mentality, in which one party ends up the winner and the other comes out as the loser.

Creating a team environment tends to short-circuit that zero-sum-game dynamic, and begins to establish a win-win scenario. Suppliers let their guard down, sharing market insight, working in a collaborative manner, and providing access to information that normally would not be disclosed. Ultimately, developing a teaming relationship with the supply base can provide the same result as working with an internal group—a personally invested sales team that wants to make sure they end up with the business on a long-term, sustainable basis. Better yet, beyond the sales team, your supplier may have invested people from multiple divisions within their own company, highly motivated to help your company succeed.

Of course, telling suppliers you want to work as a team is much different than actually accomplishing it. The natural tendency in working with suppliers is to hold them at arm's length—you do not want them to see all your cards, for fear that they may gain some advantage. While there may be some information you do not want to share, there is probably plenty more information that can safely be provided that can benefit the sourcing project and achieve optimal pricing for the spend category being sourced, which is, of course, the ultimate goal. In fact, the simple act of being responsive to the suppliers and letting them know you hear their concerns or questions can go a long way to create a team environment that can transform the whole project into a win-win scenario.

In every interaction with a supplier you must ask yourself, would I respond the same way in working with a member of my own (internal) team? Be willing to share data, provide real answers to their questions, and be responsive. Show suppliers that this project is just as important to you as it is to them, and follow up regularly over the phone or face-to-face rather than via e-mail. Verbal communication allows suppliers to ask follow-up questions and is more conducive to brainstorming, which is a clear indication you are now working in a team environment. The simple act of working as a team, rather than as adversaries, influences the supplier to share more information than they normally would. This leads us to the next step in negotiation—identifying leverage points.

Identifying Leverage Points

In the world of finance, leverage often refers to the amount of debt a company has. The more your company is leveraged, the more it has borrowed (against existing assets) in order to maintain or grow business.

In the sourcing world, leverage is information or knowledge that gives you an advantage or the other party a disadvantage. Leverage provides you with a larger opportunity to get what you want out of a negotiation. It allows you to shift the fulcrum, moving an otherwise immovable object (in this case price) closer to where you want it.

There are many ways to identify leverage points during the strategic sourcing process. Oftentimes you can identify leverage during the RFP. As proposals come in, you are provided with supplier price and service information. Price is the most obvious leverage point: If Supplier X quoted $1 for a widget and Supplier Y quoted $0.50, you now have leverage in the form of market intelligence about pricing. You can use this bit of information to push Supplier X to become more competitive.

A supplier's servicing proposal also provides you with information that can be leveraged, although that leverage can be more difficult to recognize. Analyze which parts of the RFP the supplier focused on, and determine what the supplier sees as its real value-add. Identifying the focus of a supplier proposal can give you insight into what's important to them, and this can be used as a critical leverage point during negotiations.

There are other opportunities to uncover leverage points beyond the RFP process. In the previous examples, the leverage points identified are primarily positive—additional information you can provide to suppliers that create greater motivation for them to want to *win* your business. Of course, negative leverage—or leverage that provides additional incentive for a supplier to not want to *lose* your business to a competitor—can also be just as effective.

A negative leverage opportunity is available predominantly when competition exists in the marketplace and suppliers are focused not just on getting new business, but also on making sure that their competitors do not get your business. This type of leverage can also be uncovered during brainstorming sessions or other informal conversations that often occur as a result of the team environment you have created with potential suppliers. During these informal conversations suppliers often let their guard down and talk about past projects they have worked on where they lost (or gained) business to (or from) a key competitor. Find out who those competitors were and what tipped the business into (or out of) their favor.

You should also try to find out the overriding sales strategies of potential suppliers. Determine what their goals are for the next year and for the next five years, and why a certain type of business is more attractive to them than others.

This information in itself may not be helpful unless you understand the overall market as well. The understanding of market dynamics you developed in the research phase of the sourcing project allows you to carry on more meaningful discussions with suppliers and create RFx documents that get more useful information from the supply base. When utilizing negative-leverage techniques, there are data points about the overall market that you should know:

- The size of the market for the products or services being sourced
- How much of that market your current supplier represents, and what it would mean to the market if you changed suppliers

If your volumes are substantial enough, it could cause a shift in market leadership, or it might even create an opportunity for a supplier to take out a competitor. Understanding this dynamic gives you very powerful leverage points with your supply base.

Competitive or negative leverage can be just as effective as motivational or positive leverage, but in instances in which substantial competition does not exist in the market, negative leverage tends to lose its effectiveness. In such cases your job is to create the illusion of competition.

Like everyone else, suppliers fear the unknown. While they may be up to speed on existing market conditions, they know that markets are constantly changing and competitors come and go. When the market for a particular spend category has limited competition, be sure to explore alternatives that would normally not be perceived as direct competition to your existing supplier, such as:

- Small start-ups
- New processes or technologies that would make the existing product or service unnecessary
- Companies that provide similar products and services that might be willing to make concessions to get into or advance in the business

To increase negative leverage, drop hints to the primary supplier that these alternatives are being researched. Even if you ultimately uncover nothing in your exploration of alternatives, letting the incumbent know that its business could be at risk tends to make it more susceptible to that negative leverage during negotiations.

Leveraging techniques can be used during the entire sourcing process, but they develop their greatest impact once suppliers submit first-round bids. Maximize your leveraging power by identifying areas where particular suppliers are out of line compared with their competitors. Provide them with insight and guidance as to where they are off and where they should be versus the market. In some cases you will find that suppliers made mistakes, such as quoting an incorrect product or service or building in invalid assumptions; in other cases, letting them know in this manner that you have a leveraging position can motivate them to modify their bidding strategy in your favor. Ask for refined bids, and start to hone in on suppliers that are willing to provide the most competitive offers and are working to meet the service levels your organization needs. Once these round-two bids have been submitted and analyzed, you are ready to move into the next phase of the negotiation process, developing final targets.

 ## NEGOTIATION OPTIMIZATION: DEVELOPING FINAL TARGETS

Up to this point in the sourcing process, you engage in subtle, indirect negotiations through various motivational and leveraging tactics aimed at moving supplier price points beyond what is typically presented in a first-pass offer to a level that is more market competitive. It is now time to use this information to develop final targets, using the Best Alternative to a Negotiated Agreement (BATNA) method, described previously. Before we begin this discussion, it is worthwhile to develop a deeper understanding of the concept of BATNA.

In negotiations, the BATNA is often referred to as the "plan B" offer. For example, if you are negotiating with supplier A to achieve a savings of 20 percent, and you know supplier B is willing to provide the same level of quality and service at a savings of 15 percent, supplier B is your BATNA, and serves as plan B if negotiations fall through with supplier A.

This classic example of how to use BATNA is an important one. After all, if you do not have an option to fall back on, you do not have a lot of leverage in negotiations. However, BATNA can be used as more than just a plan B. It can also be used as a tool to optimize negotiations.

As an example, imagine that you recently went to bid for office supplies. There were five products in your bid basket, and four different suppliers submitted bids in the RFx process, as detailed in Table 6.1.

TABLE 6.1   Office Supplies Bid Results

Part Description	Supplier A Total Cost	Supplier B Total Cost	Supplier C Total Cost	Supplier D Total Cost
Part1	$ 100	$ 73	$ 122	$ 70
Part2	$ 410	$ 375	$ 550	$ 392
Part3	$ 212	$ 220	$ 216	$ 240
Part4	$ 730	$ 700	$ 600	$ 712
Part5	$ 72	$ 119	$ 106	$ 102
Total Cost	$1,524	$1,487	$1,594	$1,516

While the table shows that supplier B provides the best overall cost, other suppliers are more competitive for some products. To determine the lowest overall cost for all products in the basket, add a new column to your analysis and enter the lowest total cost for each product from the four suppliers. (You can do this by using a MIN formula in Microsoft Excel.) Make sure you factor in your quantities as well, because a typical trick suppliers use is to offer huge discounts for your least-frequently-purchased products. Table 6.2 displays the results of this analysis.

As you can determine from this analysis, the lowest overall cost available is $1,329, a full 11 percent lower than supplier B's best offer to date. Of course, now it might occur to you that your best option would be to use all four suppliers, buying the lowest-cost product from each one. This scenario, however, would be highly inefficient. As discussed previously, the overall goal of the sourcing strategy is to attempt to migrate spend categories toward the tactical classification. This scenario runs counter to that goal, because the

TABLE 6.2   Office Supply Bid Results with Lowest Cost

Part Description	Supplier A Total Cost	Supplier B Total Cost	Supplier C Total Cost	Supplier D Total Cost	Lowest Total Cost
Part1	$ 100	$ 73	$ 122	$ 70	$ 70
Part2	$ 410	$ 375	$ 550	$ 392	$ 375
Part3	$ 212	$ 220	$ 216	$ 240	$ 212
Part4	$ 730	$ 700	$ 600	$ 712	$ 600
Part5	$ 72	$ 119	$ 106	$ 102	$ 72
Total Cost	$1,524	$1,487	$1,594	$1,516	$1,329

administrative cost and burden of utilizing four suppliers would far outweigh the additional 11 percent savings obtainable. In addition, suppliers would most likely be reluctant to honor the prices quoted if they are not awarded the entire basket, and this runs counter to your strategy of building a team environment.

While breaking up the spend is usually not the best tactical approach, this low-cost analysis is still useful—it represents the theoretical absolute lowest total cost the market can bear for the products you are purchasing. This lowest total cost determines the optimal cost, or BATNA, which then becomes the target for final negotiations.

Two points of caution should be considered here. First, in using the BATNA it is absolutely critical that you ensure your cost comparison is made on an apples-to-apples basis. If certain suppliers have built in (or pared out) their cost based on certain assumptions and other suppliers have not, your BATNA may not be accurate. Along the same lines, you should be sure that all unit-of-measure issues have been addressed. For instance, if one supplier is quoting a two-pack while another quotes a one-pack, this can skew your BATNA. You do not want these issues to arise during negotiations.

Second, you might have a tendency to use these targets to negotiate with the lowest overall bidder, which in this example is supplier B. However, the supplier or suppliers you choose for final negotiations should not be based on overall lowest bid alone. Instead, consider the optimal combination of cost and service. If you believe supplier D (or A or C) is a better overall fit for your organization, you should include them in the final negotiations round. Effective negotiation optimization does not just entail getting the best price. Your approach should be to combine the best overall service offering with the best price in the market. Even if supplier D cannot reach the $1,329 target, the company may approach close enough to justify awarding them the business.

A word of caution: The BATNA is an excellent tool for optimizing negotiations, but it can quickly lose effectiveness if the numbers are not based on facts. In most cases suppliers know where the market floor is for their industry and they also know their own breaking point. Presenting final targets based on an incorrect or exaggerated BATNA can backfire, leaving you with no alternatives and an upset supply base.

 ## GETTING TO "NO"

Even though one of your key objectives in your sourcing strategy is to develop a team environment with your chosen supplier that ultimately creates a win-win scenario, the final round of negotiations can tend to take on the character of a chess game, in which each side engages in moves to develop a better strategic advantage over its opponent. Many experienced negotiators are inclined to say that in this round, if your opponent accepts your offer, you have not asked for enough. Their rationale is that if you did not hear the other side say "No," you have not reached the opponent's breaking point and thus you have left money on the table. This rationale holds true in most cases; with rare exception, it never hurts to ask for more.

In the negotiation optimization process, the "No" answer is the starting point for real negotiations. "No" is the point where the supplier starts to feel some pain, but it by no means indicates that you have reached the lowest price it can offer. At this point there are several techniques for driving the price closer to your targets.

Finding Access to the Decision Makers

Often customers negotiate solely with their primary sales representative. While these negotiations can be effective, they can only go so far. Once you reach "No," your sales representative more than likely needs to go back to management for approval to provide lower pricing. Do not rely on your sales representative to make your business case for you—request a meeting in which you can talk directly to those responsible for approving your requests.

The first reason for this is simple. Allowing a third party that works for the opposing team to make your business case for you can never be as effective as presenting it directly. The message you need to relay may or may not be getting across through your sales representative, but you have no way of knowing if you do not present it yourself.

Second, in the case that your sales representative is not the final decision maker, that person effectively becomes a middleman between his or her organization and yours. From a timing perspective alone this is inefficient; as offers and counteroffers are presented, you can lose hours or even days. You also lose momentum in this scenario—it is difficult to keep working toward a common solution if both parties are not 100 percent focused on the conversation. As the days go by you can lose track of the details of the last offer (or counter), and the other party's message (or yours) gets diluted by other attention-demanding tasks. A direct conversation opens up a dialogue in which questions can be asked and answered immediately, eliminating the typical halting to-and-fro communication that a middleman tends to generate.

Lastly, many times a decision maker will take a more aggressive stance when that person is not dealing directly with the person on the other side of the table. Having a direct conversation with the actual decision maker often goes a long way toward softening that hard-line position, even if the content of your business case does not change.

Opening the Books

There are many reasons that drive a supplier to get to "No." In some cases the breaking point has been reached. In other cases, the supplier simply does not believe that you can get the price you are asking from another supplier, so the reps become overly confident that they have already won the business. To counter this mind-set, while it is inadvisable to hand over a competitor's proposal to the supplier with whom you are negotiating, some of your nonconfidential market intelligence may provide a rationale for your targets.

Beyond such market intelligence, you may also have some internal information you can share with suppliers. Even if you have developed a very clear RFx that adequately details your requirements and has answered all of the suppliers questions to date, showing them your initial data sets may give them additional incentive to improve their bid and allow them to pare out some built-in assumptions. In addition, if your market research has led you to forecast that demand involving the spend category in question is likely to increase in the near future due to mergers, acquisitions, or economic growth, provide suppliers with this data as well. If suppliers know your business is projected to double over the next few years, they may be willing to provide some concessions on the front end to secure that business during that period, or provide tiers of pricing so that once you reach the projected volumes your price will be accordingly lowered.

Opening your books in this manner does not just entail sharing data with suppliers. If you are dealing with a heavily service-oriented spend category, it might be worthwhile to provide suppliers with a tour of your facility, bring in stakeholders and end users for conversations, or arrange for a meeting with your executive team to demonstrate how developing a win-win partnership is as important to your organization as it is to theirs.

Considering the Timing

Salespeople can be as motivated by the timing of a sale as by the volume that sale represents. Bonuses and compensation structures are often based on monthly, quarterly, or annual results, and closing on your account might push the salesperson up to a new level of commission. While it can be difficult to find out whether these factors are operating in your supplier's organization, if you have built a rapport with the salesperson, he or she may be willing to disclose this information. In that case you will have developed a new leverage point. You can use this advantage to let the supplier know that you can hit a certain timing milestone for the order, but in exchange the supplier must hit your price targets. Some examples of these tactics are detailed in Chapter 14, "Leveraging Supplier Feedback."

Continuing to Ask

It never hurts to keep asking for a better deal; this is often referred to as the *beg*. Even if you know that you cannot achieve better pricing in the marketplace, letting a supplier know that their pricing approaches your target but asking for a further cost reduction nonetheless can be an effective tactic. Sometimes suppliers conclude that it is more important to offer a customer a slightly lower price than to hold the line but risk causing the customer to develop a negative impression of the supplier. Again, it helps to build a rapport through the techniques described in this chapter before attempting the beg.

 ## WHAT NOT TO DO

So far this chapter has focused on positive steps you can take to conduct negotiations more effectively. Of course, there are also many actions negotiators take that can have a negative impact on the specific negotiations or overall supplier relationship. These actions generally stem from a negotiator's inability to transition from the opponent-driven chess game mentality of direct negotiations to the continued development of a win-win team environment as the customer and the supplier begin to build a working relationship. Three such actions that a negotiator should be sure to avoid during the sourcing process are:

1. Negotiating after a reverse auction
2. Negotiating price at the contracting phase
3. Establishing artificial targets

Negotiating After a Reverse Auction

Keep in mind that a reverse auction is best used to source a spend category that you have classified as tactical, and the supplier with the lowest bid is expected to get the business—price is the major factor. Each supplier should therefore enter a reverse auction prepared to quote the lowest price it can. Because suppliers can see what their competitors are bidding, or at least what their rank is versus their competitors, the market floor can be determined rather quickly.

Even when all parties involved have a good understanding of this context, some buyers make the choice to negotiate with a supplier after the conclusion of a reverse auction. In almost all cases this is due to the customer not feeling comfortable giving the business to the lowest bidder. Reasons for taking this action include the buyer's belief that the low bidder cannot handle the business, or that the supplier's service is lacking a crucial element, or perhaps the customer just likes another supplier better. Regardless of the reason, the customer uses the lowest bid in the auction as leverage to negotiate with a preferred supplier.

In a fair and objective sourcing environment, this is the wrong approach to take. If you are not comfortable with a particular supplier's service offering, then you should not invite that company to participate in the reverse auction. As discussed in Chapter 4, only suppliers that you have prescreened through an RFI or RFP should be included in a reverse auction. Any supplier invited to this type of bid environment should be a supplier to which you would be willing to award the business, otherwise your overall price comparison is not being conducted on an apples-to-apples basis.

Negotiating after the reverse auction does your company more harm than good, because it hurts credibility with suppliers by leading them to perceive that you have not upheld your end of the bargain—you brought in suppliers that cannot meet your service expectations with the sole purpose of driving price downward. That credibility gap could make suppliers reluctant to work with you in the future.

Aside from risking damage to your credibility, inviting suppliers with a service or product disadvantage into a reverse auction can often have a negative impact on the results of the auction. If a preferred supplier perceives that the low bidder's service offering is lacking substance, it may take an aggressive stance, choosing to provide a bid that is not competitive or even choosing not to participate. If this is the case. you will have limited yourself to choose between a supplier that may not be able to serve your company effectively or a preferred supplier that is offering a higher-than-market price.

Negotiating Price at the Contracting Phase

Negotiating pricing at the contracting phase can be just as problematic as negotiating after a reverse auction. As we discuss in the next chapter, once you accept a final proposal and award the business to a supplier, you move into the contracting phase, in which you convert the proposal into a written agreement that outlines the working relationship between your organization and that of the supplier.

Often, sourcing professionals use the contracting phase as an opportunity to negotiate additional pricing concessions. Even if unit prices are not discussed, elements such as payment terms, freight and fuel surcharges, or rebates may enter into the discussion at this time. This could occur because the sourcing professional did not adequately plan the complete sourcing project and neglected to consider these factors earlier. Another possibility is that the contracting agent believes that he or she has additional leverage at this stage—the supplier is very close to getting the business and may be willing to offer more to get it.

Again, this is the wrong approach. Good sourcing practice requires that all price points and business terms be negotiated during the sourcing phase. The contracting phase should only entail clearly stating what was agreed upon in earlier phases and adding any legal terms that may be necessary. Suppliers will have already factored most of their business terms into their preliminary proposals. If a supplier provided a price based on 30-day payment terms and you request 60 days at the time of contracting, you are essentially asking them to rebid after they were awarded the business. From an ethical or legal standpoint there may be nothing wrong with negotiating at the contracting phase, but once again, you are risking damage to your credibility and establishing a bad start to a long-term working relationship.

Establishing Artificial Targets

Often, sourcing teams develop savings targets at the beginning of a project and find that the level of pricing required to reach those targets is not available in the market. Rather than adjust the targets, negotiators instead often cling to the originally projected goals as targets and proceed to browbeat suppliers to reach the desired price.

This approach is rather common in the purchasing world. Nevertheless, in order to preserve your company's credibility and to create the win-win environment that is one of your key goals, all negotiations should be fact-based, meaning that negotiation targets should be developed according to detailed research and market information. Asking a supplier to provide a price that is not available in the market may have a positive short-term effect, in that the supplier may meet your request and you will begin to save at the desired level. However, over the long term, you may find that quality or service suffers, that you begin to receive additional surcharges on your invoices, or that the supplier comes back at a later date with a demand to increase pricing, without which the supplier intends to walk away from the business, leaving you in a potentially time-constrained situation in which you must accept any offer.

At the heart of all three of the foregoing examples are the issues of credibility and sustainability; engaging in any of these negative negotiating tactics may ultimately cause you to lose the game of achieving the optimal sourcing outcome. As we discuss in the next few chapters, developing good working relationships with your suppliers is essential to sustaining the results produced during the strategic sourcing project. Setting any ethical issues aside, from a standpoint of creating a team environment, a good working relationship, and a good reputation in the marketplace, these tactics should be avoided.

 ## IN SUMMARY

Each indirect spend category entails unique negotiation tactics and strategies. Generally speaking, product-related categories involve a group of suppliers that are fairly open to negotiating on price. Conversely, suppliers that provide services may believe apples-to-apples comparisons of their offerings to the competition are impossible, and therefore may be less willing to come to the table.

You may also run into internal challenges when sourcing these categories. Often, end users and stakeholders have been working closely with an incumbent supplier and, unless properly guided, may mistakenly end up on the wrong side of the table. They may believe that during the sourcing event their preferred suppliers presented the best offer, and may truly have convinced themselves, out of fear that service may suffer or even that forcing a supplier to lower its prices might put it out of business, that their suppliers cannot afford to provide a lower bid. To them, getting to "No" means you have pushed the supplier too far—they would prefer coming to an agreement that, in their opinion, makes good business sense and doesn't put any undue pressure on the supplier's margins. In their eyes, a well-paid supplier translates into a happy supplier, which in turn translates into better service and a good working relationship.

These conditions provide all the more reason to create an open team relationship with suppliers during a sourcing engagement, sharing information, and working together toward a common goal. Keeping negotiations fact-based and backing up your targets with market research helps to keep stakeholders on board and to minimize pushback. After all, the best negotiation is the one that results in a perceived win for everyone.

7

Get It in Writing

The Contracting Phase

THE CONTRACTING PHASE of a strategic sourcing project converts the business terms and concepts developed during the RFx (request for *x*: information, quote, or proposal) stage and confirmed during negotiations into a written document agreed to and signed by both the supplier and customer. Many variables determine the type of language and terms that should be considered when writing a commercial contract, such as the nature of the item being purchased (a product or a service), the scope of work, the number of locations that will fall under the agreement, and commitments made by both parties during negotiations. This chapter is not intended to be a legal guide or to review the exact language that should be included in every type of commercial agreement. That is your legal team's business. Instead, this chapter discusses best practices from a purchasing perspective—terms that should and should not be included in a contract, ways to use contracts to ensure service levels are met, recourse for disputes, and when to include your legal team in the contracting process.

 ESSENTIAL COMPONENTS OF A CONTRACT

Organizations have varying approaches to constructing contracts. Some contracts outline all the terms of the relationship between buyer and seller in a page or two. Others can easily exceed 100 pages or more. Why such a difference in page count and, therefore, content? You might expect the answer to have a lot to do with how critical the product or service is to the organization. Spend categories that fall into the tactical or leveraged classifications of the sourcing strategy grid might be expected to have shorter agreements and those in the critical or strategic classifications to have a longer list of terms. This is not necessarily the case. More likely, the longer agreements belong to organizations that have large legal teams and risk management groups responsible for protecting the company against liability in the event that something goes wrong, as well as ensuring that none of their obligations under the agreement are in conflict with other operational or financial business plans.

There is nothing inherently wrong with a verbose contract that is loaded with terms and conditions extending out over multiple pages, other than the fact that reading through and understanding a 100-page contract can be quite time-consuming and can run up expensive legal bills. Specifically for indirect spend, you should consider the terms and conditions that are truly relevant to the relationship being established, and which are superfluous generic legal terms. Generally, once the contract is signed, no one ever looks at it again unless something goes wrong. For this reason, it is prudent to balance the need for legal protection with common sense. There is no harm in ensuring the agreement you develop is as concisely written as possible—the more concise the agreement, the more quickly it will flow through the legal process, minimizing delays in implementation and the commencement of real cost savings.

With the foregoing in mind, this chapter discusses several elements—some relatively simple and obvious, others more complex—that constitute the basic framework for indirect spend commercial agreements.

Term and Termination

The primary element in every commercial contract is the term, which sets the start and end date of the agreement. In the case of indirect spend, agreements are typically short-term, meaning one or two years, but can extend to three or even five years, depending on the category. Term clauses also provide the rules for renewing an agreement at end of the stated term, as well as the protocol for terminating the agreement before expiration.

Renewals

Renewals are handled in several ways in a contract. First, the contract may be silent on renewals. This means that at end of term, the agreement expires, and it is up to the buyer and seller to determine the path forward from there. This can be a risky approach, particularly if you do not have a good contract management system alerting you of expiring agreements, as suppliers may also not let you know about contract expiration and casually increase pricing to more profitable levels.

If renewals are covered in the agreement, they are usually enacted in one of three ways: through a term autorenew, a month-to-month extension, or an extension in writing.

In an autorenew scenario, once a contract expires, the term is automatically extended, typically in one-year increments, unless either party provides the other notice of intent not to renew the agreement. Normally, this entails providing written notice to the other party 30 to 60 days prior to the date of expiration.

In a month-to-month extension, the agreement automatically renews, but only in one-month increments, until the parties come to agreement on a longer term or give notice of termination.

From the standpoint of flexibility and leverage for the buyer, a month-to-month extension is typically the most favorable type of renewal clause. The clause essentially grants you the same levels of pricing and service you have been receiving under the year-to-year agreement, but with a greatly reduced timing commitment. The supplier is aware of this as well, and will either push to eventually renew at full term, or keep quiet in the hope that you do not realize the contract has expired.

Finally, a contract may state that the agreement can only be extended if both parties agree to the extension in writing. This essentially terminates the agreement at end of term and forces both parties to make a decision about their future relationship.

Early Termination

The early termination clause defines the rules for exiting an agreement prior to the expiration date. Contracts manage early termination in several ways.

One of the most common early termination clauses is the default clause. Default allows either party to discontinue an agreement if the other party fails to meet its stipulated obligations. For example, if a supplier provides a quote for a given price and agrees to it under the contract, but then finds it misquoted and cannot honor the price, it has defaulted. Once the default occurs, the nondefaulting party must notify the defaulter, in writing, of the failure.

Most default terms also include language regarding the right to cure, meaning that the defaulting party has a window of opportunity (typically anywhere from 15 to 90 days, and sometimes more) to take corrective action. If the default is corrected during that period, the contract continues under existing terms. Most default provisions include wording concerning the filing of a petition of bankruptcy. In most commercial contracts, a bankruptcy filing by either party results in automatic and immediate default of the agreement, and it is up to the nondefaulting party to decide whether it desires to continue with the agreement as is, create a new agreement that protects the party from additional risk, or terminate the relationship altogether.

Most contracts have a default clause, but some also have a clause stating that either party can terminate the agreement at any time, even if no default occurred, normally with some type of advance written notice (typically 15 or 30 days). Depending on the type of agreement and the products or services being purchased, early termination may be stipulated with some type of penalty, particularly if volume commitments are not met. For example, if a particular contract is worth $100,000 to the supplier, meaning over the life of the agreement they are expecting $100,000 in payments, and the customer gives notice of termination after only $50,000 of that obligation has been met, an early termination penalty clause might state that in order to discontinue the agreement, the customer must provide a payment in the value of 25 percent of the remaining obligation, which in this example is $12,500.

Lastly, the contract may be silent on early termination. If this is the case, the options for terminating prior to the expiration date are limited. Many contracts do not have minimum commitments. In this case, the easiest way to terminate the contract early is simply to stop purchasing from the supplier.

Indemnification

The indemnification clause, also known as a *hold harmless* clause, outlines the amount of financial responsibility one party will accept if the other party is sued for reasons associated with the agreement.

For example, an office supplies contract may contain an indemnification clause stating that each party agrees to indemnify and hold harmless the other party against any losses or legal fees incurred due to third-party claims arising from the conduct or actions of the indemnifying party. Now let us assume that one of your employees has an accident with a pair of scissors purchased from your office-supply vendor and decides to sue both you and the supplier. Since you have indemnified the office-supply company against third-party claims in the contract, your company is responsible for paying legal fees or other expenses incurred by the office supply vendor as a result of the lawsuit.

Most commercial agreements include an indemnification clause, and most suppliers will require you to indemnify them from suits such as the one described previously. When determining language for such a clause, you should ensure that the level of indemnification is relevant to the relationship. While blanket indemnification—indemnifying against any loss that may occur— may make sense in partnering agreements or other types of contracts, under normal circumstances it is an excessive stipulation in a commercial agreement.

Indemnity clauses inserted by a supplier's legal team may appear to be standard boilerplate language, but some contracts may have language that is not acceptable, such as stipulations that indemnify the supplier but not the customer. If a supplier demands specific indemnification and you are unclear of what the impact of that indemnification is to your organization, consult your legal advisor.

Liability

While the indemnification clause covers lawsuits and other expenses that are due to the involvement and detriment of a third party, the liability clause sets rules for the claims, losses, and legal fees in the event the buyer and supplier enter into a dispute. Most frequently, this clause sets limits to the liability either party can incur. For example, a liability clause might state, "In no event will either party be liable for any indirect, incidental, or consequential damages, whether based on contract, tort, or any other legal theory. Supplier liability for the products sold is limited to the replacement value of the products."

This or similar clauses can be found in many commercial agreements. Essentially, such clauses state that in the event of a dispute, the maximum amount the defending party will be responsible for paying is limited to the value of the goods sold.

While the limit-of-liability clause is present in most commercial agreements, the maximum amount (or limit) can be defined in several ways. In some cases, it is defined as the value of the goods sold (as described previously); in others it is the total value of the contract. Often, the maximum amount is assigned a specific dollar value. For example, the clause might state that liability limits are "$50,000 or the dollar value of the contract, whichever is greater."

From the perspective of the buyer, the higher the liability limits, the better; however, most courts will not support unlimited liability, even if it is written into the agreement. As a buyer, the goal is not to establish unlimited liability in a contract, but rather to ensure that any limits in liability will still reasonably cover your losses in the event of a failure of the product or the supplier.

Warranties

Most contracts include a warranties clause, which simply states that the seller has the right to sell the product and that the product is what the seller says it is and does what it is advertised to do. In addition, most warranties guarantee that a product will be free of defect for a certain period of time, or else be replaced.

The Uniform Commercial Code stipulates that all purchases have an implied warranty. However, it is important to include warranty language in an agreement as a statement of fact, in order to verify that you are entering a contract for the products or services specified in the agreement, and not merely agreeing to accept product "as is" with no warranty.

Title, Risk of Loss, and Freight Terms

In an agreement for goods, the question of when title of ownership is transferred from the supplier to the customer is an important one. A risk-of-loss clause outlines who is responsible for damages to goods incurred during the period between the moment a sale occurs and when the goods are received by the customer—essentially during transit, including the process of loading and unloading the goods. Many agreements do not specifically include a risk-of-loss clause. If that is the case, freight terms dictate how risk of loss is handled.

On a very basic level, freight terms outline who pays for freight and when the payment is made. In your contract, you may have negotiated a delivered price, in which the freight charges have been absorbed into the cost of the product, or accepted prepay and add terms, in which the supplier pays the freight charges and adds that amount to your invoice. In these cases, you are using free on board (FOB) destination freight terms. Under this arrangement, the supplier ships the product to your designated delivery point, and you do not take ownership until the product is received. This is an important distinction, because if the product is damaged or destroyed during shipping, it has no effect on you, other than a delay of shipment.

Conversely, your agreement may not cover delivery and you may plan to pick up the goods at the supplier's place of business using your own trucks or a preferred common carrier, and pay for freight on a separate bill. In this instance you have selected FOB origin, or collect, freight terms. Under this arrangement you are accepting ownership at the supplier's place of business, and any damages that occur during transit are your responsibility.

The decision you make as to which freight terms to use depends upon where you can get the best price, how your accounting works, or the easiest way to process an invoice. However, this decision also has a major impact on your risk of loss exposure, as outlined above.

It is important to note that freight terms dictate how risk of loss is handled unless you include a clause specifically stipulating risk-of-loss and transfer-of-ownership details in your agreement. In that instance such a clause dictates how risk-of-loss events are handled, regardless of your freight terms.

Payment Terms

All commercial agreements define payment terms that usually include:

- *Setting a time limit on when payments are due.* Standard terms are usually 30 days after an invoice is issued or product is received (whichever is later). This is the most common payment term to negotiate, as most buyers attempt to extend terms beyond 30 days, while suppliers generally try to shorten the time span.
- *Providing an incentive for early payment.* Some suppliers offer an incentive for payment within a certain period. For example, a supplier may provide a 1 percent discount if payment is received within 10 days of the invoice being issued. If your company has adequate liquidity, you should take advantage of payment discounts whenever possible. In this example, the discount is equivalent to receiving an annual interest rate payment of 18 percent.
- *Establishing penalties for late payment.* Typically, each day beyond the established time limit that payment is not received causes the buyer to incur additional interest charges beyond the original amount due. This is the obverse situation to the early payment incentive, so it is beneficial to try to avoid late payments, so that the "interest" does not flow in the opposite direction, to the supplier.

While payment terms are primarily focused on setting timelines and rules for remitting payments, some agreements also include language concerning the methods of payment that will be accepted. Increasingly, suppliers prefer electronic funds transfers (EFTs) or wire transfers instead of payment by check, and some agreements may state that EFTs are the only acceptable form of payment.

Many suppliers also accept credit card payments. It is important to note that if a credit card is used for payment, the supplier will most likely not honor early payment discounts, even if the payment is made by the stipulated time, due to the high cost of processing credit card transactions.

Force Majeure

The force majeure clause provides an exemption from liability in the case of extraordinary events, such as a war or natural disaster. A classic example of an invocation of force majeure clauses was during and after Hurricane Katrina. That event was so devastating that many raw material processing facilities along the Gulf Coast were shut down for weeks or months. Suppliers, unable to get their products to customers, declared force majeure, meaning they were not able to honor the terms of their commercial contracts. This impelled customers to seek required products elsewhere or in some cases buy products from the existing supplier but at a much higher price.

Many buyers neglect to include the force majeure clause, believing it to be standard legal jargon that has little or no bearing on their commercial agreements. This can have disastrous consequences, as in the Hurricane Katrina example. While most force majeure clauses are fairly straightforward, the way the clause is written can have a major impact on how and when you receive required products during times of shortage.

First, consider the types of events in which a supplier can declare force majeure. Typical force majeure events include war, natural disaster, and other "acts of God." Some suppliers might also include events such as crimes, strikes, or riots, all of which might be deemed acceptable as force majeure by the buyer under normal circumstances. A force majeure clause may be considered unacceptable by a buyer when a supplier includes events for which it would normally be expected to assume the risk and liability. For example, a supplier may state that a processing equipment malfunction should qualify as a force majeure event; however, you as the customer would expect the supplier to take reasonable care of equipment so that such malfunctions are avoided.

Another aspect of force majeure to examine carefully is the mutuality of the agreement. Particularly in services agreements, if a supplier declares force majeure, the typical expectation is that the customer stops payments until service resumes. However, in agreements that include monthly maintenance charges (such as software agreements), suppliers often include boilerplate language that allows them to stop providing service but does not allow the buyer to stop payments. In other words, when force majeure has been declared in these circumstances, the customer continues to pay, even though monthly service will have been halted. This serves to preclude you from contracting with another supplier.

If the service is strategic to your business or the value of the contract is high, not only should you stipulate the ability to stop payments in the event of force majeure, but you should also include the right to cancel the contract should the force majeure event disrupt normal service levels beyond 30 days.

Under normal circumstances, a force majeure clause is not very likely to come into play during the life of a buyer and supplier relationship. However, it is important to consider the ramifications of this clause for the few instances where it may become relevant.

Other Terms to Consider

Many other standard clauses are typically found in commercial agreements, such as nonsolicitation, confidentiality, and choice of law, among others. Depending on the type of product or service being purchased, these terms could have little impact on the relationship, or could become rather significant. When reviewing these terms, make sure you understand the reason they have been included in your contract. They might be truly generic in nature and can be removed. If they are customized or if the supplier considers them to be essential, it is important to make sure you understand the rationale for their inclusion, and consult your legal counsel if necessary.

Most commercial agreements for indirect spend categories are "written on supplier paper," meaning the contract template is provided by the supplier. That being the case, terms and conditions that are not beneficial to the supplier usually are not included in the template, while supplier-favorable terms often are. As the customer, there are terms you should try to incorporate in any commercial agreement that you typically would not find on supplier paper, such as the right to audit, and terms you should be wary of, such as the right of first refusal.

Right to Audit

The right to audit clause provides you, the customer, the ability to audit a supplier's internal documents to validate that they have honored the terms of the agreement. Most often the audit clause refers to price, but it can include service level metrics and other factors as well.

As an example, suppose you enter into a gross-margin agreement with a distributor of electrical components, in which it is agreed that the supplier can add a specific margin (e.g., 18 percent), to its cost to produce and deliver goods. In such an arrangement, the method that the supplier uses to define its cost (before margin is added) can have a great impact on how you are charged.

If you as the buyer have the contractual right to audit, you can gain access (either directly or through a designated third party) to the supplier's cost structure and validate that you have been charged correctly. This entails reviewing not only the supplier's internal reporting documents, but also invoices from its suppliers and any other related materials.

Many people assume they have the right to audit regardless of whether the clause is actually written into the agreement. It stands to reason that if you believe that you are being charged incorrectly, the supplier should be willing to provide documentation to resolve the matter. While this may seem reasonable, suppliers can often become less forthcoming with information if they believe the relationship is not doing well. Even if they appear willing to cooperate, they may use various stall tactics to deny access to the data you require. Including a right-to-audit clause in your agreement contractually obligates the supplier to provide you with the required data to investigate the situation. A right-to-audit clause also sets ground rules for such an audit, including:

- *The frequency of audit requests.* The typically stipulated frequency is once a year.
- *A limit on the length of time eligible for review.* Suppliers try to set a limit on how far back in history you can review, such as one or two years. You should make an effort to negotiate agreements that retain the right to audit for the full life of the relationship.
- *A list of parties eligible to gain access to the supplier's internal documents.* In some cases, suppliers prefer to have a third party audit their internal documents (rather than the customer directly). You as the buyer want to make sure you have the option to use your own internal resources or a third party of your choice to audit the supplier's internal information.
- *A limit on the length of time over which overpayments can be recovered.* Suppliers try to set a time limit on recoveries, such as one or two years. Best-in-class agreements retain the right to recover overpayments for the full life of the relationship.

Right of First Refusal

A right-of-first-refusal clause bears a relationship to a termination clause. It gives the customer the ability to terminate the agreement early, if a lower price is discovered in the marketplace. Such a clause grants the incumbent supplier the right to match the discovered competitive pricing. For example, a clause might state, "Should buyer identify lower cost alternatives for like products, buyer shall provide supplier with notice of lower pricing. Supplier will have 30 days to provide a revised proposal. Should buyer find the new proposal unacceptable, buyer has a right to terminate the agreement."

If a supplier wants to include the right of first refusal in a contract, there are a few aspects you should consider. First, be mindful of the impact this clause could have on exploring competitors. Alternate suppliers may find this clause acceptable in markets where pricing models are well known and well established, such as in telecommunications, where pricing is openly published, or for commodity-driven products such as energy. In markets where pricing is specialized and competitors exhibit distinct service levels, asking one supplier to match the price of another may be viewed as unethical. You may get the short-term gain of the cost reduction with the incumbent supplier, but over the long term alternate suppliers will be less willing to provide you with competitive quotes because they know your incumbent gets the first chance to match the quoted prices.

Second, if your contract already has a clause allowing for early termination, you should avoid also including a right of first refusal. If more competitive pricing is available in the marketplace and early termination exists, you have the discretion to move the business or give the incumbent a chance to match pricing. Adding a right-of-first-refusal clause annuls this flexibility and guarantees the incumbent a second chance, even if it does not deserve it.

 ## ATTACHMENTS

The main body of a contract establishes the basic terms and conditions of a commercial agreement. The attachments detail price points, discount levels, and price change mechanisms. They also provide context for the scope of work and detail service-level requirements and other servicing metrics.

Pricing and Price Change Mechanisms

Attachment A typically details the specifications and price of the items being purchased. In a contract in which pricing is not fixed for the duration of the term, it should also cover how price changes are handled. Some price change mechanisms can be very general in nature. For example, a software agreement may state that maintenance costs will increase by no more than 8 percent per year for the life of the agreement. A contract for elevator maintenance service may allow for increases based on changes in union hourly rates.

Other agreements may have more precise price change mechanisms. For example, if you are purchasing a product that includes a relatively high cost of a constituent raw material, your contract might specify an index from which future price changes are calculated, a formula for determining the new price based on these changes in cost, and a starting point for pricing based on the index. In agreements where pricing is index-based, it is important to note that price changes can flow both ways. If the raw material index goes up, so does your price. If the index goes down, your price should reflect that movement.

Particularly in the case of an index-based price change mechanism, you will also want to include a schedule specifying the standardized frequency of pricing reviews and modifications. This schedule should be well defined in your agreement, otherwise you may experience the supplier proactively alerting you of upward price pressures, but conveniently neglecting to notify you as indices decline.

Scope of Work

Much as an Attachment A for a goods contract details the products that are being purchased and how much they cost, the attachment covering the scope of work for a services agreement provides a precise definition of the services and their price points provided by the supplier. Individual services might be priced separately or lumped together as part of an overall service offering, or you may determine that a hybrid of the two methods is best. For example, in a contract for janitorial services, the scope of work specification might include dusting and vacuuming the office three times a week for a fixed weekly price. However, you may also need windows washed periodically. Rather than rolling the window washing cost into your fixed price, your scope of work can detail the cost for this service as a separate line item.

Service Level Requirements and Servicing Metrics

Service level metrics (and problems that result from unsatisfactory service) can be difficult to define and quantify after a contract has been written and a working relationship begins. Defining minimum service levels in writing in an attachment to the contract helps avoid disputes that may arise later due to unclear expectations between buyer and supplier. Beyond merely defining minimum service levels, the attachment should detail how service levels will be tracked, how the supplier will resolve issues arising from insufficient service, and penalties incurred by the supplier for not meeting these requirements.

There are two factors to consider in defining service-level metrics. The first and most obvious involves determining the service levels you really require. Next-day delivery may be important for your company, or you may need a supplier that can provide consignment of vendor-managed inventory. You may require specific reports on a weekly or monthly basis. These specific service level requirements were more than likely identified at the beginning of the project and included as part of the scope of work when relaying those requirements to suppliers. Because they have been part of the discussion from data collection through sourcing, they should be relatively easy to identify and include in the contract.

Once you have determined specific service level requirements, the next step is identifying other key performance indicators (KPIs) that can help maintain or enhance the relationship with your new supplier. Particularly for supply agreements that include multiple locations, KPIs can help foster compliance and sponsorship throughout the organization and assist in the development of a healthy, long-term commercial relationship. In general, KPIs ensure the contract achieves the following results:

- *Compliance with industry standards.* KPIs ensure your new supplier is at least providing the same service levels as other suppliers in the marketplace. As has been previously discussed, end users and other stakeholders can be resistant to changing suppliers and procedures. Once they do embrace change, however, it is essential to make sure the new supplier meets or exceeds the standards of other suppliers in the industry, to reassure end users of the efficacy of the change.
- *Consistent service levels.* A successful commercial relationship can be difficult to maintain if a supplier serves one location differently than another. KPIs provide a target to meet in serving all locations, ensuring a minimum acceptable performance level for your account.

Order fill rates, inventory commitments, emergency response times, and emergency delivery times are all examples of relevant KPIs. However, the proper KPIs to include in a contract vary greatly depending on the product or service being purchased. If you are unsure of what KPIs to include, ask your supplier's representative for guidance. More than likely he or she will be happy to share the standards the company uses to track performance internally.

Letter of Intent

Besides the specific terms and conditions contained within a contract, there are steps you can take to define timelines, roles, and responsibilities for potential suppliers that will ensure a smooth transition from the contracting to implementation phases. One of the most important of these steps is preparing a letter of intent.

Particularly in large organizations, the effort required to shepherd contracts through the approval and signing processes can be time-consuming. Some companies require that all commercial agreements over a certain dollar value receive approvals all the way up to the CEO level. Add to that the challenge of expediting a new contract through your legal department, where such requests often end up at the back of a queue and months could pass before the contract is actually signed. This poses a problem to a sourcing team trying to implement pricing with a new supplier as quickly as possible.

In the meantime, a letter of intent is an effective communication tool that can provide a new supplier with the assurance that your organization intends to enter into an agreement with the company, provided certain conditions are met. Often a supplier will agree to serve a new account at agreed-upon pricing levels while the contract meanders through the legal process, as long as a letter of intent has been signed. Although it is not a legally-binding document, it indicates a good-faith intent to engage the services of the new supplier.

The following is a representative example of a typical letter of intent:

Dear <Supplier Z>,

This Letter of Intent constitutes an agreement in principle for <Customer A> to enter into a contract for the purchase of fasteners and other related products through <Supplier Z>, subject to the following terms and conditions:

Contract pricing becomes effective April 6, 2010, regardless of the contract signing date.

The contract will be for a term of 24 months from the effective date.

Pricing policy will include a schedule of net prices and a pricing strategy for all other items. Under this agreement, the pricing strategy will be consistent between items in the net price schedule and all other items <Customer A> may purchase from <Supplier Z>.

The final contract is subject to legal review and approval by <Customer A's> legal counsel.

Please sign below to confirm your agreement of this Letter of Intent as presented.

This sample letter of intent details the business terms that both parties found acceptable in the negotiation stage and states that the customer's legal department must approve the final, binding agreement. The supplier and customer can begin a win-win business relationship in good faith based on that premise, allowing the customer to begin saving money immediately and the supplier to grow its revenue stream.

 ## CONTRACT MANAGEMENT

Many companies neglect to implement a standardized method for managing and monitoring newly-signed supply contracts. Often, once a contract is executed and a pricing policy is in place, the buyer files the new agreement away or passes it on to the legal department, then moves on to new projects. As time goes by, Sam sings and plays his tune, and the contract may get lost in the press of new business, or the buyer who initially drove the sourcing project changes position or leaves the company altogether, and fails to transfer responsibility for the initiative. The contract is forgotten until someone in the company realizes that the sourcing initiative in question has not been reevaluated for many months, or even years, or until the supplier calls and indicates that the contract is set to expire in the next week and the company will be placed onto a retail rate schedule if the agreement is not renewed by then. To make matters worse, no one is in charge of keeping track of expiration dates or contractual obligations, but management randomly assigns the contract to you for follow-up, and you find yourself in Rick's Café Americain, lamenting over an empty bottle that "Of all the gin joints in all the towns in all the world, this contract walks into mine!" In fact, in many organizations, simply tracking down the original terms and parameters of the commitments your company has entered into, also known as rounding up the usual suspects, can be a daunting task.

There are several reasons why it is important to develop a consistent methodology for keeping track of commercial commitments. If you are a publicly traded company, the Sarbanes-Oxley Act passed by Congress in 2002 requires that signing officers of a company must certify they are responsible for establishing and maintaining internal controls when disclosing financial information, which makes them liable if financial information is incorrect. Without easily identifying the number and type of contracts in place, and the pricing and obligations tied to those agreements, signing officers cannot reasonably provide assurance that financial disclosures are in fact accurate and correct.

Beyond reporting to shareholders and complying with federal regulations, there are several ways that contract maintenance can impact your business operations. First, from time to time, a supplier may dispute contract terms due to misunderstood scope-of-work statements or unfamiliarity with obligations. Having contracts handy and reviewing them periodically will ensure that both you and the supplier are complying with all contractual obligations. Second, as we will discuss in Chapter 8, "Implementation and Continuous Improvement," suppliers often fail to honor pricing commitments made in the agreement. If you do not have a copy of the contract readily available, auditing invoicing and verifying that correct pricing is being charged becomes rather difficult.

Last and most important, contract expiration dates and renewal clauses need to be closely reviewed and tracked so you can address renewals in a proactive manner. Relying on the supplier to alert you of contract end dates instead puts the pressure on you for renewing the contract or risking falling back to retail or inflated rate schedules—these conditions work in favor of the supplier. Keeping track of end dates can help you plan sourcing initiatives and renewal strategies for the next contract term well in advance and without time constraints. Removing such pressure puts the leverage back in your favor, as you now have the bandwidth and time to request pricing and proposals from alternate suppliers, work internally to identify issues and develop new requirements, and create a renewal based on changes in your business needs and forecasts. Essentially, it gives you a chance to do your homework before reacting to an unplanned expiration.

Tracking expiration and renewal clauses can be accomplished fairly easily by creating a spreadsheet with start and end dates of contracts and other important terms and reviewing it on a regular basis, or by putting a reminder on your calendar for the appropriate time. However, neither of those solutions help much if roles and responsibilities shift within your organization. More collaborative toolsets are available that can help you manage contracts. These tools allow you to set up rules to run reports on expiring contracts or receive e-mails indicating when contracts are due to expire. Some of these tools are available for free on the Web, such as

WhyAbe.com (www.whyabe.com/contractindex.php); others may require a subscription fee. Regardless of how you track contractual obligations and contract expiration dates, contract management is essential to ensure your next sourcing initiative is as successful as your last.

 ## MAKING THE BEST USE OF YOUR LEGAL TEAM

Depending on the size of your organization and the processes in place for contracting, you may not have much of a choice in how you can utilize your legal team. If you do have flexibility in how to engage the department, there are some best practices for you to consider, including the time to bring legal into the discussion, the setting of clear roles and responsibilities, and the steps for partnering to negotiate the most effective agreement.

In companies without clear contract management methodologies, it is often the case in procurement projects that the buyer finalizes the commercial terms of a deal with the supplier's salesperson, then hands the contract over to legal as a last step. The contract then drifts to the bottom of the inbox pile on the lawyer's desk, to be reviewed at some later date. When the lawyer finally gets around to looking at the contract, he or she has little or no understanding of the need for the product or service being purchased, or the context of the business relationship presented in the agreement. As such, the lawyer will begin to revise the document with standard legal formatting, terms, and conditions, and take out aspects perceived as risks to your organization, even commercial terms the buyer agreed to that establish the working relationship between both parties. Disputes now begin to arise between legal and the supplier's salesperson or legal team, causing major delays in contract execution and implementation. At times, agreements even fall apart at this stage.

There are commonsense ways to avoid these issues and ensure a smooth flow through the legal approval process. First, rather than waiting until you receive a contract from the supplier, bring legal into the process early and get their input during the data collection or RFx stage of the process. Explain what you are attempting to accomplish during the sourcing process, and the background of the spend category being sourced. Ask whether your legal advisor has any initial thoughts on clauses or information that should be included in the agreement.

When initiating these discussions, provide the legal team with your project plan timeline, and let them know when you expect to move into the contracting stage. Providing advanced warning will allow them to plan their time accordingly, ensuring that the agreement will be reviewed promptly, and not end up at the bottom of the inbox pile.

Once you do have an agreement ready for legal, avoid just handing it off and walking away. Provide context during handoff: Explain why certain conditions exist and the overall goals of the business relationship you are entering—this is particularly important for a services agreement. Give legal a summary of requirements for the spend and a high-level overview of the perceived risks for both you and the supplier. If you have a contract template from the supplier, provide legal with a clear distinction between commercial terms that go to the heart of the relationship being established and other standard terms included by the supplier but not discussed during sourcing and negotiations.

Lastly, if legal has any questions that require a meeting with the supplier, be present for those meetings, even if they are lawyer-to-lawyer. Without your guidance, the legal team can make changes that have unexpected consequences or bring the contracting stage to a standstill due to a disagreement on a certain term. If nothing else, being present for these discussions will minimize the back-and-forth confusion that can occur if neither lawyer is clear why certain terms or language are present.

Overall, be sure to take an integrated team approach with legal. Continue on as the project manager during contracting to ensure that timelines are met and the messaging between your organization and that of the supplier is consistent. Do not let legal lead the conversation, and do not hand off responsibility to them; after all, they are not tied to the end result—you are.

 ## CONTRACTING PITFALLS AND LANGUAGE TO AVOID

Along with language that should be included in any contract, there are certain terms and conditions that can be found in many agreements that do not belong there. Often these clauses are added by the customer in the hope that they will provide additional price protection or ensure that if better pricing becomes available, the supplier (rather than the customer) will be responsible for noting and instituting the new lower pricing. The intention of the customer here is twofold. First, the customer is trying to put the obligation on the supplier to remain competitive. This will theoretically save the customer time in that the buying company should then no longer have to pay attention to the market—the supplier will do that for them! Second, the customer is adding language that it feels justifies the decision to contract with a particular supplier. If a supplier guarantees the price is the most competitive it can offer, why would we look at anyone else?

Customers believe adding these types of clauses will save them time and effort, but in the long run they often provide a pricing advantage to the supplier. We will discuss two such clauses in this chapter, the most-favored-nations clause and the continuous-improvement clause.

Most Favored Nations

The most-favored-nations clause guarantees that a supplier will provide you with the lowest price it offers in the marketplace. For example, if you negotiate a price of $10 for a widget and next month the supplier agrees to charge $9 for the same widget to another customer, it will update your pricing so the next time you buy a widget, the price will be $9. An example of this verbiage is as follows:

> In the event of a price decline, or should you at any time, during the life of this agreement, sell the same materials or service, under similar quantity and delivery conditions, to _____, at prices below those stated herein, the agreement vendor will immediately extend such lower prices to _____.

This language is usually found in government contracts or contracts for extremely large companies and volumes, and the clause is always added by the customer, not the supplier. Typically, the purchasing staff (or legal, or finance) has added this clause to make it appear as if they negotiated the absolute best rates in the market, and to ensure that they never have to look at or think about the agreement again. A buyer often falls prey to the belief that "I sourced it, this supplier provided the best price, and he is guaranteeing I will always have the best price. I'm done!"

The first problem with this clause is that the language actually gives the supplier leverage not to lower margins with any customers, regardless of volumes or market conditions. In a real-world example, we once conducted a negotiation call with a supplier who was a distributor of maintenance products that was quoting a 10 percent discount off of list pricing on an electrical bid. We explained that most of our purchases were not repetitive, but that we could standardize on certain manufacturers that were willing to provide special pricing to the distributor based on our volumes. We asked the distributor to pass along some of that price relief to us. The supplier stated that because the company is subject to most-favored-nations clauses in other contracts, and those contracts provide for a 10 percent discount, the company could not exceed the discount for us, even on items where he is getting a much better price. To do so would force the company to offer the same discounts on all the company's contracts, and, understandably, the supplier was not willing to do that. The supplier openly admitted that the company could not be competitive due to contracts with other customers. So we achieved no additional discount, even though the volume we were quoting was magnitudes greater than the existing contracts containing most-favored-nation clauses.

We envision similar scenarios for most customers who have written most-favored-nations clauses into their contracts, in which buyers go back to the supplier for price relief due to a declining market. We can already hear the response: "Well, under the terms of our agreement, you are already getting our best price. We cannot go any lower than that!" Such clauses ultimately give the negotiating leverage to the suppliers.

The second major flaw in this clause is that it does not effectively prevent a supplier from providing a lower price to other buyers without passing that price along to you. A colleague of ours used to be in the software business and worked on large government contracts. His company was awarded an agreement in which the bid was actually higher than the contracting office's standard price for similarly sized commercial customers. As with many government contracts, the government purchaser required most-favored-nations language in the final agreement. To get around the limitations of such clauses, the supplier had created a separate company, Company B, with the sole purpose of being the executing party for all government contracts. The government contract would be signed under Company B, while all commercial agreements would be signed under the original company, Company A. Government customers receive the best pricing provided by Company B, but Company B only sells to the government, so that best pricing is higher than Company A's commercial rates. In this case, the supplier exploited a loophole in the structure of a most-favored-nations clause. This may appear unethical, but suppliers will protect their margins, and if customers choose not to do their due diligence, instead relying on the dubious protection of most-favored-nations clauses, then this can often be the result. Remember the phrase *caveat emptor*, or buyer beware; if the buyer had done some basic market research, it would have realized pretty quickly how out of the ballpark the pricing was, but it chose to take the easy way out, and subsequently paid dearly for it.

There are times when a most-favored-nations clause makes sense, but even when it is included, it is not an excuse to skip your homework. Always consider the market and the purpose of the clause before spending time negotiating this clause into an agreement. In the first example, the supplier provided a broad range of general maintenance products. Does the most-favored-nations clause mean you are getting a better deal, or are you getting the same generic discount that everyone else gets? Does this clause give you a competitive advantage, or does it simply ensure that smaller customers will now get the same discounts that you receive? In the second example, consider what the clause actually says. Are there loopholes? What pricing does this apply to—is it all products and services provided by the supplier, or just certain net prices and discounts referenced in the addenda?

Lastly, if you are a very large customer or getting a custom deal, you should ask yourself, "Why am I adding this clause?" Markets are constantly changing: New suppliers add capacity, distribution, and so on; raw material demands fluctuate; and industries consolidate or break up. Markets should be continuously monitored. Make sure when you add this clause that you are doing it for reasons that will benefit you, and not just to demonstrate what a great negotiator you are. If you do the latter, you may end up eating your own clause.

Continuous Improvement

The continuous improvement (CI) clause comes in many forms, but the basic idea is that a supplier will agree to assist in providing cost reduction and/or enhanced services to the customer over the life of the agreement. Examples of this include reducing inventories; reducing energy costs; avoiding costs; and saving on administrative costs, such as speeding up the ordering and payment processes.

In many cases, the supplier will commit to both soft- and hard-dollar savings targets in these areas and include mechanisms to calculate the cost savings in the contract. Cost savings percentages are based on estimated annual transactions and spend and, in every case, include a term to the effect of "results are predicated on customer's participation in cost reduction proposals. If customer does not implement the cost-reduction proposals suggested by supplier, the targets offered here shall be considered null and void."

Essentially, the customer has to implement the programs for the cost savings to work, but the supplier gets credit regardless. Herein lies the problem, as the following example illustrates.

On one occasion, as we started a project with a new customer, the buyer insisted on the importance of CI clauses. The buyer's contract language included details about how the supplier and customer would have quarterly meetings to discuss and implement cost savings opportunities. The buyer insisted, "We need a commitment to CI in every one of our contracts!"

We asked the buyer what specifically happens during the quarterly meetings—are they effective, do they produce the desired results, and so on. The buyer informed us that so far, it has not held any quarterly meetings.

The buyer, in his commitment to help the company reduce costs, was adamant that contract language had to be put into every contract regarding continuous improvement. After that, the buyer saw no responsibility to follow up, and since the supplier had an out, it did not feel the need to push the issue.

The CI clause cannot be effective unless you actually intend to allocate resources and follow up on CI initiatives. If you do not foresee that happening, the clause becomes meaningless. Spending time and resources negotiating CI terms into an agreement when a supplier partner will typically agree to these programs informally is a waste of effort. Weeks or months of hard-dollar savings are lost while the contract sits in legal, or meetings are held to develop cost-savings estimates or clarify what was being agreed to. In the end, the supplier always has a way out, and the buyer always has an excuse for why it was too busy to move ahead with the arrangement.

Overall, it is important to consider why you are establishing terms in a contract that can more than likely be agreed to informally. Never develop contractual obligations based on fear or to show what a great negotiator you are. After all, establishing them in writing does not automatically equate to cost reduction. Instead focus on the business terms that best establish the intent of the working relationship, then work with the supplier to implement the most effective cost-savings initiatives.

 ## WORKING OUTSIDE OF A CONTRACT: PRICING AGREEMENTS AND HANDSHAKES

A handshake agreement, or so-called gentlemen's agreement, is a quick way to get pricing in place without getting a legal team involved or dealing with your organization's contract approval process. It also gives you the flexibility to terminate the relationship at any time. However, while a gentlemen's agreement may save you some time and effort on the front end, it could become the basis for headaches later on. If, after implementation, the new supplier fails to meet service level requirements, maintain quality standards, or honor pricing, you may have little legal recourse for recovering costs. For example, let us suppose that your supplier agrees to charge you $1.00 for a widget. A month after you start buying, the supplier changes your price to $1.50, a 50 percent increase. You can go back to the supplier and request a concession, but the supplier is under no obligation to give you one, and has no incentive to do so, other than the fear of losing future business. If you cannot resolve the dispute, your options are to change suppliers or accept the increase. Written documentation of price points and acceptable price change mechanisms help alleviate this issue.

The same can be said for inconsistent or unacceptable supplier service levels. For example, you may hire a cleaning service to vacuum the floors of the office three times a week and take out the garbage twice a week. You come to agreement via handshake that you will pay $200 per week for this service. After a few weeks you realize that the cleaning service is only vacuuming and taking out the trash once a week, but you continue to receive bills for the amount of $200. You call the supplier, but your old sales rep has left the company, and now there is no documentation to back up your claim that services have been degraded. While these types of disputes are surely resolvable, without a written contract they can become a much bigger headache.

 ## IN SUMMARY

This chapter was intended as a guide to best practices in terms of contractual content, as well as the best methods for moving your organization through the contracting process. It should assuredly not be used as a replacement for the advice and consultation of a legal professional or risk manager. Different types of commercial agreements can have very different levels of impact on an organization, and you should always have your legal team provide their opinion before signing an agreement.

Chapter 8, "Implementation and Continuous Improvement," discusses how to maintain the newly developed supplier relationship and realize the savings projected during sourcing and negotiations. The contract is the basis for this relationship, and should help to ensure that the pricing and service levels you sourced and negotiated are converted into a contractual obligation for the supplier, and that the new relationship between customer and supplier is long and mutually beneficial.

CHAPTER EIGHT

Implementation and Continuous Improvement

N YOUR PERSONAL LIFE as a consumer, it makes sense that most of your responsibilities end once you select a supplier. In most cases, you go to the store, you pick out what you want and purchase it—thus ends the transaction. If you are having work done on your house, you may have a few contractors come out, you select the one you like best, and then it is up to the chosen firm to get the job done. You are the customer after all, and satisfying the customer is an important role of the supplier.

This view of a customer/supplier relationship often carries over into the business world. Traditional thinking suggests that once a contract is signed, the work of the customer is complete and any further responsibilities fall upon the supplier. Most people assume that the implementation phase and subsequent account management function will be led by the supplier, with little or no obligation put upon the customer. After all, the suppliers are the experts. They have worked on implementations hundreds if not thousands of times, and they know their business well. Their job is to serve your account and ensure a satisfied customer; your job is to pay for those services or products.

This traditional view of the customer/supplier relationship still exists within many organizations, and it is a primary reason why many strategic sourcing initiatives end in failure. In 2005, an industry-leading analyst firm,

AberdeenGroup, issued a report called "The CFO's View of Procurement." In this study, AberdeenGroup found that only 34 percent of projected savings from strategic sourcing activities are actually realized. To put that another way, 66 percent of the savings available in most sourcing projects is left on the table.

In our experience, there are two reasons why the vast majority of savings opportunities are squandered: lack of an implementation plan and lack of a supplier management strategy. These issues are linked to the same root cause, which is that the sourcing team, end users and other executives fail to realize the importance and impact of change management during a strategic-sourcing engagement.

In this chapter we discuss how a customer-led implementation process ensures that new supplier relationships or simplified, re-signed contracts are successful, and that savings are actually realized. We start by addressing common mistakes made during implementation, discussing the reasons that change management is often overlooked, and reviewing ways to overcome obstacles. We also provide an overview of actions to take after implementation, both internally (savings and compliance reporting) and externally (supplier relationship management and continuous improvement initiatives).

 ## THE CHALLENGES OF IMPLEMENTATION

Implementation is the often overlooked final step in converting the concept of cost reduction into a realization that impacts the bottom line of your business. However, implementation is often the biggest challenge in the strategic sourcing process. The reason is simple: People resist change. End users have established relationships with their current suppliers and are accustomed to a certain process and way of doing things. Quite often they have become friends with the salesperson, delivery person, or others within the supplier organization, and hate to see their friends lose business. The result is a slowed or even stalled implementation, as end users fail to see the bigger picture and try to keep their preferred suppliers engaged or try to protect them from smaller margins or loss of business. It is during this stage that you will encounter challenges to your initial analysis, strategy, and savings projections. During your implementation, you may encounter several different types of pushback, or roadblocks, that you should be aware of as you work through the change management process.

The Facts Do Not Always Speak for Themselves

Completing a solid analysis of savings identified during the strategic sourcing process does not necessarily translate into rational business decision making. Rather than focusing on the results, many end users look for gaps in the analysis or comparisons that are not apples-to-apples. In some cases, end users are simply doing their homework, and once they have determined that the analysis is solid, they will proceed with your recommendations. Others attempt to question anything in the hope of stalling or derailing the initiative. For example, an end user might say, "I talked to that supplier before; I didn't think it could handle our business."

This type of skepticism is not based on concrete evidence and therefore is very difficult to overcome. As a project lead you might think it is best to try to moderate challenges to your analysis. For example, you might suggest that the skeptical end user meet with the supplier to achieve a higher comfort level before proceeding to implementation. However, placating end users in this way is a mistake, particularly if you have done your homework and believe the alternate supplier to be a valid option.

It is important to continue to be as objective as possible as you receive challenges from end users. Do not allow intangible or unanswerable issues to slow down or stop the project. If end users are unspecific about their concerns (they have a bad feeling about the supplier, they did not like the sales rep, and so on) do not placate them. Instead, ask them to be more explicit in voicing their concerns and require them to specifically demonstrate how their issues can be resolved. In many cases, simply requiring the end users to present challenges backed by data or objective questions eliminates their pushback and allows you to move to the next step. If end users can present meaningful concerns, set a timeline for addressing them and immediately schedule a follow-up meeting to discuss the outcome. Otherwise, the project begins to stall and you encounter the next issue: misinformation.

Misinformation

As is often said in politics, perception becomes reality. Even if you provide a clear response to end-user questions and concerns, it often seems like their original premises stick. People within the organization will remember the challenges and continue to restate objections that have already been effectively addressed. Misinformation can spread like wildfire throughout the organization. If you keep your implementation timeline on track, this lack of facts can be irrelevant. People always talk and rumors always abound. However, if you find your timeline is slipping or your plan is falling off track, you need to find new ways of communicating your message to counter misinformation. It is at this stage that executive sponsorship becomes helpful. If you have high-level sponsors who can help get your message out through the organization and cut off rumors, now is a good time to use them. Have them meet with the end users or issue e-mails that detail how the concerns have already been heard and addressed, and now it is time to move forward.

Missing the Big Picture

Along the same lines as misinformation, an end user who does not have all of the information may be as detrimental to your success as one who is simply misinformed. For example, it is very common, as implementation proceeds, to hear end users immediately start to complain that they used to receive better pricing from a supplier that they found for a very specific item, often something as minute as a roll of toilet paper. They will prove that they were paying $0.59 a roll versus the $0.65 that the new supplier shows in the catalog. They then use that information to show every other user how they did a better job negotiating than the procurement team, and they may continue to purchase off-contract. The piece they are missing is that there might be a yearly rebate from the new supplier that offsets the higher unit price, or that you need to lump that spend into a larger bucket (and take a small loss) in order to adhere to a volume commitment to your new supplier that drives savings that far offset a single loss item.

Unfortunately it is difficult, and sometimes impossible, to share the entire big picture or explain a contract to each and every end user. It is also something that usually does not show itself in the first month of an implementation; it may happen months down the road. Careful auditing, which we discuss later, can help eliminate this issue.

"We Tried This Before and It Did Not Work"

End users, particularly those with several years of experience or seniority within your organization, also use past experience as a justification for why change cannot happen. If at any point in the past another supplier was under contract and that supplier failed, you will likely encounter the "We tried this before and it did not work" argument. End users often use this argument to justify why the current supplier is the only supplier in the marketplace that can properly serve your business. Again, the way to counter this argument is by converting their subjective concerns into objective analyses. Try to discover precisely why the former supplier failed, and how the new supplier has taken care to avoid the same issues or, in the case that the new supplier is the supplier that failed, make the supplier document what has changed in their methods of doing business to address the issues.

Lack of Planning

Many times implementation issues can be traced back to an overreliance on the supplier to lead and manage the implementation process. This can often happen in a poorly planned implementation, in which a kickoff meeting is held with the supplier, but not much happens in the way of follow-up. Months go by before the new supplier's program is properly implemented, if it is ever fully implemented at all. Without a plan that identifies steps, timelines, roles, and responsibilities, implementations can drag on or even fail.

All successful implementations start with a plan, which is generally provided by the supplier. Although this can expedite matters, rather than accepting the plan at face value, you should thoroughly review it yourself to ensure that it is properly tailored to your organization, with rollout dates and appropriate lines of communication established.

The Absence of a Dedicated Team

A lack of proper planning inherently includes the lack of a dedicated team to carry out the plan. However, even when plans exist, companies often neglect the most important part of planning: assigning staff! Instead of assigning dedicated resources to an implementation, committees are formed to oversee the process. These committee members have other day-to-day responsibilities that often take precedence. Because they do not see implementation as one of their primary responsibilities, the project loses momentum and often stalls.

When forming a team to assist during implementation, it is important that the members of the team are not just helping out in their spare time. They need to be (to some extent) dedicated resources, with specific tasks assigned to them and timelines tied to those tasks. The team should include a person from the procurement team as the project lead, end users within your organization, and members of the supplier staff, to ensure a smooth transition. Additionally, the team should include a high-level sponsor, such as a C-level executive, who can provide assistance should problems arise.

Companies are always trying to do more with less, and you will often find that getting resources dedicated is a daunting task. However, having these resources ensures a swift implementation and allows your company to start saving money sooner.

 ## OVERCOMING CHALLENGES

As we discussed previously, the major hurdles you face during implementation should have little to do with the supplier. If you performed the strategic sourcing process in an objective manner, then you have more than likely selected a supplier that can properly serve your business, and conducting effective implementation is a part of those selection criteria. Instead, managing change within your own organization, often referred to as *change management*, tends to become the biggest challenge in implementation.

Every implementation has specific challenges inherent to the type of spend, the end-user personalities or concerns, and the level of executive sponsorship or control you have over the category. However, regardless of the specific characteristics of the project, there are things you can do to help implementation move along and ensure its successful completion.

Be the Savings Cheerleader

The counter to every argument presented by end users and other internal stakeholders should include a restatement of the savings opportunity. While the expected savings will not speak for themselves, and misinformation and other challenges will continue to present themselves, it is important for everyone involved to remember exactly what is at stake in terms of hard dollars that will have a meaningful impact on the bottom line.

Particularly if momentum wanes, keeping the savings dollars in the forefront of everyone's mind helps keep the project on track. Quite often, as hurdles are encountered, people forget the process undertaken to identify the savings opportunities, and maintaining the status quo is certainly easier than addressing challenges. As project lead, it is your job to continually lead the cheer—restating both the savings and the benefits of the process—to ensure people make choices and take actions based on sound business decisions, rather than attempts to remain in their comfort zones.

Keep in mind that, strictly speaking, expected dollar savings do not tend to motivate all the people involved, particularly line workers. In these cases, work to motivate the change through the use of relationships or subjective rationale. For example, instead of saying the project will save you $60,000 annually, explain that the implemented project will save the company enough money to save someone's job.

Never Lose Focus

As we discussed earlier, one of the biggest challenges during implementation is misinformation, which typically comes into play when an end user or stakeholder challenges a premise, but it eventually turns out that the challenge was invalid. For example, let us suppose that you just completed a freight project and discovered that an additional 10 percent discount was available from a new supplier. However, the new supplier also has a fuel surcharge that is 10 percent higher than the incumbent. There are still savings to be realized, though, because the discount is taken off the gross price and the fuel surcharge is a factor of the net price. In other words, the additional discount dollars are still greater than the impact of the additional fuel surcharge. You present the new savings opportunity to end users, and they comment that the fuel surcharge is going up. Because they are unfamiliar with how the fuel surcharge works, they falsely believe the savings numbers are incorrect and ask you to go back to improve the fuel surcharge cost. They also ask for more time to review the numbers and make sure they understand them.

In this case we have confused end users who do not trust the analysis provided to them. They quickly share their opinions with others in the organization, and suddenly everyone is asking you about your analysis and whether there really are potential savings on the freight project. At this point it can become easy to lose focus on the end result. You might even begin to mistrust your own assessment!

Of course, end users typically ask for more information to help them understand your analysis. This is perfectly acceptable—if that information will lead them to make a decision. Quite often, an analysis is challenged in order to prolong a process or allow an end user to avoid making a final decision. Once an analysis or recommendation is challenged, it is easy to get bogged down in circular decision making, where once one challenge is addressed another appears, and then another, until we are back to the original challenge again, with end users and other interested parties forgetting that the original issue was already addressed.

Projects can quickly get out of hand once a recommendation is challenged, but there are several steps you can take to counter lack of focus and keep the project on track. First, address the concerns and next steps in writing. Provide a clear picture of what issues need to be addressed, and ask end users to confirm, in writing, that they agree with the next steps.

Second, immediately schedule a meeting and set due dates to answer additional questions. Often the biggest hurdle you encounter once someone challenges an analysis is getting all the interested parties back in a room together again. We have seen clients and their end users drag out an analysis review for as long as one year before reconvening. Get a meeting on the calendar and make sure you have all questions answered in time for that meeting.

Lastly, try to make the end user accountable. The primary reason why a recommendation is challenged is because end users have grown accustomed to the status quo and are reluctant to change. However, if the success of the project is tied to their annual objectives, they have a stake in seeing the project through to its completion. Of course, tying a sourcing engagement into annual objectives is easier said than done, particularly if you do not have authority over the end user. This leads us to the next way to overcome challenges: maintaining high-level support.

Maintain High-Level Support

Developing strong executive sponsorship is a critical component to any successful implementation. Without high-level support, projects often stall and savings are never fully implemented. Unfortunately, many project managers do not provide their executive teams with regular updates or enlist them to help troubleshoot internal issues with change management, and the project often suffers as a result. There are many reasons for this. Some project managers see change management as their responsibility, and failure to convince an end user to support their decision might be seen as an admission of a lack of leadership or effectiveness skills. Others might work in a company where the overall corporate culture is decentralized in nature, and executive-level sponsors see it as the responsibility of individual business units, divisions, and end users to appropriately manage costs.

Regardless of the reason, avoiding communication with high-level sponsors is always a mistake. Without executive support, project managers may lack the political capital or clout to enforce change-management decisions if end users decide to push back, leading to stalled or failed implementations.

There are many ways that you can easily maintain high-level management support within your company. You could simply create a status report and submit it to the high-level sponsor or sponsorship team on a regular basis. However, a written report does not always properly relay what is going on with a project. If possible, try to get 15 minutes with the sponsor every week or every other week to provide updates. Do not just start these updates during implementation; keep the executives involved from the beginning of the project. In this way, sponsors are able to provide their input along the way, which invests them in the end result. In addition, this allows them to see that the process was designed and executed in an objective manner, and keeps them up to speed on potential issues well in advance of them becoming problems.

MONITORING IMPROVEMENTS AFTER IMPLEMENTATION

Once you have successfully implemented a new contract or supplier program and the supplier is providing products or services, you may think your work is done. However, a program that is not monitored and reviewed on a regular basis will begin to lose its effectiveness. This is particularly true for multisite implementations where multiple end users or buyers work with the supplier and order product independently from one another.

Best-in-class suppliers work hard to integrate themselves into your organization. They understand that one of their primary responsibilities is to build a rapport with different end users and make themselves part of the team. Ultimately their goal is to become the default supplier, so when end users within your organization need the products or services they provide, they automatically think of them.

With that in mind, one of the main purposes of your strategic sourcing initiative is to implement opportunities for cost savings, and as the project is implemented, it becomes your job to ensure projected (or expected) savings convert to realized (or actual) savings. Failure to monitor and continuously improve and enhance supplier relationships is one of the major reasons why savings are not realized. When it comes to realizing savings and maintaining supplier relationships, the old adage, "A watched pot never boils," does not apply. New programs and savings opportunities need to be monitored closely to ensure correct pricing and internal compliance, and supplier relationships need continuous communication to run smoothly and ensure success. This requires a combination of data tracking and analysis, and both internal and external negotiations.

Tracking Your Savings

After implementation, you should have a good idea of the savings available through the new supplier program, based on historical volumes and old and new price points. However, you should set aside time either monthly, quarterly, or semiannually to review spend details, price points, and invoices to validate that actual savings match your original projections. There are several reasons for this.

First, an audit of invoices may allow you to catch errors in the supplier's pricing. Particularly in an area like telecommunications or office supplies, suppliers often fail to upload the correct price points into their systems, causing billing errors. In addition, suppliers may pass along price increases (either intentionally or by mistake), add on ancillary charges you were not aware of, or misapply freight or payment terms. All of these issues require corrective action, including having your supplier fix mistakes in its system and issue credits for improper billings.

You may feel that independent audits of pricing are not necessary because you know that accounts payable has established internal rules for paying invoices so that invoice prices must match purchase order prices. Therefore, as long as you have the correct price in your system, you believe you have nothing to worry about. While this checks and balances system might very well keep unit pricing in line, and even take into account freight and payment terms, it likely does not address other ancillary fees that might come up. More importantly, there are many categories of indirect spend that do not require a purchase order (telecommunications, office supplies, payroll processing services, and so on) or require a purchase order that includes only total price and not unit pricing. In any spend category in which you do not create a purchase order that includes the expected unit price for an item (based on contracted rates), there should absolutely be a regular procedure for manual checks of pricing.

The second reason to track savings is to determine whether buying trends have changed. Even though your initial negotiation and contracting was based on historical usage information, historical purchases do not always reflect future business. After reviewing the data, you may find end users are buying items they had not purchased in the past. They may have even started buying new categories of product from the new supplier. These new items require your attention, as price points may not have been negotiated and additional discounts may be available.

Along with determining if the same *mix* of products is purchased as in the past, you want to determine if the same *volumes* are purchased as in the past. Perhaps you have acquired a new business unit, and volumes have doubled. The increase in business may warrant additional price concessions or move you to a new volume tier discount, and normally you cannot expect the supplier to be proactive in identifying these changes and providing lower pricing.

However, there is a much broader reason why you should be aware of changes in volume. From the perspective of the finance department, savings are tracked by looking for a reduction in the actual budgeted amount spent for a particular good or service year-over-year. However, procurement people tend to track differently—they look at actual unit price reduction. The difference here is substantial. For procurement, the savings goes up as volume grows: the more volume, the more savings. For finance, as volume grows, so does overall spend. This means that even if you have a price point reduction of 10 percent, if your volume grows by 20 percent over the same period, the overall budget will not reflect the savings, and finance may call your projections invalid. Being aware of these changes and providing an assessment of them to finance are important steps to take to demonstrate the success of the program.

Further, you may find that volumes are lower than expected, which brings us to our next postimplementation analysis: tracking lost savings and ensuring compliance.

Tracking Lost Savings and Ensuring Compliance

While tracking the success of the program by analyzing and reporting actual savings is important, identifying areas for improvement is just as crucial. Tracking lost savings and ensuring compliance is a good way to check that you are optimizing the savings available through the new supplier relationship.

The first step in tracking lost savings is identifying noncompliant spend. Noncompliant spend can be defined as money spent with a noncontracted supplier, a supplier that was not awarded the business. Identifying noncompliant spend requires you to perform a spend analysis using general ledger, accounts payable, or purchase order reports. As we discussed in Chapter 3, the type and cleanliness of the data dictate which reports to choose, but regardless of the report, your goal is to identify suppliers that compete in the same market as your awarded supplier—suppliers that sell the same or similar products or services.

The easiest way to identify competitive suppliers is to review the original supplier listing from the baseline report. A properly constructed baseline report identifies any supplier that your organization bought product from before the sourcing project began. These are the most obvious culprits for noncompliant spend from locations or end users that never moved to the new supplier. Review the list of former suppliers and then perform a search of the new spend reports for each supplier name. Keep in mind that different spellings or abbreviations may come up, so it might be best to sort by supplier name before beginning your search. If you identify any spend with these old suppliers, put the spend information associated with the new suppliers aside to be reviewed later, and return to the original report. Once you have searched for all former suppliers in the baseline report, go back to the list of suppliers identified during the research phase. Now, perform a similar search for any of these suppliers as well.

These two searches, one for former suppliers and the other for alternates denied during the research phase, will more than likely capture a good amount of noncompliant purchases, but there may be other suppliers that you overlooked during the baseline and research phases. To do a thorough job, there are several other searches you can perform.

The first alternative search is by category. If you are using data pulled from a purchase order system, use the fields that categorize the spend data. For example, if you purchase corrugated boxes, those purchases might be listed in the category of packaging.

Take a look at the purchase orders for products from the new supplier and determine the categories under which these purchases are listed. Then, sort the data by category and look for purchase orders in the same category but from different suppliers. Note that not all purchases within the same category are necessarily noncompliant purchases. Using the corrugated box as an example, you might find that within the category of packaging there are also bags, plastic bottles, or steel drums—all items you would not likely purchase from a corrugated box manufacturer. By the same token, if the new supplier is not a box manufacturer but rather a distributor of packaging supplies, these items may be considered noncompliant.

Searching by category requires a closer look at the data set to determine which items are truly noncompliant. If you identify noncompliant items, pull them out of the data set and add them to the noncompliant spreadsheet.

Lastly, you can do a similar search using part numbers of product descriptions. This is the most granular search for noncompliant spend. Sort the data by supplier and search for the new, compliant supplier. Take a look at the part numbers assigned to purchases from this supplier, as well as the product descriptions. Highlight all the purchases from the new supplier and then do a new sort on product number. Visually scan through the spreadsheet to look for the highlighted data. Then see if there are any purchases with the same product number that are not highlighted, indicating that the purchases were from a noncontracted supplier. Pull this data into the noncompliant spreadsheet, then return to the original data set, perform a sort by product description, and repeat the steps.

You may feel that merely identifying noncompliant purchases is all you need in order to go back to end users and other interested parties and work with them to stop purchasing from the wrong supplier. However, remember that the facts do not necessarily speak for themselves, especially with end users who are resistant to change in the first place. Calculating the missed opportunity in terms of lost savings, then correlating the results to a relationship argument, such as the earlier example of saving someone's job, can help build a better business case to get laggard end users on board. In addition, if you identify noncompliant purchases and do not track lost savings, you cannot demonstrate how repeated purchases have a continual negative impact on the organization. Tracking lost savings essentially keeps missed opportunities in the forefront of people's minds, and every month that goes by without change makes your business case stronger.

There are two ways to track lost savings. The first is to use projected savings estimates with the new supplier. The second way is to perform an apples-to-apples cost comparison. The scope of the project, available savings, and amount of resources you have to assist in the analysis all dictate which method you use.

Calculating Projected Lost Savings

The simplest way to determine lost savings is by using the original savings estimates you projected when making the business decision to move to contract with a particular supplier. For example, you may have completed an office supplies project and projected that the new supplier will save you 20 percent on office supplies. If the noncompliant spend represents $100,000 in purchases, you could estimate that approximately $20,000 ($100,000 × 20 percent) in savings was lost because purchases were made from the wrong supplier. Obviously, this is a fairly high-level and imperfect estimate.

To get closer to actual conditions using projections, you can look at the savings by supplier. For example, let's say that your company has three locations, and before the commencement of the sourcing project, each location used a different supplier, with different price points. Each location would therefore experience different savings rates associated with the new program. Take a look at the savings by baseline supplier in Table 8.1.

Now take a look at the noncompliant purchases. In our example, out of the $100,000 in noncompliant spend, $16,000 was spent with Supplier A, $0 with Supplier B, and $84,000 with Supplier C. Therefore, the lost savings was actually $21,880 [($16,000 × 16%) + ($84,000 × 23%)]. These numbers get us much closer to the actual lost savings opportunity and provide a more detailed assessment of the value of the new supplier.

TABLE 8.1 Baseline Spend and Projected Savings

Baseline Supplier	Baseline Spend	Savings Projection
Supplier A	$ 85,000	16%
Supplier B	$ 12,000	4%
Supplier C	$170,000	23%
Total	$267,000	20%

Calculating Actual Lost Savings

Still, even a breakdown of lost savings by supplier might not be enough to convince end users that they are losing money for the organization. Some might say that using projections does not tell the actual tale of the lost opportunity, even arguing that the new supplier costs them more, pointing to one or two items where prices are higher. Also, as we have already discussed, end users do not always see the big picture, in which a supplier volume rebate may actually lower the unit costs to levels below what end users perceive they are paying. This brings us to the most accurate way to calculate lost savings: using line-item detail of purchases.

In this scenario, run a purchase order report, identify, isolate, and track noncompliant spend in a spreadsheet, and insert a column for Contracted Supplier Price. Then go down the list of noncontracted purchases line by line, inserting the price that would have been paid had the buyer used the contracted supplier. This is by far the most time-consuming way to calculate lost savings, particularly if you are dealing with a spend category in which products identified by many different stock-keeping units (SKUs) are purchased. However, there are ways to build a cross-reference table and use a simple lookup function or a macro to make the process less time-consuming. Overall, this methodology should only be used if you need to build a very strong business case to convince end users to move forward with the new program, or if the number of SKUs is very small.

 SAVINGS AND COMPLIANCE BEST PRACTICES

After the execution of a successful implementation, you may not feel the need to track off-contract purchases, but reporting lost savings helps build credibility for the program throughout the organization and eventually leads to end users consistently utilizing the preferred supplier. There are several best practices to consider when analyzing and reporting savings and identifying lost savings opportunities.

Automating the Analysis

As mentioned in Chapter 3, several spend analysis toolsets can readily provide useful reports and analysis, allowing you to completely bypass the manual process of data mining. Spend analysis tools can be expensive, but depending on the scope of projects you are working on, they could be a worthwhile investment. Keep in mind, however, that data analysis tools do not solve problems with poor data sets, and often require an extra step (and often a fee) for cleansing and classifying your data sets.

If you cannot justify the expense, you can also develop some level of automation internally. Using a database or spreadsheet tool, you can develop a macro that automatically applies predefined logic—for example, pulling noncompliant spend out of large data sets based on specific criteria, adding projected (or actual line-item) lost savings, and converting that data into reports. If you are tech-savvy, you may be able to develop an internal toolset on your own. If not, talk to your IT team, as they most likely have the knowledge and skill set to help you construct such a tool.

Making the Reports Meaningful

Reporting on achieved and lost savings on a company-wide level does help executives understand the success or failure of the program, but does little to identify where the specific problems reside. The more granular the reporting, the more meaningful it becomes. To achieve this level of insight, break out the reports by division, location, or even end user where it makes sense. Tracking savings in this way assigns to divisions or end users accountability for complying with the new program and informs them that their spending habits will continue to be scrutinized until they move to the contracted supplier. In addition, recognizing end users who are properly participating in the program grants them additional credibility as good corporate citizens. Those who use the right supplier and save money for the organization should be acknowledged for their success; those who fail to use the correct supplier should be identified and questioned.

When tracking actual achieved savings and lost savings opportunities, you should also consider the time period captured in reports. Month-to-month or quarter-to-quarter tracking helps identify issues that require immediate resolution; however, it does little to show overall trends in the program. That is why running totals from the beginning of the program should also be tracked, to help demonstrate whether compliance has improved, deteriorated, or remained steady over the life of the program. This information comes in handy when trying to determine which actions taken during implementation helped make the program successful, and which had little (or detrimental) effect.

CONTINUOUS IMPROVEMENT INITIATIVES

Tracking savings and compliance helps to keep a new program on track internally, building credibility with high-level sponsors within your organization as well as with your supplier. However, the best programs are those that are self-managed to a degree, meaning that the supplier is well-recognized throughout the organization and the value they provide is clearly understood, and therefore end users are more inclined to make purchases correctly. Continuous improvement initiatives further establish the supplier relationship and integrate the supplier into your organization by focusing on enhanced service levels and total cost of ownership (TCO).

Continuous improvement initiatives look not just to pare *down* costs through a unit cost reduction, but also to pare *out* costs, which can produce savings well beyond the initial unit-price cost reductions available from strategic sourcing. Paring out costs can include reducing demand, and thereby volume of purchases; integrating technologies to make the order to invoice process more efficient; and reducing the amount of time needed by internal resources to manage inventories.

There are as many different types of continuous improvement initiatives as there are categories of spend, and we cannot cover them all here. However, we review some of the most common and most effective continuous improvement initiatives that companies can undertake.

Volume Reductions: Doing More with Less

Prior to utilizing strategic sourcing, you may have had a category of spend that was decentralized, with many end users ordering and using products based on their perceived needs, with no oversight of what was being purchased or when. Internal systems may have included minimum and maximum inventory levels, but those levels may not have been based on hard facts, but rather on end users attempting to ensure that enough safety stock was available to handle emergencies, or on their own mistakes and lack of oversight. Now that the strategic sourcing component of your initiative is complete, you can work with the new supplier to put in tighter controls around inventory levels and safety stocks, establish the right amount of inventory, and potentially reduce or eliminate consumption of unneeded products. Three of the most common volume-reduction methods are discussed next.

Vendor-managed inventory (VMI) is one way to produce a favorable impact on consumption. VMI takes the responsibility for maintaining inventory levels out of the hands of internal resources and passes it to the supplier. VMI is most common in the area of maintenance supplies, in which managing a stock room can become a full-time job, but it can be used effectively in other areas as well, including packaging supplies and administrative items, such as office supplies.

In a VMI scenario, most of the necessary work takes place in the beginning: setting up strict guidelines in advance that include clear minimum and maximum levels and defining the exact SKUs that should be stocked on your shelves. Without including this step, supplier representatives have a tendency to overstock bins with product that is not necessarily needed. When clear rules are established you will most likely see an immediate reduction in consumption, because inventory levels are clearly identified and the likelihood of frivolous or unneeded purchases is greatly diminished.

Implementing a supplier-stock and/or consignment inventory program is another way to reduce volumes and improve overall cash flow. Supplier-stock inventory is dedicated inventory held at the supplier's location on your behalf. Consignment inventory is inventory that the supplier stocks at your location, but you do not pay for until you use it.

Supplier stock and consignment programs ensure prompt delivery of product and eliminate the need for safety stock, thereby reducing volumes. From the perspective of cash flow and inventory-carry costs, these types of programs also provide advantages, as the inventory is readily available but not paid for until it is utilized.

A third way to reduce purchased volumes is through supplier budget reviews and guaranteed savings programs. In a guaranteed savings program, a supplier guarantees overall costs will not exceed a certain threshold on an annual basis. This is achieved through a combination of unit cost reduction, product substitution (which we discuss later in this chapter), and decreased consumption programs. Essentially, these programs give the supplier some responsibility for ensuring your end users are purchasing as economically as possible.

Guaranteed savings programs can typically be found in tactically classified spend categories, such as office supplies. For example, an office supply company with a guaranteed savings program might establish a monthly budget for each department within your organization based on historical spending habits (products purchased, volumes, and so on). Purchases in excess of the monthly budget amounts are closely monitored and may even require additional internal approvals, which help keep consumption in check.

Process and System Integration

Integrating your current processes and technologies with those of the supplier is another good way to reduce internal costs associated with the order-to-payment process and free up resources to work on other tasks.

One of the most common forms of system integration is the *punchout catalog*. Punchout catalogs tie your purchase order system to the online ordering portal of the supplier. Using this method makes ordering more efficient, because a purchase order is automatically sent to the supplier and ties together your part number with the supplier part number, ensuring you receive the correct product. Properly implemented punchout catalogs are also able to handle multiple suppliers that deliver the same product and can automatically place the order for the lower-contracted-price item.

Taking this concept a bit further, systems integration can also tie your purchase order system to the supplier's invoicing system. In this scenario, you can receive invoices electronically through an eProcurement tool (such as Ariba or Basware) or through functionality in your enterprise resource planning system that reconciles the purchase order against the invoice. Any invoices that match a purchase order (within reasonable thresholds) can be paid electronically, eliminating the need for accounts payable to physically review the invoice. Invoices that do not match the purchase order within acceptable tolerances can be flagged by the system for further review.

Enhanced system integrations can even include the automatic replenishment of inventory, which ties your inventory system minimum and maximum levels to the supplier's ordering system. When inventory levels reach a certain level, the supplier ships additional product to the appropriate location.

Process and systems integration can virtually eliminate the need for employees to manually place orders and process payments. However, as you might imagine, these projects are only successful if the program is well-conceived and well-designed from the start. Using sloppy data or not clearly identifying business rules to be followed can easily make a systems integration task unsuccessful.

Optimization, Standardization, and Substitution

Continuous improvement initiatives can also be used to continually pare down unit costs through a combination of the techniques of optimization, standardization, and substitution.

Optimization

Optimization programs ensure that if multiple options exist, the best option is chosen every time. You might think that in a strategic sourcing initiative, selecting the lowest-cost supplier is the best way to optimize the program, but additional opportunities for savings may still exist. For example, if you are working on a corrugated box project, your supplier has likely given you pricing in volume tiers. The greater the quantity purchased, the lower the unit price. In this case, you might find that users place orders on an as-needed basis, choosing whichever volume tier fits their immediate requirement. However, if you were to set different inventory levels and hold POs until the quantity reaches a more cost-effective volume tier, you would be able to further improve costs, thus optimizing the program.

Other examples of optimization, which we discuss in later chapters, include least-cost routing for telecommunications and lane optimization for freight projects. When investigating ways to optimize, you should consult your suppliers. Often, they can provide assistance in developing optimization programs, particularly if they have been working with your organization for a while and have identified inefficiencies in your purchasing habits.

Standardization

While optimization seeks to ensure that the best option is chosen from a menu of choices, standardization is focused on reducing the number of choices available, producing economies of scale that allow suppliers to provide more competitive pricing. It also has the added benefit of simplifying the ordering and product selection process for end users, making it less likely that they will order the wrong part, or from the wrong supplier.

Continuing with the corrugated box example, you may purchase hundreds of different types of boxes to pack and ship product. The production of each unique box specification is run separately by the box manufacturer, and each time a new run starts and stops, the production machinery requires some level of manual changeover; this process incurs a large portion of the overall box cost. If your business can use the same or similar type of box for multiple uses, you can reduce changes in specifications and therefore achieve reductions in unit cost through higher volume runs without changeouts. Further, reducing the number of box specifications does not always necessarily mean standardizing on a particular box size. Instead, you can focus on the type of corrugated board used to make up the box—standardizing on this component allows you to get improved raw material pricing (because you are buying a larger quantity of just one type of corrugated board) and minimizes the amount of changes or retooling necessary to match your requirements.

The same can be said for printing. You may have multiple types of marketing materials or other print requirements, all of which are printed on different sizes and types of paper. Deciding on one or two paper types allows the supplier to buy bulk on your behalf, and pass those economies of scale on to you.

Overall, in any project in which you have similar products with many different specifications, opportunities to standardize exist. This could include using the same templates, product types, formats, and so on. As with optimization, the supplier can provide assistance in identifying inefficiencies and making suggestions that allow you to achieve a much higher level of standardization without an undue number of changes to the end requirement.

Substitutions

Substitute products are lower-cost, generic products that have the same specifications and useful life as high-cost brand-name products. Often end users buy the brand name product merely because they are familiar with the name, even if a generic functions just as well.

A common example of substitution is in the area of office supplies. Most office supply distributors have developed their own line of generic products that can be used in lieu of brand name goods. Once substitute products are identified, the easiest way to ensure they are purchased is by setting up rules with suppliers, so that even if a brand-name product is ordered (using a Web portal, via purchase order, or even over the phone), the generic product is shipped. This process is called *autosubstitution*. If you prefer a less invasive method, you can set up rules on many ordering portals so that if a brand-name product is selected, the interface shows that a low-cost alternative is available and asks whether the end user would like to purchase that item instead.

In any scenario in which autosubstitution is utilized, the products being substituted should be reviewed carefully. There may be reasons a brand-name product is used, particularly by a marketing department or a sales group. If you are unsure of the application of a particular purchase, discuss it with the department in question before establishing an autosubstitution process.

Let the Supplier Help

There are many other continuous improvement initiatives that can be considered beyond those we have discussed. Depending on the product or service being purchased, supplier-assisted initiatives can reduce energy consumption, reduce downtime, pare out freight costs, train end users in industry best practices, and reallocate resources, among other benefits. If you embrace innovation and continue to work closely with suppliers after implementation, you will find they can provide a wealth of ideas on how to reduce costs and make processes more efficient. The key is to remember that you cannot expect the suppliers to advance these initiatives on their own. You should continue to take the lead, pushing the suppliers to be more innovative and to drive organizational change. Without internal leadership, continuous improvement initiatives will not go far beyond the conceptual stage.

 IN SUMMARY

The less time you spend managing issues with compliance and other change management problems, the more time you have to focus on driving savings in other areas. Well-designed implementation and continuous improvement initiatives that include dedicated resources and real leadership help minimize these issues and help integrate the supplier into your organization.

Still, you must remain independent from your suppliers to a degree. Continually monitoring the market is a significant part of the continuous improvement process. You cannot rely on a contracted supplier to keep you informed of market conditions. Markets are fluid and new suppliers offering a competitive advantage may enter into the marketplace at any time, and it is not in the incumbent supplier's best interest to inform you of that.

Contracted suppliers should be made aware that they need to work just as hard to keep your business as they did to earn it, and that the moment they become uncompetitive or unresponsive, they will be transitioned out. The best way to maintain sustainable, long-term results is with a watchful eye, an independent mind, and the realization that there are always additional ways to further reduce costs.

CHAPTER NINE

What Not to Do During a Strategic Sourcing Initiative

ARLIER IN THIS SECTION we covered the basics of the strategic sourcing process and how to maximize your savings opportunities using proven best practices. However, many procurement professionals begin to skip steps or take shortcuts in their sourcing initiatives due to a variety of reasons, including constraints on their time or because they feel that the spend category is not critical to their business.

The number one mistake that many companies make is getting caught up in documented preestablished sourcing or request for proposal (RFP) process without allowing for any creativity or flexibility in the individual sourcing events. This usually happens when an organization develops a formalized sourcing plan, with formal documents, then trains new sourcing professionals on the process while neglecting to add creativity and flexibility into each individual sourcing event. This section discusses what not to do during a strategic sourcing initiative.

 ## CREATING OVERLY COMPLEX OR LONG RFPs

The easiest way to guarantee higher prices and a smaller potential supply base is to engage potential suppliers with an overly complicated or lengthy request for proposal or request for information document or process.

To provide some insight into this phenomenon, let us examine the example of a state transportation department that recently requested that our consulting firm participate in an RFP. In this example, our firm was asked to participate in an RFP for "Telecom Bill Audit and Recovery Services." When we received first contact for this event, we were excited about the opportunity to participate, knowing that government spending in telecommunications is a ripe category for savings opportunities. However, our optimism quickly evaporated when we received the 100-plus-page hard copy RFP.

First, this organization was not exploiting the full capabilities of current technology. This particular document was only available in hard copy form, and responses were to be submitted in typed format. This means that every firm that wished to respond was immediately required to convert all of the text from hard copy to electronic form, because most companies create and manage documents electronically these days. Because of this obstacle, we would posit that 50 percent of the potential supply base immediately decided not to bid at this point.

However, we still saw this as an opportunity, and the savings produced, and therefore our fee, could be huge. Therein lay the next problem. Telecom audits are a great way to reduce overall telecom costs, since they typically include both a recovery aspect (getting credits for lines that should have been disconnected, as well as other misbillings) and infrastructure optimization (disconnecting unused lines and circuits, changing services, and so on). However, on page 85 of the document, we stumbled across this line: "Identifying services that should have been disconnected but are still being billed is naturally a part of this effort and credits or refunds to the consultant are eligible from the date the disconnect was proven to be issued. There is no compensation for future savings nor is this a 'traffic engineering' RFP." In other words, finding lines that are no longer active, issuing disconnects, and verifying the new prices were not part of the scope of work. In fact, neither were other simple changes that could be identified when analyzing this type of data, such as aggregating and contracting long-distance spend and least-cost routing options.

The scope of work was limited to acquiring credits for misbillings, most of which occur when a company issues a disconnect order and the carrier fails to terminate the line, or continues to bill the customer, or both. While substantial savings were still available in this arena, the RFP was constructed with the assumption that the provider of sourcing services had access to proof that a disconnect was requested by the customer. In many cases, the data were not available, or could only be found by searching through the e-mail records of the person who had issued the disconnect order. It was highly unlikely that a state transportation department was going to allow the provider to rummage through e-mail records for this information.

Of course, if disconnect orders were readily available, a provider could approach the carriers and request credits. But getting the carriers to actually issue credits for past billings (in this case up to six years' worth) could take several months, and the impact would only be seen once.

The long-term cost-savings impact for any company (including government entities) resides in identifying unused lines, issuing (or reissuing) disconnect orders, following through to verify the disconnects happen, and validating them on the next bill. The impact is immediate and invoice amounts can be reduced substantially in a relatively short amount of time.

Since the transportation department was excluding any compensation to the providers for that service, the awarded bidder certainly would not undertake that activity. Since the buyer's organization had not taken such steps in the past (hence the audit), it is highly unlikely that it would be doing so in the future either. A real cost-savings opportunity escaped absolutely untouched.

The true benefit of this proposal, in terms of a typical government entity's way of thinking, is that the contract specialist who issued the RFP could demonstrate that he or she spent a lot of time writing a 100-plus page document that made absolutely no business sense and achieved little or nothing in the way of capturing effective bids from competent sourcing providers. However, the document and review process most likely kept a team of individuals busy for at least six months. Our government dollars, well spent.

This is a classic example of the necessity of streamlining the RFP process, which is just as critical to achieving optimal cost savings as the actual project. Let us examine the flaws in this approach. First, the department had targeted the wrong audience. The identification process for each supplier simply consisted of identifying contacts at companies that have "audit services" in their website descriptions. They never reached out verbally to communicate the actual scope of work with the potential supply base, and failed to communicate that the successful bidders would have to offer services that went way beyond the limited scope of the engagement outlined in the document. Second, because of the sheer length of the RFP document, many of the most effective and least expensive firms most likely chose not to participate simply due to the burden of responding to the RFP. Most importantly, the transportation department piled on so many specifications that the scope of the project became extremely narrow and likely to produce a poor return on investment for the initiative.

MORE IS LESS

When it comes to writing an RFP and soliciting responses, more is less. Too much detail or asking too many questions in an RFP, can limit the scope and quality of responses. First of all, it immediately elicits negative emotional responses from the sales teams tasked with responding, who view the unnecessary requirements as added work. We have established that negotiations and sourcing should be a fact-based process, with the emotional component removed as much as possible, therefore starting a sourcing event in such a manner sends precisely the wrong signal at the start of a project. The number of vendor responses to such long RFPs is usually rather low.

Many vendors are outright unwilling to commit presales resources to the completion of long RFPs. This is particularly true with smaller suppliers that immediately label the opportunity as an unlikely win. The problem is that many smaller organizations are often the most creative and cost-effective solution providers. Eliminating them in the beginning of your sourcing process due to an unnecessarily lengthy RFP leads to higher bid proposals from larger suppliers, and therefore less net savings on the project than desired or projected.

A long RFP only adds costs to a process, without capturing better information from suppliers. First, it lengthens the overall sourcing process, as it takes time for the customer to create the documents and send them out, then for the suppliers to evaluate the documents, ask questions, and respond. This time consumption translates into lost potential savings opportunities, as a quicker sourcing process could have led to savings being accumulated more rapidly. A lengthy RFP adds costs to the supplier, and those costs, often not transparent to the buyer, are rolled into the proposed pricing. Additionally, it adds costs to the customer's internal team, due to the necessity of reviewing multiple lengthy 100-page submissions, a very onerous task that undermines the value of asking for submissions in the first place.

Your RFP needs to accomplish only a few tasks. It should identify you, your organization, the players and decision makers, the process, and, the most important element, your core needs. Specify your needs as minimally and openly as possible, and encourage suppliers to respond with alternative or creative solutions—do not attempt to dictate the solution in your questions. A lengthy, overspecified RFP actually has the effect of masking your core needs and often does not allow a vendor an appropriate venue to elaborate on its expertise. Long RFPs often solicit unnecessary information on noncore items that can introduce difficulties later in your vendor selection process.

Before sending your RFP out to market, have your internal team review the document line by line and decide whether each requirement in the document really needs to be included. Simply ask, "Do we need this item?"

It is often helpful to first conduct a request for information (RFI) process, the responses to which can help focus your RFP. The RFI responses identify which suppliers are willing to respond to an RFP and gauge their overall level of interest. A creatively written RFI can also act as a teaser to the suppliers to get them excited about the opportunity, rather than perceiving the opportunity as a burden.

Lastly, you should consider whether you really need to issue an RFP. An RFP is meant to help your selection committee decide whether a project makes sense. However, in many cases, it may be unnecessary; particularly for cases in which the product or service you are sourcing has a rather limited range of solutions. In these cases, the RFP may just add complexity to the sourcing process and be a waste of resources.

 ## LETTING THE SUPPLIER WRITE THE RFP FOR YOU

Letting a supplier write an RFP for you is perhaps one of the biggest and most common mistakes that a large percentage of companies makes. Suppliers actually benefit greatly from this situation, and use many tactics to get customers to let them write an RFP.

The most obvious tactic occurs when you engage a supplier looking for a particular product or service, and the supplier's sales team "helps" you prepare the RFP by conveniently supplying you with RFPs from other customers. The sales reps will act as if they are doing you a favor to expedite your sourcing event. However, the reality is that the RFPs that they claim were sent to them in the past are in fact documents that their own team has custom-developed for you, in which they have constructed questions for which they give the ideal answer, or they engineer the RFP such that the supplier becomes the only provider that can respond with a favorable answer to many of the questions. This is an extremely effective sales tactic, as it ensures that the supplier provides the best response to the sourcing event while at the same time giving the buyer the illusion that the supplier is doing him or her a favor and is trying to build a positive relationship with the customer outside normal business practices.

Another, less obvious tactic suppliers use to get customers to let them write the RFP is to provide free RFP templates on the Web. Often these templates are not even branded with the organization's name, but they are guaranteed to contain questions that only the supplier that created the document can answer in a positive fashion.

Examples of Why You Should Not Let a Supplier Write the RFP

As previously mentioned, the main reason that you do not want suppliers participating in any manner in your RFP development is that they will ensure that those RFPs mainly include questions that put them in the most favorable light. However, even if you choose to use a free template from the Web or a document that was sent to you by a supplier, you should make sure that all of the questions are clearly relevant to the product or service you are buying, and to your overall business needs.

We are rather familiar with one such free RFP template from the Web. This particular document has become so prevalent in the marketplace that we have seen at least a dozen modified versions of it from buyers who are starting a sourcing process. Ironically, the document is so popular that its advantage has actually decreased for the company that created it, as many sourcing-solution suppliers have customized their own generic template responses in order to respond more quickly and accurately.

Demographics

This particular document and many like it tend to focus very heavily on demographics of the supplier's customers. The top question is "How many Fortune 500 clients do you serve?" Suppliers that deal in the Fortune 500 space often make a huge deal out of this. Therefore, it is not uncommon for them to promote the fact and get customers to use it as a disqualifier for competitors that are not so heavily invested in the big company space. Though this may be meaningful to your organization if it is in a Fortune 500 company, chances are it bears very little relevance. What is important is to focus on whether the supplier has worked with companies that are similar to yours in terms of industry, size (employees, locations, divisions), and culture, not the amount of revenue your organization brings in.

Another demographic question might ask whether the supplier has locations within 100 miles of your organization. While this may in fact be important when it comes to an on-site presence, chances are it should not be among the disqualification criteria for engaging a supplier. Service providers may be more than capable of delivering their services at remote locations, often in lower-priced regions of the country, which could in fact have a positive impact on their pricing. Manufacturers similarly may have lower labor costs that outweigh higher shipping costs by being strategically located in a lower-cost region. The sheer size and location of a supplier should not be a major factor in your decision criteria. Just remember, the more locations and people that your supplier has, the more overhead costs they have, which in turn can drive up your price.

"What is your annual revenue?" is another question that appears on most generic RFP templates. But what does this fact really tell you? Does it matter that the supplier generated $25 million in annual revenue, versus a company that generated $300 million, but was not profitable? Be extremely careful on how your score this response to an RFP. Depending on the scoring methodology, a company with $300 million in sales that has not run a profit in five years, is heavily in debt, and carries a severe risk of closure or sale could get a higher grade than a $25 million dollar company with consistent 20 percent growth and high profitability. With which company does it make more sense to develop a long-term strategy? Does your scoring methodology take this into consideration?

Features and Functions

The feature and function specifications become the real heart of the problem when you allow suppliers to write an RFP for you. They tend to load it up with features and specifications that they know only they offer and that are probably not features that you need anyway.

The common free RFP template with which we are familiar, which applies to a software solution, offers several typical examples of included unnecessary features and functions. The functionality and technology sections of the document are nothing more than a feature list of the authoring company's software, crafted as statements that make buyers think they need (and will use) every last feature of the solution.

In this document there are quite a few examples, such as:

- *Does the solution support HTML (hypertext markup language) formatting?*
  - HTML formatting is great; however 99 percent of people do not know how to use it properly, so should it really be included on your requirements list? It also creates a whole new set of questions surrounding security, scripting, remote hosting, and so on. So should it really be in this first pass RFP? A better question would be more open-ended, such as: "Does your software allow users to customize the look and feel of their content?"

- *Does the solution allow large line-item events (minimum of 1,000 lots for line items) with at least 25 price or nonprice attributes per line item?*
  - This is a good question if you are doing large line-item events of over 1,000 lots with multiple price attributes. The problem is you are probably not ever going to do that, so why does it need to be in your RFP? Again, a more open question is more appropriate, such as: "How does your system handle large line-item bid events?"
- *Do you offer a hosted on-demand environment?*
  - The answer to this is usually "Yes," but the question procurement people need to ask themselves is whether they want an on-demand environment or local hosting and licensed software. Do not let the supplier tell you what is best; do your own research. Your sourcing team should be talking with your IT team to determine whether you want to go with software as a service (SaaS) or a behind-the-firewall local installation. Do not let the supplier dictate to you which is best for your organization.
- *Is your software available in eight languages?*
  - If you work for an international company that is sourcing from multiple countries and has in-house resources that speak the languages and understand the cultures of each of those countries, this may be important to you. However, if you are sourcing primarily out of North America, do you really need a solution that likely costs more with features you will never use?
- *Does your software integrate with SAP, Oracle, or products from similar vendors?*
  - Although having integrated systems that work smoothly across all operations is an ideal situation for most businesses, in some cases it is more trouble than it is worth. Take for example the fact that 80 percent of all enterprise software deployment projects either run over budget or behind schedule. Achieving integration would be nice, but as a first step in your electronic enablement, your procurement team should be taking baby steps. The time it can take to totally integrate your in-house enterprise resource planning (ERP) system with a third-party sourcing platform can lead to large savings opportunities lost because of the delay in the implementation process. A better question would be: "How can I pass along data from your tool into my existing ERP system?"

The Yes/No Approach

Another problem with predeveloped RFP/RFI templates is the yes/no approach, in which the template is loaded with questions that can only be answered with a simple yes or no. This becomes even more of a factor if you are using an electronic RFP software tool that does not allow the suppliers to offer an answer beyond a simple yes or no. Typically, the evaluation procedure scores vendors with 100 percent or 0 percent based on their answers, when they may have better solutions that remain unknown to you because of the lack of flexibility in the answering mechanism. For example:

- *Is classroom training available?*
  - If suppliers answer no, that is not necessarily a reason to give them a score of 0. It is reasonable to assume that there are much more cost-effective ways of delivering training these days, such as Web presentations or online help videos. Again, a more open question would serve better: "How do you provide initial and ongoing training services to our end users?"
- *Can you make the flange in Type 316 SS [or insert any other material or product here]?*
  - We often encounter companies that have been purchasing a particular product from a particular vendor for many years, the only reason being that the product is what the supplier originally specified for them years ago. It is worthwhile for buyers (and engineers) to take the time to understand why they are buying a certain product. In this case, maybe a newer, lower-cost material, such as 303 or 304, would work. You will never find out if your supplier is building all of your specifications for you.
- *Does your product include a Mandarin translation?*
  - Perhaps this is important to your business. Let us assume the current answer is no, but the vendor intends to include Mandarin translation in a later release of its product, which will be available before your anticipated implementation date. The yes/no approach does not allow a supplier to adequately indicate that such an option will soon be available.
- *Is your company ISO 9001 certified?*
  - Although this may apply to many buyers' internal QC policies, it might be time to reevaluate it as a requirement. Many companies have superior internal quality control systems and simply choose not to pay for auditing by ISO, so they should not necessarily be disqualified if they answered no to the question. Additionally, they may not be in a traditional industry that would require ISO certification, or they may be certified by a different quality control program, such as AS 9000 (aerospace) or QS 9000 (automotive). Again, the yes/no approach does not leave the supplier any room to properly address your needs.

We could continue to list hundreds of examples of reasons why suppliers should not be writing your RFP for you. Many of these points can also be translated into examples of elements you should not be including in your RFP or RFI, even if you are building the document from scratch. From a big-picture perspective, there are two lessons that are worth learning from this section.

First, if you are a buyer looking for a new technology, product, or supplier, be careful of the free templates that are readily available on the Web. In most cases they are just a listing-dump of every little feature or line of code in one supplier's product or service offering. The suppliers then mask these features as requirements for which every buyer should be asking. These templates do, however, give you a great starting point so that you do not have to create an RFP from scratch, but it is important to go through each criterion very carefully and make sure it actually applies to your business, and ensure that your own requirements are reflected, not just the supplier's.

Secondly, if you are already buying from a particular supplier and do not have the specifications handy to seek alternates, it is a worthwhile exercise to build the specification in-house, or with outsourced assistance. Although you can and should reach out to your incumbent supplier for information, try to understand what it is you want to buy, and why exactly you are buying it in the way that you do. This may require you to conduct internal team interviews, in which you dive deeply into understanding end-user requirements. You should never accept unexamined answers such as "It is just the way we do it," or "We have always done it this way." Take time to completely understand your organization and your end users' requirements and build a document that lists those requirements. Do not let your supplier define your requirements, needs, or specifications.

In all cases, it is advisable to avoid yes/no questions and to develop a more open-ended dialog with your potential suppliers. Rather than asking dozens of questions that may or may not be relevant, and that may have a limited ability to capture the information you are really seeking, present a business problem or opportunity and encourage suppliers to describe how they would resolve it. Be sure to encourage alternate or innovative approaches. Building a massive, structured RFP prevents suppliers from being able to come up with such creative solutions to resolve your problems.

RFP SPAM

In order to obtain the best results in your initial attempts to identify potential suppliers and begin engaging them in your sourcing project, you should start by casting the widest net possible into the marketplace to help identify sources of supply. However, many organizations do not treat this step with as much care as it warrants, and they tend to spam the market with their RFPs or RFIs.

First, let us define *RFP spam*. Simply put, it is the practice of sending out bulk RFP or RFI documents, either by electronic or physical means, to a group of suppliers without previously contacting the suppliers; introducing yourself, your company, and the RFP process; or giving suppliers an opportunity to introduce themselves and ask questions about the process. RFP spamming is a poorly conceived method of releasing RFPs that seems to have become more prevalent recently.

Examples of RFP Spamming

There is no question that RFP spam is often done intentionally, but there are certainly occasions in which it happens innocently, perhaps due to time constraints, laziness, or inexperience. To help avoid falling into the RFP spamming trap, we have included some examples to be aware of the next time you issue an RFP.

Using Generic E-Mail Addresses

This is by far the most common mistake used in the sourcing process. In this example, buyers simply spend a few minutes researching and collecting e-mail addresses of sales departments for several potential suppliers that they find online. These generic e-mails usually read something like info@company.com or sales@company.com. They then put these e-mail addresses into their favorite e-sourcing system, or send out individual generic e-mails including the RFI or RFP document, and expect to get responses from those suppliers.

The problem is that the receiver of such an e-mail realizes that it came into the generic mailbox, and either ignores it as spam because that person knows nothing about your company or project, or comes to the conclusion, without any other information, that this is a phishing exercise, and that you intend to use the information gathered to gain an advantage over your incumbent supplier. In any event, the responses to such RFP spamming tend to be limited, and of low quality.

The Hard-Copy Spam Method

This method is exactly the same as the previous, yet is more costly. In this method of RFP spamming, a buyer collects physical addresses of supplier locations and mails or overnights a hard copy of the actual RFP or RFI. Buyers often have the misconception that a physical document makes them look more serious to a supplier, when in fact, most suppliers only want to read and respond to electronic documents, and may never open the envelope because they think it is junk mail.

Filling Out a Series of Template E-mails

Similar to the first example, this process is only slightly better, and will only produce mediocre results, at best. In this scenario, the buyer "improves" the process by filling out and sending a generic e-mail template that asks suppliers if they want to participate in an RFP, then sending a follow-up containing the actual RFP or RFI, then sending yet another follow-up e-mail that asks why they did not fill it out. As you can surmise, this is generally perceived as annoying, and produces very low response rates.

Sending an RFP to Companies that Do Not Sell the Product or Service You Are Sourcing

Contrary to what you might imagine, this is a fairly common practice, especially when it involves the procurement of services. A buyer spends a little time researching the companies in the identified target industry and bulk e-mails all of those suppliers without taking the time to truly understand whether each supplier even offers the services that are being sourced. In some cases, this is done specifically to circumvent internally established or regulated sourcing strategies that specify that the buyer must invite a certain amount of suppliers to a bid process. The reasoning is that if the supplier does not respond, then the obligation to survey the market is fulfilled and the award of the contract can go to the buyer's preferred, preselected vendor.

Reasons that RFP Spamming Occurs

Why do buyers send out RFP spam? There are many reasons, primarily unintentional, but problematic all the same. Your RFP will be much better received and responded to if you consciously avoid the traps that lead to inadvertently issuing RFP spam. Following are some of the more common reasons.

The RFP Was Just a Formality

Your organization or your sourcing team had already made the decision to select a particular supplier or solution, but internal policy or law (in the case of government procurement) may require your team to submit and receive a certain number of bids from suppliers.

Overreliance on Technology

Many organizations are under the illusion that implementing an expensive piece of sourcing or procurement technology somehow makes their sourcing events become magically more effective. As we have stated repeatedly, nothing can replace the competent, creative guidance of humans in the loop.

Lack of Resources

Your organization simply does not have the human resources, technology, market data, or time to properly conduct a sourcing initiative.

Lack of Training

Your procurement team, or an individual assigned to the task at hand, simply does not have enough experience with strategic sourcing in order to properly conduct the initiative. This often takes place when a company puts a formalized sourcing methodology (with corresponding documents) in place and expects that anyone can repeat the process and obtain optimal results without adapting the process to fit the individual initiative or properly training the assigned individual.

Elitist or Entitled Attitude

"My company is a Fortune 50 company, we are a household name, and everyone wants to work for us. Suppliers should bend over backwards to win our business and add us to their client list!" Wrong! Unfortunately, many procurement professionals, or the departments for which they are procuring goods and services, often get big heads about their buying power. Due to their (often mistaken) perception of their power and influence in the marketplace, many people think that suppliers should be tripping over themselves to win their business and that all of the hard work and effort should be completely on the supplier's side.

Lazy

It is unfortunate but true: Some procurement professionals are simply lazy and only want to do the bare minimum to get by. Often they want to simply repeat a process that is in place, or recycle an RFP from a year ago without making adjustments and reevaluating the marketplace.

Expected Results from RFP Spamming

Unsolicited RFPs rarely generate a significant response rate, and those that do elicit responses rarely have competitive pricing.

Granted, there are a few commodity items for which an unsolicited RFP might actually get you better pricing results than what you are currently paying. However, as we have stated, the approach does not provide prospective suppliers the ability to present other creative ways to improve cost elsewhere in your supply chain or produce soft savings by streamlining the process.

There may have been a category or two in the past in which you were able to find an acceptable fit via spamming an RFP to a multitude of suppliers. But by not having done proper research and formally engaging suppliers for that category, you may have missed out on an even better fit for your organization and needs.

Many procurement professionals spend only a portion of their time on actual sourcing. Even procurement professionals that specifically have a sourcing-only position spend their time sourcing many products or services at the same time. This can lead to lax or sloppy habits, such as RFP spamming. However, most sourcing and procurement managers fail to realize that most suppliers' sales representatives have one key focus, and that is to choose their customers carefully and to sell only one product or service. Skilled salespeople and management teams know that when they receive an unsolicited RFP with little communication from the prospective customer, they have almost no chance of actually winning the business.

Although most companies spend 19 percent to 30 percent of their revenue on sales and marketing, these are not fixed costs of doing business. Suppliers will not invest the proper resources and time in responding to an unsolicited request for proposal unless they are reasonably confident that they have a chance of actually winning the business. When they receive RFP spam, they prioritize it accordingly, and don't put much time and energy into it, if any. That is why the response rate and quality for RFP spam is so low.

How to Avoid Becoming an RFP Spammer

"Blind bids are for suckers." "If you do not have a relationship *before* the RFP, you will not have one afterward." These were a couple of comments we encountered in a recent sales training seminar; this is what the people who receive your RFP spam are hearing and thinking. Furthermore, the seminar specifically suggests to salespeople that they should make it a condition of responding to an RFP that they are guaranteed prebrief and debrief meetings with the issuer, regardless of the results of the RFP selection. This is a fantastic suggestion; however, it should be you and your procurement team, as the issuer, who initiate these discussions. You should not wait for the supplier to demand these meetings.

First, Some Basic Tips

Do not rely on your company's Fortune 100 status or name recognition to make suppliers hungry for your business. In fact, becoming a supplier to a megacorporation or a high-profile client can actually be undesirable to many suppliers. These suppliers, particularly smaller businesses that can be much more nimble and can provide customized solutions for their customer bases, are very careful about the size and nature of the customers they work with, and take care to only bid on business that they will be capable of supporting in the long term. Leading into a bid solicitation with a "flexing your muscles" attitude can create an immediate deal-breaker for such suppliers, in that they assume that the entire relationship after the sale will continue to be an uneven and uncomfortable one.

Do not rely on your $15,000-per-month electronic sourcing or electronic procurement software system to conduct the event on your behalf. For that matter, do not rely on your inexpensive or free e-sourcing system to run the event on your behalf either. Without proper communication and relationship building, many suppliers simply do not have the desire to respond to a bid through an electronic system. Suppliers need to know that they have a reasonable chance of winning business, and want to know the people with whom they are dealing on the other side of the transaction. Additionally, many software systems simply do not allow the suppliers to properly expand upon questions and present more in-depth or alternative approaches, or to showcase their offerings and services in order to differentiate themselves from their competitors. It is worthwhile to be aware that many suppliers view RFPs issued through electronic systems as a form of reverse auction and will be hesitant to treat the response seriously, which is why communication and relationship building marks the difference between a failed bidding event and an extremely competitive one.

The Proper Way to Conduct RFPs: Make Contacts, Make Time

Getting to know your suppliers is by far the most important aspect of the RFx process. Take time to research your prospective suppliers. Treat the process like preparing for a job interview, in which you would want to know everything about the company with which you are interviewing, just as the interviewer would want to learn everything possible about you. This is important for making sure that your respective businesses are in alignment and will be able to work successfully together.

Start with basic online research. Read about the industry, review the supplier's website, research its competitors, find relevant news articles, use subscription services, if available, to understand the hierarchy and financials of the prospective suppliers, then make calls.

Identify the proper person or persons within the prospective supplier's organization who would handle your account. Make sure you are communicating at the right level; if you manage multiple locations, or have a large spend, make sure you get a senior account representative or a national/international account manager.

Take time to speak with your prospective suppliers' account managers or sales teams. Calling prospective suppliers, asking for e-mail addresses, and letting them know that they will be receiving an RFP before you hang up does *not* qualify as taking time to speak with a prospective supplier. After you have conducted your own research into a supplier, take at least 10 minutes to speak on the phone with the proper people there. This is the very first step in building a long-term relationship with that supplier. Make sure your prospective suppliers understand your needs and wants, and find ways to assure them that the sourcing event is a real opportunity and that they have a good chance to win your business.

Take the time to explain the process to prospective suppliers. Regardless of the type of sourcing event you are conducting (RFI, RFP, RFQ, or reverse auction), inform them of the steps of the process and what they need to do at each step. Explain that you will be sending documents, whether physical or electronic, or using a sourcing software platform. Make sure they understand what is expected of them in the response. Immediately schedule a follow-up call for a time after you have sent them the RFx, during which you can walk them through the process a second time and offer them an opportunity to ask questions.

Follow up with suppliers throughout your timeline of the sourcing event. For example, if you provided 20 days to respond to an RFP, follow up regularly via e-mail, phone, or both to make sure that they are making progress and no new questions have arisen. Make sure that your follow-up calls or e-mails are more detailed than, "Just making sure you get this to me by (such-and-such) date." Continue to build the relationship by asking the suppliers whether there is anything *they* need to assist them in preparing the response.

Training

Earlier we mentioned that improper training can often serve as the root cause of RFP spamming. Often, the problem is actually caused by having too much documentation and formal process documents. Often when new hires come into your organization, they are told to review internal process manuals to learn how the company does such things. The trainees may take matters a step further and search online for other formalized methods of sourcing a particular category. While it is important to understand how sourcing events are typically done, or how they were done in the past, rigidly following a formal policy for procurement often impedes your ability to adapt and add creativity into the strategic sourcing process.

Many sourcing professionals come from standard procurement back-grounds, in which they believe sourcing is merely the process of developing a standard structured (i.e., overly complex) RFP and asking three suppliers to bid. A procurement professional should understand and execute best practices for specific commodities, not just reissue a generic RFP. For instance, sourcing telecommunications is a completely different activity from sourcing office supplies. Telecommunications sourcing efforts can yield optimal savings if the sourcing team has a good familiarity with available technologies and a solid understanding of tariffs, which can be leveraged to gain improved pricing. An RFP is not always the best practice for telecommunications projects. On the other hand, sourcing office supplies requires heavy spend analysis to determine usage patterns within your organization. In most companies, a formal best practice policy manual will not get down to this level of commodity sourcing detail, and the sourcing team may end up using the wrong strategies for their sourcing events.

Get Help

Managing multiple spend categories and staying current with market intelligence is a daunting task and cannot always be accomplished with in-house resources for every single spend category. Fortunately, there are a variety of solutions, ranging from electronic marketplaces to traditional and nontraditional consulting firms, that can help manage the categories that you just do not have the time or resources to source properly or for which you require additional support. In Part Two of this book, we cover some of those technologies as well as provide advice on engaging outside support services.

MAKING THE SUPPLIER PUT SKIN IN THE GAME

As a provider of strategic sourcing services, our organization is often asked to participate in and respond to RFPs for those services. As part of that process, we have recently begun to see a new trend that we believe is horrible and counter-productive. We call it *making the supplier put skin in the game*. Its origin is unclear; perhaps it is a response to the recent recession, or a poor tactic invented by some new professors somewhere who have no real-world sourcing experience. No matter the origin, this new sourcing tactic does nothing but limit your potential supply base and guarantee you higher-priced bids in the categories you are seeking to source.

The most common method used to require a supplier to put skin in the game involves issuing an RFI, RFP, or reverse auction in which the supplier, in some form or another, is required to invest financially to obtain the right to respond or even view the RFx material. Although this is a rather common tactic in government projects or in the use of subscription lead-generation services, it has no place in the private sector in which buyers are dealing directly with prospective suppliers. The following are examples of how this concept is employed, and why you should avoid doing so.

Scenario 1: Recently our organization received an RFP notification that provided only this bit of information: "X Company is accepting sealed bids/proposals from qualified firms to furnish the goods and/or services in the specification document. The Procurement Managed Services specifications documents can be downloaded electronically for a fee of $500. *All prospective bidders/respondents are hereby cautioned not to contact any member of X Company other than the specified contact person.*" Of course, we would only be allowed to access this person's contact information after paying the fee. The issuing company was hoping that the fee would generate the impression that this was an important, worthwhile, and lucrative opportunity. Now, as tempting as an offer such as this may appear, no serious consulting firm or supplier would ever entertain the idea of throwing away hundreds of dollars to gain access to RFP documents for an opportunity that may not even be related to its business when it cannot even speak with or e-mail a contact person to gain a brief, high-level understanding of what the RFP entails.

Scenario 2: A company that had been a prospect of ours for an extended period finally contacted us out of the blue. They were seriously considering engaging with us for sourcing services, but they believed they had developed a good method to rank our organization against other providers in our industry. They had identified a specific, upcoming, one-time purchase, and in this case the product was one with a narrow list of four or five recognized qualified suppliers. They were planning to conduct a bid by themselves with the suppliers, and would do their own negotiations with them to get best and final offers. After this step was completed, it was the buyer's intention to send us (along with several other consulting firms) the specifications and ask us (along with the other prospects) to go back to those same suppliers and try to negotiate better deals. They did not plan to provide us with their obtained pricing, efforts, and information until after we submitted our results to them. If we came back with the best bid, compared to the other consulting firms, then they would have the option of hiring us based on their internal qualifications, and there would be no guarantee that we would ever be paid at all if they concluded that our contingency structure did not achieve a significant enough difference (however they had decided to measure that) from the savings they had produced on their own. To add to this deplorable methodology, this particular RFP required us to pay $2,000 to ensure that we had skin in the game.

These two examples illustrate rather well the flaws in the skin-in-the-game approach. In relation to the first scenario, when any company makes the decision to respond to an RFP it assigns human and electronic resources to the sourcing event. *That* is the skin in the game; there are hard-dollar costs incurred by assigning resources to evaluate and respond to an RFx event. These costs are typically viewed as traditional sales costs, but nevertheless ultimately affect the price of the products or services that a company offers. Asking a supplier to put forth an additional financial investment only serves to raise the price of the product or service that you purchase from them, and will more than likely cause the most cost-competitive suppliers to choose not to bid at all. This approach tends to gain you a small one-time cost reduction, but ultimately results in the selection of overpriced vendors for the long term.

In the second example, the idea of sending multiple organizations out to beat up the same suppliers for better pricing on the same exact items is going to produce *zero* results (any respectable supplier will have already made their best offer in the initial negotiations). In fact, it will achieve nothing but damage to any relationship that the organization has built with those suppliers. Worse still, this tactic causes your consultants to deliver inconsistent messages to your downstream supply chain. You cannot have two or more teams working in parallel on the same category at the same time, unless they are working collaboratively; this can only create confusion and ill-will, as the suppliers realize that the customer has not been negotiating in good faith. Besides abusing their potential consulting partners, the use of this tactic would anger the downstream supply chain and cause many suppliers to drop out of the bid process rather than take on the onerous task of providing proposals for the same business to four or five different teams. This has the added effect of damaging the company's reputation, and therefore the quality of RFx responses, in future sourcing initiatives.

Collaboration is an extremely important component of strategic sourcing and relating to your supply chain. The skin-in-the-game tactic of making suppliers pay for an opportunity to participate in the sourcing event does nothing to help your position to develop good relationships with your suppliers that can ultimately produce benefits beyond unit cost. You can have the best of both worlds of unit price reduction and improved service levels, but you will not make it happen by opening up communications with your supply chain by saying "show me the money!"

 ## IN SUMMARY

The common theme to all of these examples of what not to do in your sourcing events is twofold: Show respect to the supplier and make your questions more open-ended.

Failing on the first point, showing respect to prospective suppliers, is one of the most common mistakes procurement professionals make. Salespeople and account managers for any business desire to grow their businesses and increase profitability. Good companies will not chase opportunities that they do not believe they have an adequate chance of obtaining. By disrespecting a supplier's time or finances (for example, by asking the supplier to pay for access to the RFP), you immediately cause that organization to place your organization's opportunity into the unlikely-to-win category, thereby decreasing the field of prospects out of which you can develop a low-cost, stable supply chain.

By making your questions more open-ended and by initiating dialogs with your potential suppliers, you immediately obtain respect. Suppliers will feel that they have an adequate chance of winning your business when they have been properly prepared for a sourcing event, when they have personal contact beyond a simple e-mail, and when they know that they are not required to dedicate dozens, or hundreds, of hours to your sourcing initiative.

The RFP approach should not be used as a substitute for developing an understanding of the market and engaging with suppliers. Often, up-front market research and preliminary supplier discussions drive the creation of the questions that should be included in your RFP and can provide meaningful information that you can use not only to qualify or disqualify suppliers, but also to drive down pricing during the negotiation phase. As a tactical solution, the RFP still provides backup to justify decisions made by the sourcing team, but it should never be used as a crutch to prop up poor sourcing event design.

PART TWO

The Tools

CHAPTER TEN

The Importance of Market Intelligence

OULD YOU WALK INTO the first car dealership you saw, with cash in hand, and buy a car without doing any research whatsoever? Of course not. When people purchase new cars, they typically start with determining their wants and needs. Next, they browse manufacturer and third-party websites to create a long list of potential suppliers of vehicles that suit their needs. Smart buyers then work their options down to a short list by doing further research, reviewing reliability studies, checking resale value, and even trying to time their purchases so that they coincide with manufacturer or dealer promotions. For quality information, shoppers browse auto websites; read magazines such as *Consumer Reports*, *Motor Trend*, and *Car and Driver*; research the results of award companies such as JD Powers; and review the National Highway Traffic Safety Administration crash reports.

Car buyers also realize that answers to other questions have a bearing on their decisions, such as:

- What is the resale value of my trade-in? Is it worth my time to sell it privately, or do I take a small loss and save a headache by simply selling it to the dealer?
- What financing options are available to me? What is the manufacturer offering? What is the dealer offering, and through which banks? Could I

get a better deal through a credit union? Could I use a home equity loan, or should I use cash?
- Should I lease or buy?
- Should I consider a relatively recent used car, or do I only want a new car?
- What other options should I take: prepaid maintenance, extended warranty, others?

Smart buyers spend an enormous amount of time considering each of the options. A vehicle can be a significant personal investment, and people want to make sure that the five-year contract they sign with the supplier (the lender) is the right choice for their family.

The same dynamic of skillfully and thoroughly using market intelligence to optimize the decision-making process applies equally to making a car purchase and engaging in a sourcing project. Market intelligence includes information that is relevant to a product or service, the companies that supply those products, and the overall market or supply chain for those products, services, and suppliers. Market intelligence is analyzed specifically to support accurate, long-term decision making. It helps identify targets for cost-savings goals and leverage points with the supply base. Further, market intelligence can provide guidelines for the development of an acquisition strategy.

When the economy is good and companies are profitable, many organizations lose sight of the importance of market intelligence and become lax in their procurement habits. However, as the recession of 2008–2009 reminded buyers, world-class organizations should always be evaluating their supply chains to identify supply risks and noncompetitive pricing, or else they will be hit the hardest when the economy takes a turn for the worst. For example, when the technology bubble collapsed in early 2000, hundreds of businesses folded almost immediately because they did not have proper supply chain and procurement strategies in place to keep their costs under control. Supply dried up as suppliers disappeared, which in turn hurt or eliminated organizations farther up the supply chain.

In the mid-2000s many economists predicted that the steel markets would remain flat. Only a few companies who had invested heavily in gathering market intelligence realized early that there was massive expansion happening in China. Armed with this insight, these companies hedged their steel purchases by prebuying at lower pricing, and were able to not only remain profitable as raw material prices skyrocketed, but were also able to actually grow their revenue.

There is a wealth of information available to procurement professionals, but not all of that information will help you make the best business decisions.

Further, the time and effort required to segregate good intelligence from bad can be a challenge, particularly if you have other roles to fill within your organization. This chapter reviews the types of market intelligence to collect to aid in the decision making process. It then explains what steps to take to ensure the data you collect is meaningful and useful for your organization. Lastly, the chapter discusses how to identify the point at which it is time to stop researching and start taking action.

 ## THE TYPES OF MARKET INTELLIGENCE

The information that is gathered to be used as market intelligence varies based on the type of product or service that your organization is purchasing and how critical that product or service is to your overall supply chain and sales of your end product. Generally, several key pieces of information need to be collected regardless of the product line.

Global Market Conditions

From a global market intelligence standpoint, a buyer needs to understand the forecasting that suppliers use to prepare for competing in a global market. Even though a product might be purchased for domestic usage from a domestic supplier, that supplier may be making plans based on forecasting for markets outside of your home country, because if demand for the products grows significantly in foreign markets, or if currency exchange rates shift so that it is more favorable for that supplier to sell internationally rather than domestically, it may cause a shortage of domestic supply, or higher prices.

For example, in 2008 Nintendo released Wii Fit software and hardware for its popular gaming console. When the game was released, it was widely unavailable in the U.S. markets. This shortage was not caused by a manufacturing disruption or capacity planning issues, however. Wedbush Morgan securities analyst Michael Pachter speculated that 2 million copies of the game had been shipped to Europe, while only 500,000 copies had been shipped to North America, despite a much larger sales volume potential market in the United States. His assumption, which was widely considered to be accurate, was that Nintendo was strategically directing its stock to Europe due to a hugely beneficial exchange rate on the euro, which meant more profit per unit sold than if it were sold in the United States. At the time, Pachter said to the *Los Angeles Times*, "The shortage demonstrates one consequence of the weak dollar. We're seeing companies ignore their largest market simply because they can make a greater profit elsewhere. They know that Americans will be just as fat a few months from now."

A procurement team needs to have a holistic understanding of the global landscape, regardless of whether the targeted product or service is only sold domestically. For example, it is beneficial to know whether there are opportunities today that suppliers can implement to help lower the costs of manufacturing and shipping of components that make up the final product. If shipping costs are a material aspect of your received inventory costs, you should be following the oil market, as an increase in crude leads to higher fuel costs, which translates to more expensive shipping charges. Or, you might research whether a particular region or country is starting to reach full manufacturing capacity. If so, the process for changing suppliers to a new geographical region can in some cases take years, adding cost and complexity to implementing such a strategy. You should constantly be evaluating the supply risk of the supplier from which you currently purchase as well as government regulations, cultural shifts, and potential natural disasters that can disrupt supply.

Benchmarking Data

In some cases, benchmarking is one of the most critical components of gathering market intelligence. Benchmarking is the process of analyzing your organization's business processes, costs, and performance, and comparing those metrics against the best practices from other industries and competitors. Benchmarking can be a difficult process, as your competitors are unlikely to make reports about their strategy and profitability readily available for you to study.

In order to gather such market intelligence, you need to build a cross-functional team that can help you evaluate your competitors' products. Your marketing and sales team can help you identify which markets your competitors are penetrating and determine the price points at which they are selling their products or services. They can also conduct research studies to determine cases in which your product was not selected by a type of consumer and discover why those customers were driven to a competitive product or supplier.

Involve your engineering teams. Are your competitors able to bring a product to market that has a final price tag that is lower than your cost for that part? What factors went into producing that final product that allowed your competitor to bring the product to market at such a low cost? Ask an engineer. Have your team, or outside consultants, review the products of your competitors to determine if they have found a less expensive manufacturing method, or perhaps a lower-cost component. Have the engineers at your facilities work with the engineers directly within your supply community to jointly develop lower-cost solutions. Remove the barriers that prevent a procurement person from working with a salesperson and get your teams collaborating.

Review and compare your total process against your competitors'. Although this information can be difficult to track down, ask suppliers that may have participated in your competitors' sourcing process about how they were solicited. Ask your suppliers whether they have suggestions as to how the procurement and supply process may be modified to lower your costs and improve your lead times. In this scenario, a supplier may be able to give you valuable tips without directly telling you what your competitors are doing.

Understanding Market Pressures

What pressures are coming to bear now, or in the foreseeable future, that may impact your supply chain and the ultimate sale of your products or services? Gathering market intelligence should include an understanding of what is happening in the economies of both your consumer's as well as your supplier's locations. This market intelligence can be used to both react to conditions and to take advantage of potential cost savings opportunities.

For example, if a particular supplier is in a region that is experiencing an increase in unemployment, it may be an opportunity for your organization to negotiate lower pricing as cheaper labor becomes available. Suppliers may be willing to lower pricing in order to retain your business if you offer longer-term contracts or commitments that can help their organizations meet their declining sales forecasts.

Perhaps your potential suppliers have had recent massive layoffs, and no longer have the in-house engineering experience they once had. Look to your internal organization to see if your engineering experience could assist the supplier. Rather than viewing the supplier as a vendor, treat them as a partner, and develop a joint competitive advantage with that supplier that is mutually beneficial to both organizations.

Are your suppliers crunched for cash? A market assessment of an industry as a whole may identify that suppliers are tight on funds because of a lack of financial institutions willing to lend, or major players who are no longer making large purchases, or other external factors. Perhaps there is an opportunity to negotiate on price by improving your payment terms in the favor of your suppliers.

Another alternative is to ask your suppliers what soft, or nonfinancial, aspect of your business is desirable to them. For example, a smaller supplier that is just breaking into the market may be more interested in using your logo on its sales literature than it is concerned about making profit from you. This can be leveraged again into lower pricing.

 ## COMPONENTS OF SUCCESS

A market intelligence initiative can only be successful if you ask the right questions and have the metrics in place to measure whether the sourcing project provided the expected results. Developing the right questions include queries to both the outside world as well as to your internal resources.

Making Time

It may sound simple, but the most critical piece of your market intelligence gathering initiative is making time for the process. Your role within the organization may include sourcing, but it likely also includes various other tactical and operational responsibilities, such as placing orders and tracking inventory, to ensure your shop floor or production departments have what they need to keep up and running. Make sure you and your management are committed to dedicating the appropriate time, people, and technology resources to properly understand the category being sourced. Also keep in mind that contract renewals can sneak up on you quickly. Depending on the category, you should begin gathering market intelligence three to six months before a contract expires. Use electronic tools whenever possible to remind you and your staff that a category is coming up for renewal.

Is Now the Right Time?

Although it seems like an obvious question, a frequently overlooked aspect of the market intelligence gathering phase is determining if the current moment is the right time to be examining the market in general. If you are still a few years away from product launch, historical data and trending analyses are going to do you very little good at the moment. Collecting data too early becomes a useless effort because the data will be stale by the time you use it.

Is your team ready to switch suppliers, technologies, or services? While having competitive information available to leverage your suppliers is a highly recommended tactic, determine beforehand whether your organization is ready or even able to make a switch.

How early are you in the life cycle of the product? If you are purchasing goods or services that impact a product that you are selling, make sure you are in the right phase of the life cycle of that product before searching for market intelligence surrounding its components. If your team is not prepared to make a specification change, or if it is prepared but marketing has already printed literature that includes a brand name of the supplier in the documentation, then it might be too late in the process.

Building the Right Team

Throughout this book we constantly emphasize the importance of building the right internal team to lead you to best-in-class results for your organization. Putting the proper team together to guide the collection of market intelligence is just as critical.

It is important that your main team members have superior technical, analytical, and communication skills, and possess thorough enough technical knowledge to analyze a product or service and understand how to break it down to a component level.

A creative way to proceed with product analysis is to start from a zero-cost model. In other words, rather than looking at a finished product and reverse-engineering the costs that go into that product, literally start from zero dollars. Imagine you have a blank table upon which you are building the part from scratch. For each component of that part that you place on the table, identify all the possible costs that you can imagine that go into making that part. For instance, how did it get there (freight), what is it made of (raw materials), how was it machined (labor and equipment)? Now, you have a base-cost price that most likely is drastically different than the price the suppliers have been charging you. In order to figure out why, you can evaluate and research each step of the cost model you identified to see how market conditions may be driving your prices. Once you have a complete understanding of each component of the cost, you gain huge leverage with the supplier when you ask them to justify their pricing later in the sourcing initiative.

From an analytical standpoint, your team must be able to break down large data sets and understand the components that make up that data. They should have strong skills in using spreadsheets, and at a minimum understand how to create pivot tables and graphically plot data within Microsoft Excel. Individuals who do not have these skills often take too long to conduct data analysis, and worse, will often cut corners in the manipulation of data.

End users and other affected parties should also be part of the team, so that they can share qualitative requirements and give their perceptions of past, current, and future market conditions. End users can help identify suppliers and provide key differentiators between competitors. While end users can provide valuable insight, they do not necessarily understand the big picture or the ultimate goal of the project; therefore, you should not let them take the lead during market intelligence or sourcing.

Keep in mind that a person who excels in one aspect of your operation is not automatically qualified for retrieving and understanding market intelligence. The best negotiators in the business are often not as skilled at analyzing data. Similarly, the best analysts in the business are often very poor at negotiating. Make sure you have a blend of both types of people on your team.

Establishing Metrics

It is important to establish appropriate metrics in order to properly gauge the success of your project. These metrics include the identification, analysis, and application of methods to examine the data obtained from the marketplace, and then developing methods for testing hypotheses in order to predict results.

Depending on the product or service you are buying and the uniqueness of your organization as a whole, your metrics can change drastically from project to project. There are two types of metrics that you need to consider: hard metrics and soft metrics. Hard metrics are a way to measure tangible things, or things that have an impact that can easily be seen. Soft metrics can be equally important, but are more difficult to measure, because they tend to be more subjective and often do not have hard statistics associated with them.

Some examples of hard metrics include examining the impact of each of the following process changes:

- Actual hard-dollar savings projections—old unit cost versus new unit cost
- Increase in payment terms—gaining extra days in the payment term process
- Lead-time improvements—actually shrinking the amount of time it takes to have a product or service delivered
- Material quality improvements—switching the raw material of your purchased product in order to increase the value of the product that you are selling

Some examples of soft metrics include analyzing the effects on the end result or product of the following changes:

- An exclusive right to become the distributor of a new product from one of your suppliers
- An improvement in material quality, which may change consumers' perceptions of the product's value
- A better relationship with your supplier that may lead to joint product development or that may gain you a competitive advantage
- Improvements in process that may reduce the overhead and labor costs of a particular function within your organization

Having the appropriate metrics in place is critical to determine whether your sourcing project was or will be successful. When you first undertake your initiative, you should identify and standardize your metrics. While conducting your market intelligence phase, keep these metrics in mind as you ask questions to both internal staff and external sourcing. The success metrics act as guidelines to determine the direction your sourcing initiative should take.

Identifying Suppliers that Can Meet the Requirements

One of the most basic components of market intelligence gathering is often one of the most overlooked. Buyers need to know how to identify suppliers that can meet quality and service-level requirements for the goods or services being purchased. Identifying these suppliers early in the process is important, because qualified suppliers can actually provide you with enhanced market intelligence that may not be available to you on your own.

Suppliers should be viewed as potential partners in your business and your supply chain. Ask them for assistance in collecting market intelligence. You may be surprised; many suppliers happily and quickly hand out relevant statistics and information that can be useful in your sourcing process. But let the buyer beware—in many cases suppliers provide facts and figures that make them look better or make their competitors look worse. While you should avoid uncritically accepting all of the information they provide, much of it can be extremely useful, as long as you give each potential supplier an option to respond or submit its own corresponding information.

When asking potential suppliers for information, they may actually give you insight, intentionally or inadvertently, into other suppliers you should be contacting. In one recent sourcing project, a market research company touted to a buyer that the company was recently awarded a top-five rating from a leading industry analyst firm. With that information in hand, it took that buyer all of five minutes to track down the analyst firm's report and identify the other four top vendors. As an added bonus, the report included the top 50 firms in the world.

As mentioned previously, having the proper metrics in place is important in all aspects of a sourcing project. This is just as true when dealing with suppliers and attempting to research market information. When dealing with potential suppliers, your metrics should be able to measure anecdotal information along with hard data. For example, you will want to be able to accommodate answers to these questions:

- How quickly does the supplier respond to your questions? Most suppliers should be able to turn around responses fairly quickly. However, if they are too quick with a certain response, it might just be a canned answer. If the supplier takes too long to respond, it might not have as much familiarity with the market as they would lead you to believe.
- Does the potential supplier give satisfactory answers to your questions? Often, suppliers attempt to answer a difficult question with a misdirected answer; if this is the case, repeat or rephrase the question until you receive an appropriate response.
- Does a supplier offer insights into the product or service you are purchasing? The best suppliers provide you with more information than you need or, at a minimum, offer more than you request. You are seeking a supplier that will share insights and valuable information that you did not already know.

Sometimes looking for suppliers that are already in the market of the product or service you are buying is not the right approach. For instance, maybe the product you are planning to purchase is unique, and no one has made it before. Or, perhaps you are looking to get out of a sole-supplier scenario without your incumbent supplier finding out. In these cases, you must attempt to identify adjacent technologies.

Identifying Adjacent Technologies

Sometimes it is just not possible or feasible to collect data about the specific product or service that you are procuring. Perhaps it is a new product, and does not have historical data available, or perhaps it is a product that is confidential in nature, and it is difficult or impossible to learn the history of the product as your competitors are the only ones with that information. In these cases, you should look to identify similar or adjacent technologies, and attempt to extrapolate lessons learned from those products and apply them to your product.

For example, a large life sciences and pharmaceuticals company was in the process of designing a new medical device that provided tactile feedback to surgeons while they were operating on patients via the latest computerized systems and robotics. The new device needed to provide some sort of physical shake or vibration to the operator, who was controlling the robotics via a control panel system. However, nothing had ever been designed like this in the medical community before. When the research and design engineers were tasked with developing or finding a medical vibrating device, they really had no precedent for medical vibrating motors. The simple fix, of course, was to research a similar technology. In this case, the similar technology was the vibrating motor that can be found within cell phones and smartphones. Although this motor was not exactly what they needed, researching it got them in touch with the main manufacturers, who were able to put their own product development teams to the task of creating a unique, medical-grade device.

In another example, a large hand tool manufacturer planned to develop a new source of supply for a unique product, a series of mining tools of various sizes that had large rubber handles molded around a series of steel rods in order to increase the lifespan and stability of the product.

In itself, rubber-to-metal bonding is not an uncommon manufacturing process; however, the buyers quickly learned that the process is typically used only on dimensionally small parts. The research team discovered that it was impossible to find hand tool manufacturers that had the capabilities to produce dimensionally larger parts that met their requirements. In order to continue the project, the buyers researched adjacent technologies that shared similar manufacturing methods.

In this example, the research team first turned to the aviation industry and then the automotive industry. What they found was that dimensionally large rubber-to-metal bonding companies used to be successful in the production of bumpers on automobiles. Car and truck manufacturers developed enhancements in appearance and safety improvements over the last 20 years that led to fewer rubber-to-metal bonding companies; however a few still existed with the old equipment, mainly large molding presses. At this point, the sourcing project became relatively easy, as identifying suppliers now provided an easy direction. Ultimately, the team identified a supplier that normally sold to the automotive industry. They had the staff, knowledge, and equipment to quickly ramp up production of the new tool.

Asking the Right Questions

Your team needs to identify internal category or subject matter experts and enlist their help. As mentioned previously, you should identify and engage with experts from other departments that the purchased product or service impacts. In the initial stages of your intelligence gathering, your team needs to identify the answers to the following questions.

When Was the Last Time This Product Was Sourced?

Insight into the timing and success of past engagements can aid your own sourcing initiative. Who in your organization led the past initiative, and what lessons were learned? If possible, find any supporting personnel, documents, and data that may still be available from this last initiative. After reviewing that data, attempt to determine what success the last initiative had and what you would do differently. Do you expect a different result this time?

How Old Is the Data that You Currently Have About the Product or Service?

Even though you may not have sourced the product or service in recent memory, chances are you still may have some current data about that product or service. Look back at old e-mails, supplier invoices, and the industry as a whole. Are prices increasing, decreasing, or remaining the same? Have the suppliers reached out to you recently to tell you about new products, and have you ignored their sales calls? Or has your organization simply continued purchasing a product off of the last contract and not made any adjustments?

How Static Is the Data?

A procurement team needs to have a firm understanding of just how static the data is surrounding the product or service being purchased. For instance, is the product a fairly mature one that has not seen any major shifts in pricing for several years, or does the product consist of components that are sensitive to changes in the market, such as steel or wood pulp? Understanding the importance of static versus dynamic data will be covered in more detail in the next chapter.

What Meets My Requirements?

As we have been stressing throughout this book, just throwing your current specifications into a document, labeling it a request for quotation, and sending it out to a variety of suppliers to retrieve pricing is not an effective way to drive savings. The same dynamic applies to gathering market intelligence.

When determining your product or service requirements, make sure that you are not just creating a specification sheet that lists only the current features of the product or service that you are using. When doing your research, attempt to identify a range of products or services that meet your needs, not just those that are exact replacements of what you are currently purchasing.

To gain a greater understanding, let us return to the car example from the beginning of the chapter. Assume you are in the market for a new car. Your spouse or friend has a new Ford Taurus that has the Microsoft Sync system. You become enamored with this system because it is able to respond to voice commands, links up to your iPod, has a GPS, and has Bluetooth capabilities for your smartphone. Now you go out to "source" a new car for yourself. If you go to car dealers specifically asking for the Microsoft Sync system, you will discover that Ford is the only manufacturer in the market that provides the system. You immediately just knocked out 90 percent of the potential supply base for your new ride. Now, if you had built your specifications based on needs and wants, rather than a specific exact replacement, you would have found that you have a plethora of options available to you. Your list would become: voice activation, GPS, Bluetooth, and iPod control. If you hit the market with that list of requirements, you would find that just about every manufacturer has at least one vehicle that meets your needs, and in total you would have no less than 50 vehicles to choose from.

For a more business-related example, let us look at the telecommunication category of indirect spend. Assume you have a satellite office that currently has five employees. That office currently has five copper telephone lines and DSL service for internet. You would like to make a change. If you hit the market with a request for pricing for five copper lines and 1.5 Mbps DSL, you will not get many competitive responses, mainly because there are few providers that can even offer both services, and the ones that do are often just resellers of the main carrier in your region.

Now, if you had done your market research a bit differently, you would have likely identified no less than a dozen options. Rather than looking for an exact, drop-in replacement for five copper lines and 1.5 Mbps DSL, it would have been more effective to search for providers of broadband and telephone services. If you solicited quotes from all the players in the market, including cable companies, with your needs rather than a solid specification, you would have received a lot more responses. You will find suppliers are able to offer much better and more cost-effective alternatives, such as fiber, VOIP, cable, and so on. They can offer five telephone lines and a higher-speed Internet connection for a much lower price than you are paying today.

In summary, as a general rule, cast the widest net possible when conducting your market intelligence. Try not to limit your searches to the exact product or service that you are buying today, and let suppliers come to you with alternatives that meet your needs.

BREAKING DOWN THE COMPONENTS

In order to uncover even more savings opportunities, it is worthwhile to track the cost of components that comprise the indirect material you purchase. The simplest way to break down the components of your purchased products is to look at the raw materials that make up those products, as well as the shipping costs for that material.

For example, corrugated cardboard boxes are a product that many companies purchase for packaging and shipping product. While we could write an entire chapter on sourcing corrugated, for now we will focus on the importance of market intelligence in the matter. The costs that make up a corrugated box include the material, labor, shipping costs, profit margin, and customization charges such as printing. Since the majority of most products' cost is made up of the raw materials, this is also the logical place for a procurement professional to look to cut costs. In the corrugated example, the raw materials can be traced back to wood pulp. So, while conducting the market research phase, identify the costs of pulp as well as fuel (for delivery surcharges). Fuel is fairly easy to track; there are plenty of websites that publish the going rate of a barrel of oil, the mainstream media reports it, and you drive by gas stations every day. However, pulp is not as easy to track. Fortunately, a publication, *Pulp and Paper Weekly*, publishes an index called the Kraft Liner Board index. This index shows the current and historical rates of the pulp material that is the major component of corrugated packaging materials.

With fuel prices and pulp prices in hand, a sourcing team can easily identify trends in raw material components for their corrugated spend. This information allows you to validate whether a supplier is justified in raising prices, or could provide you with the firepower to open negotiations to lower pricing.

Tracking these costs also allows you to identify the optimal time for sourcing, as well as the appropriate times to stock up on inventory. In the next chapter we will review just how you can leverage indexes to provide a cost-savings opportunity and lower your supply chain risks.

 ## IN SUMMARY

It may sound silly, but the last phase of gathering market intelligence is knowing when to stop. Like any investment of time, you reach a point of diminishing returns. At some point you discover that finding additional information takes substantially more time and effort, and the data points you uncover become less useful or relevant to your exercise.

In general, you should stop the collection of market data when you feel you have enough information about the product, market and economic conditions, as well as information about the supply base, that will help you in your negotiations with your prospective suppliers. You should have enough data to intelligently raise counterarguments with the supplier about price increases and, at a minimum, have a firm understanding of the supplier's cost models.

Although this chapter mainly focuses on identifying historical data that can be leveraged to drive better prices or lock in future sources of supply, you also need to look for trends in the future that will impact your purchasing patterns.

We briefly discussed market speculation, as it related to oil and raw materials but it is also important to look at sales forecasts for similar technologies. It is worthwhile to know, in general, whether the market for a particular product growing or shrinking. If the market is growing, are your competitors out trying to lock in sources of supply that may prevent you from getting product? If the market is shrinking, are your suppliers stable and diverse enough to continue manufacturing the product or service that you are buying?

What else is down the road? Is a revolutionary new product on its way to market that will force you to change the products you buy, or abandon a product altogether? The point is, you need to research the future aspects of your business, rather than just examine historical trending data. As a general rule in research, if you ended your data collection after you browsed the first two pages of Google, you did not do enough.

The next chapter discusses some of the tools you can use to collect market intelligence to help you identify the best source of supply and negotiate class-leading pricing.

CHAPTER ELEVEN

Tools to Assist You in Gathering Data and Expediting the Sourcing Process

IN CHAPTER 10, we discussed the importance of gathering market intelligence and how it can be used to leverage better pricing and better results for your organization. Fortunately for supply chain and procurement managers, a variety of tools are available to assist in gathering data as well as expediting the actual sourcing process. In this chapter we discuss, at a high level, some of the most important tools of which you should be aware.

 ## TRADITIONAL INDUSTRY PUBLICATIONS

One obvious but often overlooked method of staying informed is to subscribe to the biggest publications that relate to your industry, as well as any publications in the procurement or supply chain space. The good news is that most publications are free, and can be delivered either in electronic or hard copy format.

By reading case studies in these publications, you can learn from others' successes and failures and perhaps even incorporate the ideas and strategies that have worked for other organizations into your sourcing process. Analysts, researchers, and practitioners also contribute to publications and may talk about specific information that relates to a product or service you are buying, such as cost of oil, prices of plastics, or the capacities of shipping companies. One of the most important things that industry publications provide is an ongoing update on the market and the direction in which trends are moving. Even cursory reviews of these publications provide enough information to keep you abreast of market movement, leaving you better prepared to negotiate your next agreement.

Indexes

We briefly mentioned the use of indexes in the previous chapter on market intelligence. Often, paid subscriptions to specific industry magazines include access to indexes for that particular magazine's target focus. For example, the magazine *Pulp and Paper Weekly* includes historical and current access to pulp source supplies and Kraft-liner board, which can be used to help you negotiate pricing or provide a price model for corrugated and office supplies.

Another paid publication that is widely considered an industry standard is *American Metal Markets* (*AMM*), which publishes a monthly magazine as well as a daily newsletter and maintains a robust website with information on all things metal-related. Most importantly, *AMM* offers a 10-year historical metal news and pricing archive for paying members. These are just a few examples; doing a bit of worthwhile research will likely reveal that there are similar publications, sometimes many others, for your industry.

Blogs

Industry blogs are another overlooked and easy-to-access source of information. Blogs that discuss strategic sourcing, procurement, or supply chain are becoming a growing medium respected by professionals and even analyst firms. In fact, some of the leading blogs are starting to diversify their businesses to actually offer analysts of their own, competing with the likes of Gartner and Aberdeen. Bear in mind that blogs do not need to be industry-specific to be valuable; there are several types that may be useful.

Practitioner Blogs

These are the blogs that the actual professional practitioner and consulting firms publish. These blogs are sometimes a bit biased, leaning toward a particular technology or service, and often include company-specific press releases and case studies. Although they may offer great insight into a particular commodity or business process, it is often a one-sided viewpoint, and open dialog through comments on a post is often moderated so that competitors are not able to opine on the topic (and its one-sidedness).

However, some of the better blogs, such as www.StrategicSourceror.com and Next Level Purchasing's blog, http://blog.purchasingcourses.com, provide objective views of a wide array of topics from industry news to procurement best practices. The information in these articles may help influence your supply chain decision-making process. These blogs, although run by consultants or company owners, tend to be less biased and offer informative pieces that help gain the confidence of potential customers.

General Business Blogs

General business blogs are typically run by independent or third-party individuals or companies. These blogs usually generate revenue by selling advertising space and minor consulting services to their sponsors. Examples of this type of blog include www.SpendMatters.com and Blog.SourcingInnovation.com. These blogs often cover procurement and supply chain news and offer informative pieces on a much more regular basis than other types of blogs.

Because these blogs are run by third parties, other consultants and suppliers regularly offer information to them for review and publishing, which is not something that is typically done for blogs run by consultants or software developers. The writers usually have less biased opinions toward particular services or product types, but are often criticized for promoting their sponsor's solutions over other equal or better solutions for the end user.

Overall, these are the most successful type of blogs in the space, as the writers typically come from the consulting world and have a firm understanding of the overall market and process that procurement departments live through on a day-to-day basis. However, they can often be a bit technical and difficult to read.

Commodity-Specific Blogs

These blogs are dedicated entirely to a singular type of commodity. They are similar in nature to the general blogs described previously, in that the writers are often highly experienced former practitioners who have switched careers to move into publishing. These blogs are great when following a specific commodity is critically important to you, however they are less useful for most indirect spend categories. An example of this type of blog is MetalMiners. As with general blogs, be aware that commodity-specific blogs also tend to be a bit preferential toward sponsors that advertise on their sites.

Periodical Blogs

The final type of blog worth checking into is one that is published by a periodical, such as a magazine or e-magazine. These blogs supplement the monthly or weekly periodicals that they publish. They are typically a great way to catch up on any news that has happened regarding a specific article that was published a couple of weeks ago. They also typically offer the most commentary from a variety of sources, in this case, actual procurement managers from the readership community. Although these blogs often have a variety of interesting commentators and authors, they typically do not offer best practices about any particular commodity, and when industry experts do chime in, it is usually only to promote a product or service of their own organizations.

GROUP PURCHASING ORGANIZATIONS

Although this may sound odd, an extremely useful tool in your strategic sourcing portfolio is a group purchasing organization, or GPO. GPOs were created to leverage the group purchasing power of multiple business entities. In simple terms, several companies band together to offer a larger variety and volume of goods, particularly in indirect spend categories, to suppliers who, ideally, offer lower prices in order to secure the business. Most GPOs earn their revenue by collecting a small administrative fee that is paid directly by the supplier, based on the volume of products or services, in the form of sales dollars, that the GPO can bring to the table.

GPOs pitch that they have deals or prices available for specific products or services that individual organizations would not be able to obtain on their own. This includes competitive net pricing, improved discounts, and other enhanced value-added services. Your job as a sourcing manager is to determine in which categories a GPO might be beneficial to you by independently evaluating their programs against your current vendor cost structures. If you determine that joining a GPO is a good idea, try to get any membership fees waived, and make sure that you do not commit to a specific dollar amount of spend. Most GPOs will accept these terms.

Once you have joined the GPO, use the offers that the GPO has just as you would for any other supplier. In cases where you have smaller spends, the GPO may in fact have superior pricing in its contract for the products you are interested in. However, if you have a significant spend, particularly if you carry the largest spend out of any of the other GPO members, you might do better negotiating a deal directly with the supplier. While this may be the case, GPOs provide access to the pricing and enhanced terms immediately, while a renegotiation could take time and effort that offset any additional concessions.

When considering the use of a GPO for a particular spend category, also keep in mind that there are soft-dollar benefits to using that GPO. In theory, the GPO should be managing the overall relationship with that supplier and the category as a whole. You could collectively benefit from the quality assurance checks and evaluations that other members are conducting on the supplier and you will not be required to have as many face-to-face meetings with the supplier's sales team on an ongoing basis. You may also gain greater insights into a particular commodity, based on your interactions with purchasing managers and teams from other companies that belong to the GPO.

To summarize, using a GPO is an excellent way to gain additional market intelligence by gaining pricing intelligence and collaborating with other professionals in your market. However, GPOs do not always have the optimal pricing and discounts, and you will be forgoing the benefits of developing a direct relationship with your supplier.

IMPORT RECORDS

Working with overseas suppliers can often produce savings above domestic suppliers. One of the best ways to identify an overseas supplier is to learn which ones your competitors are using. Fortunately, websites and tools now exist to facilitate this process easily and inexpensively. If a company is shipping a product from overseas, it must come through a port; when it does, the bill of lading is copied and stored in government records.

Currently, two online companies offer easy-to-use and inexpensive solutions to help you gain access to those bills of lading: Panjiva.com and ImportGenius.com. Both of these sites charge a tiered monthly fee based on the amount of data you require. A subscription allows you to search for information about a particular product that was imported into the United States.

Once a product has been identified, the bill of lading includes useful information such as the point of origin of the product (usually the supplier), the point of destination (typically the customer), what the product is, what it weighs, and the quantity of product for that shipment. This information can help you identify alternate sources of supply, by using suppliers that your competitors have already identified.

PUBLISHED INDEXES AND REPORTS

Many valuable indexes are published by trade groups or government agencies and can be used to develop market intelligence around a particular product or service, as well as ultimately to assist in driving prices down during negotiations.

Consumer Price Index

One such index is the *Consumer Price Index* (CPI), which is published monthly by the United States Bureau of Labor Statistics. This index shows the monthly changes in prices paid by urban consumers for a representative basket of goods and services. It is generally considered an effective way to measure inflation. The CPI measures the percent change of those goods or services in a particular market, and is a measure of the real value of money.

Data from the CPI sometimes find their way into negotiations, and sometimes are even considered in a supplier's formula for developing pricing for their products or services. Because it is one of the most closely watched national statistics used to understand the state of the economy, the CPI can often drive wages, salaries, pension, and regulated contract prices.

Since the CPI is a free, government-published report, it makes sense for a procurement manager to become familiar with it. It can be used as a predictor of economic trends and may provide insight as to when to lock in pricing for a particular product or service.

ISM Reports

The Institute of Supply Management (ISM) is a not-for-profit organization that was originally founded in 1913 as the New York Association of Purchasing Management. The ISM consists of thousands of members, including purchasing, supply chain, and logistics professionals. It is widely considered the most reputable certification body in the nation for purchasing managers.

In addition to providing training and certification, the ISM is widely known for producing two key seasonally adjusted reports, entitled *Manufacturing ISM Report on Business* and *Non-manufacturing ISM Report on Business*. Both reports are partially based on an index that ISM generates, called the Purchasing Managers' Index, or PMI. The PMI, a general indicator of economic activity in the United States, is published on the first of every month. It is a survey of the purchasing habits of hundreds of purchasing managers. PMI results in a number that indicates the health of the U.S. economy; generally, a number below 50 means the economy is contracting, while a higher number means the economy is expanding.

The *Non-manufacturing ISM Report on Business* is a seasonal report that is based partially on the PMI and partially on other factors determined by the results of surveys of purchasing managers. It is considered a key indicator to help predict the services markets in the United States and can help you determine how pricing should be reflected by service providers, based on the overall strength of the market.

The other major report that industry analysts generally anticipate is the seasonally adjusted *Manufacturing ISM Report on Business*. This report derives its information from the official ISM Manufacturing Index, which is a national manufacturing index based on surveying purchasing managers and executives at roughly 300 industrial companies. Overall, the index and subsequent report calculate nine separate subindexes, including new orders, production, employment, supplier delivery, inventory, prices, new export orders, imports, and any backlog of orders. Using this report, a buyer can predict the general health of the industrial production marketplace, and subsequently can help predict manufacturing employment, as well as pricing moving forward. This can be of inestimable value in a sourcing project.

 ## THE WEB

While an obvious location to discover information is the World Wide Web, there are several techniques that can help you get beyond the first page of results in Google.

Search Engines

Most people are familiar with the leading search engine, Google, and often forget that other search engines produce different results. Being aware of various search engine options and how to maximize relevant results can completely change the way you use the Web for information. Do not just stop your search with Google. Hit all of the major engines, including Bing and Yahoo. Each search engine, while yielding some duplicates, also produces results that are unique.

Also, don't quit your Web research too soon. If you only look at the first page or two of results returned by your search engine, you have stopped too soon. Better suppliers or valuable information may be buried later in the results, but the keywords on their pages may not line up with your query, or they simply may not have optimized their pages to achieve a higher page rank in the particular search engine being used. It is critical to delve deeper than the top results to identify smaller or new suppliers. For instance, a Fortune 500 company is likely going to produce a page-one search-result hit. On the other hand, a mom-and-pop shop probably will not have a very high page rank, but it may have better pricing and an offering that better fits your needs.

Expand your search terms, and learn and adapt your search techniques as you go. Let us look at a basic example: You start a search for the word "pallets." After reading about pallets for a while, you notice that some suppliers also refer to pallets as *skids*. Searching again for the term "skids" might produce worthy suppliers that you might not have otherwise found.

Another way to adapt your search is to generalize it by moving up-category. This allows you to get more hits and hone in on your true specifications. For example, assume you are searching for "forklift fleet management services," but you just cannot find much information. Try moving your search terms up to a more general level, such as "material handling."

You can also use Google and other popular search engines to "spy" on your competitors and suppliers. While not true corporate espionage, the Internet is useful for finding specific information, such as PowerPoint presentations and Excel documents, that gives you insight into the competition and your supply base. For instance, with Google, you can search specifically for a specific file type. If you use the string "filetype:ppt" combined with a keyword, you can target your searches for Microsoft PowerPoint presentations that relate to that keyword. For example, go to Google and type something like "xyz company filetype:ppt" and you will likely find PowerPoint presentations that were created by, or that refer to, the XYZ Company. Or, try substituting the phrase "xyz company" with a statement such as "manufacturing in Mexico," and you will likely find presentations that have a direct bearing on that which you were seeking. This technique also works for pdfs, Word documents, Excel spreadsheets, and more. Just change your search to filetype:*file-extension*; for example, filetype:xls for Excel and filetype:doc for Word. If you don't know the standard filetype extensions, Google can help you with that as well.

You can also search a single site for references to other sites, or for documents or file types. The search term "site:xxx" allows you to search within a specific site (when you replace the "xxx" with a URL). Suppose you want to find the term "strategic sourcing" on Source One Management Services's website (a consulting firm). Type "strategic sourcing site:sourceoneinc.com" in the search engine's search term box. Or using what you learned about researching quality reports earlier in this chapter, you can search for white papers (usually saved as Adobe PDF files) on Source One's site. The search term would appear as "filetype:pdf site:sourceoneinc.com."

Many individuals often quit their Web searching too soon, or do not include broad enough search terms to identify the information they require. With a few extra minutes and creative thinking, you can identify and extract slightly harder-to-identify information, or information that was not necessarily meant to be discovered easily.

Directories

Anyone who worked in purchasing before the days of the Internet probably remembers the iconic green books that were known as the *Thomas Register*. Thomas Publishing Company first published these reference books over a century ago, and they were ever since considered the best source for identifying suppliers or product and service manufacturers. At offices across the country, you could find bookcases and desks stacked with 10 or 20 of the big green books.

While the hard copy versions are showing their limitations and are less frequently used, the need for such information has survived into the digital age, and has spawned an entire Internet industry of supplier directories. The Thomas Register has moved online to become ThomasNet.com, and other companies have made efforts to quickly move into the space.

Supplier directories are mainly websites that categorize suppliers or vendors into a particular area of expertise. They also typically provide more demographics and statistics than a search engine and allow you to compare suppliers side-by-side. For instance, if you searched for "pallet manufacturer" on Google, over 250,000 results would be returned, and they would be nothing more than links to manufacturer websites, with the occasional map or phone number scattered among them. Supplier directories organize the information much differently and can typically display more accurate and complete results, including a company overview for each supplier.

The directories offer filtering capabilities, so you can quickly narrow your supplier list. Each site offers unique filters, but some typical examples include:

- *Zip code*—a radius filter, so you can find suppliers near you
- *Certifications*—filters for suppliers certified with any quality assurance associations, such as ISO9001, QS9000, or industry-specific certificates

- *Employees*—filters that indicate how many actual employees a company or location has
- *Revenue*—filters that indicate how large the organization is in terms of dollars

Supplier directories can simplify supplier identification in a way that typical Web searches cannot. However, like most tools, they do have a few shortcomings or downsides. Most supplier directories are subscription-based, meaning the supplier pays to advertise and get listed. However, most directories still allow nonpaid suppliers to be listed, but they show up lower in search results and the listings will only include high-level information about their business. A few supplier directory sites are pay-only, meaning suppliers are only included if they pay a fee. Although we recommend you still use these sites, you really should supplement your searches with other directories that offer nonpaid solutions.

 ## SOCIAL NETWORKING

Social networking sites are starting to find their way into more and more business atmospheres every day. Sites like Facebook and Twitter were originally developed to tap into the consumer-based audience, but have quickly changed to support businesses as well. Other sites, such as LinkedIn, were specifically designed to focus on businesses and people looking for connections or jobs.

There is value in participating in these social networks; however, we do not suggest that you jump around Facebook clicking on the Like button for companies simply because you have heard of them. Instead, search the site for companies with which you wish to do business, or even your competitors. You may find useful information on their pages: press releases, discussions with customers, photos, product announcements, and so on. Often, suppliers' social pages are updated before their websites, because they do not need a Web programmer to make the change. Additionally, you may get lucky and discover that one of your competitors has foolishly posted confidential information about its products, or simply "liked" a certain supplier with which you are looking to do business, which may indicate that it uses that supplier.

When on a supplier's social or Twitter page, you may even want to directly ask a question or send them a message within the site. Many companies have entire social media teams, which are effectively customer service agents that monitor and respond to social media inquiries. These service reps typically respond much faster than typical e-mail interactions. On Twitter, you may actually have a direct connection right to the person who can answer your questions.

It is a good idea to join social media groups within your field of expertise, or in a field about which you are attempting to learn more. Sites like LinkedIn actually have user-generated forums in a variety of topic areas. One forum of particular interest is the Strategic Sourcing Group, which is made up of many procurement and sourcing individuals at hundreds of companies, but also consists of some of the leading consulting firms' individual analysts. Dialog in these forums is typically very open, and it is a good place to ask a question about how to source or collect data in a particular category.

To learn a bit more about that supplier's sales representative who is prospecting you, try to find his or her LinkedIn or Facebook page. LinkedIn shows you a short (usually public) resume of the individual, which you can use to figure out how long that person has been with the supplier's company and to learn what that person knows about the industry in general. If you see that the person has had four jobs in three years, it might be time to ask that supplier for a higher-up salesperson with a little more experience and consistency.

Although many argue that business discussions should have no place in the social media world, published for all to see, the reality is that the social Web can be a place to extract valuable information about and insights into individuals and businesses you may work with. Just be extremely careful that you do not inadvertently publish or disclose any confidential information about your business or product lines.

RESEARCH REPORTS AND WHITE PAPERS

Why start your market research from scratch when there is a chance that someone else already did it for you? Many of the leading analyst firms, such as Gartner and Aberdeen, periodically publish research reports and white papers that discuss the state of a market or even predict the future of that market.

White papers discuss the activities of many of the lead players in a particular industry, and it is common to find reports that actually rate each of the suppliers in that market. Examples of reports and white papers may include topics such as leading procurement consulting firms, manufacturing in South America, or IT spending over the next decade.

These research reports or website subscriptions can often be purchased at a reasonable cost. Additionally, reports are typically sponsored by third-party consulting firms and providers, who sometimes distribute white papers for a period of time without a charge. Before you pay for a report, check to see whether there were any sponsors, and then look to see if that report is free on the sponsor's website.

Other white papers and research reports can actually be obtained from providers and suppliers themselves. Many organizations often utilize their own resources to create a research report about a particular product or service. These reports can also be useful for gathering hard data, but their overall conclusions are typically biased and should be taken with a grain of salt. Unfortunately, this is also a problem with the leading third-party firms, who are often criticized for favoring their sponsors and customers in their reports. With all research papers and reports, it is best to focus on the data provided and draw your own conclusions, rather than blindly take the conclusions of the report.

 ## ELECTRONIC SOURCING TOOLS

As we have discussed, electronic sourcing tools, or e-sourcing tools, automate parts of your sourcing process and provide a central repository for your suppliers, RFxs, and supplier bids. One of the great benefits of these tools is that, at the conclusion of an e-sourcing event, they can provide you with reports useful for analyzing the results of the event. Additionally, some tools help facilitate compliance with legislation, such as Sarbanes Oxley, so you have accurate records of the actual business processes and financial transactions conducted by your company.

Different e-sourcing tools provide a wide range of features and functionality, so price points for the software can vary considerably. Many tools can be used in a stand-alone capacity for a single event, or can be fully integrated with your organization's enterprise resource planning (ERP) system, such as SAP or Oracle. The most popular tools are Software-as-a-Service (SaaS) systems, in which the software actually resides in the cloud on the Internet, though behind-the-firewall or customer-hosted solutions still exist. With so many options and variables, understanding the pricing for these tools can be a challenge in itself. Some providers charge by the user, others charge by the event, others charge a hefty monthly fee, while yet some others take a percentage of the spend transaction.

E-sourcing tools have traditionally been employed by large companies with huge budgets, but within the last few years they have become a feasible technology for even the smallest of companies. In fact, completely free e-sourcing toolsets like www.WhyAbe.com are now available for both buyers and suppliers.

While we could write an entire book on e-sourcing tools and features, and the selection process for acquiring procurement software and ERP systems, we limit ourselves here to helping you develop a basic understanding of e-sourcing tools.

The basic idea behind e-sourcing tools is to provide enhanced functionality to help expedite the sourcing process. The features of these tools can include assistance with supplier identification (such as using the tool provider's preregistered suppliers) and help with creating and administering a sourcing event, whether it is a request for information (RFI), request for proposal (RFP), or reverse auction. The tools create a centralized communication panel for your sourcing event, so you only have one location for viewing all of your suppliers' responses.

One of the most common problems that we see with companies using e-sourcing tools is that they rely too heavily on the feature that conducts the sourcing portion of a project for them. In other words, buyers become overconfident in the ability of the tool to solicit potential suppliers, and become lax in their actual communication efforts with suppliers. In the following sections we outline some of the other common critical mistakes buyers make while using e-sourcing tools.

Neglecting to Invite Suppliers to Bid

Perhaps the most basic mistake that buyers make while conducting an e-sourcing event is neglecting to invite suppliers. Believe it or not, many purchasing professionals spend a fair amount of time to create an e-sourcing event on an online tool, then never invite any suppliers to participate. This is a very common mistake on marketplace sites, such as WhyAbe.com or ThomasNet's RFP tools, where buyers are able to post their listings in a public forum, under the assumption that suppliers are monitoring that forum to check whether a new project exists that matches their qualifications. Simply put, it is a mistake to post an RFx and assume suppliers will come flocking to bid. Instead, you must proactively invite suppliers to participate. Most suppliers, especially in a recession, do not have sales forces that actively search online for leads, and there are simply too many websites for them to continually check.

Running an e-sourcing event without inviting suppliers is like having a party without inviting guests. The chances of anyone showing up are slim to none. Moreover, researching and inviting the right suppliers is critical to the outcome of your sourcing initiative. Schedule time with invited suppliers to review your specifications, your award process, and the toolset. Engaged and educated suppliers provide cleaner and more accurate bids.

Neglecting to Contact Suppliers Prior to the Event

As we have discussed, one of the most critical aspects of any sourcing event, regardless of whether you are using e-sourcing tools, is to contact suppliers before your sourcing event and get them interested in participating. This is especially important in regard to using sourcing tools.

Buyers often have a preconceived notion that if they are using a tool, then it eliminates the need to reach out and contact the supplier outside of the automatic e-mail that the tool sends out to the invited supplier. Suppliers won't take an event seriously unless they are able to actually speak with the buyer. Most suppliers see an unsolicited e-mail inviting them to bid as simply a phishing attempt to get pricing from them to use as leverage against the incumbent supplier. So, most suppliers will simply not bid.

Take the time before the event to contact your suppliers, introduce yourself and your company, and make them aware of your sourcing process. Offer to schedule a follow-up discussion once they have received your specifications to answer any questions they may have. These simple communication steps can produce a significant impact on the results of your project.

Inviting the Wrong Suppliers or People

Inviting the wrong suppliers or people to an event is an inexcusable problem that occurs all too often. In these cases, one of two things happens: either a buyer invites suppliers that simply cannot supply the sought-after product or service, or the buyer invites the wrong contact person (often as a result of using a generic e-mail address from the company's website) from the supplier, and the correct internal contact never knows about the event. Larger suppliers could literally have dozens or hundreds of people that may be responsible for responding to RFx events across their massive organizations. If you invite the wrong person, do not expect that the e-mail will ever make it to the correct person. The person you sent it to may consider the invitation to the event to be spam, may not have the time to forward it on to the right person, or might simply not care to forward it along.

We previously discussed various tools that could be used for supplier identification, and also discussed the importance of communicating with the supplier verbally before the event itself. Fortunately, if you take these steps, with an emphasis on the verbal contact portion, you will never have an issue with your invitation getting to the right person.

Including the Wrong Specifications

So you have taken the time to find suppliers, and you reached out to them to discuss your event, but no one is bidding, or suppliers are indicating that they do not want to participate. What went wrong? Typically it is because your specifications are incomplete, are overdone, or simply cannot be understood. We have discussed throughout this book the importance of giving suppliers the proper information and a means of open communication. During your open communication stages before the actual sourcing event, make sure you schedule time to allow suppliers to ask you questions. If too many suppliers refuse to participate, it is likely that your specifications are overly cumbersome.

Neglecting to Familiarize Suppliers with the Tool

When conducting an e-sourcing event, make sure that all participants using the tool, including suppliers, are comfortable with it and trained on the ways to use it properly. Often, buyers create an event using a toolset and assume that suppliers will be able to navigate through the features of the tool and submit their responses properly. The reality is that many suppliers have never participated in an online event before or, conversely, have participated in many and may be confused with the process for the individual tool.

This is yet another area that can be addressed with open communication, indicating once again its importance and the reason we stress it so much. When speaking with suppliers, make sure you walk through your tool selection to give them an opportunity to ask any toolset-specific questions prior to the event. If suppliers are confused by the tools you elect to use, your event will likely result in poor bids from your suppliers—or none.

Conducting the Wrong Type of Event

It is important to make sure that you are conducting the right type of sourcing event. Running a reverse auction with 50 line items creates a situation in which suppliers are unlikely to participate because of the complexity of the bidding process. Similarly, if you have a single item that is highly commoditized, it may be ideal for a reverse auction instead of an RFP.

Do not conduct a phase of an event if it is truly unnecessary, just because it is the next step in the sourcing process sequence. For example, several of the tools available in the market force the buyer to follow the tool's process. One in particular requires the buyer to first conduct an RFI (asking the qualitative questions) before conducting a reverse auction or RFP. While this may be appropriate for some products and services, asking suppliers to participate in an RFI for simple commodities for which a large quantity of qualified suppliers exist results in wasting the time of those suppliers who choose to participate and influencing many others to simply elect not to participate. Tools should follow your processes, not the other way around.

The bottom line on e-tools is that they help you become efficient and organized and can help to expedite your sourcing process. However, they will not eliminate the need for the human element of supplier identification, specification preparation, and supplier engagement.

 ## CONSULTANTS

Many organizations simply do not have the in-house expertise, time, or resources to properly conduct all business functions. This is just as true of strategic sourcing initiatives as any other business practice. These organizations consider strategic sourcing to be just one of the functions of the procurement department, and have not dedicated resources specifically for the task. Instead, the company relies on the procurement department to continue to support daily purchasing, inventory, and engineering activities while also sourcing products and services. While this may work in some simple indirect spend categories, more complex categories require far more information, experience, and attention than many purchasing agents have.

Most organizations handle contract renewal in a haphazard way. For example, a typical telecommunications contract is signed for a three-year term. A month or so before the contract expires (or renews), the purchasing team realizes that this is about to happen and, along with a couple of people from the information technology department, starts to research the marketplace and learn about new technologies. While they will likely be able to find some savings, given their timeline, they will never get best-in-class pricing and service levels.

Additionally, the incumbent provider will not be threatened by competition so close to contract expiration, because, for example, voice and data network migrations take careful planning and may require a 3- to 12-month implementation phase, depending on the size and complexity of the network. The current carrier will quickly recognize the ad hoc sourcing effort as a scramble to try to generate favorable terms for contract renewal and offer some minor pricing concessions, which will not even remotely approach terms that might be offered if it knew that the customer had provided ample time for proper market research and potential migration to a new carrier.

The best-run organizations that understand the value of strategic sourcing continually research tariff filings and billing platforms (and the different pricing and discount structures each entails), look for new technologies, and constantly search for credits, disconnects for unused circuits, and a variety of other factors.

So, how is your procurement team supposed to be one of those best-run organizations that is an expert in every single category, have access to paid-subscription sites for historical data, and have the time to source something properly while making sure the shop floor still has the raw materials to get product out the door? In most organizations, the team simply cannot do all that. You may need outside help from a procurement service provider. These consulting firms have readily available all of the staff, time, and tools that have been outlined in this chapter, and are significantly less expensive than building your own team and databases every three years when a contract is up for expiration.

What Is a Procurement Service Provider?

A procurement service provider, or PSP, is a third-party organization or consultant who can supplement internal procurement departments. PSPs have their own staff that assist in a variety of tasks for their clients. These tasks include strategic planning; implementing best practices, supplier rationalization, and supplier collaboration; strategic sourcing; and negotiation.

According to an Aberdeen Group Research Abstract entitled "You Will Outsource Procurement: Here's Why and How" from October 2002, "Enterprises utilizing PSPs have been able to improve spending coverage, reduce costs for goods and services, employ industry best practices, leverage the latest procurement technologies, and streamline source-to-pay processes—all without taking on the risks and assets required to achieve such results." In another article, "Strategic Sourcing in the Mid-Market Benchmark: The Echo Boom in Supply Management," the Aberdeen Research Group writes about potential new approaches for midmarket companies' sourcing initiatives, due to findings that show that these companies currently have mostly fragmented or limited sourcing efforts. Specifically, to remain competitive, midmarket companies should develop "increased reliance on third-party consultants to help define strategic sourcing process and train internal employees on commodity costing models, sourcing automation tactics, and category and supply market assessments."

Why Use a Procurement Service Provider?

In most organizations it is very expensive and difficult to maintain domain expertise in every category of spend. Using a PSP avoids the burdens of procurement infrastructure for nonstrategic categories. A PSP can provide a rapid analysis of an organization's spend and implement changes, negotiate with suppliers, and use proven industry best practices. A good PSP becomes an extension of the organization's existing procurement resources in an unobtrusive fashion.

Most procurement service providers have access to all of the tools outlined throughout this chapter and, typically, the fees that you pay to the provider cover use of and access to all of those tools. Additionally, PSPs bring subject matter expertise to the table as well as historical data and case studies of projects for other clients. Rather than individually licensing tools and indexes or purchasing research papers for a category that you are likely to source only once per year or every three years, it often makes more sense to pay a fee to a PSP who can do it faster, better, and with greater results.

How Do You Use a Procurement Service Provider?

The manner in which you choose to work with a PSP is up to you. Some organizations choose to completely outsource their procurement departments to a dedicated procurement company. However, this is not possible for most customers due to the complexity of their businesses and the goods and services that are purchased to support them.

Every organization is unique, so there is no single answer that works for everybody. Procurement service providers can be used to replace your current procurement department, to supplement your current resources in strategic or nonstrategic product areas, to provide electronic tools to make your procurement department more efficient, or simply as consultants for implementing best practices.

The important idea to bear in mind is that you do not have to outsource your entire procurement network in one fell swoop. It is usually best to select a target area and gain top-level support within your organization before contracting with a procurement service provider.

Which Provider Is Right For You?

There are quite a few procurement service providers out there, and new companies are moving into the market every day. Select an organization that has a variety of skills and abilities in their offering. Typically, the best providers offer a combination of tools, consulting, and implementation skills. This provides your organization with the best possible result, as each piece individually does not provide the results that an entire solution can offer. In some situations, it may be acceptable to engage a consultant that only works with a single spend category; however, these providers are very narrowly focused and will only produce results for a small aspect of your business.

Many procurement service providers only offer a portion of a solution, such as electronic tools or commerce, or they take over your process, produce some results, and never transfer the knowledge back to your team. Make sure that the provider you select offers a long-term solution for you that includes a knowledge transfer phase that enables your team to produce similar results in the future without reengaging the provider.

Some providers go above and beyond to ensure that your team is trained and has the resources to replicate results in its sourcing projects. For example, Source One Management Services actually leaves its customers with free e-sourcing tools so that the customer does not need to license or purchase tools in the future.

Follow these steps when selecting a procurement service provider:

- Select an organization that has been in existence longer than five years. This may help to eliminate the new consultants who have moved into the market recently and are simply looking to make a profit off of your organization, often at the expense of your vendor relationships.
- Select a procurement service provider that covers a variety of procurement product and service areas. Instead of contracting multiple procurement service providers, find a single provider that has experience or qualifications to handle all of your target procurement areas. It is not advisable to hire multiple consulting firms that each specialize in one or two target areas. It will be draining on your resources to manage the multiple contacts and projects, and most single product area service providers do not respect your relationship with your vendors.
- Check references. Any established procurement service provider should be able to provide you with references that are in some way related to your organization. When checking references, make sure to ask specific questions, not just for an opinion. For example, ask what categories the provider helped source, how long did it take, what results were produced, and how the staff interacted with the provider.
- Research the backgrounds of the individual team members that may be working on your project. In many companies every member of the team has an identical background to the others (because they all left another corporation). You should attempt to find a team that has different experiences, backgrounds, and education.

What Is a Contingency-Based Strategic Sourcing Provider?

Simply put, contingency-based sourcing consultation agreements are contracts with a sourcing consultancy in which the work is performed exclusively on a gain-sharing model. This aligns the interests of the customer and the consultant by making the end goal for both parties maximizing cost reduction (and in some cases, cost avoidance) while maintaining or improving the levels of quality of procured goods or services. Contingency agreements typically bill at a percentage of dollars saved as a result of the success of the project for a period of time defined in the contract.

For instance, if you are currently paying $10.00 per unit for a specific item, a contingency-based sourcing consultant may be able to lower that price to $8.00. You in turn may pay them 35 percent of the savings ($0.70/unit) on every unit purchased for two years after the results have been achieved. The net result for the pay period is a $1.30 per unit savings and, after the term expires, you continue to enjoy the full $2.00 savings.

Contingency agreements have many advantages over standard fee-for-service models. First, they guarantee results, or else you pay nothing. Second, the provider invests out-of-pocket all the up-front costs of resources, people, and time, as many will not bill their clients until results are achieved. Lastly, contingency agreements encourage providers to produce the maximum savings available, while building a sustainable supply chain. If they recommend a supplier that fails, they do not get paid. If they cut a project short, with mediocre results, they earn a mediocre pay. Many fee-for-service contractors typically stop putting in the effort once they reach a level of result with which they think their customer will be comfortable.

Contingency agreements may include projects ranging from one-off capital expenditures to ongoing indirect spend, or even strategic mission-critical, direct spend categories. Many organizations have standing agreements with providers so that they can call them in on any project at any time. Regardless of the way you choose to engage a provider, contingency-based providers offer subject matter expertise and resources with limited or no risk, as they are driven to expedite and maximize results to earn their fees.

 ## SELECTING A PROCUREMENT SERVICE PROVIDER

As with suppliers for goods and services, the selection process you use for identifying a procurement service provider should be carefully considered and meticulously carried out. You should conduct a proper sourcing event, with a focus on the interview process of the provider. Next we outline some potential pitfalls of which you must be wary while selecting a sourcing partner.

The Bait and Switch

This is one of the most common tactics we see employed by many procurement service providers and it is one of the most important aspects to look into when going through your vendor selection process. Make sure that the firm you engage can provide backgrounds on the individuals who will actually be working on your projects. Many providers are simply franchises that anyone with a few thousand bucks in hand can join, without being truly qualified. These franchises have impressive websites, extensive client references, and superior sales teams, often consisting of seasoned professionals with expertise in exactly the commodity areas in which you are seeking help. The trouble is that the team you meet in the sales process is not necessarily the team that will be working on your engagements. They hand the work off to local franchises, outsource the work, or give the work to junior resources within their organization, and the project ultimately ends with mediocre results. You should ask and be assured that the people to whom you are introduced in the sales process will also be your contacts throughout the life of your engagement.

Is the Provider Sustainable?

For how long has your proposed supplier been providing a contingency model? If the company is reacting to market demand and has just recently configured such an offering, chances are it is not yet perfected. A contingency-based model requires an enormous up-front investment by the service provider, as it is in fact providing services and resources for free until savings can be achieved. If a provider is not experienced in this type of model, and does not have the financial strength to support it, it would be motivated to assign the lowest cost resources, grab low-hanging fruit, and close the project as quickly as possible in order to see some return on investment. This of course leads to mediocre savings for your organization.

Is the Provider Getting Paid on Both Ends?

Find out how your prospective sourcing provider is truly being compensated. Many providers are simply agents or resellers for a variety of suppliers. They find you cost savings from your current price, bill you for their work, but also collect a fee from suppliers as a commission or finder's fee. Sourcing providers that are collecting revenue from both ends have an inherent conflict of interest that will always drive them to recommendations for their clients that result in the maximum revenue potential for their own organization. This is especially true in areas such as telecommunications, in which it is relatively easy to be set up as an agent for multiple carriers. Your sourcing provider should work exclusively as your agent, and should be an extension of your procurement team, with only your interests in mind.

Hard-Dollar Savings Versus Soft-Dollar Savings

Make sure your sourcing services provider is only going to bill you for actual realized hard-dollar savings. Unless you are engaging the sourcing consultant for a true business process evaluation engagement, the language of their contract should not allow for soft-dollar savings, such as the savings that can be obtained through elimination of staff or internal process improvements. The best strategic sourcing services providers will be able to obtain profitable results for their clients without attempting to fight over the soft-dollar savings of process improvements, which inevitably become a point of contention between a provider and its customer.

Additional Costs

Make sure your contract with a sourcing provider details any and all costs for which you will be responsible for the life of the engagement. Read the fine print—many consulting firms have additional fees beyond the percentage that was agreed to in the contract. These providers can turn travel reimbursement fees or technology licensing during their engagements with you into profit centers for themselves. The best providers will not have any hidden fees and will not even require the customer to be responsible for travel costs for their analysts.

Anticipated or Estimated Savings

When conducting your RFP or negotiations and contracting with a contingency-based procurement service provider, make sure that they have skin in the game to ensure you realize the savings you are anticipating with the project. This is different from the skin-in-the-game scenario for working with suppliers of products and services (which is to be avoided), because the skin in the game in this situation is not a transfer of funds, but an alignment of the interests of the customer and provider through a properly executed contingency-based contract. Many contingency contracts require the customer to pay a fee based on the estimated savings that are delivered in a report toward the end of the project. This is especially true of very large consulting firms and firms that are new or unproven with the contingency model. The results that are delivered in a report often do not achieve 100 percent implementation and do not account for any changes in your business or demand for the product or service.

You should never sign a contingency contract that requires you to pay based on a group of analysts' research and paperwork, without seeing the actual hard-dollar savings implemented. Similarly, be careful if a provider wants to bill you for an average of savings. In this case a provider may track the first two months of savings and then bill you the average amount for the life of the contract. While this works for some static spend categories, it is a poor idea for a category that has seasonal spending variations or a variety of line items, not to mention that you will be forgoing the monthly analysis and audit required to report the hard-dollar savings upon which you are being billed.

Getting Help with Implementation

To expand on the previous point, make sure that the provider you choose is committed to the success of your engagement by ensuring that it sticks with you and helps with any implementation details at the end of the engagement. In some cases, implementation is simply a matter of signing a new pricing agreement with your incumbent supplier, and only takes a few days. However, in more complicated projects, implementation can require testing, on-site visits, coordination with multiple departments, vendors, and business units, and even staff training. Your procurement service provider should be helping your business with each step of the implementation, not just delivering you a report and telling you to do it on your own.

Assistance with Auditing and Compliance

To ensure you are actually receiving the expected savings results, your contract with your sourcing provider should stipulate that it assists with ongoing auditing and compliance for as long as you are paying for its services. Many providers start to bill on estimated or average savings after a project has been implemented, yet never ensure that the suppliers are remaining compliant with their contracts or that the customer is doing what it needs to do to obtain maximum savings. Things change: new employees, new systems, new internal policies, and business downturns all can contribute to the derailing of the anticipated results of a sourcing engagement. Not only should your sourcing provider be keeping an eye on the progress of the project for you, it should also constantly be monitoring the market, looking for ways to improve the project even during implementation, and hopefully bring even more savings to the table.

Concluding Thoughts on Using a Procurement Service Provider

Contracting with a contingency-based PSP can have a substantially positive impact on your organization's bottom line without assuming a lot of the risk and costs of a traditional fee-based consulting firm. However, there are many aspects of the relationship of which you should be cognizant to make sure you get the right firm for your business. Do not be afraid to open dialog with your proposed supplier and offer creative suggestions for improving your contract that include tiered incentives or a hybrid model of fee and contingency. If your provider is unwilling to deviate from the standard contract, look elsewhere to another provider who is looking for a mutually successful engagement.

 IN SUMMARY

The important takeaway lesson of this chapter is that you should not rely on a single piece of information or component of market intelligence methods when sourcing a category. The more information, tools, and resources that you have at your disposal, the better equipped you are to negotiate stronger agreements with your suppliers. If you do not have the time or money to find and leverage the right tools, hire a consulting firm that can help.

CHAPTER TWELVE

Increasing Stakeholder Engagement

TOO OFTEN, A PROCUREMENT TEAM undertakes a sourcing initiative for an indirect spend category and neglects to include all of the stakeholders for that category. The usual assumption of the team members is that the category is not a material contributor to the organization's final product or service, and therefore is not critical to the successful conduct of business. Unfortunately, they then neglect to include the many stakeholders in the team that do actually have interest in that spend category.

 ## WHAT IS A STAKEHOLDER?

A *stakeholder* can be defined as any person, group, or department that has influence in a spend category or is influenced directly or indirectly by that spend category. On the simplest level, the stakeholders are, of course, the end users and the category owners who are responsible for sourcing the spend. However, stakeholders can range further afield, including finance departments, management, shareholders, customers, and even marketing teams that may have joint marketing and branding arrangements with the suppliers.

Stakeholders can play a variety of roles in the sourcing process, and their participation can ultimately swing the results of a project, either to a positive or negative outcome. It is absolutely critical to engage all of the stakeholders in a spend category early in the sourcing process, and to keep them constructively involved throughout the process, so they feel that their concerns are understood and they don't intentionally or inadvertently derail the project later on.

Not only can stakeholders provide valuable insight into the existing supplier relationships, quality levels, and specifications, but many of them can also play a key role in the negotiation process. This is especially true in cases where the preference is to maximize savings with the incumbent supplier. Regardless of the project and the goals associated with it, having proper stakeholder engagement can turn what would normally be lackluster results into spectacular ones.

It is essential to identify and include all potential stakeholders as early as the data collection phase of the initiative. In addition to identifying the stakeholders themselves, also include their requirements, roles in the process, and sensitivities about the spend. Not only does performing this due diligence help to streamline process, but it also helps avoid issues later. As an example, let us assume that a certain end-user requirement is overlooked that is critical to a certain individual stakeholder's process. If you move through the sourcing process without determining that requirement by engaging that end user, you may work through the request for proposal (RFP) and negotiation phases and believe you are on your way to establishing a final contract when you finally uncover the requirement and have to start all over. Now, you have to back up and explore that specific requirement and reevaluate whether the chosen supplier can address it and determine how it will affect the pricing and terms upon which you have already mutually agreed. Gaining as much perspective as possible in the beginning allows you to avoid such time-consuming problems and work toward an established goal with a global perspective that includes both internal and external considerations.

In order to get the most from your stakeholders early in a project lifecycle, you should conduct a project kickoff and continually hold interviews with each stakeholder. The kickoff and interviews help to identify roles and shape the strategy around the project. During the project kickoff, any existing contracts, information about the existing supplier(s), and details concerning the items and their specifications should be identified. Following the initial presentation, stakeholder interviews can yield a surprising amount of new information and unconsidered factors. You may learn of failed relationships with certain suppliers and the details of why they failed. Or, you may hear of success stories with other suppliers and unique advantages they bring that justify a higher cost.

There are several key items that you should strive to learn from your stakeholders during the interview process. Specifically, you should ask for information such as feedback on the current supplier, experiences with alternate suppliers, identification of all spend in the category as well as spend in similar categories that could be leveraged for the sourcing engagement, and insight into current and future requirements.

While conducting your interviews, take special note of contrasting responses to each of your questions, depending on the role and perspective of the person you are asking. In some instances, the information you uncover may have a sensitive political nature within the organization, so take care to be discreet. You may find that different stakeholders have drastically different experiences with the suppliers and spend category, yet have been unwilling to share their viewpoints because of a contrasting point of view of another stakeholder. This is another reason that these interviews, often skipped, can be such a helpful tool in the process. Gathering this information from multiple sources and evaluating it side-by-side results in a comprehensive view of the current situation and provides insight as to what should change and what should stay the same. Also, it gives you enough information to take back to the decision makers in the category so you can collaboratively agree on whose needs and which requirements are to take precedence in cases of overlapping specifications or conflicts.

Each of your various stakeholders has something to contribute to the sourcing process, from fact-finding and research to negotiating outstanding items on the final proposal. Identifying and appropriately engaging all interested parties is essential not only for maintaining a smooth and fluid process, but also to ensure that optimal results are obtained.

WHO ARE THE STAKEHOLDERS?

Identifying each and every stakeholder as early as possible in a sourcing initiative is critical to its success. There are several stakeholder groups common to all organizations, and each unique business and spend category will draw a different circle encompassing concerned stakeholders. While moving into the interviewing stage of your sourcing initiative, it is not uncommon to learn of more stakeholders that were not initially identified. This should not be a cause of alarm, as it is common, but those new stakeholders should then be immediately engaged in the process moving forward.

Next, we outline the primary groups of stakeholders that are common to most spend categories and organizations. You should be sure to include these stakeholders in any strategic sourcing project, when appropriate. As previously mentioned, there will likely be other specific stakeholders in your organization that you will be able to identify from this foundation.

The Decision Makers

Decision makers range from finance departments to marketing personnel to operations managers; each holds a certain degree of influence on the decision, depending on the organization, category and goals of the sourcing process. The specific people weighing in on the final decision should be clearly identified in the beginning of the project, as they need to be kept abreast of the process, players, and considerations throughout. Otherwise, important factors can easily be overlooked, and weeks' or months' worth of effort can disintegrate at the tail end of a sourcing initiative as an uninformed or underacknowledged decision maker slams the brakes on the whole process. The decision makers' input at the onset of the project, and subsequent contributions during the process, is typically the most valuable of all stakeholders' input, because the decision makers' wants and needs must be satisfied and their dislikes need to be worked through, or else they can ultimately derail any decisions that have been made. Without addressing these sensibilities, a supplier that has a great organizational fit may not win the business due to various, less significant, subjective factors that were not accounted for during the sourcing process.

A huge mistake that many sourcing professionals make is failing to keep decision makers engaged throughout the entire sourcing initiative. It is easy to decide early on that the folks who will be making the final go-forward decision are too busy to be bothered with day-to-day supplier engagement and negotiations. However, bringing them in at the end of the project, when all quantitative and qualitative negotiation is complete, creates a great potential for unconsidered factors and pricing considerations, regarded as critical by the decision makers, to stall the project. This creates more work, and makes renegotiating more difficult as suppliers have already put forth their proposals and fought their internal battles over pricing. A balance point between the minutiae of the negotiation process and reporting major milestones can be established, and when decision time comes, the final presentation of offerings should not hold any surprises for the decision makers.

The Influencers

Aside from the actual decision makers, it is also extremely important to identify and engage with any individuals or departments that can influence the spend category. Identifying everyone who can influence a category can sometimes be difficult as the influencers are diverse, sometimes elusive, and can come from areas within the organization that are not easily identifiable as being affected by the spend category. Some influencers are a positive force, while others can act as impediments.

There are many types of people that can influence the success of a supplier or change in supply strategy. For instance, one type of influencer can include a current or prior employee who still has decision influence (like a board member) or has moved to a new position within your organization, but still has a relationship with the incumbent supplier. In nonprofit scenarios, you may find that a person or supplier has donated considerable money to the organization, and therefore new considerations come to the table beyond unit price and quality. A final example may be department heads affected by the purchasing decision because they have a relationship with the same supplier for a different spend category. In other words, the group buying janitorial supplies may be buying them from the same supplier that provides maintenance, repair, and operations (MRO) or electrical items.

The impact an influencer has on the decision-making process and ultimately the purchase can vary dramatically. Identifying as many influencers as possible early on allows you to include them in the process and nip any potential conflicts or upsets in the bud. In some instances the party may choose not to participate at all. This may or may not be the ideal case, as those people may have valuable input about the quality of the supplier and relationship. However, identifying those people up front allows them to make decisions about their own participation, as opposed to them finding out about the project on their own later and trying to insert themselves then, potentially derailing the project. Conversely, if influencers decide to participate, they may have additional, valuable insights about the relationship that will help the negotiators nurture the relationship rather than sour it, making it a positive experience for the supplier and all the internal stakeholders, both direct and indirect.

The End Users

An end user is any person or group of people who is directly subject to the impact of a purchasing decision because of their day-to-day utilization of the product or service being purchased. In other words, they are the people that use the product or service that your company purchases. Since these people are intimately close to the final results of your strategic sourcing project, their feedback is indispensable. They can help identify where soft costs increase as price decreases or why a certain alternative offering may present significant conflicts with current process and workflow. Also, end users tend to have a knack for identifying important qualitative considerations that would be overlooked without their input.

The role of end users tends to appear relatively insignificant on the surface, but it is imperative to include them because once you dig in, their input can be extremely diverse and valuable. End users also have the ability to derail a project or make a new supplier fail if they feel they were not included in the process. The bottom line is, they are going to be a major part of implementing and living with whatever decision is made, so it is worthwhile to include them in the process from the start.

Other Interested Parties

Ultimately, each organization should consider all possible parties that may have an interest in the category or supplier. These people can be difficult to identify but the effort is worthwhile, as they may have a significant impact on the decision-making process. A few examples include administrative assistants, relatives working for a supplier, board members, or investors who own a supplier's stock. In the same way, certain suppliers may be preferred by some or all of the organization due to other relationships outside of direct sales and purchasing. Suppliers who donate to the organization may get preference in the purchasing decision, but care should still be taken to ensure they are offering competitive pricing and no conflict-of-interest situation is created.

 ## THE VALUE BROUGHT BY STAKEHOLDERS

Quite often stakeholders can bring tremendous value to a sourcing engagement, as long as they are given appropriate roles and kept informed and involved at all times. Over the next few pages we illustrate examples of how to effectively utilize stakeholders as a resource.

Building a Project's Foundation through Data Collection

Data collection is the phase that builds the foundation for the rest of the project. During this phase it is easy to get bogged down and overwhelmed with ostensible dead ends, especially without the support of the stakeholders of the given spend area. Knowing the account and supplier relationship history (often undocumented) will help you avoid running into those dead ends. Learning about pain points that stakeholders may be experiencing with the current supplier, sensitivity to other suppliers in the same space, and ways that the supplier goes beyond expectations provides valuable forms of feedback.

The spend category's history may come from a variety of sources beyond invoices and purchase orders. This is why it is important to engage everyone early in order to identify who can provide sound information for building your data-collection framework. Getting a grasp on the background of the current supplier relationship and spend is the first step, followed closely by gathering data from invoices, contracts, internal documents, and databases. However, identifying who has the actual data can be quite a challenge.

Data can come from a variety of sources, all of which should act as checks and balances relative to one another. There are five primary sources of data from which to create an overall big picture of spend: general ledger, purchase orders, invoices, contracts, internal communications, and supplier documentation. Many different people in a wide range of roles might be involved in collecting this data. Finance, purchasing, operations, accounts payable, legal, end users, and the current suppliers themselves are all likely to play a role, and there may be others. Working with all of these stakeholders makes it possible to gather the most data with the least effort. It is important to be as thorough as possible in this data collection, because data may come from a variety of sources and go completely undiscovered during your sourcing process, which, of course, would be detrimental to the results of your sourcing project.

Uncovering as much data as possible early in the process helps optimize the time, effort, and results yielded from your initial analysis in preparation for a sourcing initiative. Not only does the data from various sources help to fill knowledge gaps in each of the five primary source areas, it also allows for cross-referencing and auditing, as the data should be congruent across all types of sources. This analysis allows for identification of past misbillings or other errors that can be corrected for potential recovery. It also enables firm assurance that all of the data is correct going forward, so that everything is being appropriately considered and addressed in the new contract. The more data you have available, the better. Having a positive outcome is highly dependent on your ability to identify stakeholders that reveal the facts you need at the beginning of the project.

Enriching Your Research

Parallel to the data collection phase of the project, research is another task where work may be mitigated and results may be bolstered by engaging the appropriate stakeholders. A specific area in which stakeholders can assist in speeding up results is supplier research.

For a variety of reasons, the category of spend under your purview may not be one to which you or your organization has paid particularly close attention, or has traditionally not been included in your review but has been added since the last contract. No matter the reason, there are stakeholders, especially end users, who can add value in identifying potential alternative suppliers and offerings that would be a good fit for your organization. Also, often overlooked, administrative assistants, who have shaken numerous hands and collected volumes of business cards from salespeople dropping into the office or gathered phone numbers of calls that they have screened from business solicitors, may be able to identify suppliers who would have otherwise remained unnoticed. While it is getting easier all the time to find competitors in the marketplace via the Internet, it is also easy to overlook small local shops that may be just as good or a better fit than the big players (more flexibility, local presence, faster reactivity), or adjacent technology suppliers that may offer something that fits your need but not your exact product description.

The other area of research, products and service offerings, can be a little trickier since the offerings themselves—pricing metrics, discounts, and so on—tend to change, especially if the last contract was signed several years ago. This is where research and collaboration pays dividends. All of the requirements previously identified by stakeholders need to be considered while doing research. The focus needs to be flexible and optimistic, but not overly so.

If the category is one in which there is true uncertainty about which suppliers can best serve your business, then multiple suppliers should be identified as potential replacements if they meet or come close on most criteria. The suppliers can then be asked how they would meet your business needs, and a more informal process can help you craft your decision criteria. Unless there is an absolute must-have criterion that a supplier cannot meet, they should remain in consideration until all potentials have been identified. They can be further thinned out later as supplier interviews begin. Engaging multiple stakeholders with various points of view and concerns allows you to identify best-suited suppliers, as each of their focuses will be a bit different during the research process.

What may be a lesser concern to one stakeholder, and therefore easily overlooked, may be at the top of another stakeholder's list. Working through these relationships will ultimately reveal overlap between potential suppliers chosen by the various stakeholders. These suppliers are much more likely to be good fits, not only for the organization as a whole, but to each group of stakeholders, which bodes well for the future relationship.

Defining Your Business Requirements

Before renewing a contract or going to market, your business requirements should be defined and reviewed. If quality, process, inventory, ordering, and so on have changed, this point in the process is a great time to ensure that issues are addressed before signing a new agreement. Requirements and their respective thresholds will come from various stakeholders, much the same as the other phases and steps in the sourcing process that we identified. Some opinions about a certain requirement may conflict and a middle ground may need to be established, or one threshold may take priority over the other depending on the stakeholder's position, or any number of other factors may influence the list of requirements. This should be ironed out as much as possible before addressing requirements with the supplier or suppliers.

If all needs and wants have been addressed before the sourcing process has begun, they cannot easily be influenced or diluted by suppliers. That is not to say that supplier feedback is not important. In most cases, certain preidentified requirements will need to be changed or adapted due to supplier limitations anyway. Creating a list of ideal requirements established from the input of all stakeholders before the project has begun and conceding specific points as needed, based on selected suppliers' abilities to meet those requirements, is the best way to ensure you are not forgetting important factors. It also puts your project in the best possible position to have all requirements met at the highest possible thresholds.

The first step is identifying the requirements themselves. Again, all stakeholders have different opinions and thresholds at which these requirements should be met, but ensuring their alignment is equally as important. A classic example of a requirement conflict is between information technology (IT) and finance. IT wants to maximize voice and data network uptime and minimize complaints, and is largely unconcerned with the cost. Finance tends to want to keep costs down, usually at the not-understood expense of uptime and a poor user experience. Identifying these issues early gives you a good chance to help both parties find some common ground. Left unrecognized or untended, a potentially significant gap in requirements may exist, and you could go on to negotiate the wrong services (too expensive, or ones that will not provide the service levels required by IT and end users) or not obtain the requirements important to a critical stakeholder or group of stakeholders, thereby potentially complicating and prolonging the process.

Once the requirements have been identified, they need to be evaluated, conflicts need to be defrayed, and, in some cases, orders of importance should be established. Ideally, this should be done before suppliers are solicited for any type of response, in order to cut off any potential internal roadblocks you may have in your organization, such as end users trying to skew the results because they favor one supplier over another. By gathering the different perspectives from everyone from finance down to end users, responses will likely be diverse. Making decisions about wants versus needs early in the process aids in proactively addressing all items throughout the sourcing process, and also helps guide requirements that were not previously considered due to a change in supplier, process, or technology.

Going to Market

When going to market, you should not just let purchasing play the lead role while everyone else fades into the background. Some or all stakeholders may participate in motivating suppliers and assessing bids. Additionally, keeping all stakeholders involved also provides the benefit of easing the transition phase to a new agreement, process, product, or supplier, as all of these items will not be suddenly dropped into their laps for them to figure out how to use on their own. Most importantly, leveraging your stakeholders in the actual negotiation in the pursuit of achieving additional savings is the most valuable way you can take advantage of your team's participation.

Throughout the chapter, we have discussed how stakeholders can play a key role in collecting data, establishing choice suppliers, providing feedback and history on the incumbent, and identifying requirements. The careful preparation and consideration of all those items bears fruit in the RFP process. All factors should be included in the RFP itself, guiding suppliers' responses to include all information required to make an informed decision.

Once the RFP has been issued and suppliers get to work, you may not hear much from them until they return their bids. Your stakeholders can take an active role by reaching out to suppliers to ensure they understand the RFP, answer questions, and help motivate the supplier to compete for the business. During this time, stakeholders can be leveraged in conversation with the suppliers. For example, when dealing with the incumbent, you could explain that finance has established an imperative for savings across the organization and there is a requirement for X percent savings or finance will mandate taking the business to market. Alternatively, there may be a case where there are qualitative requirements that a supplier is not including. You can leverage your end users by getting them to explain to the supplier that the pricing is where it needs to be but the supplier simply must address requirement X or the end user will not get behind a change of supplier. Not only does staying involved with the suppliers help generate thorough and timely bids, it also helps get you closer to where you want to be throughout the process in smaller increments rather than waiting until all bids are returned and then coming up with a strategy to get a list of improvements, both quantitative and qualitative, from a choice supplier.

Taking Advantage of the Benefits after Implementation

You cannot take full advantage of the benefits of a newly negotiated agreement until it has been completely implemented. If there is a change of supplier, implementation is almost always more work than a simple renegotiation with the incumbent. Regardless, new pricing needs to be implemented on the supplier side but needs to be validated for compliance with the new agreement on the buyer side. Adoption of new processes may also be required. Having secured your stakeholders' involvement all along helps to ease this transition as they should, at a minimum, be aware of where the process began, what has happened intermediately, and how things ended up the way they are now.

If you do not take the time to involve end users and operations personnel in the whole process, implementing a new program or supplier and then suddenly dropping the heavy lifting into those end users' laps leaves them more or less paralyzed. It also opens the door to animosity over changes that will make a negative impact (even if it is only a perceived one), as those now responsible for managing the change may feel overwhelmed by it and often believe they could have done better if they were more involved. These types of issues will be completely avoided by simply keeping stakeholders involved throughout the process. They will have had their input considered, and if contributions were not adopted, they will at least understand why. They will see how the pricing translates between suppliers, or how and why process changes may be necessary. In addition, they will be familiar with these concepts before the implementation phase begins and can prepare accordingly. Having the support of the people who actually need to deal with the category and suppliers on a day-to-day basis is absolutely critical to reaping the savings you worked so hard to negotiate. Engaging stakeholders throughout the process has multifaceted and ongoing benefits that ultimately help smooth the path to realized savings.

 IN SUMMARY

Whether approaching a contract renewal with an incumbent supplier or going to market to find new suppliers, stakeholders are an indispensable tool throughout the process. Identification of all stakeholders, no matter how slight their involvement in the category may be, is pivotal to maximizing results and minimizing the timeline to realized savings. All interested stakeholders have valuable input, feedback, and knowledge of the category and current supplier relationships that may or may not be documented and, in many cases, those stakeholders are not even known to the management teams. They can help you build a history, understand more precisely how to approach the market, and ensure your RFP yields best-fit solutions for your organization.

Including every stakeholder possible throughout the entire process helps to mitigate any risk of them working to cause the supply chain to fail in the future. It can help to ensure that there are no surprises for those responsible for implementing any changes that may have come about during the RFP and negotiations. Stakeholders will also feel that they have played a positive role in producing a successful result for themselves and the company, and will therefore have an easier time and be more driven to get the new agreement and pricing implemented.

PART THREE

Examples from the Field

CHAPTER THIRTEEN

Supplier Collaboration

THROUGHOUT THIS BOOK we have discussed the importance of having open specifications, requirements, and dialog with your potential supply base. The goal of this openness is to produce a collaborative environment within your supply chain. In most cases, this process begins with the initial contact with your potential suppliers, and includes an open, personal dialog with those suppliers' sales representatives.

We cannot emphasize enough the importance of making a phone call or even a face-to-face visit instead of merely sending an e-mail requesting information. E-mail communications alone are only likely to produce the same sort of effort from the potential supplier as you put into contacting them. Suppliers will not be invested in the initiative or the relationship and will do the bare minimum required, if they do anything at all, to address your e-mail.

Your goal in a sourcing effort is to get the supplier as personally invested as possible in the process. This includes, when feasible, getting the supplier to commit resources beyond just the sales force to your project in order to produce creative or collaborative solutions for your particular need. These resources could include management, technical teams, and research and development teams. Typically, the more individuals who are involved on the supplier side, the more solutions and concessions you can ask for, as they will not want to lose the opportunity after they have committed their own resources to such an extent.

This chapter illustrates a few examples of how supplier collaboration produces superior results for certain projects. Additionally, we cover some examples of projects that originally seemed to be straightforward strategic sourcing projects but, through collaboration, produced far superior results and savings than ever could have been imagined before.

 ## OPENING UP YOUR REQUIREMENTS

As we already mentioned, your project's success is critically dependent on your ability to communicate your needs to your potential supply base. Equally important is your ability to be flexible about the solutions that are offered by the suppliers.

As we have already discussed, when you develop your sourcing strategy, whether it is a reverse auction, request for proposal (RFP), or informal negotiation, make sure you open up your requirements to allow suppliers to introduce their own cost-effective solutions for your needs. In other words, do not restrict your requirements so severely that suppliers can only propose one solution— the one presented in your document. Open up the dialog with your suppliers, explain what you are looking to accomplish, ask them how they can help you get there, and pay attention to the responses.

Discover a Better Solution

Let us look at an example involving computer servers. Assume that your information technology (IT) department put together a specification for three midrange servers, complete with uninterruptible power supplies and backup hardware. Now, most IT or procurement professionals would simply take those specifications out to the leading computer manufacturers and ask them to place a bid. Or they may take their task a bit further and ask suppliers to participate in a reverse auction. While both of these tactics can help to lower the price from the expected budgeted price, they are likely not the most cost-effective solution for your business.

Conversely, if you open your requirement up and approach your suppliers with the need you are attempting to fulfill instead of a specification for hardware, you could likely get very different solutions offered by the vendor. For instance, a supplier may recommend that instead of three midrange servers, your organization should purchase one high-end server, running virtualization technologies such as VirtualMachine (VM). VM systems can run multiple environments and/or operating systems simultaneously on the same server hardware. This allows you to buy less equipment, including all of the ancillary devices, such as DVD drives, tape drives, power supplies, and surge protectors. Employing technologies such as these not only lowers your one-time costs, but can lower your ongoing costs as well, through the reduction in monthly electricity costs and easier management requirements for the systems' administrators.

However, if you had merely approached suppliers and told them to bid an exact specification, it is unlikely that they would have ever made major product suggestions that could benefit your company. To achieve even greater cost reductions, take your suppliers' recommendations and go back out to market with their competitors for an even better solution.

Find Acceptable Substitutes

Opening up your requirements does not need to be as complex as the previous example, in which the decision makers must have a complex understanding of technology. In fact, it may be as simple as letting your suppliers know that you are open to alternate solutions, or product substitutions, beyond what you have requested in the RFx process.

For example, when sourcing printer toner, rather than specifying exact model numbers of Hewlett-Packard-brand toner, let the suppliers know that you are looking for a solution to provide toner and list the printer models that you have in your company. Suppliers will likely come back with alternatives to the original equipment manufacturer (OEM) toner, such as generic or remanufactured product, that can lead to savings north of 50 percent.

Don't stop at price though; tell the supplier of any concerns that you may have with their alternate solution—don't just disqualify it. In this toner example, you can work with the supplier to ensure you are satisfied with the product, quality control process, and product return policy, so you have no fear of switching product lines. Additionally, you can ask for testing periods (at no cost) as well as contract language that will allow you to get out of the contract if there is unsatisfactory supplier or product performance.

These examples show how your company can benefit greatly by offering suppliers the opportunity to propose an innovative solution to your problem or need, rather than dictating a solution to them.

GIVING SUPPLIERS WHAT THEY NEED

The easiest way to build supplier collaboration is to give suppliers everything they need to help you reach your goals. This includes being up front and honest about the price points and levels of service that you are expecting for a particular product or service.

The information and market intelligence gathered during the research portion of your sourcing engagement is not just useful for leveraging pricing from your supplier, but can also be used to help steer the supplier in your desired direction. If you provide factual evidence of declining prices, or a solid argument as to why you should become a preferred customer, you are likely to drive successful results in your project.

Use Market Intelligence

Telecommunications spend is a ripe area for all companies to open up requirements and explore alternative solutions. The Telecommunications Act of 1934 specifies that pricing agreements and contracts need to be published by telecommunications carriers, and that the carriers cannot be discriminatory with their pricing. This means that telecommunications carriers must file a tariff any time they develop specialized pricing for a client.

If your company has identical or similar geography and infrastructure as that which is already defined in an existing tariff, then you can request to receive the same pricing agreement as that tariff specifies. The problem is, most telecommunications sales representatives do not have the time or resources to research the tariff filing on your behalf. You can help sales representatives and yourself by presenting them the tariff filing that matches your organization's situation and demanding the same pricing structure. Often, sales reps do not have the authority or the ability to create attractive customized pricing plans for their customers. However, by simply steering them in the direction of a filed tariff, they can use that document in their internal battles to get you a more attractive pricing offer.

Involve Technical Teams

Another way to work collaboratively with telecommunications providers is to get their engineering teams working directly with your own technical resources. Having a procurement person develop a deal directly with a telecom salesperson is probably the leading cause of high prices in telecommunications. Work collaboratively with your IT department and the carrier engineers to develop a solution that may not only be more cost effective, but often offers higher levels of service. Unfortunately, the sales teams within telecom carriers often don't even know all of their products and services and, more often than not, do not even understand the solutions. They could be trying their hardest to give you better pricing, but they can only work within the confines of tariffs and the existing infrastructure. Working directly with their engineering teams, you may be able to investigate new products and technologies that serve the same purpose but are substantially less expensive. Ironically, in many cases, the sales representatives are happy to offer these solutions (once they become aware of them), even at a lower total cost, because their commission plans may actually incentivize them to drive customers to new products and services.

In both of the foregoing cases, you provide the supplier with your end goal, which is always lower cost and a higher level of service, rather than detailed specifications. By assisting the sales team at the telecommunications carrier, you are effectively enabling lower prices for your organization, while more than likely increasing service levels at the same time.

 ## HELPING SUPPLIERS WITH THEIR SUPPLY CHAIN

Throughout most of this book, we focus heavily on data collection, analysis, and working directly with your suppliers. However, one step that is commonly overlooked while sourcing indirect spend categories is to look further down the supply chain, to your suppliers' suppliers, and even to *their* suppliers. In these scenarios you work closely with your first-tier suppliers and assist them in reviewing their supply chains to see if there are opportunities for cost reduction with their suppliers, which will then, in turn, translate into savings in the product you purchase for them.

Improve Supply Chain Efficiencies

A few years ago the authors of this book were engaged to assist in a strategic sourcing and cost-reduction initiative to supply gas containers to a national chemical manufacturer that was under severe pressure to reduce the costs of its indirect and direct materials, but was already receiving best-in-class pricing from its supply base. The organization asked us for help in finding creative ways to reduce the price, since traditional sourcing methods were not producing any savings opportunities.

The first step of this project was to break down the components of the finished product that our customer was ultimately selling. In this case, the end product merely consisted of a gas or chemical, the container it was sold in, and freight costs (receiving and shipping to distribution points). However, diving deeper, we learned that the container itself consisted of two parts: the vessel and a valve cap that sealed the contents in the container.

Upon further investigation, we learned that the chemical manufacturer was in fact purchasing containers with the valve preinstalled, but was also buying valves independently from another vendor. We learned that federal regulations had changed, and all existing containers were required to have their valves swapped with a new type of valve that had improved safety features. Our customer was selling new containers with the proper valve, but also had a separate profitable division that was responsible for replacing the valves on the millions of containers that were already in the marketplace.

Immediately, we identified an opportunity for price improvement, because the product lines all had similar quantities of component materials associated with them. We knew if we could go to market with the entire valve spend, it held the potential of being much more attractive to suppliers than two separate spends of half the size, as was the current case. However, as the matter currently stood, we also knew that we were not going to generate substantial savings, and we needed a way to identify further opportunity. The solution lay in aggregating the valve spend and getting the container supplier out of the business of manufacturing containers with valves attached.

Before we went out to market with the entire spend of valves, we held internal discussions about how the container manufacturer would handle us telling them that they would be losing the valve components of the business, and we also needed to conduct internal studies to determine the cost impact on our client's staff of having to assemble in-house the container and its valve. We decided the best course of action was to be forthcoming with our supplier and see what suggestions it might have.

Our team was careful in their approach in dealing with the supplier, due to internal concerns that the supplier might be upset that they were losing a piece of business. However, to our surprise, the supplier was extremely happy to meet with us and, in fact, had discovered the same pain point: the valves. The supplier was the leading manufacturer of chemical containers in North America, and was running into similar issues in that the valves supplied with the containers were almost as expensive as the containers themselves. The supplier meeting led to a brainstorming meeting with procurement teams from that organization and the chemical manufacturer. Ultimately it was decided that we could use the combined spends from both organizations to leverage the valve-supply base. With the aggregate spend of both organizations, the volume was four times what any individual segment had previously purchased on their own.

After helping the supplier conduct a global sourcing initiative for the new valve spend, savings of 39 percent were ultimately achieved. However, we now had a new issue: the second-tier supplier did not want to receive multiple orders from different companies and purchasing managers, nor did they want to ship to multiple facilities in North America. Our supplier and our client got together again, and turned this problem into an opportunity. There was, in fact, a freight saving opportunity for shipping all of the valves in full containers to our existing supplier, rather than partial containers to our client and the supplier. Additionally, we learned that the supplier had excess manufacturing and staffing capacity and could act as the intermediary for placing orders for valves for a low margin.

As an end result, our client is now purchasing valves directly from the container manufacturer, at a reduced price, and is receiving the benefits of the lower-priced valves on the assembled containers that it purchases. The container manufacturer not only reduced their costs, but increased their profit margin with other customers who did not receive the benefits of the lower valve pricing.

COLLABORATING WITH SUPPLIERS IN SIMILAR INDUSTRIES

As we discuss in several sections of this book, adding a bit of creativity and some out-of-the-box thinking to the sourcing process can often produce big results. One way to accomplish this is to explore suppliers in similar industries to the one that delivers the product or service you are looking to purchase, and see whether they have any suggestions or ideas on how to reduce your costs and improve your supply chain.

Change the Process to Improve Efficiencies

We encountered a unique project a couple of years back in which a client asked us to help reduce the costs of methanol, a high-purity solvent. The client had already attempted to find a lower-cost supplier, but was unable to identify any suppliers whatsoever beyond the two suppliers it was already using.

The solvent the company purchased was used in a final product line and was purchased in bulk, direct from manufacturers, and repackaged into smaller quantities for sale to other businesses. The solvent had several strict chemical property and quality requirements, with the most critical being that it had to be 99.9 percent pure.

As it turned out, the customer had done a very good job identifying the qualified suppliers in the marketplace, and there were in fact only two suppliers that could provide the chemical, both of which they were currently using. We decided to branch out to similar manufacturers and distributors and explore whether they could offer a solution.

We were able to identify another manufacturer that sold the solvent; however, they only produced it at a 75 percent purity level and had no interest in investing in new manufacturing capability to produce the 99 percent requirement. So, our team then reached out to that manufacturer's distributors to see whether they knew of any additional sources of supply.

While the distributors were unable to find a new source of supply, we identified one supplier with a potential solution. It assigned an entire internal team to our request and immediately asked for a meeting with our client's engineers and procurement team to discuss the need. The distributor's representatives expressed that they were very interested in winning the new business, and came up with a solution that worked for everyone. Their engineers, working with a team from the customer, reverse-engineered the process of filtering in order to create the solvent that had the purity levels our client required, and determined that the infrastructure and equipment requirements needed to create the purity level were not all that unique.

Ultimately, the supplier, anxious to get into a new market, invested in the equipment required to purify the 75 percent solution from the one supplier to the 99.9 percent level that our customer required. Our customer now had a third source of supply and more importantly, now had a substantially lower price for the product. The distributor was also extremely happy, because it now had an entirely new product line and already had sustainable orders to support the investment of the equipment required to make the product.

 IN SUMMARY

As this chapter has demonstrated, collaborating with your suppliers can produce surprising and profitable results. Often, supply-chain collaboration is an overlooked component of the sourcing process when it comes to indirect materials and services. Procurement teams, IT managers, and manufacturing workers tend to think of all indirect spend categories as commodities and often overlook the importance of the supplier's knowledge about the product or a particular industry. Collaboration is normally done only once a supplier has been awarded the business.

Collaborating with your entire supply chain (including your suppliers' suppliers) can often produce sustainable results that equate to large cost savings opportunities. Just as important, it encourages partnerships with your suppliers, which may lead to your company being the first in line for new product developments or other supplier benefits.

CHAPTER FOURTEEN

Leveraging Supplier Feedback

NUMEROUS FACTORS PLAY A PART in executing a successful sourcing event and ultimately reducing costs. As we discussed in previous chapters, many of the components focus specifically on equipping yourself with market data and a good team in order to effectively negotiate lower costs with suppliers. However, as we have discussed, becoming the perfect customer is another atypical method of optimizing cost savings. By understanding what the supplier's wants and needs are, and demonstrating you can meet those requirements, you can often motivate the supplier to provide pricing or enhanced services that might not otherwise be available.

In this chapter we illustrate several examples of projects in which we were able to leverage supplier feedback to build a business case for why we were the perfect customer. In doing so, we were able to convince the suppliers that they did not just want our business, but in fact needed it.

AVOIDING THE RFP PROCESS

As we have previously discussed, avoiding the RFP process altogether is one technique for becoming the perfect customer, because it actually has the ability to build confidence in your suppliers, as they believe you are working in a collaborative environment and that you represent a serious opportunity.

Recently many suppliers, particularly in the services industry, have been walking away from many RFPs and potential new business opportunities if they conclude that they do not have a good chance of winning the business. A weak economy compounds this issue, with companies scaling back and working to get more done with fewer resources. Sales teams have become selective in reviewing which business opportunities look real and which are long shots, and allocate resources appropriately. In the past, RFP issuers disqualifying suppliers due to a late bid (or no bid) was a common practice, but these days you could be severely limiting your competitive landscape with that approach.

So what is a strategic sourcing professional to do when suppliers still need to be evaluated and qualified, but are unwilling to commit to a formal written response? We have found a successful sourcing strategy has been to look for opportunities to shift away from formal RFPs and utilize supplier presentations as the initial qualifier during the sourcing process.

Supplier presentations have traditionally been reserved for the later stages of the sourcing process (with some exceptions), after the list of potential providers has been narrowed from 10 or more down to 2 or 3. This saves time and effort on the buyer's side, and allows the sourcing staff to bring in a cross-functional team and any interested end users to survey the sourcing landscape, but only from a select group of suppliers that best meet the customer's requirements.

Moving supplier presentations to the front end can be a great deal more time consuming, because each supplier needs one to two hours of your time up front. You can limit the time investment, though, by mapping out exactly what your requirements for the new supplier are in advance of any meetings. Once you do that, you may find that out of the 15 potential suppliers, only 3 or 4 are really a good fit for your organization.

Allowing suppliers to give a presentation rather than provide a written response can make impartial qualitative comparisons a difficult process, but there are easy ways to force a format. Start by giving suppliers a list of key concerns, and make sure they are going to cover each of them during their presentations. Before the presentations, show them your scorecard system and make sure they understand the importance of each category of the scorecard.

Having been on both sides of the table during a prequalifying presentation process, we have seen it used effectively. On the sales side, during one of these presentations our team spent five hours in a meeting room with a potential customer, including multiple end users and other decision makers. While it became clear early on that we were not the best fit for what this customer needed, it was still preferable to spending a few days (and nights) constructing a written response to an RFP document and expecting the same result. In addition, we had the chance to meet face-to-face with a large group of purchasing professionals, which was a great networking experience. The likelihood is that if there is a better fit down the road, they will remember us more clearly from that meeting than from a written response.

On the sourcing side, we have found the process actually cuts timelines dramatically. Allowing suppliers to utilize their standard format (or sales pitch) and add to it based on your company's primary concerns means they do not have to reinvent the wheel, just customize it a bit. A huge benefit in this tactic is that you can typically set up a supplier presentation within a week rather than waiting two to four weeks for a written response to come back. Plus, suppliers are much less likely to ask for a time extension if they have already confirmed a face-to-face meeting.

Overall, we recommend bypassing the initial proposal process for presentations whenever possible. Suppliers are often much more motivated and engaged when taking this approach, and it becomes clear very early on whether the suppliers actually listened to your concerns or just gave them lip service. In some cases a written response may still be required, and a formal quote will definitely be needed, but as a prequalifier, the process works well.

MAKING YOURSELF THE IDEAL CUSTOMER

Procurement professionals and business managers spend a lot of time making sure that the vendors in their supply chain are the perfect supplier. You can define your ideal supplier in many different ways, but most are looking for low-cost yet high-quality products or services, innovative and leading-edge technologies, combined with a collaborative environment in which the supplier is actively looking for ways to help you to decrease your operating costs, increase your revenues, or both.

Conversely, leading suppliers are doing the same thing by focusing on finding the perfect customers. Suppliers have a similar list of attributes that they consider important. These attributes could be creditworthiness, ability to pay quickly, name recognition of your organization (and permission to use it in marketing), geographical advantages, product volumes, favorable ordering methods, inspection methods, timing of the award, and your likelihood to use the supplier exclusively.

So, how do you determine what is important to a specific market or supplier? It may sound obvious, but the simplest way is to ask them. At the start of the process, just as you review your requirements with your salesperson, ask him or her what the company looks for in a customer. You will be surprised at just how many suppliers will openly discuss with you what is important to their businesses or to the sales reps personally. Once you determine what is important to suppliers and their sales teams, use that information to leverage the supplier by turning yourself into the ideal customer for that company.

For example, if the supplier is interested in faster payment terms, work with your accounting team to see if immediate or shorter payment terms are possible. If you can accomplish that, you may be able to ask for more aggressive pricing from the supplier. If your organization has a respectable or well-recognized name, get your own public relations and marketing departments involved to see if you can do joint marketing or branding that could benefit both parties. This again can translate into lower prices from your supplier.

Further, the salesperson may have different needs and wants than the organizations he or she represents. Ask your salesperson about these as well. It is likely that the person is on a quota or commission schedule that offers quarterly or end-of-year bonuses. If you time it right and can get a deal done in order for the rep to hit a bonus, the rep may be willing to drop margins substantially. On a spot-buy basis, we have even seen salespeople sell products at a loss or on zero margin just to earn commission bonuses on their cumulative targeted sales figures.

Throughout this book we encourage an open dialog with your supply base, and heavily discourage the use of long, drawn-out standardized documents and processes that do nothing but create busy work for suppliers. Your dialog should not be one-sided; it is not just all about what you need. It is important to also consider what the supplier wants.

 ## EXAMPLES OF LEVERAGING SUPPLIER FEEDBACK SUCCESSFULLY

Following are some real-world examples of sourcing projects that have leveraged supplier feedback, with details about how that feedback led to better pricing for each organization.

Improving Solutions by Asking Questions

When sourcing telecommunications, specifically on multilocation or complex networks, it is extremely important to solicit the supply base for feedback on how various suppliers would address your network issues and what innovative solutions can solve your problems or accomplish your goals. In most scenarios, the procurement or information technology (IT) department puts an RFP out that simply lists the company's current infrastructure (copper lines, T1 circuits, frame relay, and so on) and asks suppliers to quote their pricing. However, what should be taking place is much different. The RFP should speak to the needs of the organization, such as bandwidth requirement and features on the voice package. After describing the current and future state, the RFP should ask suppliers to quote the accommodation of current requirements as well as provide alternative solutions that would improve the current state and lower prices at the same time.

We recently conducted a telecommunications strategic sourcing project for a building supply company with over 200 locations in the United States. When we were first engaged, the customer had already conducted an RFP, basically asking suppliers to provide a new quote for its existing infrastructure, and the lowest-priced supplier (an alternate to their existing supplier) came back with a best offer, which would produce 8 percent annual savings.

Our first step was to cancel the formal RFP and open up a dialog directly with the suppliers. Initially, our conversation started with the supplier that bid the lowest during the RFP. We simply outlined the existing infrastructure and what we were seeking to accomplish (adding bandwidth while lowering prices). We then asked the supplier how to best meet those goals. The account manager at the telecom provider quickly came back with one of the engineers and described a new type of network that accomplished all of our goals at a much lower price. The supplier explained to us that the new network was currently the type that the carrier preferred to deploy and that the supplier could offer much more aggressive discounts than merely upgrading the current configuration.

Using this information, we were able to approach the incumbent supplier and ask for a similar solution. That company came back with a quote for a similar type of infrastructure that was 35 percent less expensive than existing prices, and provided a higher level of service. If our customer had never asked the supplier for help, it never would have learned about or implemented the new service.

Finding Real Motivations

We were recently engaged to help identify the lowest price of a specific software package that is only sold through resellers. However, our client had already done its due diligence and had received very aggressive pricing from its preferred technology vendor. Our client needed the software in the next 45 days, but was unwilling to make the purchase until the next fiscal quarter (which started in 15 days).

Initial conversations with the supplier showed that there was no way it could lower prices beyond current pricing because the product was currently being offered at cost, as a good faith measure toward the customer. A quick look into the market showed that no other reseller was able to come remotely close to the price the incumbent was offering.

In this case, our hands were a bit tied, yet we were still under pressure to produce some savings results or value-add for our customer. We reached out to the supplier and explained the exact situation and asked them what could be done. The supplier was adamant that the software was at the lowest margin they could offer but also expressed a slight concern that the order for the software would not be placed in the current fiscal quarter. Opening up the dialog a bit and asking what the real concern was yielded the fact that the salesperson was actually very close to hitting a bonus target for the quarter, based on volume of sales across all of his product lines.

We were able to leverage this information. By waiting until the last couple days of the fiscal quarter and reaching back out to the supplier, we learned that the salesman was still just a little short of his bonus target. We were then able to come to an agreement that benefited both parties. The salesman agreed to sell us the product at cost, with no markup whatsoever, as well as extend payment terms of 30 days for our client. Ultimately, our customer saved an additional 5 percent off of an already low price and did not have to pay for the software until the date they actually needed it, and the supplier's sales representative was happy that he made his quarterly bonus target, even though he lost any commission of sale on the individual software license.

Discovering Soft-Cost Benefits Through Open Dialog

Strategic sourcing is not always about getting a lower price; sometimes it is about building solid and stable relationships with your supply chain. We experienced this in a project in which we were able to leverage supplier feedback, leading to some soft-cost and value-added benefits rather than straight-up cost savings.

We were engaged to help an organization with the purchase of new computer hardware for the entire enterprise. However, as in many cases, our customer was actually very experienced in strategic sourcing for this particular category. The discussions quickly shifted from price only to more open dialogs that involved meetings with engineering teams at the supplier and the information technology department at our customer.

Our customer was doing very high-end graphical work and required powerful desktop workstations, servers, and specialized accessories. The sourcing process quickly identified that there really was only one supplier that the company should be dealing with, yet we were still searching for a way to sweeten the deal. We were already having very positive conversations directly with the supplier's engineers, yet we still needed more motivation for our customer to pull the trigger on a multimillion-dollar systems upgrade.

So the simple thing to do, and the thing that was initially overlooked, was to ask the supplier what it wanted out of the relationship. The supplier quickly responded that even more important than the actual dollar amount of the sale was gaining the ability to include our customer (who is a respected brand name) in the client portfolio. However, there was one small glitch, in that our customer had a clause in all of its supplier agreements and contracts that specifically forbade the use of the company's logo by suppliers without express written permission.

To find a way around this impasse, we started a conversation with the marketing departments of both the supplier and the customer. In the end both companies agreed that they were very compatible in both a business and a cultural sense. In the meetings the supplier expressed an extreme desire to use the customer's logo and name in their own marketing materials. The customer agreed because the supplier indicated that it was willing to spend millions of dollars developing television commercials that jointly marketed both companies' solutions.

In this case we were able to leverage everything we learned to create a win/win final result. The customer spent the same amount it would have if the conversations had not taken place, but now reaped the additional benefit of millions of dollars' worth of free advertising coming through joint marketing efforts with the supplier.

Finding Leverage Points by Expanding the Scope of Sourcing

In a recent sourcing engagement, we were assisting a national company with over 500 locations to identify a new source of supply for their laser printer toner cartridges. The process itself was rather lengthy, as it included a change-management component that involved explaining to the existing user base the benefits of moving to non-OEM equipment and overcoming their concerns and perceived fears. The project also included an extensive testing period.

The list of qualified suppliers was narrowed down to two, both of which had passed quality testing and had quality assurance programs in place that our customer was comfortable with. However, pricing offered by both suppliers was nearly identical, so a clear winner could not be selected.

We reached back out to both potential suppliers to explain the situation and were open about how each was equal in our ranking process. Unfortunately, both suppliers explained that they were at the maximum discount that they could offer and had nothing more to offer from a service level perspective. However, one supplier seemed particularly more concerned that their organization may not win the business.

We decided to leverage that concern to see if there was anything else the company could do. Our tactic was simply to wait and make no decision. As the supplier followed up over the next few weeks, we replied that we had not made a decision but may be leaning in the favor of the other supplier, which happened to be the incumbent.

In the end, we achieved a breakthrough. Our potential supplier had been holding internal discussions for the entire period of time and asked for a face-to-face meeting. Once the meeting took place, the company was not able to offer lower pricing on the toner, but actually came back with discounts on existing contracts that we had in place, such as mail room supplies and postage ink.

By maintaining an open dialog with our potential suppliers and leveraging their fear of losing the new business, we were able to successfully achieve savings in categories outside of the current scope.

 IN SUMMARY

Leveraging supplier feedback can take many forms. In essence, it boils down to having open and honest communications with your suppliers and soliciting them to invest resources beyond the typically assigned account managers or sales representatives.

By leveraging the information that your supply chain provides, you can actually achieve deeper discounts in the products or services you are buying, and improve the overall relationship and integration with each of your suppliers.

CHAPTER FIFTEEN

Data Analysis

Transforming Data into Information

WHILE DATA IS SOMETIMES VALUABLE ON ITS OWN, its true worth is derived when it becomes meaningful and useful information. The path from data to information is not always apparent nor is it necessarily easy to navigate. By way of a few examples and explanations, this chapter provides some insight into how the value of data can be uncovered. Specifically, we discuss examples of using data analysis to discover pricing trends, target and optimize cost savings opportunities, and drive contract compliance.

After you complete the data collection phase of your initiative, the analysis of that data starts with cleansing the data set, which involves identifying corrupt, invalid, inaccurate, inconsistent, missing, or duplicate data and taking an action according to predefined rules. The action taken differs on a case-by-case basis. For example, duplicates may be deleted and corrupt data may be corrected or tagged.

While cleansing data, it is important to look for variations that a simple matchup in Microsoft Excel might not catch. For instance, a common mistake that many organizations make when entering purchase orders is creating an item that is already in the system, which leads to duplicate data. Although items have identical or similar descriptions in the system, they have unique part numbers. Therefore a sort-and-compare task in Excel is not going to reveal them as duplicate items. This illustrates the importance of human eyes reviewing the data, even if the work must be outsourced.

Ultimately, data should be as clean, complete, and reliable as possible after being cleansed, which means the rules by which anomalies are addressed need to be carefully considered and implemented. Before beginning data cleansing, it is critical to create a backup data set of the original data or a proper method to retrace your steps back to the original data; these steps are lifesavers if the results of cleansing end up being questionable or the scope of the analysis shifts.

Once source data is clean, it can be bolstered with additional entries, such as category data and unique identifiers. With any relevant additional fields added, the data is ready to be manipulated and analyzed into meaningful information. The derivatives of such an exercise are infinite, hinging on the data itself and the purpose and scope of the analysis.

EXAMPLES OF OPTIMIZING DATA SETS TO FIND TRENDS

A critical component of data analysis is the ability to optimize the data sets and determine trending and patterns that may be useful in your strategic sourcing process. Optimized data provides insights that allow you to negotiate with your suppliers from a stronger position, and can also help build the specifications for the target products or services.

Optimizing your data set is critical to supporting the conclusions you draw in your subsequent sourcing initiatives. An optimized data set can actually change the course of your sourcing process, and will help to drive the best savings opportunities available. A few examples will illustrate the importance and value of data optimization.

Optimizing for Average and Peak Requirements

An important decision that all telecommunications managers face is determining how many phone lines are needed to serve all users and conditions in an organization. For example, a business with 50 users may need to be able to make 10 to 50 concurrent calls, depending on the activities in which the end users are actually engaged. In a call center, for example, the number of simultaneous calls will be much higher than in a regular office with intermittent inbound and outbound phone usage throughout the day. While there are ways to estimate the number of call paths required to serve all users based on the types of users they are and how many outbound and inbound toll minutes are on the invoice, it is difficult to be sure without properly analyzing the data.

Some modern telecom equipment, such as a private branch exchange, or PBX, has reporting mechanisms that actually provide good recommendations for how many call paths are required to serve users. Unfortunately, in many cases, that is about the extent of the information you can get. The reports do not show trends or actual usage statistics, which would provide a context for what those numbers actually mean to you. There are in fact some systems with robust reporting tools that can report such details; however, many organizations do not opt for those features when purchasing their PBX equipment since they did not foresee at the time a significant enough return on the investment nor a need for such tools on a day-to-day basis. When the reporting tools are not available, there are ways to draw the same conclusions on your own.

You can usually get call detail in electronic format for all outbound and toll-inbound calling directly from your telephone service provider's online Web portals. Getting local usage can be somewhat more difficult and may require a special request to your provider. However, other types of inbound calling are more difficult to find as they are not reflected on the invoices for your account. To get this information, you can ask your provider to run a traffic study on the lines or circuits to determine their usage. Typically a month's worth of usage is an ample amount to determine any trending and high- and low-usage periods. However, it is important to keep seasonal usage in mind, especially if your business is prone to such trends.

Once you have all of the data for both inbound and outbound calls, compile it into a spreadsheet. Using Microsoft Excel, you can tally simultaneous calls for each minute of each day. See Figure 15.1 for a sample of data.

You can then run reports or create graphs from that data. This will allow you to see the peaks (usually around lunch hour) and troughs (the middle of the night and weekends) in your usage. See Figure 15.2.

You may be surprised to find that usage only spills over to a secondary telephone line by a few call paths once a month. While the report you ran on the PBX may indicate that you need a certain number of call paths, you did not have the context to see that perhaps you only needed that number for a few minutes each month, and therefore can probably replace an expensive multiline circuit with one or two traditional stand-alone lines for the rare and brief overloads. By building a simple table, you can make an informed decision about the number of lines required, and save hundreds or thousands of dollars per month in the process by eliminating excess lines.

	B	C	D	E	F
1	Date/Time	5/10/2010	5/11/2010	5/12/2010	5/13/2
2	0:01	0	3	1	0
3	0:02	0	4	1	1
4	0:03	1	4	1	2
5	0:04	2	4	1	3
6	0:05	2	4	1	3
7	0:06	2	4	1	3
8	0:07	2	2	1	3
9	0:08	1	3	3	7
10	0:09	1	2	2	8
11	0:10	1	2	2	8
12	0:11	1	3	2	8
13	0:12	1	2	2	8
14	0:13	1	3	0	6
15	0:14	1	3	1	4
16	0:15	3	3	1	3
17	0:16	5	3	5	4
18	0:17	5	2	5	3
19	0:18	5	3	4	3

FIGURE 15.1   PBX Inbound and Outbound Data

Developing Appropriate Spend Categorization

Maintenance, repair, and operations (MRO) purchases present another prime example of cases in which data optimization can reveal greater cost-savings opportunities. Typically, MRO spend categories consist of hundreds, if not tens of thousands, of unique parts that a manufacturing business uses. These items can range from air filters for forklifts to three-inch lag bolts used in packaging products. So, before taking your MRO spend to market, you need to optimize the data to enable you to build appropriate market baskets and to target appropriate suppliers.

For example, when sourcing MRO, most organizations simply throw together a spreadsheet of the prior year's purchases (without the unit prices) and send it to several undifferentiated suppliers. They ask the suppliers to bid on each line item and tally up the responses. However, what they do not factor in is that each supplier is typically going to have a particular category in which its pricing is particularly strong and others in which its pricing is simply not competitive.

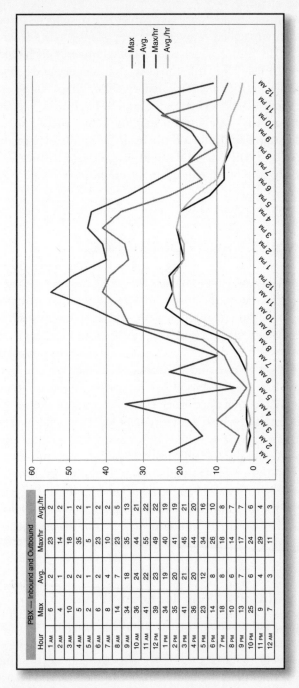

Hour	PBX — Inbound and Outbound			
	Max	Avg.	Max/hr	Avg./hr
1 AM	6	2	23	2
2 AM	4	1	14	2
3 AM	10	2	18	1
4 AM	5	2	35	2
5 AM	2	1	5	1
6 AM	6	2	23	2
7 AM	8	4	10	2
8 AM	14	7	23	5
9 AM	34	18	35	13
10 AM	36	24	44	21
11 AM	41	22	55	22
12 PM	39	23	49	22
1 PM	34	19	40	19
2 PM	35	20	41	19
3 PM	41	21	45	21
4 PM	36	20	44	20
5 PM	23	12	34	16
6 PM	14	8	26	10
7 PM	18	8	18	8
8 PM	10	6	14	7
9 PM	13	7	17	7
10 PM	25	6	24	6
11 PM	9	4	29	4
12 PM	7	3	11	3

FIGURE 15.2 PBX Inbound and Outbound Data Graph

By using your data to appropriately categorize your spend before the bid, you have the ability to solicit suppliers for only a portion of the entire spend category, and can determine which is most competitive for each type of spend. For example, nuts and bolts go into the fasteners category and belts and bearings fall into the power transmission category. Other typical categories include plumbing, electrical, HVAC, safety, paint, and so on. Even if you continue to solicit bids from potential suppliers on every line item, you now have a method for sorting and optimizing the data returned to determine whether some suppliers are more competitive in individual categories. The ultimate savings solution will likely be a blend of implementing multiple suppliers instead of a single one.

 ## DATA ANALYSIS AND COMPLIANCE

The proper knowledge and data analysis tools help buyers evaluate the effectiveness of new agreements and ensure that suppliers implement proper rates and prices. The spend data required to achieve both of these aims is more than likely accessible from your purchase order system. In most cases, taking the necessary steps to cleanse the data prepares it for effective comparison to the structured list of items, rates, and discounts established in your agreement.

The objective here is to establish two data sets (or sometimes more, depending on how adoption compliance is determined) to enable the development of comparison heuristics by which the data can be placed in separate buckets: one (or more) that tracks compliance, and one (or more) that identifies instances of noncompliance. Again, the buckets in which the data ends up may vary, but it is advisable to maintain all data points rather than drop irrelevant or out-of-scope data. This way you can review each bucket once the analysis is complete and verify that all the original data has been properly addressed, allocated, and maintained. In other words, maintain the integrity of the original data set; do not remove columns, records, or any other data that on the surface appears to be useless.

Identifying and Controlling Noncompliance

Let's say you are a manufacturer with multiple locations across the country. You develop several national agreements for maintenance parts used to repair machinery and want to make sure all the sites buy under these agreements rather than using their preferred individual local vendors. You inform the sites of the agreements and get accounts set up, but typical track records for complying with new purchasing arrangements are rarely perfect the first month, and many sites may choose to keep buying in the old way until they are corrected by management. In order to encourage and enforce compliance, it is incumbent upon you to identify cases in which parts are being purchased from the incorrect supplier and to remind the facilities or people doing that purchasing that they have unnecessarily cost the company money by not purchasing under the correct agreement.

In order to accomplish this, spending needs to be monitored and filtered by a rule set that can identify which facilities buy under which contracts. This may vary by facility and contract, so the problem may be more complex than it first appears. However, identifying and applying the metrics by which data can be pulled into its correct compliant or noncompliant bucket allows easy compliance monitoring going forward, so it is worth the time and effort to develop it. See Table 15.1.

Many benefits, both direct and indirect, derive from this exercise. It is perhaps the easiest analysis to link directly to hard-dollar savings. Additionally, the reporting mechanisms developed to identify compliance can also be used to calculate and report savings. And last, but certainly not least, the results of the analysis can also be used to identify and address operational inefficiencies, streamlining the overall process.

 ## DATA ANALYSIS AND TARGETING SPEND

For situations in which cost reduction is imperative, identifying target spend categories and the people making purchases may not be as straightforward as you would hope. Spending may not be uniformly or intuitively categorized and it may be decentralized. By taking a top-down approach, you look at aggregate spend categories and drill down until you can itemize the spend, then categorize it to fit naturally into the targeted buckets you have identified.

For example, if you are trying to save money on shipping, look at your financial data, preferably one year's worth, and identify all the suppliers from which you purchase inbound and outbound shipping services. Be extremely careful in gathering that data, as often it is incorrectly classified in ERP systems, or the freight component of a product's price is bundled into its total purchase price. Once you have identified those suppliers, pull invoices. Alternatively, you may be able to get shipment data from the supplier's online account management portal or by having the account manager run the reports you

TABLE 15.1 Compliance Filtering

Category	Keywords	Suppliers	Compliant Location	Noncompliant Location	Compliant/ Noncompliant
Motors under 100 hp	Motor	Motor supplier 1	Location 3		Noncompliant
General industrial		General industrial supplier 1			Compliant
Safety supplies		Safety supplier 1		Location 1	Compliant
Safety supplies		Safety supplier 2	Location 1		Compliant
Mill parts		Mill parts supplier 1	Location 3		Noncompliant
Safety supplies		Safety supplier 3			Noncompliant
Motors under 100 hp		Motor supplier 2		Location 2	Compliant
Lubes and greases	Fuel, lubricant, grease, oil	Lubes and greases supplier 1			Noncompliant
Motors under 100hp	Motor	Motor supplier 3			Noncompliant
General mechanical		General mechanical supplier 1		Location 1	Noncompliant
Safety supplies		Safety supplier 4			Noncompliant

require to build a shipping history. Regardless, it is extremely valuable to know who is requesting or authorizing the majority of the spending in the category you are looking at, data that is most likely available from your purchase order system.

Once you have gathered all of the supplier, spend, and buyer data, it is time to cross-reference it. Cross-referential data analysis is a perfect tool to check that you have indeed identified all the spend from the top down. For example, if a supplier gives you spend data and you cannot match it with data you pull from the general ledger, then it may have been placed under a different budget code or under a different name (e.g., USPS instead of U.S.

Postal Service), and it is potentially missing from your original analysis. Cross-referencing allows you to identify it and enables you to go back and find other areas in which the spend might be uncovered. From the purchase order information you can usually identify the key stakeholders in that spend category and interview them regarding their contribution to the spend, as well as their requirements and preferences. The more stakeholders you can identify in your analysis, the easier the process will be. Sometimes it is simply impossible to figure out who the owners of the spend are. However, ascertaining the majority is usually good enough, as you will identify the remainder during the interview process.

In this case, the data analysis tends to transform as you discover additional details. Developing a broad and flexible framework for the data you gather will help avoid inconsistencies that would need to be accounted for later. The foresight required to produce such a framework will come from general sourcing experience, as most categories have some commonality, but category-specific sourcing experience is most valuable. As you work through the process and cross-reference data sources, you will discover that certain sources contain data that others do not. However, following up with the source's provider (e.g., a supplier for usage data) will most likely yield the same data, ensuring you have captured everything.

The goal of this type of analysis is twofold. The first goal is to ensure you have captured all the data. This objective influences the second goal, which is to target spend areas within a category. As data is gathered, compiled, and referenced against itself, it is important to keep in mind how what you are learning impacts your end goal of targeting spend.

DATA ANALYSIS AND TRENDING

Data trending reports are yet another useful vantage point from which you can view data. They reveal indispensible information in cases in which the per-unit price of an item varies in relation to the index or cost of one or more of its primary constituent parts. Likewise, in cases in which various factors influence normal usage, trending is a necessary tool in the optimization of inventories or prepurchased services that need to be increased during peaks and reduced or eliminated during lulls. Regardless of the situation, it is important to first identify whether or not there are trends that have an impact on the targeted product or service, and then to actually perform the analysis required to identify precisely what that impact is.

Accommodating Seasonal Trends

Wireless communications offers a great example of accommodating seasonal trends. Suppose you are managing wireless spend with one or more providers for an accounting firm. You are well aware that the first few months of the year are the busiest for your firm; therefore, you look at previous years' invoicing to see when voice usage and text messaging peaked and make necessary adjustments to your plans to ensure you do not incur significant overages. The trend is most likely obvious and fairly consistent in this case. Additionally, you will want to consider the number of phones deployed, whether there are any users that incur usage substantially greater than their peers, and how many users are remote or on the road compared to those that remain in the office. Further considerations may apply, but all of these factors affect decisions about your plans over the next few months.

Table 15.2 is an example of peak usage for both text and voice and how it can be made easily apparent.

By graphing this data, you can quickly get a good visual representation of the true usage incurred by your team throughout the year. (See Figures 15.3 and 15.4.) Although your sourcing process should take into account the peaks and valleys of your historic usage, you can focus on providing plans that are optimal for the majority of the year using an accurate reflection of daily usage.

TABLE 15.2   Peak Usage

	Jan.	Feb.	Mar.	Apr.	May	Jun.	Jul.	Aug.	Sep.	Oct.	Nov.
All users on 250 txt msg, 450 min, pooled											
User 1	228	100	286	444	483	250	84	142	233	66	204
User 2	193	258	349	474	293	149	211	248	155	103	150
User 3	125	316	379	487	455	108	137	7	21	131	238
User 4	211	392	422	424	288	234	131	19	94	170	157
User 5	192	139	319	282	468	116	134	67	42	187	165
User 6	176	301	244	479	403	136	246	154	82	39	144
User 7	281	149	406	421	408	238	155	188	26	205	89
User 8	51	206	409	416	489	228	231	46	67	13	248
User 9	225	184	257	463	257	206	211	164	248	189	87
User 10	208	100	346	468	341	225	123	191	118	69	187
Total Mins	3970	4234	4483	4713	3675	4062	3117	3019	3830	4266	3289

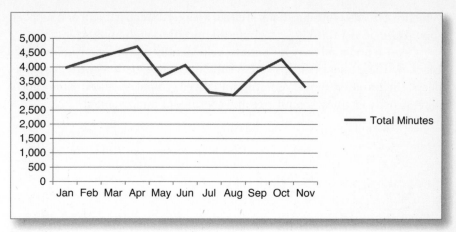

FIGURE 15.3   Total Minutes Used

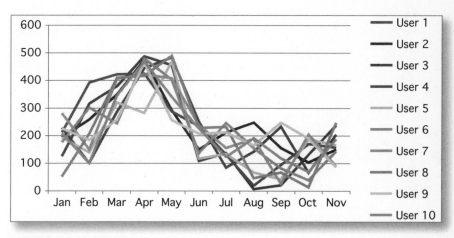

FIGURE 15.4   Minutes Used (by User)

 IN SUMMARY

In many cases, data analysis is performed to search for answers, but it is also a valuable tool that can be used to identify appropriate questions. There will be occasions when all relevant and useful information is not easily available or accessible. In those situations, the data that is available should be reviewed and carefully considered. It may be possible to reveal a few answers with what you have, but follow-up questions to either an internal department or a supplier should also be identified prior to undertaking a thorough analysis.

Cleanse and analyze your data to help identify gaps in your knowledge. Learning these answers helps you in subsequent negotiations with your suppliers. Once your strategic sourcing initiative is complete, those same efforts serve to drive ongoing compliance and continuous improvement.

PART FOUR

IV

How to Do It

16

CHAPTER SIXTEEN

Office Supplies and the Sourcing Process

THE OFFICE SUPPLIES CATEGORY is one of the most universal spend areas in sourcing. And why wouldn't it be? Everyone uses pens, pencils, paper, paperclips, envelopes, highlighters, and staples. Because office supplies are commonplace across companies and even industries, you would think that pricing would be relatively standard, and that most companies would get about the same level of pricing, but nothing could be further from the truth.

Think of it this way: Your organization has short- and long-term goals and objectives. While office supply spending may not seem like it plays a vital role in these goals, it very well can. Tactical costs like office supplies affect the bottom line and set unwritten rules about how your organization operates. Efficiency can be achieved throughout all aspects of the business plan—from what you buy and how much you pay to who controls the spend and how orders are placed.

The main focus of sourcing office supplies is to create a more efficient and streamlined process while simultaneously lowering acquisition costs and developing sustainable implementation plans to keep budgets in line. This chapter demonstrates the necessary steps involved in sourcing office supplies, which will also lead to a more practical understanding of the details of sourcing projects in general. Not only is it important that you have a clear understanding of your purchasing profile, but you also need to understand your leverage for negotiations. All of this is discussed, as well as how to acquire the most value for your company's money.

 UNDERSTANDING THE BASICS

Just as you would when sourcing any other product or service, the first step in sourcing office supplies is to gather all of the appropriate documents you need to develop the spend analysis. This includes contracts with any current suppliers and any other pricing agreements already in place. Within these contracts you will find the following:

- The contract pricing list, also called *core items*. This is the list of prenegotiated products for which the supplier has provided net pricing. These products typically have a fixed unit cost for the length of the contract, while some items, such as paper, can fluctuate based on a predetermined index or market rate.
- Noncontract pricing and discount structures, including any discounts off of manufacturer list costs.
- Incentives and rebates that are applicable to your company.
- Applicable manufacturer programs that your company can or does participate in. For example, there might be additional discounts for purchasing branded products or deeper discounts on particular items or remanufactured products.

In addition to your contract's pricing details, you also want to identify all term conditions, commitments, and any penalties for early termination. Pay careful attention to termination penalties, as they can pose a financial risk to your organization if you trigger them. Keep in mind that even if an early termination clause exists, this does not mean you cannot exit the contract. As you move along in the sourcing process, you can compare your savings opportunities against the termination penalties and risks; in most cases you will find that the savings opportunities outweigh the risks and penalties.

There are many different types of savings opportunities in the category of office supplies; it is worthwhile to develop an understanding of the different opportunities and how to acquire them. We discuss many of these strategies later in the chapter. For now, we focus on the savings advantages your company more than likely currently enjoys. Some common rebates or incentives for which you might currently be contracted can include:

- *Volume rebates.* These might consist of the supplier rebating you a percentage of your net sales up to a preset maximum limit. Often, this is done on a monthly or quarterly basis.
- *Volume discounts.* These may apply to particular products, such as paper or toner. The more you buy at any given time, the less you pay per unit for that particular order, or the more you buy over a longer period of time, the greater your discount becomes.
- *Order rebates.* Some suppliers may offer rebates based on how you place orders. For example, if you place orders electronically as opposed to manually through hard copy order forms, the supplier might reimburse a certain percentage of those net sales dollars back to your company. Electronic orders are more efficient to handle for the supplier, therefore they may offer discounts to encourage them.
- *Additional business rebates.* Suppliers want as much of your business as possible and might offer incentives if you purchase products from them that you would normally purchase elsewhere. This can include technology, furniture, and even services such as printing.
- *Private label rebates.* If your company purchases self-branded products from the supplier, it might provide additional discounts or rebates for using private label instead of name-branded products. An example of a private label product is Staples Stickies instead of Post-It Notes.

Each of these rebates, discounts, and incentives is developed to encourage the buyers to do more business with the supplier. This information is important in the spend analysis so that you can account for the true pricing of each item when you begin to baseline current spend profile details.

 ## SPEND ANALYSIS

Office supply spend is normally classified by companies in the tactical spend classification, meaning, more often than not, that the cost of the processes to acquire the goods are more than the price of the actual goods themselves. Tactical purchases in an organization are less critical and should be approached as such—by looking to improve the procure-to-pay process and heavily leveraging your requirements in the marketplace. As you continue in this process you will find that there are many local and national suppliers that can likely provide you with the products and services you have targeted. Such a crowded marketplace ensures the competitive landscape necessary to obtain lower prices and value-added services.

Once you determine who your current supplier or suppliers are and you collect all the contracts and pricing agreements, it is time to obtain details about your target products and how much you actually pay for them. This can come from purchase orders, quotes, invoices, forecasts, and, most importantly, historical usage reports. Your supplier can provide this report for you; often, you can obtain these types of reports through your existing online ordering systems. A current 12-month usage report is adequate to give you a good idea of the items you are buying, along with quantities and costs. When requesting a report from suppliers, make sure to ask that the spend be broken down to the product level. Also make sure that the details of the report include supplier part numbers, manufacturer names and part numbers, cost types (core or noncore), and supplier categories (such as toner, paper, and so on). You may also run an internal usage report to compare to the supplier's information to ensure all the spend information has been gathered.

A comparison of core and noncore prices can reveal savings opportunities. Divide the data from the supplier usage report into core and noncore purchases (the products for which you are paying net pricing versus the products for which you receive a discount off of list price). By doing so, you will be able to compare the core items with the core contract price list more easily. Suppliers typically establish lower pricing for core items than for noncore items, because these are generally the items that you purchase most often. You will also be able to compare the discount structure listed in the contract for noncore items with prices you are actually paying. Noncore items, or noncontract items, are priced less aggressively with a lower discount percentage because they are not purchased as often as the core list of items. However, you must be careful later in the process, because in order to bolster their profits under the contract terms, suppliers may purposely offer huge discounts on items you do not purchase frequently, while offering marginal fixed pricing on the products you purchase most often.

This comparison analysis assists you in auditing your existing purchases to see if you have been paying what you agreed to pay per your old contract or pricing agreements. It also helps you identify the items for which you may want to receive quotations from alternate suppliers when sourcing the category. Once you have divided the spend into these two categories, you will be able to determine the percent of spend that is geared toward core items and the purchases that are noncore. Generally speaking, the ideal split should be around 70 percent core and 30 percent noncore; anything within a 10 percent range of those percentages is acceptable. If you find that the total spend for your core purchases is at or less than 50 percent, this is cause for concern. This analysis will allow you to determine whether there are frequent noncore purchases that should be moved to your core list.

Overall, this assessment provides your organization the opportunity to reevaluate the sales service you are receiving from your current supplier. Your historical spend analysis may help you reach the conclusion that your existing supplier is always acting in your best interest, proactively moving items to your core list, or you may find that most purchases are all falling in the discount category, and that your supplier is reactive to your demands and not proactive in helping you achieve your savings.

Once you have analyzed your core and noncore categories, it is time to perform the actual audit. Review the core purchases and compare them to the core price list in the contract to confirm that pricing is in line with the contract. Another aspect to review when evaluating the core list is units of measure. When evaluating your purchasing history, you may find that the unit pricing listed at purchase time often does not align with the unit pricing per the contract. The contract price list may show one cost for one unit, but if the item is sold in a different unit of measure, the actual billed cost could be different. Line up the core price list with purchasing usage and review it item by item to ensure an accurate cost analysis. If the unit of measure does not match, convert the usage unit of measure to that shown in the contract to represent the correct cost.

Each purchase in your report is assigned to a category, such as toner, writing implements, kitchen goods, and so on. For noncore purchases, you can analyze where within these categories the majority of your spend falls, and whether these items should be receiving any special discounts or rebates per the contract. This can also help when sourcing the category from alternate suppliers; depending on their noncore discount structure, you can use the analysis to compare the new bid to the current structure.

Finally, while the category of office supplies as a whole may fall into the tactical classification, you can take a further step and classify the different subcategories. Detailing the spend by class adds the benefit of being able to identify the risks involved in purchasing different products in these subcategories. In other words, it is valuable to determine which products can be substituted for like alternatives and which need to be of a higher quality for your individual business needs. Toner is a good example of a product for which you can readily find substitutions, but you also need to consider qualitative aspects beyond just cost. Remanufactured products can significantly reduce your toner costs, but you need to evaluate them thoroughly for both quality and yield-of-prints to ensure they will operate as efficiently as the product from the original equipment manufacturer (OEM). On the other hand, when purchasing general office supplies such as staples, pens, and notebooks, you are less likely to risk much when purchasing the less expensive product. However, certain departments, such as sales or the executive suite, may purchase certain items for a particular reason, and these considerations should factor into your final strategy.

 ## EVALUATING THE COMPETITIVE LANDSCAPE

Once you complete the spend analysis and develop a profile of office supply purchases, you can begin to research and evaluate the market landscape. Office supply providers are plentiful, on both a national and local level. While you are probably most familiar with the bigger players, it is often helpful to also research the market for lesser-known suppliers. By expanding your scope to different-sized suppliers, you gain a better chance of finding one that can meet the specific needs of your organization. Local providers often have the ability to offer competitive pricing while providing more value-added services, but obviously may not be able to serve your national needs. However, comparing the pricing and level of service to national-scale suppliers will help you determine a benchmark target.

Qualifying alternate suppliers requires you to understand your company's needs. When conducting supplier interviews, prepare a list of qualifying product and service specifications. The list will differ depending on your organization but the most common points include:

- Payment and invoicing terms
- Freight and shipping methods and terms
- Special product or brand availability
- Customer service requirements
- Order methods—for example, via the Web, phone, or fax
- Reporting capabilities
- Support for any technical requirements
- Lead times

In addition to determining which players are viable in the marketplace, you want to educate yourself on market conditions. For example, the pricing for paper products can fluctuate throughout the life of the contract due to the commodity-driven market for wood pulp, as opposed to that for pens and pencils, which more than likely have fixed prices. You should also have a firm understanding of what the landscape is like for the suppliers themselves. Are they all profitable, or has the recession forced consolidations and bankruptcies?

Finally, it is important to understand that certain products are loss leaders for suppliers. In other words, they will sell you something at a price that may even be below their cost. They will do this in the categories that buyers focus on the most, but which really do not have a significant impact on the overall spend. For instance, they may sell you boxes of pens at an 80 percent discount from retail price in the hope that amateur buyers will compare that price to the display price in their local strip-malls and conclude that they are getting an awesome deal. Those buyers then tend to trust that they are getting aggressive pricing from the supplier across the board, when in fact they may be paying a grossly inflated price in a more important area, such as paper or toner.

DEVELOPING YOUR SOURCING STRATEGY

The first step to developing a sourcing strategy is to understand the pricing models of the individual suppliers and the products themselves. Understanding how suppliers establish the price for an item will help you develop your request for proposal documents. Office supply pricing, as discussed previously, generally involves a core list of items with prenegotiated unit prices as well as a discount structure for noncore items. With that in mind, there are several considerations in developing a strategy to approach the bid process. For example, you may ask yourself whether you are open to changing to a new supplier or whether you are more concerned with using market data to leverage better pricing from your incumbent supplier. Ensure that your approach factors in any changes your business might experience in the future, such as a downturn or expansion, particularly if they involve multiple locations.

Do not wait for the suppliers to suggest which items should be considered core and which are noncore. Instead, develop your own ideal list of core items and include them in the request for proposal (RFP). The following information is important to include in the bid document:

- Supplier product number
- Manufacturer
- Manufacturer part number
- Detailed product description

- Any other codes or numbers that will help the suppliers to cross-reference the products for quoting accurately
- Unit of measure (UOM)
- Estimated annual quantities of each line item, which are determined by your spend analysis

For the most part, you can develop this bid document using the usage information originally collected from incumbent suppliers, with minor tweaking. The more data and information you provide to suppliers, the faster you can expect them to return responses. Providing accurate estimates will also help suppliers determine whether your high-volume items represent desirable business; if so, you can use this information to help leverage lower costs.

Your RFP should list more than just the products purchased; it should provide a universal format for the suppliers to use for responses. You should request that suppliers fill in the following information in the RFP response:

- Proposed item number.
- Proposed item description.
- UOM—suppliers should try to base their quotes on the same UOM you currently use for purchases. If this is not possible, you will need to know what UOM they are using so you can complete an accurate apples-to-apples comparison.
- Manufacturer list price.
- Net unit price.

You should also provide a section for the suppliers to quote substitutes for all items, as valid substitutes can provide substantially more savings than an apples-to-apples quote. For example, if your organization typically purchases OEM toner, ask for private-label brands or remanufactured items. If your company wants to start in a less risky category, ask suppliers to quote substitutes for common items, such as pens.

Make sure the noncore list is detailed by category in order to make the analysis easier. Most office supply providers will price the noncore items either with a discount structure or by an average discount off manufacturer list price. They also like to provide these discounts by category. For example, many suppliers prefer to respond to noncore item sourcing requests as follows:

- General office supplies: 20 percent off list price
- Ink/toner: 11 percent off list price

- Paper: 12 percent off list price
- All other catalog purchases: 7 percent off list price

Another option is to negotiate a flat average discount off list price across all categories. The highest flat discounts are available if you also negotiate a *margin floor*, or minimum allowable price, which allows the supplier to offset some of the risk associated with flat discounts across categories.

Of course, the RFP should address more than just price. Determine important considerations for your business beyond cost savings. For example, analyze whether you need:

- A telephone-accessible customer service department
- Special delivery and shipping methods
- Additional incentives and rebates to assist in the transition to a new supplier
- Specific terms in the new agreement
- Budgetary controls or enhanced reporting

These are just a few of the possible questions you need to detail before distributing the RFP to the suppliers. While each question may not apply to your organization, you and the suppliers need to develop a clear picture of the results desired from the sourcing initiative.

Once you have prepared the bid document, you should also develop overview questions that are typically found in a request for information (RFI) document. Since office supply spend falls in the tactical classification, it is unnecessary to conduct a stand-alone RFI initiative; you can just have the suppliers answer the questions during the RFP process. Some important information to include in your RFP document is as follows:

- *Company overview*—A short overview of your company, including the location of your headquarters and a brief explanation of the company.
- *Program goals*—A short paragraph detailing what your goals are for this RFP, and for the initiative in general.
- *Your contact information*—Provide contact information for the person conducting the RFP so suppliers know where to submit questions.
- *RFP response directions*—Directions for the suppliers concerning the methods for submitting responses (for example, by e-mail, via postal mail, or through an electronic sourcing tool).

- *Executive summary*—Suppliers should provide an overview of their organization; this may help verify that they have the qualifications to provide the support and services you are seeking.
- *Invoicing and payment*—Request information on payment terms and the suppliers' preferred invoicing method and frequency (monthly, weekly, by e-mail, by postal mail, and so on). Include any points here that are pertinent to your contract terms.
- *Rebates and incentives*—The supplier can indicate any rebates and incentives that are part of the bid.
- *Account management*—When sourcing services, you want to be sure that the supplier you are working with has a plan of action regarding how your account will be managed, including contacts for placing orders, resolving disputes, and establishing return material authorizations.
- *Order capabilities*—Detail how you currently place orders and ask suppliers how they would accommodate or improve upon that model.
- *Supplementary information*—Include any other pertinent questions or concerns in regard to the contract or any other service or product specifications. For example, it may be important to your organization to learn whether a supplier participates in recycling programs, and what value they can add to the contract. Or perhaps suppliers can offer other green initiatives. Perhaps the supplier's budgeting tools are important to your organization.

Include any other information that you believe will help compare suppliers with each other and the current service you are receiving. You can also include any additional services to the scope of work, such as quarterly price and usage reviews or consignment and storeroom management services. Try to include everything up front to avoid having to go back to each supplier seeking new pieces of information once the RFP has been released.

Finally, develop a firm idea of the scope of the responses you are seeking. Ask yourself whether you are looking to expand your current offering, lower your prices, or develop a whole new strategy for purchasing office supplies. Answering these questions internally will help you develop a scorecard for evaluating responses. This scorecard allows you to impartially analyze the bids you receive from alternate suppliers in an objective, fact-based manner.

One of your overarching goals when sourcing office supplies is to optimize the process. Focus on how the process currently operates and explore ways to make it more efficient. Some possibilities include streamlining order placing and processing, consolidated invoicing, and involving the supplier to help manage core pricing and budget controls. On a more sophisticated level, involve your information technology (IT) department and look into potential integrations with your existing ERP or procurement systems.

 ## IMPLEMENTING STRATEGIES BEYOND BIDDING

There are strategies beyond the RFP process that can generate additional cost savings and pricing enhancements. In the office supply market, manufacturers are willing to extend special pricing to you if you agree to standardize on their products (that is, use them exclusively). The most common of these arrangements is the Hewlett-Packard (HP) Big Deal, in which HP provides additional discounts in exchange for increases in volume. Of course, if you cannot generate adequate volume in a given spend category, it may not be worth the effort to negotiate with the concerned manufacturers. Review your spend profile and identify areas in which you spend the most money, as well as areas in which you buy the most product, then focus on direct manufacturer negotiations in these areas. For example, if you find that you spend a substantial amount of money on tape and sticky notes, you can negotiate along these lines with a manufacturer such as 3M.

Working with manufacturers in this manner can be done directly or through your preferred office supply distributor. Working through a distributor can often get you to the right people in the manufacturer's organization faster, can help in negotiating the distributor's markup on the agreed-to pricing (thereby allying the distributor more closely to your goals), and allows you to hand off management of the standardization program to the distributor.

Another way to reduce costs and save valuable time and effort is to have a group purchasing organization (GPO) manage your office supply spend. Because GPOs leverage the total volume of all their members when negotiating with suppliers, the discounts available to you through a GPO may in some cases exceed the discounts you would be able to achieve on your own. In addition, you may be able to outsource the supplier management function of this tactical spend category to the GPO, which can maintain the supplier relationship, renegotiate when warranted, and assist in troubleshooting service and compliance issues. While the prices you obtain may not be the lowest in the marketplace, this is offset by gaining additional advocacy with suppliers, networking opportunities with other GPO members, and access to best practices and the latest category market intelligence.

QUALIFYING SUPPLIERS AND GOING TO MARKET

At this point you have developed an idea of which suppliers are in the market and what requirements they will need to meet in order to facilitate a bid. Now it is time to qualify suppliers based on your previously developed criteria. Determine whether they have the capabilities to manage the account effectively. Discuss the RFP with suppliers, including timelines and overall requirements.

Contrary to the way most businesses conduct a sourcing event, such as a three-bid process, you should attempt to maximize the number of suppliers participating in your bid. As long as suppliers can meet the needs of your organization, include them in the bid process. While they might not win the business, alternate supplier proposals can deliver a wealth of market intelligence and leveraging opportunities. This gives you the ability to use the competitive market of office supply providers to your advantage.

A few days prior to the release of the RFP, notify those suppliers who have been qualified that the RFP will soon be distributed. Once you send out the RFP, call the suppliers and make sure that all their questions are answered. Try to address concerns quickly to avoid delays down the line. Also be sure to remain available for questions during the RFP process.

Follow the guidelines we outlined in Chapter 4, "The RFx Process" and Chapter 9, "What Not to Do." In order to maximize the effectiveness of your RFP event, make sure the suppliers are engaged and are confident that they have a genuine opportunity to win the business. Similarly, ensure that you are dealing with the correct level of representative within the supplier organization. For example, if you are planning to purchase products from multiple locations across the country, you should not be working with a regional account representative, but rather a national representative. Office supplier sales teams deal with hundreds of RFPs every week, and you want your bid to stand out as a high priority. Soliciting feedback and listening to the supplier are two easy ways to draw positive attention to your company and get the vendor excited about your opportunity.

 ANALYZING AND ASSESSING THE RESULTS

Once you have obtained the completed bids from participating suppliers, compile the results from the RFP document. Make an initial comparison of the suppliers based on how their responses align with your organizational goals for this project. This can help you determine what information is important and what is tangential to your final goals. This assessment will also help you to ascertain any value-added features in the offers. You can also weigh the offers against one another to figure out which are optimal choices and which benefits will be outweighed by the costs required to implement them.

The next step is to analyze the returned bids. Compare the baseline unit costs to the bids, and be sure to extend all unit costs out by the quantity indicated in the proposal. When evaluating the suppliers' bids, first review the responses to ensure that the units of measure align with those on the current contract, as not all suppliers can provide products in the same package configuration. If they do not line up, you need to convert them to match the UOM of the product you are currently buying. Tables 16.1, 16.2, and 16.3 provide examples of unit of measure issues found in supplier quotes.

In this example, you must determine a conversion factor to normalize the individual unit price for an item and then compare it to the baseline. As you can see, this conversion factor is simply a comparison of unit costs multiplied by your annual quantity to determine the proposed net extended cost. Extending out the net costs for your estimated usage is important, as it is the only way to accurately reflect how a line item's price impacts your total annual office supply spending. When analyzing the bid, focus on both high-cost items and higher-volume purchases to determine the best way to leverage those purchases to obtain lower pricing.

Reviewing the bid line by line is important to ensure that the proposed items and units of measure line up with those established on the core list. Alternate suppliers need to line up the core list of items with products that they supply; sometimes errors can occur, or the supplier will purposely misrepresent

TABLE 16.1   Baseline Data

Baseline Product Description	Base Unit Price	Base UOM	Quantity Based on Usage	Baseline Extended Cost
POST-IT, FLG, ASSRT, STD	$ 0.87	EA/100	18	$ 15.66
ENVELOPE, PADDED, 9.5 × 14.5	$34.78	CT/100	8	$278.24
LABEL, REINFORCE, WE, 200	$ 0.25	PK/200	17	$ 4.25

TABLE 16.2   Proposed Data

Proposed Item Description	Net Price	UOM	Conversion Formula	Net Price to Match Base UOM	Net Extended Cost
POST-IT FLAGS, SM, 140 CT, 4COLOR	$ 2.46	PK/140	($2.46/140)*100	$ 1.76	$ 31.63
9.5 × 14.5 KRAFT BUB MLR	$16.80	PK/25	$16.80*4	$67.20	$537.60
REINFORCEMENT, P/S, ECON, 1M/PK	$ 2.07	PK/1000	$2.07/5	$ 0.414	$ 7.04

a line item in an attempt to appear more competitive. If you miss these errors, your analysis may be inaccurate and, in some cases, create large discrepancies. Another important aspect to consider is whether the alternates are quoting similar products. For example, check to ensure that quotes for OEM toner are equivalent to your current purchases and not remanufactured (unless specifically requested). The supplier should clearly spell out proposed substitutions, but if it fails to do so, it will lead you to perform an assessment that is not apples to apples.

You should also review proposed substitutes for accuracy and equivalency. While these products can vary slightly in style and type, they should still be very similar to the original item. If you approve of the proposed substitutes, line up those items in your scorecard analysis.

TABLE 16.3   Bid Comparison

Baseline Product Description	Base Unit Price	Base UOM	Quantity Based on Usage	Pastore Paper Products	J.P. Office Supplies	Small Town Office Products	Lowest Potential Price
POST-IT, FLG, ASSRT, STD	$ 0.87	EA/100	18	$ 0.77	$ 1.01	$ 0.87	$ 0.77
ENVELOPE, PADDED, 9.5 × 14.5	$34.78	CT/100	8	$36.10	$28.88	$35.99	$28.88
LABEL, REINFORCE, WE, 200	$ 0.25	PK/200	17	$ 0.25	$ 0.31	$ 0.34	$ 0.25

Once you receive each bid document and have aligned the proposed items with the core list from your contract, you can calculate the savings potential. However, you want to do more than just estimate the total savings potential for each supplier; you want to find the best possible price for each item. If you have too many line items to do this, focus on the top 80 percent of total spend—this is likely to encompass only 20 to 30 percent of all items.

Your goal at this point is not to calculate total savings potential, but merely to identify the lowest possible price for each item, regardless of where it came from. Table 16.3 shows an example of comparing the current pricing baseline to each of the three suppliers who placed bids. Keep in mind that the price displayed for each supplier is the normalized price after factoring in any UOM conversions.

As you can see, there is an additional column called "Lowest Potential Price." The information in this column is generated by a minimum value formula in Excel that identifies the lowest price from each of your new bidders. Make sure that your incumbent price is accounted for in this formula as well. The lowest potential prices identified are known as the *best alternative to a negotiated agreement*, and will be used as your negotiation targets. You are now ready to begin first-round negotiations with suppliers.

Keep in mind that asking suppliers to requote on every single item is usually not the best idea. First of all, suppliers may feel that the rework is superfluous and may be unwilling to engage in the extra effort if they do not believe they have a good chance of winning the business. Second, if you are working on a bid with hundreds or thousands of items, suppliers will not know which items to address, and may come back with a lackadaisical response. Third, from a timing perspective, asking suppliers to rebid every item could double the length of the bid process.

Rather than having suppliers rebid every item, extend out the lowest potential prices to see where the real savings potential resides, in terms of dollars to the bottom line. Of those line items, take the ones that will have the most significant impact and go back to each supplier, asking them to hit the new target prices. This gives suppliers a smaller scope to manage, allowing them to put their best foot forward. At this time you should also review the noncore discount structure proposed by each supplier. Similar to line-item pricing, take the best discounts available for each category and ask suppliers to match them.

When the finalists receive the targets, they will most likely not need as much time as they did for the initial proposal, since you are only asking them to focus on a few items. This is also a good opportunity to request any additional information you did not find in the proposal or to ask them to expand upon any value-added features they offered as part of their bids. In addition to any missed information, you should request a sample implementation plan at this point. This gives you a good idea of the minimum time required to move to a new vendor if this is the decision taken.

When the target bids are received, normalize the units of measure again and align them in a new spreadsheet. Align the baseline pricing with the new pricing, along with any viable substitutes. Calculate the savings and align the new bids with the baseline costs to determine which supplier has the most competitive bid in terms of cost (see Table 16.4).

Once you enter the updated bids into your spreadsheet, you can extend out the total cost for each line item and for your total contract-spend items list. Your potential supplier will most likely start to become evident at this point, but you still need to compare the value-adds, implementation plans, and any other supplementary information requested in the proposal. With all of these factors aligned, you can narrow down the finalists or make your final selection. Some questions to consider during this evaluation process include:

- Have all of your questions and concerns been addressed?
- Are the payment and invoicing terms in line with your organization's terms? Has the supplier optimized this process in any way?
- Are the freight terms and shipping methods in accordance with your expectations?
- Has the supplier satisfied your company's needs for special products or brand availability?
- Does the supplier have the desired customer service requirements? What value-adds does the supplier offer in this area?
- Are the ordering methods appropriate for your needs?
- Does the supplier have the required reporting capabilities?
- Can the supplier support your company's technical requirements?
- Has the supplier offered relevant value-added programs?

Make sure that all pricing-related concerns are addressed as well.

- Is the core pricing in line with your expectations and have you achieved best-in-class pricing?
- Is the noncore discount structure competitive?
- Has the supplier offered rebates, sign-on bonuses, or any additional discounts?

You may have other questions or concerns beyond this list, so be sure to address them prior to making your final decision. Supplier selection should be

TABLE 16.4 Total Bid Cost

Baseline Product Description	Base Unit Price	QTY Based on Usage	Baseline Extended Cost	Pastore Paper Products	Pastore Extended	J.P. Office Supplies	J.P. Extended	Small Town Office Products	Small Town Extended
POST-IT, FLG, ASSRT, STD	$ 0.87	18	$ 15.66	$ 0.77	$ 13.86	$ 0.88	$ 15.84	$ 0.87	$ 15.66
ENVELOPE, PADDED, 9.5 × 14.5	$34.78	8	$278.24	$34.99	$279.92	$29.00	$232.00	$28.88	$231.04
LABEL, REINFORCE, WE, 200	$ 0.25	17	$ 4.25	$ 0.25	$ 4.25	$ 0.20	$ 3.40	$ 0.32	$ 5.44
			$298.15		$298.03		$251.24		$252.14

based on the total cost of ownership, which includes pricing, service, ability to implement savings in the shortest amount of time, and ability to sustain or increase savings over the life of the contract, to name a few factors. If one supplier stands out in terms of price and another excels in service, conduct additional rounds of focused negotiations to ensure you optimize your selection. Do not be afraid at this point to go back to the suppliers and ask for further pricing concessions, or to ask if they can improve their service levels to be comparable to the offering of another. Often at this stage, suppliers are willing to provide cash incentives, including transition bonuses, in which they pay you a fixed amount to offset the cost of transition, or end-of-quarter or end-of-year rebates, which incentivize you to achieve specific volume thresholds or growth.

CONTRACTING AND IMPLEMENTATION

Once you have identified the optimal supplier solution, it is time to move on to contracting and implementation. If you selected your incumbent supplier, contracting could be as easy as signing a new document and ensuring the pricing is in place, and then moving on to the implementation of new services or other account changes that were agreed to during the RFP process. If you are transitioning suppliers, a full rollout and training program may be required.

The contract itself should specify when the pricing is implemented, typically within 30 days of the customer signing the contract. Make sure the contract terms specify that pricing goes into effect after *you* sign the contract, not the supplier, as suppliers are notoriously known to sit on the contract without signature. Unfortunately, many suppliers purposely delay signing the contract and implementing pricing in order to sell to your organization at a higher price for a bit longer. Hold your supplier to the estimated signing date, and if it continues to miss it, make the company aware that you have an alternate supplier who is hungry for the business.

The contract, whether with your incumbent or a new supplier, should specify all rebates and value-added programs directly within the document or in the attached addendums. Do not sign a contract that refers to addenda that have not yet been drafted. Price guarantees or term agreements, as well as payment terms, penalties, and additional scope of work details, should also be included in the contract. If your selection involves the implementation of a new ordering platform or integration into an existing system, make sure that firm timelines are established for their completion as well.

During the RFP negotiation process you collected sample implementation plans from the suppliers. At this point you should request a detailed plan, including dates for the suggested rollout of the new contract. Each organization's plan varies depending on the ordering process and system updates that are required. You should work with the supplier to develop your own implementation plan that includes notifying key end users of the change. If your company uses a punchout catalog, you will need to work with IT to remove the previous supplier's data and assimilate the new vendor's catalog. If your users have the ability to place orders on purchasing cards, ensure that they receive hard copies of the new vendor's catalog to help enforce the adoption of the new supplier.

Frequent and clear communication with end users is the key to ensuring that implementation of a new supplier goes smoothly and that subsequent purchases are compliant with company policy. With office supplies contracts, it is essential to safeguard all savings opportunities available through a new supplier and contract. Not only do you need the end users to purchase from the new supplier to get the savings, but you also need them to take advantage of the value-added programs put in place by the new supplier. You should not just be telling your end users what to do; you should be attempting to transfer knowledge and empower them to drive a successful implementation. End users need to be trained on any new technical systems or online ordering processes, and to develop an understanding of the available incentives, such as substituting private-labeled products for name brand items to achieve additional cost savings. They also need to be introduced to the customer service program, whether it be an onsite representative or through a phone system.

Creating an Autosubstitution Program

One important step during the implementation phase is creating an auto-substitution program, in which the supplier works with you to determine which high-cost brand-name products can be substituted with a generic or remanufactured equivalent. When an individual searches for a particular item, the supplier's website or ordering system automatically substitutes a lower-priced product that serves the same function. For instance, when an end user attempts to order HP 4350 yellow laser toner, the system automatically substitutes the order with a remanufactured toner equivalent at a much lower price.

Autosubstitution helps you avoid the headaches of training every single person that places orders on every substitute they should be using.

Additionally, most systems allow you to track detailed purchasing information, so you can see the individuals in your business who consistently order more expensive product replacements that deviate from your preferred substitute items. You do not need to have technically complex or high-priced items to use an autosubstitution program. In fact, basic items like pens, sticky notes, and notepads are ideal for replacing with off-brand products at a lower price.

Guaranteed Savings and Budgetary Controls

Distributors are often willing to provide other cost reduction services, such as guaranteed savings programs and budgetary controls, that need to be addressed during implementation. Guaranteed savings programs generally stipulate that the supplier guarantees your spend will not exceed a certain percentage or dollar amount over the course of a year, based on a baseline set of data. If your company does spend more than this amount, the supplier pays your company the overage in the form of a credit or rebate. Because suppliers are still focused on maximizing profit when a guaranteed savings program is in place, they work very closely with buyers to ensure the lowest-cost items are purchased and that controls are in place so that excess amounts of product are not purchased. Guaranteed savings programs can be very useful to companies concerned with making major changes in the way they purchase, and such programs essentially outsource the control of office supply purchases to the distributor.

Depending on the size of your organization, you may also benefit from participation in a budgetary control program. While the actual details may vary from supplier to supplier and company to company, the basic premise is that the supplier works with you and your team to establish budgets for individual departments or cost centers. You aid the supplier in developing the parameters, but the goal is to ensure that departments are not spending excessive amounts on supplies. The supplier works with you to determine a set monthly limit; once the department has reached that limit, it can no longer place orders. Depending on the individual parameters established, your company can allow a process to be put in place that requires the department to request approval for purchases above the limit. Another important point to consider is that departments cannot roll over unspent dollars. An annual review of the budgets also helps to ensure that all departments receive the appropriate amount for their headcount and needs, and are purchasing the correct mix of contract and noncontract items.

MONITORING COMPLIANCE

When implementing a new supplier or a new contract, there is always the potential for a few hiccups. From end users not ordering the right brand of supplies or ordering from the wrong vendor to suppliers slowly increasing prices or pushing higher-margin items on end users, monitoring your purchases is critical to achieving the savings targets that you estimated.

Immediately after implementing your new program, you should begin to monitor the core pricing and noncore discounts for correspondence with the contract. Periodically, download a list of past purchases and focus on examining the highest dollar-amount items. Verify that the purchase prices match the prices established in your contract, or calculate the discount percentage from list pricing to ensure that noncore purchases are correct.

Beyond monitoring the quantitative aspects of the relationship, you should also make sure that the supplier continues to bring qualitative value to your account. Many purchasing professionals and other stakeholders leave the job of continuous improvement to the supplier. However, without some leadership from your organization, even the most willing and eager supplier cannot create change. You should track the efficiency of the customer service program to ensure that the vendor provides you with the required levels of service. Any value-added programs or incentives should be reviewed to determine effectiveness and troubleshoot issues. For example, ask these types of question to guide your monitoring efforts:

- Do your end users constantly need to make returns?
- Are your autosubstitution programs working properly?
- Are your billing terms accurate?

Keep note of each of these items and discuss them with the supplier as soon as they come up.

In addition to monitoring the supplier, you should monitor the compliance of end users. Make sure that they are not only purchasing from the preferred supplier, but also making an effort to purchase from the core pricing list. While the noncore purchases can still represent savings opportunities, you will optimize savings by purchasing core items whenever possible, as these items were priced more aggressively. Try to obtain direct feedback from the company's end users. These individuals are the ones most affected by the new contract and processes put in place; if there are improvements that can be made up front you should address them as soon as you can.

Keep in mind that the new supplier should be providing your company with opportunities for optimizing and streamlining the ordering and delivery processes. Purchasing office supplies should not be a time-consuming task for end users.

Revisit the core pricing list and value-added programs on a quarterly basis with the supplier. Review these items with the account representative to determine if there are any relevant or worthwhile alternations. You should review the spend usage and determine whether your core versus noncore purchases are still within the targeted 70 percent/30 percent split range. If you find that end users are not purchasing from the core list, try to find out why and work with the representative to adjust the core list to better suit the buying needs of your company.

 ## IN SUMMARY

To maximize the savings potential for office supplies purchases, it is critical to have a solid understanding of your end users' needs. Additionally, you must have a firm grasp on other aspects that are critical to your business, such as payment terms or technology requirements.

When sourcing a tactical classification of spend, you should focus not only on acquiring optimal savings opportunities but also on streamlining the entire process. The soft-dollar savings achieved in a streamlined process can often outweigh the hard-dollar unit cost savings. Focus on the ways your company can take advantage of all of the value-added programs, incentives, rebates, and discounts available from the supplier.

Communication is a vital part of sourcing the category of office supplies. It is essential to communicate with the end users and discuss their needs, the methods of implementing the changes, and the steps of continually optimizing the process. Communication with the supplier adds continuous value as your mutually beneficial business relationship grows. As you navigate the intricacies of this process, you will find that your company has unique and exclusive needs and requirements. By following these basic steps and using these tips you can build an effective supply chain that is beneficial to both your organization and the supplier.

CHAPTER SEVENTEEN

Negotiating Local and Long-Distance Telecommunications Services

THE SPEND CATEGORY OF TELECOMMUNICATIONS is ripe with savings opportunities. There are two primary reasons for this. First, the information technology (IT) or management information system (MIS) teams responsible for making decisions about infrastructure and configuration are often not focused on cost or trained in negotiations and strategic sourcing. Second, the accounts payable team or other parties responsible for paying the invoices are not necessarily familiar with the services or contracts and cannot make a determination as to the accuracy of any given charges. The combination of these circumstances normally leads to inflated cost structures and opportunities to achieve savings through an audit of infrastructure and contracts and reprovisioning and recontracting of services.

IT and telecom directors care most about maximizing uptime and minimizing complaints about their systems and resources. Naturally, that objective drives their tendency to choose more robust, and usually more costly, solutions to ensure they are keeping the company's voice and data systems running smoothly. The problem is that there are usually less expensive, more streamlined solutions that readily meet the company's telecom needs, but they may not have the time, resources, market intelligence, or understanding of the provider's pricing structures and offerings to make an informed decision. The result is to revert to their primary objective of managing a solid infrastructure, giving very little consideration to cost.

Once the resources and services are contracted and in place, service and billing begins, and in many cases the team who worked through the contracting phase will not closely examine the services they are buying for another three years, until the time comes to renew or change the contract. While the group that audits the invoices may have been involved in the purchasing phase, neither their focus nor their vocation concerns telecommunications, therefore their ability to audit invoicing against the contract and against their own logic is limited because they lack the familiarity with telecom systems required to understand the implications of each circuit, line, usage rate, and so on. Over time, incremental billing errors accumulate. Invoices appear fairly level from one month to the next, but two or three years into the contract, they may have crept up 20 percent or more.

Without a telecom task force in place to collaborate with the technical and finance groups, it is easy for telecom services to be purchased at suboptimal rates, and for additional dollars to seep through the cracks due to inadequate audits. While establishing such a team is not always an option, there are several practices concerned parties can implement to reduce and maintain costs on all telecommunications services.

SOURCING PROJECT OBJECTIVES

Identifying the goals of a sourcing project in the world of telecommunications is critical, as the nature of such technology inevitably leads to scope creep. Some technical innovations yield hard-dollar savings that can be directly derived from decreased invoice amounts, while others demonstrate soft savings, such as saving staff time. The primary goals of the project should include the following.

Hard Savings
- *Optimize inventory:* Ensure you have only the technology you need, with a slight allowance for incidental growth.
- *Optimize configuration:* Use resources first that have the lowest usage rates, then use the more expensive resources for overflow or backup. Also, evaluate and ensure that routing and interconnectivity are as efficient as possible, but not unnecessarily robust.
- *Best-fit technology:* Reevaluate requirements to allow you to choose the most appropriate service for each of your applications, including some technologies that may eliminate the need for current or future upgrades.

Soft Savings

- *Maximize uptime:* Apply appropriate resources; ensure that management and maintenance of equipment and connections are being handled internally or by a third party.
- *Consolidate invoicing:* Minimize the quantity of invoices that need to be tracked while staying flexible in carrier diversity. You will find that it is easier to track and pay a single or small number of invoices as opposed to the potential dozens that can accumulate due to ad hoc service additions over the years.
- *Failover diversity:* Optimizing carrier, pole, and demarcation point (DMARC: the locations where telecom lines enter buildings) diversity, as well as configuring resources to fail over to one another, allows your organization to continue uninterrupted business even in the event of many outages.
- *Create a flexible contract:* Maintain a maximum amount of flexibility to be able to exit your contract early with little or no penalty. This frees you to move to new, better, and sometimes less expensive technology or to renegotiate your existing contract sooner in order to get better rates and discounts.
- *Future technology preparation:* Keep forthcoming technologies in mind before entering a contract. For example, if the organization's existing network is configured as frame relay, but your company has plans to implement voice over Internet protocol (VoIP) over the next few years, now might be the time to migrate to multi-protocol line switching (MPLS) technology.
- *Clean inventory:* Cleaning up and documenting inventory makes auditing and addressing various changes easier.

Organizations can more than likely discover other savings opportunities, both hard and soft, given that the combination of telecom requirements and configurations is unique for each organization. While the products and services available in telecommunications are numerous and ever-changing, we limit our focus to the most common services. However, the principles that drive the effective management of these options can be applied across the implementation of almost any telecommunication service.

 ## TELECOMMUNICATIONS SPEND

Telecommunications spend at its most basic level can be broken down into two primary categories: monthly recurring charges (MRC) and usage charges. Savings can be readily derived from both.

Typically any or all of the following steps can reduce MRC:

- Removal of unused or underused facilities (lines, circuits, and so on)
- Removal of unused or underused features
- Change of technology
- Change of carrier
- Price negotiation

It is necessary, during any sourcing event, to understand, from soup to nuts, all the components that make up the spend. Otherwise, it becomes rather easy for vendors to give you discounts in one area while increasing your costs in another less-understood area. A typical example: A telecom provider offers you an irresistible price on a new piece of technology. It looks like an unbeatable bargain, but once you take the time to consider the shipping and installation charges (and whether they are grossly inflated to compensate for the low list price), the new technology may not look like such a good deal. Understanding all components of telecom spend allows you to eliminate some charges and reduce others.

Drilling down a bit, we can identify the components of some of the common items that nearly all organizations include in their telecom spend. For the sake of simplicity, we focus on the three most common and nearly ubiquitous spend areas in voice communication.

Copper Lines

Most houses and many businesses are still using the standard pair of copper wires that have been in use for many decades. From a technical perspective, the different types of copper lines require distinguishing, but from a financial perspective, it is rare to see a significant price discrepancy amongst them, so we will discuss all copper lines as equals. A single copper line has a bandwidth capacity of 64 kilobits per second (Kbps); however, due to some overhead on the line capacity, 56 Kbps is the net speed available to you. This capacity was used by the old 56K modems on your home phone line, if anyone is old enough to remember those.

The charges from most carriers for these lines include the line charge itself and any features that may exist on the line, such as call forwarding, voicemail, directory listing, and so on, along with applicable taxes and surcharges.

Circuits

There are two primary types of circuits. One is known as time-division carrier 1 (T1), essentially a copper pair with an increased bandwidth of 1.544 megabits per second (Mbps) that can be channelized, or broken up, into 24 distinct call paths with capacities of 64 Kbps each. The advantages of this type of circuit are that T1s are typically less expensive per call path than 24 individual copper lines, and they have higher service level agreements (SLAs) in place, which means that the average time to effect repairs is quicker than with individual copper lines.

The other type of circuit is a primary rate interface (PRI). The advantages of a PRI circuit are similar to those of a standard T1; however, the PRI also offers digital call quality, enhanced features such as custom outbound caller identification, and the ability to use all 23 channels (one of the 24 channels is dedicated to operational signaling) for both inbound and outbound calls, whereas T1s typically need to be segregated and specified for one or the other uses. The advantage of this direct inward dial (DID) calling is that your organization no longer needs to rely on extension calling, in which a caller using the main number and then has to dial an extension to reach a specific person. Instead, every user on the system is assigned his or her own number, which is indexed on the PRI. When an outside caller dials that number, the call comes into the PRI switch, which directs it to the intended recipient. Therefore, instead of having 75 individual lines dedicated to one person each (which would be far more expensive than a PRI), or having a single main number with an overabundance of extensions, each user can have a dedicated DID number (usually costing 10 to 30 cents each) on the PRI.

Circuit costs get broken down into two billing components, but can also have a number of additional items added on depending on the carrier. A typical circuit's cost (carriers tend to bill differently) is comprised of a port charge and a local loop or access charge. The loop charge is the cost for the pair of copper wires between your DMARC and the carrier's PRI switch at the central office. Most carriers are least flexible on the loop charge, especially outside their own territory, because it is typically fixed due to distance involved and the carrier will often have little or no margin to reduce costs.

The port is the size of the bandwidth that you are paying for and hence is available to you. Since we have established that the loop can handle up to 24 simultaneous calls, it is helpful to think of the port as the bottleneck or reduction point at which you are delivered only what you pay for. A PRI or T1 port is 1.536 Mbps, though fractional circuits can also be purchased. For example, if your organization only requires a maximum of 12 simultaneous calls then, with some vendors, you can purchase a 768 Kbps port. An alternative metric used on voice circuits is a channel charge. The terms *channel* and *call path* are used interchangeably, so in the previous example, instead of a 768 Kbps (half of

1.544 Mb) port, you would see a channel charge for 12 channels (11 bearer [B] channels and 1 data [D] channel if it is a PRI circuit) on your invoice. Fractional voice circuits are a rarity today because the cost difference is marginal between a full T1 or PRI circuit and fractional service, or the equivalent in copper lines.

Some additional items typically go hand in hand with the port and loop charges. These include DID number charges, features, and surcharges. By way of example, DIDs, while not part of the circuit cost themselves, can add a significant portion to your bill. So if you have negotiated a $400 PRI charge (port and loop) and you have 400 DIDs costing $0.20/each, that's another $80 or 20 percent.

Usage

The third telecom spend area, and the only one that is typically variable by month, is usage. While it varies each month, there are ways to fix your usage costs or at least make them predictable within a few percent.

Usage can be broken down into inbound (toll free, or 8xx) and outbound calling. From there it can be segmented further into:

- Local
- Long distance
  - *Intrastate:* Calls with the origination and termination in the same state
  - *Interstate:* Calls with the origination and termination in different states
  - *IntraLATA:* Calls with the origination and termination in the same local access transport area
  - *InterLATA:* Calls with the origination and termination in different local access transport areas
  - *International:* Calls with the origination and termination in different countries

Each of these call types has its own associated per-minute rate. Various vendors have their own methodologies for billing calls and minutes, such as incremental (for example, six seconds), rounded, or a connection charge plus the per-minute rate. They may also use a specific formula for calculating the per-minute rate on combinations like those outlined above. These distinctions need to be carefully considered to ensure you are calculating your rate comparisons in an apples-to-apples manner.

An additional usage area to consider is directory assistance (411) calls, which typically range from $0.50 to $2.00 per call. This charge can add up quickly on your phone bill, especially if you have a lot of users who do not always have easy access to a computer. Directory assistance calls can be turned off in your switch or can be rerouted to a free service to achieve savings. Overall, any or all of the following can reduce usage charges:

- Eliminating unnecessary usage
- Changes in technology
- Optimizing switch programming
- Utilizing features that reduce or eliminate per-minute rates
- Price negotiation

As previously mentioned, there are ways to make your usage much more predictable, but at a minimum the per-minute rates—specifically for the most common call types for your organization—can be drastically reduced merely by negotiating a *fraction of a cent* off of your current rates. Before focusing on negotiations, let us take a look at what you can do to reduce your costs without going to market or recontracting.

 ## REVEALING SAVINGS THROUGH AUDITS

There are two internal audits that may reveal savings from the invoice bottom line: contract compliance and inventory audit. Both require some collaboration between the invoice reviewers and the technical group that actually understands the application of the items on the invoice. Sometimes these are the same person or group of people, but many organizations are not lucky enough for this to be the case.

Auditing invoices for compliance with the contract can be tricky, to say the least. It is helpful to first identify an inventory of lines, locate those items on the invoices, and then attempt to correlate them to their respective contracts. But identifying the inventory in its entirety can be difficult. Circuits and lines get added willy-nilly over the years, ending up on disparate invoices, and people forget what they were purchased for or where they are located. How can the invoice auditor ever be confident that he or she understands 100 percent of the telecom spend?

The key to inventory identification is triangulation. By using a method made popular on many crime shows, where the good guys find the bad guy by calculating the distance of his cell phone from three different towers to figure out his location, you can employ a similar strategy to understand your telecommunications spend. Though it is a bit of a misnomer in this case, the idea remains the same. You might discover the ability to pull information from many more than just three resources and documents in order to identify a complete inventory. For instance, these sources provide valuable clues:

- Contracts
- Invoices
- Carrier customer service records (CSRs)
- Internal records of circuits, lines, trunks, etc.
- Visual tours of telecom closets and facilities
- Accounts payable records of the telecommunications category (and related) spend, as well as spend by vendor
- Voice and data networks and diagrams
- Interviews of telecom and IT personnel, help desk employees, administrators, and end users

You will find that you get a fairly solid understanding of your spend from your various carriers' customer service records by collecting all, or even some, of this information and cross-referencing it. But then you may very well notice that you have missed a few invoices that were categorized as facilities in the general ledger and are approved by plant operations because they are dedicated to alarms, for example. Walking around the facility, you might find a lit smart jack (circuit point of entry into your building) for an old Internet T1 line that you have not used since the company upgraded the network and centralized Internet service at headquarters. The person paying that invoice had no idea it should have been disconnected years ago. Hence you will have just proven yourself a master sleuth, and found an opportunity the save the company money.

Donning your detective hat once again, simply visiting the telecom closet and checking all the lit smart jacks might reveal an old circuit that is being paid by another department but has not been connected to anything in the building for years. Calling each phone number for each phone line that's being billed could reveal dozens of lines that ring with no answer, many of which may not even be extended to a desk in the facility or do not have a phone connected to the extension. Lines that are questionable but otherwise appear to be completely unused can be prudently eliminated by having them physically disconnected in the building at the point of entry before calling the phone company and ordering a formal disconnect. This way, if some people complain that their phones are not working, the lines can be quickly restored at no cost and with no risk of losing the number.

In addition to cleaning up the actual resources, invoicing should be cleaned up, too. Unwanted third-party charges, also known as cramming and slamming charges, tend to find their way onto invoices from time to time. For instance, the crammers call someone at your organization (or at least claim they called) to get permission to add a charge to the invoice, such as a directory listing or moving the long-distance service to their platform. Often, when you attempt to remove these third-party charges or request credits against them, the crammers claim that they have recorded proof that someone at your organization authorized them to make those changes or add those charges but, unsurprisingly, they often have a bit of trouble finding the recordings. When they are able to play back the recordings, you discover it is usually of someone who is not authorized to make changes to telecommunications, and the conversations can only be vaguely construed as permission to add the charge through some very creative interpretation. Regardless, these charges sometimes look legitimate but can add up quickly, especially if many local invoices exist.

The process of identifying and understanding the inventory can be somewhat slow and painful, but it is worth the effort. Inevitably, you will find a number of resources and charges that can be cleaned up and eliminated immediately, which not only saves the company money each month going forward, but also makes auditing the invoicing against the contract simpler. Ideally, new lines, circuits, and other services will be added under existing agreements and accounts. If other groups or individuals order outside of the established accounts in the future, your clean inventory and sound understanding of your spend helps you identify those new orders quickly so they may be tracked and optimal savings can be sustained without inventory creeping out of hand again.

 ## OPTIMIZATION OF RESOURCES

Once the inventory is cleaned up, it becomes easier to envision how resources can be optimized. Before going to market for telecom services, a telecom director should consider whether inventory is optimized. Signing up for a new three-year agreement only to realize later that a few circuits could have been replaced or removed is frustrating and can be avoided. Optimization involves gathering a month (or more) of invoicing and getting a handle on usage.

If usage comes from one or more facilities, there may be options for centralizing calling at headquarters, a data center, or through a hosted private branch exchange (PBX). Conversely, it might make the most sense to keep each facility separate and to optimize each individually. Centralizing calling produces two savings opportunities:

1. Interoffice calling will be free, as it can be transported over the wide area network (WAN).
2. Pooled resources allow facilities to borrow from one another; therefore less capacity is needed to cover the same facilities due to complementary usage patterns (especially with facilities in multiple time zones).

For example, a certain facility may need only 18 simultaneous call paths, but a PRI is almost always cheaper than 18 copper lines and certainly provides improved quality and features, so technically a PRI leaves you overtrunked, or nonoptimized. This tends to happen to all facilities, plus or minus a few call paths. When all resources are pooled, trunking can be reduced and all facilities can share resources with one another, allowing for a more efficient capacity allocation. Most resource consolidations involve session initiation protocol (SIP) or VoIP technology; however, such upgrades to the PBX at each facility can be costly. Return on investment for a VoIP migration can vary widely depending on your usage and configuration. For example, if most facilities in the organization do not spend much time talking to one another, there will not be substantial savings through VoIP, because the per-minute rates to call outside of the company (standard local and long-distance calling) will be the same or only marginally better than what you could currently obtain. But if much of the usage is between facilities within the organization, that calling would become free on a VoIP platform.

Of course, VoIP is only one method for optimizing resources (through centralization) and usage (by eliminating otherwise billable interoffice calls). A good, general, and thorough cleanup and streamlining of resources can often produce around 40 percent savings; in some cases, much more. Auditing inventory produces savings by:

- Eliminating old, unused or underused resources
- Consolidating dedicated resources into a shared resource via the PBX
  - Converting outbound-only lines into extensions on the switch
  - Converting dedicated lines, such as faxes and conference bridges, to DIDs, which are usually $0.30 or less, as opposed to a dedicated copper line that may be costing $30
- Identifying old, expensive technology that can be replaced by newer, less costly technology

Consolidating resources is another area in which to achieve savings. Resources may have been left segregated due to limited personnel supporting a change or implementation, or due to gradual, ad-hoc trunk-count increases in which there was no other focus than to quickly add resources for one reason or another. Regardless of the reason, fax machines, conference bridges, mail machines, outbound-only noncritical modems, and other resources may have their own dedicated lines when they could either be configured as extensions on the switch (which would be free, assuming capacity in the switch exists) or be converted to DIDs (a few cents each) and transported in over the T1 or PRI. In fact, organizations using PRI circuits would be wise to make such changes not only for financial benefit, but also because the call quality is better over a digital circuit, and fax transmission will be cleaner and faster.

Another way savings can be quickly realized is by replacing old technology with new, less expensive technology. This includes some of the aforementioned changes, but also such changes as moving away from DID trunks to T1 and PRI circuits and SIP and VoIP technology or adopting multiuse circuits based on fiber that can be split into any or all of the functions of Internet connection, private line, and PRI services. These are only a few examples in which critical thinking about existing infrastructure, instead of just recontracting existing services, can easily yield significant savings.

 ASSESSING THE MARKETPLACE

Depending on the service for which you are entering the market, the ability of a carrier to meet your requirements will vary. Most carriers with a national presence are able to properly serve you, provided you are not in a rural area where the central office, post office, and pharmacy are all owned and run by the same person. Before getting into specifics, we should become familiar with the various types of carriers.

At the highest level, carriers can be divided into two categories: incumbent local exchange carriers (ILECs) and competitive local exchange carriers (CLECs). A local exchange carrier (LEC) is a company that can provide you with dial tone. The ILECs that cover the majority of the United States include Verizon, AT&T, and Qwest\CenturyLink, with Windstream and Frontier covering the remaining small portion. The CLECs are many, and their service areas range from local through statewide and regional to national. Agent channels and resellers, representing a third category of players in the market, are important to consider because, even though these carriers are reselling identical services as the ILECs and CLECs, they buy them wholesale and mark them up as they are able. Therefore they can compete against the identical service from the identical carrier based on the profit margin with which they are comfortable.

There are a few features to look for when going to market that can not only help produce savings, but also help to optimize your infrastructure and billing. Two such questions to ask include:

1. Can the carrier provide creative solutions or innovative technologies that will help save the organization money?
2. Can the carrier aggregate invoicing and provide management tools to save staff time and keep spend organized?

Aggregation of invoicing has many benefits. Of course, it is not always optimal to do so for all services, as you may get the best pricing for a given service from one provider but better pricing on a different service from another provider. Additionally, carrier diversity is also important, as putting all your eggs in one basket can backfire in the event of a carrier regional outage. Nevertheless, aggregating invoicing for a certain service, such as copper lines across locations or even at a single location, can produce some great advantages. For starters, accounts payable can work with a single, simplified invoice rather than several or even dozens of local invoices. This also standardizes your rates, making your invoices easier for nontechnical auditors to review each month, as opposed to the necessity of tracking various lines billing at various rates across various invoices. Local accounts can be notoriously slippery—they are low-dollar invoices that usually are not given much attention. Many continue to be paid for years after they should have been disconnected. In other cases additional costs creep onto the invoice; these often are of little significance individually, but the aggregate sum across many accounts can significantly add up and chew into your telecom budget.

By consolidating your services and accounts to a handful of carriers not only do you reap these rewards, but you garner yourself a single point of contact for each primary account with each carrier. This is a major benefit for local lines, especially across locations. Otherwise, every time a complaint comes in or a new line needs to be ordered, you find yourself looking up the LEC and calling customer service and dealing with endless waits and transfers before achieving resolution. Having an account manager who handles issues and orders takes a huge load off the day-to-day burden on your internal support team. In addition to an account manager, most carriers and resellers now have self-service online portals to allow you to manage your account. You can perform custom invoice analysis, file trouble tickets, and place new orders all from a single Web page, thereby cutting down on wasted time spent on the phone with a customer support agent who knows nothing about your infrastructure, configuration, or organization.

It almost goes without saying, but aggregating services with one or two carriers also enables you to leverage your volume. This may or may not be significant depending on the size of your organization, but it may be an important leverage point, especially if your telecom spend was primarily decentralized before. You may go from countless local invoices with various carriers across 60 locations to a single, aggregated invoice for all 500 lines at those locations. That is enough spend to leverage additional discount points against other spend areas with the same carrier, such as the wide area network. At that point, you will be able to offer the sales manager at your provider of choice a significant amount of new business with which to revisit pricing and develop additional discounts.

Working with carriers that stay competitive by deploying new technologies is also a great way to save money and keep ahead of the technology curve. Of course, migrating to different technologies can be expensive in terms of one-time and capital costs, so care should be taken to plan the timing and appropriateness of a change. A few examples of technology upgrades that, in many cases, can lead to monthly savings include migrating from frame relay to MPLS, utilizing VoIP to aggregate calling across locations, using third-generation (3G) and fourth-generation (4G) wireless services as backup for networked locations, and taking advantage of flexible fiber products that can deliver multiple services such as PRI, Internet, and private lines over the same cable.

 ## IMPLEMENTING CHANGES IN SERVICE

Choosing among carriers is only part of the battle when going to market. Understanding the best methods for implementing changes in services is also crucial. For example, you may acquire great monthly recurring pricing, but the one-time costs for implementation or requisite equipment purchases may be expensive and offset most or all of the anticipated savings. Also, knowing the optimal route from point A to point B in your telecom migration strategy allows you to avoid or at least to plan for downtime. In relation to the primary services previously described, we can look at the details of moving those services between carriers.

Copper lines can be moved between carriers fairly easily. In the case of rebillers, it merely entails a paper change, with no physical changes to the lines. When moving between LECs, the lines are removed from the old carrier's switch at the central offices and added into the new carrier's switch. This causes a short period of downtime while the work is being done, so the work usually occurs outside of business hours or during nonpeak hours, such as early in the morning or around lunchtime.

Migrating PRI services is a little bit more involved. There are two ways to accomplish a move from an existing carrier to a new carrier. One is to make sure both the existing circuits and the new circuits are all on and working correctly in the switch. Doing a conversion in this manner ensures limited or zero downtime but also incurs additional costs, such as installing additional PRI cards in the switch, and typically a longer period in which both the old and new circuits are billing simultaneously. The other way to do the conversion is called a hot cut, in which old PRIs are pulled out of the switch and the new circuits to be tested are added. The problem is that removing the existing PRIs from the switch takes all of your inbound numbers on that circuit offline and probably compromises most, if not all, of your organization's ability to make outbound calls. The benefit of doing a hot cut is that most of the other one-time costs previously described are significantly mitigated or eliminated.

Regardless of your chosen migratory path, it is necessary to move the phone numbers that were previously delivered on the old PRIs to your new carrier so that they can be delivered on your new circuits. This is accomplished by requesting a port order from your new carrier. To prepare the order for execution, the carrier will likely ask for a letter of authorization to do some back end work with the old carrier. Most carriers require two to four weeks to establish and execute a port order. When the day comes to move the numbers, you convene with the new carrier and your switch vendor on a conference bridge call. When all participants are ready, you ask the new carrier to trigger the port, at which point you can make test calls that your vendor will work to confirm are coming in on the new circuit. The process is reversible if a significant issue arises, but if it all tests okay, then the port is complete, your new circuits are active, and the old one can be eliminated.

IN SUMMARY

There is much to achieve in a telecommunications audit. It is important to establish and maintain focus on your goals as you undertake the initiative. In most cases, establishing a clean inventory, optimizing resources, minimizing disparate bills, and producing savings are worthy objectives of the project that uncover opportunities to save money before even going to market. Collaborating with all stakeholders, from IT and accounts payable staff to end users, helps to ensure that you maximize your return. When the time to go to market arrives, keep new technologies in mind and be sure you understand all billable elements of the services you are buying.

If you properly execute all of these steps, you are sure to have a telecom infrastructure that not only costs less every month, but is also much easier to understand and manage, which frees more staff and resources to focus on growing your business.

CHAPTER EIGHTEEN

How Cell-Phone Management Drives Continuous Cost Savings

A PRIME CANDIDATE FOR COST REDUCTION in just about any industry is your cellular wireless spend for both voice and data services. For many organizations wireless can be confusing because it tends not to be a centralized spend category, which can offer significant challenges for tracking the various carriers, plans, phones, and so on in order to make an effort toward optimization. However, once you learn to navigate the airwaves, wireless can become an area where significant savings may be achieved with relative ease.

FINDING THE DECISION MAKER

The first and most critical step in your wireless sourcing initiative is to find the correct decision maker. This is the first step of every project but, with wireless, you will be amazed at just how important this step is to a successful saving initiative, because many different department budgets may be involved. There may be a sales department that handles the sales team's accounts, an information technology (IT) department that manages BlackBerrys, a fleet department that governs push-to-talk phones, and an executive secretary who is in charge of C-level executive phones. See how convoluted this has already become? When laid out in this logical and aggregate manner, it sounds ridiculous to have so many levels of influence for something like wireless, but many companies that have built up their wireless services in an ad hoc fashion over the years work with this model.

The success of your wireless sourcing project strictly relies on finding the single person within your organization who can pull the trigger and supersede everyone else. This person might be in purchasing or IT, or may be the chief executive officer (CEO), chief information officer (CIO), or chief financial officer (CFO). Whoever it may be, it is important for that person to possess the ability to override the decisions of midlevel managers.

Wireless spend is often complicated further by multiple wireless providers, corporate-liable (the company pays for the service) and individual-liable (an employee pays for the service and is reimbursed by the company) plans, and individual requests and demands for specific mobile devices. With the recent advances in smartphone technologies, individuals are much more likely to argue that their choice of device is critical to their productivity, although they often just want a device that aligns best with their personal preference. These issues, which should be easily addressable, tend to escalate quickly when end users do not get what they want. All of these situations are good reasons to have a strong, senior upper-level sponsor manage these decisions.

 ## KNOWING YOUR CONSTITUENTS

Wireless usually crosses more departments and affects more users than most other spend areas in your organization. It is also a category that most managers want to control. To compound the problem, some departments have mandatory requirements for their users (text messaging, data plans, etc.). Generally, wireless can be an extremely difficult category to manage due to the various layers of management, requirements, and end users.

After you identify who in your organization has an appropriate global view of and influence on wireless, your next step is to identify all of the players who have authority over wireless spend within your organization and involve them early to gain their input throughout the process. During this step, seek to answer the following questions:

- What geographical regions need to be covered by your new contract?
- What are your IT department's requirements (e.g., which phones and operating systems are supported)?

- What requirements for voice and data exist for each user, and is it necessary for everyone to have both?
- Are there any international requirements (such as people who travel internationally, or make international phone calls)?
- Are there particular mandatory features that new phones should have (such as push-to-talk)?
- How are cell phones paid for? Does the company own the plans or are staff members reimbursed?

Just as not identifying the right boss or sponsor can derail a wireless project, so can making the mistake of not having the right people involved early in the process. Often wireless sourcing projects proceed all the way to the negotiation phase before a new person gets involved and raises a flag as to why the new carrier will not work. Your goal early in this effort is to engage as many people as possible and gather all the information that is critical to project success, so that these types of situations can be avoided.

 ## KNOWING WHAT YOU OWN

After you have recruited the ideal company decision maker, and have determined all of the players that impact the project, the next step is to learn the details of the inventory. Unfortunately, this is not always as easy as you might think. Most organizations assume they are aware of their entire inventory but, in reality, they only know the surface layer of their wireless spend. Sourcing wireless spend can be extremely complex. First, there are many providers in the United States that many people have never even heard of. For example, well-known providers include Verizon, AT&T, Sprint, T-Mobile, Helio, Clear, Cricket, BlueGrass, Beyond, Virgin, and a host of others. The situation becomes even less clear from an equipment standpoint. With a dozen major equipment providers, a half-dozen operating systems (webOS, iOS, Windows Mobile, Palm OS, Symbian, BlackBerry, and so on), and hundreds of available phone models from which to choose, getting your hands around all the different options becomes a highly technical and detailed project. All this does not even take into account the plethora of technical issues surrounding wireless, such as the differences between code-division multiple access (CDMA) and global system for mobile communications (GSM) systems, as well as multiple frequency bands and second-generation (2G), third-generation (3G), and the advancement of fourth generation (4G) technologies such as

WiMax and long-term evolution (LTE), which are both being rolled out as of the writing of this book.

Of course this can all be overwhelming to absorb, especially if you are not already somewhat familiar with the various carriers, devices, and operating systems in existence. However, digging through the mountain of information about wireless technologies can typically be aided and expedited with the assistance of your IT department, which tends to be well informed about the current inventory and the marketplace.

Your next step is to determine how equipment and plans are currently handled within your organization. Some factors to consider are:

■ Do you have people who submit expense reports for contracts that they own or does your company have its own contracts with carriers?
■ Do users sign individual agreements that get billed directly to your company?
■ Do you have users who have family share plans?
■ Do some of your users carry multiple devices (such as a cell phone, BlackBerry, and aircard) and are those devices contracted with single or multiple carriers?

Without properly finding answers to all these questions, ample room is left for users' devices and plans to fly under the radar.

You cannot control your wireless spend until you control your wireless inventory. There is no single silver bullet to ameliorate this situation, but here is an example of a comprehensive approach.

■ Get each wireless carrier to generate a report of all of the users billed, detailing devices and amounts, for each of your company accounts and subaccounts.
■ From your accounting department, obtain copies of expense reports that include wireless charges.
■ Get a listing of all employees from the human resources (HR) department. If possible (and this is at the discretion of HR and the employees), also get a listing of individuals' personal phone numbers. This information can be used to leverage the carriers later, as well as for seeking personal discounts for your staff (as an added benefit).
■ Consult the general ledger to discover whether all costs derived from the obtained carrier and expense reports have been captured in the wireless spend GL categories.

One advantage of going through this difficult process of tracking your inventory is that once you know what you are paying for, you learn what you can get rid of. For example, there may be spare phones on your plans that have not been used in the past six months, and that are not even on stand-by status. Yet somehow you are still footing the bill for them. Dump those devices. If you are worried about early termination, you can get rid of those devices without penalty in the contract negotiation, which is covered later in this chapter.

Creating an inventory from scratch and then managing it closely does not merely cover head counts; the activity has much broader implications. While it may be a tedious exercise, it is worthwhile to get your arms around your current inventory, as this is the foundation from which you can build sustainable wireless savings.

USAGE: MINUTES

In the wireless world, usage designations fall into a variety of buckets. Usage typically refers to voice minutes, but could also mean data transmission. There is also text message usage, as well as usage associated with a mishmash of optional features. To compound the situation, there are several subtypes of usage within each of these categories. To increase billing opportunities, wireless companies tend to invent terms, plans, and tiers at their convenience, which often makes it difficult for the buyer to accurately compare offerings across telecommunications providers. Following is an overview of the most common types of voice minutes you will encounter. It is important to know the details of these types of usage and be able to compare them to the corresponding type from other carriers.

Peak Minutes

Calling minutes used between the hours of 7 AM and 9 PM, Monday through Friday, are commonly designated as peak minutes. These minutes are typically the primary candidate area for savings that most buyers examine when purchasing wireless plans because they deplete your plan's monthly pool of minutes the fastest. However, having a solid understanding of your usage patterns and comparing the actual peak times across carriers can provide huge savings opportunities for your business. Keep in mind that some carriers, such as Sprint, offer extended peak minute plans. For instance, as of the writing of this book, Sprint's peak-minute period actually ends at 7 PM, which provides the consumer with two extra hours of off-peak minute usage compared to competitors. Several other carriers offer to close the peak minute window even earlier, at 6 PM, but for an additional charge. Later in this chapter, we address some strategies for comparing minute plans.

Nights and Weekends

Nights-and-weekend (nonpeak) minutes periods are comprised of the usage that falls outside of the peak usage time frame. These minutes typically are not counted as usage against your allotted monthly pool. As previously mentioned, the definition of nights and weekends will vary by carrier and can potentially change according to the plan purchased. A final, important note: Some carriers also categorize holidays as nights and weekends.

Shared or Pooled Minutes

Most carriers allow groups of users to share a large pool of minutes. These plans are commonly referred to as shared or pooled plans. A shared plan typically consists of a large bucket of minutes from which all users on the plan pull. The minutes bucket can also be a pooled collection in which the minutes from each user's plan contribute to the pool. Finally, some buckets are a hybrid of the pooled and shared models. Later in this chapter we discuss best methods for configuring these arrangements.

Within-Network Usage

These are minutes used between people using the same provider (for example, Verizon to Verizon calls or AT&T to AT&T calls). Verizon refers to this as *IN* usage. Sprint and T-Mobile refer to it as *mobile-to-mobile* usage. Some providers have unlimited mobile-to-mobile calling on all plans that do not reduce monthly peak minute allotments. Other providers may not include this in every plan, but offer it as a feature for an additional monthly charge. Still others may let you choose a certain number of people who will have unlimited calling privileges. This type of usage is an extremely important consideration if your organization's users often call one another on their cell phones.

Push-to-Talk Minutes

Not all carriers offer this feature. This is also known as walkie-talkie or direct-connect minutes. This is the feature that Nextel popularized, with that unmistakable chirp and associated poor reception that is perceived by many people as obnoxious. As with all other features, it depends on the provider whether this comes standard with your plan or costs extra. Also, depending on the carrier, you may need to choose from a limited variety of phones that support this functionality.

Overage Minutes

Overage is made of up the billable minutes (not nights-and-weekends or within-network) beyond that which is allotted in your plan or pool of peak minutes. Costs of overage minutes can run as high as $0.49 per minute, which in most cases is significantly higher than your plan rate. In order to protect yourself from overage, always arrange in you wireless plans for at least a 10 percent buffer over average peak minutes used.

Roaming Minutes

Minutes generated by calls originated outside your provider's service area are designated as roaming minutes. For instance, let us suppose that you bought your phone in Chicago and have a Chicago area code; you will generate roaming minutes if you take a vacation to Cabo San Lucas and call the office to check on things. Those minutes will be charged as roaming with correspondingly astronomical rates. The reason for this exorbitant charge is that you are using the network of a provider with which you have no contract. International calls are the most common triggers of roaming charges. In the early days of wireless, roaming often occurred within a country. These days even the smallest providers often piggyback on a large nationwide provider's network, so it is a situation that does not need to be worried about domestically. To help you manage this situation, most wireless providers provide a list of international rates on their Web page.

Rollover Minutes

Rollover minutes are not offered by all carriers. They are unused minutes from your monthly peak minute plan that move into the next month's bucket of available peak minutes. Rollover minutes can be confusing, as they often have expiration dates on them as well, such as 30, 60, 90 days, or even six months. So, although you may not use all 100 minutes in your plan in a given month and the unused minutes roll into the next month, they may actually expire, if still unused, by the end of the third month.

In the wireless world, your usage drives the type of plans you buy, which in turn drives your wireless spend. Your goal is to create an optimized plan that allows you to comfortably squeeze as much value as possible out of your plan. This can be a difficult task, but it can add up to significant savings. If you are starting from scratch, a significant up-front time investment will be required, but the bright side is that the investment will more than pay for itself. Once you have the right program in place, periodic maintenance is usually all that is necessary to sustain ongoing savings.

There are two ways to go about determining your users' usage: by manually reviewing your invoices or by obtaining a downloadable report from your wireless provider. Some providers are much better than others at making this information available and providing a useful level of detail. However, some providers only furnish high-level detail in their reporting, or provide dozens of reports that require a database expert to piece together. In many cases this is an intentional tactic on the supplier's part, because the supplier knows that useful and understandable reports lead to easy comparisons of pricing plans. Unfortunately, sometimes the best choice is to get your hands dirty and pull out the paper invoices and manually enter the data into your own spreadsheets.

For simplicity's sake, the following instructions will assume that you are only analyzing a single provider's offering. The main details to examine are peak minutes purchased versus peak minutes used. Most plan descriptions will list the number of minutes bought, and there is also usually some table with minutes available and minutes used in a usage table per user. CD-ROMs and online reporting *should* have these figures available; if not, you should contact your provider to obtain this information. Once you have found it, perform the following actions:

- Create a spreadsheet and enter the peak minutes bought and used for each user for the most recent three months, at least.
- If the business is cyclical, try to capture the three or four peak months.
- Derive an average of the peak minutes used—this is calculated by dividing the total peak minutes used by the number of voice plans.
- Compare average peak minutes used to total minutes available.
- If average usage is less than 85 percent of available minutes, you are oversubscribed and can reduce the number of minutes purchased.
- If average usage is more than 90 percent of available minutes, buy more.
- If average usage is more than 100 percent of available minutes, you are in overage territory, and need to take immediate action.

Carriers love it when you tap into overage territory, because this is when their most lucrative billing occurs. Overage charges are easily discernable on the individual user's usage summary sheet. They may be labeled something like "billable," "voice charges," or "usage adjustment." The charges can also be gleaned from the front page of the bill. If you see any exorbitant amount of charges for usage charges, voice, cellular services, and so on it is almost always due to overage usage (or a great deal of directory assistance).

There is an important caveat to this: Just because all users may be with one provider and they are all under corporate liability, this does not necessarily mean that they are all sharing minutes. It is not uncommon for people to be added to a corporate profile of sharing users yet be subscribed to an individual plan. As you check plans (for providers that have not just grouped all users into one big bucket), look for the word *share* in the plan name, and look for that word or some other indication in the usage box.

This will have two implications in your analysis. First, you have to take those nonsharing users' minutes out of your calculation of total minutes available. Those particular minutes are available only to that person. If that user has triggered overage billing, stop the hemorrhaging and get the user more minutes immediately. Do not wait for that person to be absorbed into the pool. Second, look at the possibility of adding individual users to the pool (and growing the pool accordingly to accommodate them).

Pooled Minutes

From your investigations, you now know how many users you have and what their usage patterns are. Now it is time to shop around for the best plan(s) to fit your wireless usage needs. The problem is that each wireless provider has its own unique (or at least somewhat unique) plans to accommodate business usage. Which one is best? There really is no best. There are just better and smarter fits for your particular needs. To keep things simple, let us assume you are already consolidated and sharing across users.

The first thing you should realize is that there are two different types of shared plan approaches. We will loosely call them pools and buckets. A pooled plan means every user contributes some minutes for all to share. Then there is a bucket, or shared plan, which is a large aggregate of minutes to which individual user's plans do not contribute, but rather from which each participant withdraws. Of the major wireless players (Verizon, Sprint, AT&T, and T-Mobile), only Verizon uses the pool method. Every user makes some kind of peak minute contribution, which can vary by user. AT&T and T-Mobile use the bucket, or shared, approach. They have business enterprise plans in which a large chunk of minutes is purchased for all to use.

AT&T puts a limit on the number of lines each bucket can supply and charges a line fee for each line. T-Mobile has no line limit per bucket and each bucket comes with an included number of lines at no monthly fee. A line charge is assessed for each user over the set number of lines. In this approach, no one technically has allocated minutes the way Verizon has.

Sprint has constructed a hybrid of the two approaches. A single user can purchase up to 4,000 minutes to add to a pool, much like in Verizon's plan. But Sprint also allows for so-called add-on users. These users do not contribute to the pool of minutes, but they can withdraw from the minutes bucket, much like under AT&T and T-Mobile plans.

In most instances in which you reconfigure plans, you will remain with the incumbent provider. That usually narrows the scope of your research. If you are considering migrating service to another provider, then there is much more work to do.

Knowing the structure of different plans also steers the emphasis of your analysis. Some plans offer unlimited within-network calling but no free nights and weekends. You will want to evaluate those elements of usage along with peak usage to build the best plan. If you experience a lot of weekend usage, it is important to figure that into your minute needs.

Look for the details and special offers too. For a short period of time, Verizon offered what they called Option 1 and Option 2 plans. Option 1 plans offered the standard number of peak minutes (450, 900, 1,350, etc.) along with unlimited nights and weekends. With Option 2, for the same price, you would receive more peak minutes (550, 1,100, 1,650, etc.) but no unlimited nights and weekends. If you have no, or limited, night and weekend usage, Option 2 is more cost effective. This is a good example in which due diligence can produce significant rewards.

Your ultimate goal in learning about pool minute plans is to optimize the commingling of your employees' plans in order to obtain the best pricing possible for groups of plans and pools, while still meeting your organization's total requirement for wireless minutes.

The moral of the story is that once you have a solid handle on your usage you should start scouring the Web and making phone calls to wireless sales representatives and learn their offerings inside out. Devise different scenarios to see which plan of attack provides adequate coverage at the best price. Unfortunately, there is no magic bullet when it comes to managing a wireless spend, but due diligence and hard work will pay off.

 USAGE: DATA

Historically, wireless spend consisted of primarily voice plans, minutes, and messages. The rapid expansion of smartphones and aircards into the mainstream has made data usage an equal, if not more important, portion of your bill. As with all things wireless, tracking the usage patterns of your staff and predicting their future requirements can be tricky. It is best to start by reviewing several months of usage to capture the kilobyte (KB) or megabyte (MB) usage by each user and compare it to what is allowed by the plan.

Be extremely careful when comparing data plans across carriers, as they may measure usage differently (e.g., using KB instead of MB). Additionally, pay careful attention to carriers who label their data plans as "unlimited," because often that unlimited plan actually has a cap of 2 to 5 gigabytes (GB), so it is not truly unlimited. Some carriers simply throttle your bandwidth if and when you reach the cap, while others hit you with huge surcharges or terminate your service.

While it is tempting to simply opt for the unlimited plan for each aircard or smartphone user, it can actually be extremely financially beneficial to actually determine each user's habits to see whether any of them can get by on a limited plan. For instance, users who simply read e-mails without attachments may benefit from a smaller plan. Users who need data but do not need e-mail access may also choose a lesser plan (in Verizon's case, corporate e-mail users are billed at $45 per month, while a straight unlimited plan without corporate e-mail is only $30 per month).

 ## USAGE: FEATURES

In addition to minutes and data usage, features can substantially impact your monthly billing. It is important to identify all types of features that your users are purchasing. There is often a considerable opportunity for savings by removing unneeded features, decreasing feature speed and size, or adding features to ensure that no overages are incurred. Following are the most common features that you should review in your sourcing efforts.

Messaging

Most carriers offer several levels of messaging plans. This can range from unlimited messaging for all types of messages, to unlimited text or picture only, to smaller allowances of messages, such as 200, 500, or 1,500 messages per month. Different carriers may use different terms to define messaging but generally SMS refers to text messaging, while MMS refers to multimedia messaging, which includes video, photos, and audio files. Carriers also offer unlimited mobile-to-mobile or in-network messaging plans that provide users unlimited messaging with other users in the same network. In order to understand your users' messaging habits, you must carefully analyze individual employees' historical invoices and continue to do so in subsequent audits once your contract is implemented. Otherwise, if your employees are not on the right messaging plan, you could quickly incur significant overage charges.

International Discounts and Roaming Plans

International travel can be very costly. International calling and roaming plans provide discounts for users who call overseas from the United States or who make calls while roaming outside of the United States. It is critical to capture this usage and the charges associated with these calls, not only for choosing an appropriate international plan, but to request additional up-front incentives when developing a contract (see notes in the contract management section that follows).

Insurance

Depending on the nature of the business, insurance may or may not be necessary. For example, a construction company whose technicians are always outside working on a construction site may warrant adding an insurance plan for a few dollars per month. This is another area where an up-front cash incentive may negate the need for purchasing insurance; it is also discussed in the contract management section that follows.

Downloads

Downloads may include ringtones, alerts, broadcasts, videos, and so on. These downloads can often be obtained through internal software that is included with the device (such as Verizon's Get It Now), or could be obtained through third-party stores, such as the Microsoft Marketplace, Android Marketplace, or iTunes. In most cases, there is no business need for these services, so it is worthwhile to consider establishing an internal company policy banning the use of any of these services, and you should speak to both the carrier and your internal IT staff to explore whether access to these features can be removed entirely from the device.

 ## CONSOLIDATING PROVIDERS

While pooling or sharing minutes, as previously discussed, presents opportunities for substantial savings, just because all users have been grouped into one account that is invoiced on one bill does not necessarily mean that all of those users are automatically participating in a pool or bucket of minutes. You must take additional steps to make sure you have most efficiently optimized these types of plans.

Consolidating to one provider or as few providers as possible presents a huge savings opportunity. It costs less to have peak minute coverage when minutes are shared as a group than on an individual basis. You end up purchasing fewer minutes because people who have high usage can use the minutes of people who have low usage. A person who uses 2,000 minutes a month can have a 450-minute plan and not go into overage, because that person is borrowing minutes from others on 450-minute plans who only use 100 minutes a month.

Let's start with the basics of consolidation. You typically have to have at least five users to be eligible for business share plans. If you have less than five, an alternative would be to arrange a family share plan. Just because you are a business does not mean you cannot take advantage of a family share plan; the plans are governed by the number of lines, not the name of the entity.

Assuming everyone is on the same carrier but not on the same account, you need to get the phone numbers and account numbers of all the people you want to consolidate. Forward that list to your account rep for that provider, who can then help with the consolidation. Different carriers have different approaches to this. Some are easier to deal with than others.

Moving individual-liability phones (phones owned privately by the employee) to a corporate plan (as corporate-liability phones) is a bit more challenging. Before beginning, you should understand your carrier's process so you can review it with your individual liability users and streamline the migration. Most providers require waivers signed by the employee and a copy of a recent bill, and in some cases the employee is required to call customer service and verbally authorize the corporation to take over the line. Making employees aware of all steps and benefits will help you get them moved in one fell swoop rather than having to go back and forth between the provider and the user for each requirement.

Early Termination Fees

If you are migrating users from one provider to another, be wary of early termination fees (ETFs). If your fleet of phones is scattered across the country and is comprised of a hodgepodge of users and carriers, it is financially advisable to move people from smaller providers like Helio, Virgin Mobile, and US Cellular to larger ones like AT&T or Verizon. If you plan on doing this, make sure you know what the contract expiration date is for those users being migrated. ETFs typically range from $150 to $200, and can reach as high as $375 if the user has a smartphone. Keep in mind, some early termination fees can be leveraged even if the user is just shy of fulfilling their term commitment, so you need to do a financial justification to see if it may be less expensive to wait the remaining months for the contract to expire before migrating the user to a new contract. ETFs may also have a prorated formula attached to them, which varies by carrier. With a prorated ETF, the fee for early termination may go down each month as users approach their contract expiration date. If a new contract has recently been signed, it is usually advisable to eat the ETF and move the user. If the user has 18 months left on a two-year contract and the ETF is $200, you will more than make up for the amortized $11.11 per month ETF.

New Plan Profiles

When consolidating users, be ready with a new profile of plans. Some providers require that you have new plans prepared prior to migration. For example, if you consolidate individual users to a business enterprise plan with AT&T, their individual plans do not carry over. You have to know how many minutes are needed so you can buy the appropriately sized pool of minutes as soon as everything is consolidated. This is not as pressing an issue with Verizon or Sprint. Individual users carry their plans with them and start to share those minutes as soon as everything is consolidated and they have a share plan. With Verizon and Sprint, the difference between a share plan and an individual plan is $5. Verizon, for example, has a 450-minute individual plan for $39.99, and there is an extra $5 fee to share those 450 minutes. You do not have to change anything else, but you have to specifically request this. Just because you are asking to consolidate lines does not mean your provider will automatically change the individual plans to share plans.

Consolidating multiple accounts into one may or may not require signing a new contract with that provider. It is important to be aware of this fact when undertaking the wireless audit and cleanup process. Because the accounts are with the same provider, it is easy to assume that accounts and plans can easily be changed and consolidated, but that is not always the case. It is always a good idea to check with your account representative prior to planning or making changes so you can plan according to their process and requirements.

Before selecting your provider for future negotiations, make sure that the carrier meets all of your business users' needs. For example, if you have users who travel overseas, you should keep in mind that domestic providers in the

United States offer different types of cellular service, such as CDMA and GSM. Each has benefits and drawbacks. GSM is widely considered the international standard, and often means that your device will work in other countries without any issues, although the international roaming rates still come into play. That being said, CDMA carriers, such as Verizon, also offer dual-mode phones that provide both CDMA and GSM capabilities for international usage. Other providers offer loaner phone programs for international travelers; however, this can be expensive and inconvenient for the traveler.

International calling and travel is just one consideration. Others may include device availability, push-to-talk capability, and network coverage. As with any sourcing project, you should make an effort to understand all requirements, what is being provided now, and what the wants and needs are for post-consolidation management.

 ## CONTRACT MANAGEMENT

If you have a significant number of wireless users whom you are renewing or moving to a new provider, you have leverage when it comes to adding your terms to a new contract. The number of lines that qualify as giving you leverage can be a moving target, depending on the provider, the timing of the business cycle (end of quarter, end of fiscal year), and, in some cases, your account representative and his or her motivation to get a renewal.

Waivers

There are several items you can get waived relatively easily in the contract. Here's a short list.

Activation Fees

Most wireless providers charge an activation fee of about $30 for new users. In reality, activating a new phone costs little or nothing to the provider; it is just another way for carriers to line their pockets. You will probably not encounter much resistance when requesting to have all or a portion of activation fees waived.

Coterminous Contract End Date

You should ask that all contracts terminate at the same time. Doing so is good planning, as it will ultimately allow you to move your business in one fell swoop at the end of the agreement rather than piecemeal as users come off contract. This also benefits the provider, since it is able to lock more users in for a longer period of time. Assume a phone you are consolidating is six months into a two-year contract. By having a coterminous contract end date, that wireless provider now has that phone for 30 months, not 24. They will probably not say no to that.

Early Termination Fees

There are two points to address here: Establish a sliding scale of ETFs and get a percentage of your headcount of users waived. A sliding scale will reduce the ETF by a certain amount for every month the phone is in service. A standard amount is $5 per month. So if a phone is under a two-year contract with a $200 ETF, but needs to be cancelled after 12 months, the ETF will drop to $140 ($200 − (12 × $5)).

Percentage of headcount subject to ETFs is another leverage point. What this means is that you can negotiate to be allowed to eliminate a certain amount of lines without incurring any ETFs. Suppose you have 200 devices and negotiate the right to cancel 10 percent of your current headcount without incurring ETFs. That means you can get rid of 20 devices and not pay a cent. Ten percent is a standard number; shoot high and see what you can get, but never go for less than 10 percent.

Equipment Pricing

Having a uniform fleet of phones helps in the management of wireless contracts, and there are many quality phones you can get for free when you enlist with a provider. When it comes to higher-end devices, like smartphones, you can demand a discount if you have the numbers to back it up. The discount will depend on how many units you need to buy and the timing of your request in relation to the wireless provider's sales cycle. If you do not have an immediate need, collect and hold orders for new phones, then place them all at one time; the volume can then drive a better price. Also, ask for phones at the end of the provider's quarter; they are more likely to grant your request in order to meet sales goals.

Accessories

It is not hard to get free accessories, such as car chargers and belt clips. Again, this depends on the number of lines you will be contracting.

Bluetooth headsets can also be highly discounted but are less likely to be included for free.

Current Pricing

If your company is still under an old contract, you may not immediately be eligible for the most current pricing. This does not require any kind of specific action, but it is worth monitoring, so that when contract renewal rolls around, you are prepared to gain the best advantage. If there is a new pricing program with the provider and you are under an old agreement, you may not be eligible for the new pricing until a new contract is in place. Be sure you have done your research and are up to date with the market and your needs to get the best pricing.

Autorenew Clause

Once the contract term has expired and a new agreement is not yet in place, the company and user plans should be established to convert into a month-to-month arrangement instead of automatically renewing for an additional term. Carriers will readily remove any such autorenew clauses, but only if you ask for them to be taken out.

Contract Terms

The following list outlines critical contract items to be included in your negotiation with your wireless provider. Each of these items is negotiable and has a direct impact on your initial and future spend.

Grandfathered Plans

Often, you may be able to find old plans that carriers no longer advertise but that are still available. You can ask for one of those plans to be included in your new contract. An easy way to accomplish this is to determine whether your existing users have plans that are no longer offered by the carrier. Sometimes these older plans offer better options than the plans carriers are currently offering. For example, Sprint used to offer a voice plan in which the peak minutes carried all the way until 9 PM (their standard plan currently maintains peak rates until 7 PM), but the plan was $5 less per user than the current plan. While a high-level examination appears to reveal that gaining the extra two hours of off-peak rates favors the new plan terms, in-depth usage analysis may show that, on average, only some users are using only a few minutes in the 7 PM to 9 PM range, and that the $5-per user savings of the older plan far outweighs the cost of paying for the limited use of the extended peak minutes period, thereby justifying the change.

Discounts

Discounts are one of the most critical aspects to negotiate in a contract. Besides analyzing which plans are right for your company, you can leverage the entire spend to achieve a discount off of voice, data, and features. You may also want to investigate group purchasing organizations (GPOs), which in some cases can offer significantly higher discounts than a sales representative can offer. Additionally, explore whether state contracts are available based on your industry. For example, the State of New Jersey's Verizon Wireless contract offers significant discounts to certified educational institutions.

Cash Incentives

If you do not plan to replace the majority of your equipment, ask your carrier for an up-front cash incentive in lieu of free equipment. You can later dispense that cash to purchase new equipment as required. Shoot for a target of $250 cash per voice user and $500 per smartphone plan (voice and data).

International

There are some carriers that do not offer international packages, but allow for discounted international calls. These carriers give additional cash incentives up front or monthly to accommodate these significant usage charges. For carriers that do offer international plans, ask for any additional international calling plan charges to be waived.

New User Credits

You should also receive up-front cash incentives for new subscribers as they are added to the account, even if you do not add them at the start of your contract. If you achieve up-front cash payments in your negotiation, make sure your contract specifies that you will continue to get incentives for each user who is added during the entire term of the contract.

Equipment Discounts

Although it is often worthwhile to ask for up-front cash incentives, an alternative is to ask for free equipment or heavy discounts on high-end devices. You may also ask for flat-rate pricing for devices during the term of the contract, so you do not need to worry about current promotions each time you buy a new device.

Consolidation and Growth Incentives

If suppliers have the opportunity to gain new business, they will likely offer higher discounts and more up-front cash and other incentives to motivate customers to move their business.

Insurance

While not covered in great detail in this chapter, insurance and warranties may be a line item that can be negotiated in a contract. Before you even attempt to negotiate this line item, do a historical analysis of your users' habits to discover whether you have specific users who often break or lose equipment and could benefit from insurance, instead of blindly adding a line-item charge across your entire user base.

When you move to the contracting and negotiation phase with your prospective suppliers, ask for everything up front rather than each component individually. Carefully evaluate the response of the carrier's representative and then request that certain items be added back in to wrap up the negotiation.

 ## OWNING THE LINES

One factor often overlooked in the challenge to successfully manage all the foregoing details concerning the renegotiation of a wireless contract is to establish a corporate wireless policy. In other words, you need to own the lines. Many companies have no policy whatsoever and this hampers any effort to control costs.

Many organizations have a mix of devices they pay for on a monthly basis and those that are expensed by users. Expensing wireless devices and plans usually leads to wasting money. Normally a cap is established on the amount of money allowed to cover the expensed bill. Often, that amount is taken for granted and allowances run as high as several hundred dollars. With an allowance like that or even remotely near it, the user probably has a family share plan where their spouse and kids are covered by the corporate dollar. Plus, when you go with an allowance limit, most people signing off on it will not dig into the bill to see what they are paying for as long as it does not exceed the cap.

The way around this is to arrange corporate ownership of all lines. Construct a corporate wireless policy that clearly states that all reimbursed usage that is paid for by the company is owned by the company. That means whenever a new user is added to the company wireless profile, that line is owned by the company. If any user leaves the company, the device and data remain with the organization.

Implementing such a policy can be challenging. Various providers have different methods of legally transferring ownership of phones and the process can get cumbersome. One thing that simplifies the matter is that many people—when faced with losing ownership of their own lines—will opt to have the company buy them a phone that they use for business, allowing them to keep and pay for their personal phones. Be sure the wireless policy clearly states that this option is available to them. This may lead to a large up-front cost when implementing the policy, but it will almost certainly pay for itself in savings. Plus, as discussed earlier in this chapter, if you have a large enough number of phones to buy and get a new contract signed, you may be able to get all or most of the phones for free.

Once you have ownership of all lines, you have control over the plans and can control who gets what in terms of smartphones, aircards, features, and so on. Controlling those costs can save the organization significant money. Also, billing is consolidated, which eases the burden on accounting, which no longer has to process dozens or hundreds of expense checks for wireless usage because now there is one invoice per provider.

 ## THE ONGOING AUDIT

Unfortunately, it can take several vendor billing cycles to get all contracted plan changes invoiced properly. Periodically, you should look at your monthly bills and, if possible, access online carrier tools to make sure your bills are coming in as you expect them.

Throughout the life of your contract, you should periodically reevaluate your overall equipment and line inventory to ensure that users are still active and you are not paying for employees who have been terminated. You should also do a periodic review to ensure that changes in users' habits do not warrant a shift in their minute or data plans.

In your monthly review of the wireless bill, make sure that there are no overage charges for any of your users. Also, look closely for feature charges that you did not approve, international roaming, text messaging overages, and calls to 411.

A relatively easy way to review your plans on an ongoing basis is to take the average cost per user for voice and data plans and compare it to each month's prior average. To accomplish this, average the cost per user for voice and data plans. This is calculated by dividing the total monthly costs for the plans (including discounts, taxes, and surcharges) by the number of users. For example:

Voice plan has 700 users
Monthly recurring charges = $32,000
8% discount = $2,560
11% taxes and surcharges = $3,238.40
Total monthly charges = $32,678.40
Average cost per user = $32,678.40/700 = $46.68

When there are multiple types of data plans—domestic BlackBerry, international BlackBerry, aircards—it is best to separate out and calculate the average cost per user by data type.

If, when you compare your results month over month, you see your monthly average cost-per-plan rate trending upward, you can take appropriate steps to adjust your plans.

 ## MAINTAINING YOUR PATIENCE

The final word of advice to keep in mind when dealing with wireless providers is *patience*. We have worked on quite a few wireless projects for a number of clients in various industries, and we have only discovered one carrier team that was exceptionally responsive to the customer's needs. A few were marginally responsive, which is usually the best to be hoped for. Still other wireless teams were practically absent. A project that comes particularly to mind is one in which we made plan changes in June that were not put into place until October. That was despite monthly invoice audits reminding the supplier that they had done nothing!

Through the years and our many sourcing projects, we have interacted and communicated with several people knowledgeable about the wireless industry who have given us valuable insights into some of the primary reasons behind this lack of care and responsiveness.

Sales Driven

Wireless is a sales-driven business. Once a provider gets you to sign a two-year deal, they believe that they have captured you. Odds are you are not going to change providers midcontract and take a huge hit on all the ETFs. Once wireless reps get a contract signed, they move on to the next one without looking back.

Delay Tactics

As with many contract-driven sales initiatives, unfortunately you need to deal with supplier delay tactics, such as suppliers or sales representatives purposely dragging their feet and delaying the contracting or negotiation phase of your sourcing initiative. Suppliers may employ this tactic because they speculate that you may decrease your monthly spend, and they want to keep their existing revenue flow for as long as possible.

Turnover

Most sales-intensive fields have high turnover rates. If you are mediocre or poor at selling and you are not making adequate money, you are more than likely going to jump ship pretty quickly. This happens quite frequently in wireless. The subordinates and call center employees in this high-stress industry who might help out on your account are also subject to high turnover rates.

Team Reshuffling

As a result of turnover, to compensate for voids in capability that cannot quickly be filled, people may shift from wireless team to wireless team. Also, representatives with large workloads may be asked to take on additional responsibility, so they do not have time to attend to every account the way you would want them to.

The bottom line is that any major reshuffling of your wireless profile, including anything from plan changes to consolidation to transfer of ownership, takes time. Even something as seemingly simple as sending your wireless rep a spreadsheet of voice plans to change can routinely take at least two months—one month to get the bulk of it changed, then another month to fix mistakes and oversights.

Another word of advice to accompany patience is *persistence*. Sending an e-mail to request some changes and then assuming they have been taken care of, or waiting for the representative to send an update or, even worse, waiting for the next invoice, will get you nowhere. Keep close tabs on your representative and try not to lose your cool when, despite your being on top of your game, you discover that your account representative is not. These things take time. It is not just you or your organization. Many share your frustration. It is worth the effort to remain patient and persistent, and the savings will be the proof.

 ## IN SUMMARY

Wireless spend is often segmented across multiple departments and can be a challenge to rein in. Before beginning a wireless audit, it is critical to identify who is managing each segment and who the primary decision maker is across all of the spend. The real work begins with getting your hands dirty by creating an inventory and auditing usage and features.

In tandem with your audit, it is important to research the market and to review requirements so you can choose the correct devices and plans for your users. Obtaining market knowledge helps you to optimize your plans and ensures all your users are able to be productive without technological impediments. Gaining control over your inventory, your requirements, and your service plans allows you to strategically negotiate with and consolidate providers in a manner that makes the best sense for you and your organization. While wireless can certainly be a challenge, especially if it has not been centrally managed, the hard work pays off in savings that are easily sustainable.

CHAPTER NINETEEN

Getting the Best Small Package Rates

S MALL PACKAGE, small parcel, letters, overnight, expedited—while referred to by many names, it is a common spend category present in almost every type of business. On the surface, small-parcel shipments do not appear to be a very complex category to source, primarily because there is a limited number of suppliers. FedEx and United Parcel Service (UPS) ship the majority of expedited packages, while the U.S. Postal Service, couriers, and smaller regional players serve the rest of the market.

The limited supply base creates several challenges when sourcing this category. First, purchasing and logistics managers often view the Big Two as being equal in terms of service and price, thereby oversimplifying proposal analysis and overlooking large segments of cost and quality improvement opportunities. Second, in such a small market, carriers know exactly what their competitors can and do offer, and know how to tailor their proposals to appear advantageous in comparison to the competition. Third, limited competition makes negotiations and achieving cost reductions difficult. The Big Two have nearly identical playbooks when it comes to negotiations, including shifting the focus of discussion onto service while downplaying the importance of price, stalling or delaying discussions to get the pressure of time on their side, and utilizing their chains of command to delay and add confusion to cost discussions.

This chapter provides an overview of the factors you need to know to ensure you are actually choosing the lowest-priced provider for your business. It details the most effective ways to gather and analyze data, how to leverage market intelligence to motivate carriers, and what to look for in contracts and proposals that carriers do not tell you. Lastly, the chapter details the types of technology and other service changes you can make to reduce or eliminate the internal costs associated with scheduling and processing shipments.

 ## GATHERING THE DATA

As with most sourcing initiatives, one of the most important steps of the project is gathering your own data and specifications. This is particularly true for small-parcel shipping. The best negotiating in the world will not get you anywhere when it comes to producing hard-dollar savings for small parcels if you do not have a proper understanding of your shipping history and profile.

There are three ways of collecting historical data for small-parcel projects. The first two are reactive, meaning you only begin to collect the data once you determine that it is needed for cost reduction efforts. The third is proactive, which means you already have it on hand before sourcing begins.

The first method of collecting necessary information is through your own historical invoices (if they are available) or by requesting access to online portals from your existing carrier and extracting the data into a spreadsheet or database in order to analyze the types of shipments you are sending out and receiving, where they are coming from and going to, service levels, weights, and costs. Unfortunately, doing this with paper invoices could literally take hundreds of hours, and the online portals sometimes do not go back as far as you need, or do not have all of the information you need to get what you are looking for.

An easier way to collect data is to ask your existing carrier (or carriers) for it. You should be specific in outlining the data you are seeking, and ask them to commit to a delivery deadline. Of course, in all likelihood they will miss that deadline anyway. Small-parcel carriers are notorious for delaying any sourcing initiative because they know that the outcome will most likely be lower prices or a change of suppliers. For them, any review of shipments and costs is perceived as a losing situation. Because of this, many carrier sales representatives use a delay tactic to attempt to drag your process on as long as possible, in the hope that you will just move on to another spend category.

Overall, the most effective way to collect data is to already have it on hand. Proactive shippers make sure they receive weekly or monthly usage reports from carriers when developing a new relationship or recontracting with a carrier. If you are already receiving reports from your carriers, then data collection should be a breeze; if not, setting up such a reporting mechanism is one of the first tasks to accomplish.

Regardless of the method of data collection, when you request information from your suppliers, you should be trying to establish your entire shipment profile across all of your locations for at least one year. Specifically, you should focus on:

- *Service types:* Gather a listing of all shipments and the service type for each shipment. Examples include ground, overnight letter, overnight package, and so on. Make sure you understand what each service type means in terms of guaranteed delivery times.
- *Zone:* Determine the shipping zone for each shipment. FedEx and UPS use very similar zone structures (although different naming conventions) for the majority of the continental United States. Knowing your zones allows you to better compare competing offers later in the process.
- *Weight:* Track the billed (not measured) weight of each shipment.
- *Zip to zip:* In addition to determining the zone, gather the destination and delivery zip code of each shipment.
- *Number of pieces:* Determine the number of pieces, letters, or packages each shipment included.
- *Times:* Ask for the shipment time and date as well as the destination time and date. This information is important for auditing your supplier in the future and applying for credits.
- *Pricing/costs:* Ask for a pricing breakdown, which should include the gross price (list price), net price (after applied discounts), fuel surcharges, and any accessorial fees.

With your historical data, you can build a shipment profile for your business, with a focus on the highest-cost shipments and the most frequently used shipment types and zones. This becomes absolutely critical later in the process in the evaluation of offers from each carrier.

 ## UNDERSTANDING PRICING

The typical purchasing group goes to market for small-parcel shipments with the two major players, FedEx and UPS. However, most buying groups are not experienced enough to understand the offerings of each organization, especially since at a surface level they appear to be identical. Both carriers offer similar service types, with slightly different names and very similar pricing structures.

When responding to a request for proposal (RFP), each carrier typically returns a list of service types with a percentage off of list discount prices. They then rely on their customers to see that their discounts are greater than those of their competitors, thereby hoping to win the business. What most customers fail to realize is that the list or gross prices against which the discounts are applied vary between carriers, and is based on the carriers' own published tariffs, called the *Daily Rate Guide* or *Service Guide*. Because the tariff rate or list pricing is different for each carrier, looking at discount percentages alone is meaningless. One carrier may provide a larger discount than the other, but if their list pricing is higher, the overall cost for the shipment could be more.

To illustrate this issue, let us explore a typical situation. A very common shipment is a one-pound package shipped within the same zone with a next-day, 10:30 AM delivery commitment. In its RFP response, UPS may offer a 30 percent discount for such a service, while FedEx offers a 34 percent discount. At first glance, FedEx appears to be the better deal. However, before drawing that conclusion let us take a look at the actual tariffs published in 2010. UPS refers to this type of shipment as "UPS Next Day Air, Zone 102, 1 Lbs." and quotes a standard tariff rate of $18.80. FedEx calls this same service "FedEx Priority Overnight, Zone 2, 1 Lbs.," and lists a standard tariff rate of $20.25. If you factor the tariff (list price) into each offer, you will see that UPS's 30 percent discount, which nets out to $13.16, actually generates a better price than FedEx's 34 percent discount, which yields $13.37. The difference in this single example is minor ($0.21), but it can quickly add up over the course of shipping several such packages over the life of a contract.

Unfortunately, there is no uniform difference in prices between the two suppliers' tariff guides. In other words, each zone, shipment type, and weight has a different delta (degree of separation) in price across each carrier, with one carrier showing an advantage over the other with respect to a particular line-item cost, but not on every single variation. Because of this, it is critically important to analyze the published documents from each carrier for the service types and line items that you use most. You do not need to review every one of the thousands of combinations, but should focus your attention on the most frequent shipment types that your business uses most.

On a positive note, each carrier maintains the same tariff rates for ground shipments. Therefore, if your business does most of its shipments by ground, then it becomes very quick and easy to evaluate discount proposals.

Surcharges are another important aspect to consider when reviewing costs. These charges are sometimes called ancillary charges, surcharges, or fees, but regardless, they can add up quickly. Some common charges include a fuel surcharge, hazardous materials fees, dimensional weight surcharges (for shipments that are light in weight but dimensionally large, like lightbulbs), penalty charges for incorrect zip codes or addresses, and residential fees. Make sure you understand each type of charge, and compare all of them across offers. Keep in mind that some surcharges, such as fuel, are a standard percentage multiplied by the net fee for shipping your product, so they quickly compound costs for a high-priced shipment type.

 ANALYZING THE DATA

Once you collect a historical listing of shipments, it is time to analyze the data and develop a sourcing strategy. The first step is to aggregate the data. If you have multiple locations or utilize multiple carriers for your shipments, make sure you consolidate the information into the same spreadsheet or database. Once you have done this, your data set may be rather large. Reviewing and digesting thousands of rows of shipment history and multiple columns of data may seem like a daunting task. However, there are several assessments you can perform to get a better handle on your data set, including a service type analysis, a zone analysis, and an accessorial analysis.

Service Type Analysis

A service type analysis provides a summary of service levels required for the majority of your shipments. Summarizing shipments in this way helps determine where you should focus efforts during sourcing and negotiations. For example, if most of your shipments fall under the three-day service level, focusing efforts on improving your next-day rate may not make much sense.

In order to develop a service type analysis, you first need to standardize service level descriptions in your shipment history. UPS and FedEx have different names for the same or similar service types, so creating a new column with a standard name for each type helps get a better understanding of which services are being utilized. At the same time, UPS and FedEx use different codes for their zones. For example, a FedEx Priority Overnight Zone 2 package is the same as a UPS Next Day Air Zone 102 package. Table 19.1 provides a cross-reference of UPS and FedEx service types and zones for all expedited domestic shipping.

TABLE 19.1 Service Type Cross Reference

FedEx Service Description	FedEx Zone	UPS Service Description	UPS Zone
FedEx 1st Overnight	2	Next Day Air Early AM	102
FedEx 1st Overnight	3	Next Day Air Early AM	103
FedEx 1st Overnight	4	Next Day Air Early AM	104
FedEx 1st Overnight	5	Next Day Air Early AM	105
FedEx 1st Overnight	6	Next Day Air Early AM	106
FedEx 1st Overnight	7	Next Day Air Early AM	107
FedEx 1st Overnight	8	Next Day Air Early AM	108
FedEx Priority Overnight	2	Next Day Air	102
FedEx Priority Overnight	3	Next Day Air	103
FedEx Priority Overnight	4	Next Day Air	104
FedEx Priority Overnight	5	Next Day Air	105
FedEx Priority Overnight	6	Next Day Air	106
FedEx Priority Overnight	7	Next Day Air	107
FedEx Priority Overnight	8	Next Day Air	108
FedEx Standard Overnight	2	Next Day Air Saver	132
FedEx Standard Overnight	3	Next Day Air Saver	133
FedEx Standard Overnight	4	Next Day Air Saver	134
FedEx Standard Overnight	5	Next Day Air Saver	135
FedEx Standard Overnight	6	Next Day Air Saver	136
FedEx Standard Overnight	7	Next Day Air Saver	137
FedEx Standard Overnight	8	Next Day Air Saver	138
FedEx 2Day	2	2nd Day Air	202
FedEx 2Day	3	2nd Day Air	203
FedEx 2Day	4	2nd Day Air	204
FedEx 2Day	5	2nd Day Air	205
FedEx 2Day	6	2nd Day Air	206
FedEx 2Day	7	2nd Day Air	207
FedEx 2Day	8	2nd Day Air	208
FedEx Express Saver	2	3 Day Select	302
FedEx Express Saver	3	3 Day Select	303
FedEx Express Saver	4	3 Day Select	304
FedEx Express Saver	5	3 Day Select	305
FedEx Express Saver	6	3 Day Select	306
FedEx Express Saver	7	3 Day Select	307
FedEx Express Saver	8	3 Day Select	308

Once you have standardized service types and zones across all shipments, run a pivot table by service type and sum up the total net spend. Sorting this pivot by spend shows you service levels on which you spend the most money. Now add to the analysis a count formula for shipments and divide total spend by total shipments. You now have an average cost per shipment for each service type. As you will likely see in the data set, the higher the priority of service chosen for shipments, the higher the cost per shipment.

The service type analysis not only demonstrates the service levels on which you spend the most money, it also gives you an idea of where you might want to change service levels to receive additional cost reductions. This concept is more fully explored later in this chapter.

Zone Analysis

The zone analysis extrapolates the service type analysis to demonstrate not only what service levels are utilized, but where shipments are going. It is important to understand the service level being utilized by zone for several reasons. First, this level of information is helpful to carriers when providing bids. It shows them how far, on average, your packages travel and by what shipping method (air or truck).

But reviewing data by service level and zone can provide a larger benefit. Moving shipments to a different service type based on the ship-to zone can result in cost reduction without a change in actual service levels. For example, if you are shipping packages to zone 3 via next day air, you can switch to ground and get about the same level of service. This cost reduction strategy, called *mode optimization*, is discussed in detail later in the chapter.

Accessorial Analysis

Accessorial analysis provides detail on the types of additional charges you incur. Understanding this is important for two reasons. First, these charges are negotiable. For example, if you find that many of your packages are assessed a fee for shipping hazardous materials, you can negotiate a lower price or even get this fee waived. You may also decide that it is worthwhile to change internal processes in order to avoid fees. If you are often penalized for putting the wrong address on a shipment, you may decide to cleanse your address file or start using carrier software to print shipping labels to achieve greater control and consistency.

Detailing accessorial fees based on a shipment history provided by your carriers can be a daunting process. Both FedEx and UPS incorporate these fees into shipping data, but they present the data in different ways. UPS generally provides completely separate lines of data with descriptions of fees. For example, one row of data demonstrates a shipment going from Chicago to Los Angeles; the next line shows that shipment incurred a residential delivery fee. FedEx, on the other hand, normally adds a column called *miscellaneous charges*. This one-size-fits-all column includes fuel and other accessorial charges lumped together, and without invoices it is difficult to reconcile which fee types were incurred.

The easiest way to gather this information is to ask the carriers for a separate accessorial report. Carriers can provide the data by shipment or in summary fashion over the course of a month or year. If you use multiple carriers you can consolidate the data in a manner similar to your shipment manifest, standardize the fee types, and run a summary pivot table to see where the majority of your accessorial spend falls.

SERVICE LEVEL AUDIT

The standard analysis of service types, zones, and pricing discussed earlier provides shippers with a good understanding of their shipping profile and can be passed along to carriers during a sourcing initiative. A service level audit is another assessment that should be considered; however, its purpose is much different. It is performed to determine which shipments over an allotted time period were not received within the specified service level (with some exceptions and stipulations). For example, such an audit uncovers cases in which you requested next day service by 10:30 AM, but the package did not arrive until 2. The reason for this audit is simple: Both UPS and FedEx offer guaranteed service levels, meaning that any time they do not get the package to its intended destination on time, you should get a full refund on your shipment.

It is possible to perform a service level audit yourself using the shipment history provided by the carriers. In some cases, UPS and FedEx respond to standard requests for data by providing default reports that demonstrate when a package was picked up and when it was delivered. Using this information and a spreadsheet, you can create several formulas to identify which shipments were delivered late. Once this is accomplished, you can use this analysis to request a credit from the carrier, which can be a lengthy and frustrating process.

Third-party audit firms are numerous and are often paid on a contingency basis, meaning they receive fees only if actual recoveries are made. If you do not have the in-house resources to perform an audit, it is worthwhile to consider using one of these firms. Regardless of the strategy, auditing data is an important component of the small-parcel cost reduction strategy, and should be done on a regular basis.

 ## GO-TO-MARKET STRATEGIES

There are two basic go-to-market strategies you can utilize for a standard small-parcel strategic sourcing project. We call these strategies the *posturing strategy* and the *new business strategy*, and they are based on the spend profile and characteristics of a typical midsize to large company in a market that has two dominant players. If you are a smaller company or can utilize the postal service for expedited shipments, other strategies are available. Overall, the strategy you choose will be based on your current shipping profile and your comfort level in competing the Big Two against each other.

Positioning Strategy

If you have no intention of switching suppliers, and you have no additional business to incentivize your incumbent supplier with, you only have a single option: to position yourself as willing to leave the carrier if you do not get price relief. Utilizing a positioning strategy can be very tricky. The most critical aspect of the strategy is to make sure your entire team, down to the shipping personnel, is on board with the strategy. If your supplier catches any wind that the effort is just posturing, they will provide few, if any, cost concessions.

When using a positioning strategy, you should approach your suppliers by giving them target discounts for each of your shipment types. Don't be afraid to be aggressive in the discount percentages; you could be surprised how deep the carriers may be willing to discount. If you are completely uncomfortable with developing targets, start with a clean slate and ask the carriers to come back with their offers, explaining that you expect to see price relief. When they return with their offers, you should counteroffer with more aggressive discounts than they are providing. Explain to them that you are getting better offers from their competitor, and if they ask to see those offers, explain that it would be unethical for you to reveal them, just as you would not share their offer with the competitor.

One advantage of a positioning strategy is that it can produce results much faster than a standard RFP process that goes to multiple suppliers. Additionally, it is easy to calculate savings, as you do not have to worry about comparing list pricing and surcharges across suppliers.

New Business Strategy

The best leverage you can gain with your incumbent or potential supplier is presenting them with the opportunity to win more business than they currently have. If you are using multiple carriers, consider shifting a portion of the spend from one carrier to another, or incorporate more locations that may not be currently purchasing under your national contract. Make sure you have a national contract in place that can cover all of your locations.

When going to market with a new potential supplier, the entire spend is new revenue to them, and you will likely see aggressive pricing to win it. When you approach your incumbent supplier for price relief, you should be using a dual approach. The first aspect of that approach is representing that the supplier has a chance to win additional business, and the second is that you are seeking bids for your business and expressing the position that you are ready to leave because of the competition's willingness to provide aggressive pricing.

Once you have determined your strategy, it is time to request proposals. This process, of course, starts by contacting your carrier rep and making that person aware of next steps. Keep in mind that if you have multiple locations, your local sales representative is usually not the best person to speak with; you should immediately request that your conversations be escalated to a national account manager.

 ANALYZING THE BIDS

Previously, we explained list pricing or tariffs. Understanding these documents is critical to analyzing the true cost when comparing one vendor to another. In the ideal world, a procurement team would analyze every single combination of zone, shipping, service type, and weight across each carrier to determine the variance from supplier to supplier. However, most companies do not have the resources to conduct such an analysis. Instead, you should focus on the largest group of items that make up your top spend, using the 80/20 rule. For instance, in most companies, there are probably less than 20 service types, weights, and zones that make up approximately 80 percent of your entire spend.

Developing target price points can be very difficult unless you have access to data for other similar businesses. You may want to consider engaging a procurement service provider to help with the initiative, as it would most likely know the right targets for your profile. Keep in mind that your carrier is not going to be aggressive with pricing if you have hundreds of shipping types across multiple categories, or if you have a large spend that is nonetheless spread across dozens of locations, with no one location being particularly significant. The carriers are generally more motivated by commercial business over residential, as well as the shipping origination of your product; some locations are more profitable than others. These are all areas that a third-party consultant could help you understand.

If you did not provide target discounts to your suppliers during the bid process, be prepared for them to come back with aggressive discounts for areas in which you do not do much shipping. On paper the pricing may look attractive, but if you were to do the analysis, you would discover that your overall annual spend is not going to decrease by much. One tactic you can use is to take the most aggressive percentage discount, add more to it, and ask the supplier for that new discount percentage on every one of your shipping types.

Keep in mind that due to overhead, carriers usually offer much lower percentage discounts for ground shipments than for all other spend types. Depending on your spend, a typical ground shipment discount may begin at 5 percent and usually does not exceed a 20 percent discount. For other types, however, without knowing your exact spend profile, shipping types, originations, weights, and all the other aspects of your business, it is difficult to determine projections on the size of discounts and savings targets for which you should be aiming. Nevertheless, assuming you have only a few locations and a spend near $500,000, you could expect to see discounts of 50 percent to 60 percent in most areas. For spends greater than $750,000, expect discounts greater than 60 percent or even 70 percent.

 CONTRACTING TIPS

Once you have finalized the actual pricing terms of your agreement with your suppliers, you should do a final round of negotiations to change certain contractual terms and conditions. In most cases, suppliers readily agree to the following clauses, provided they are confident that they will win your business at the end of the day.

First, you should negotiate a minimum increase each year. As mentioned earlier, each carrier increases their tariff rates (list pricing) on an annual basis. You should request terms in the contract that your discount increases on the same scale as any increase in list pricing. So, if they increase their list pricing by 1 percent, you would get an increased discount percentage for each service type in order to index your costs to the same rate as when you originally signed the contract.

Even though the focus of your RFP is on the top shipment types and zones you use every day, you should also ask for discounts in your contract for the tiers, zones, service types and weight groups that you do not use as often. First, you still want to receive a discount for the few occasions that you ship something outside the norm; second, you do not want to be locked into a long-term contract and have your business's core shipping patterns change into a category for which you have not anticipated discounts.

Make sure guaranteed delivery times are built into the contract. For example, if you pay for next day morning delivery, make sure you have a guarantee that the carrier delivers your product by 11:30 AM. You should also make sure the contract language gives you the right to audit the carrier's records and request credits or refunds for the carrier's missed delivery times; otherwise, guaranteed delivery times are meaningless.

Make sure any costs for training, deployment, or hardware get waived. Your sales representative likely has the ability to waive all hardware costs including computers and printers (but not the consumables, like paper and packaging). They usually also offer free training for your shipping personnel, provided you ask for it.

Pricing Tiers

Over the last few years, the Big Two have shifted their pricing strategy from dedicated discounts regardless of volume to tiered discounts based on an average level of spend, normally based on a 52-week rolling average. Pricing tiers have advantages and disadvantages for the shipper, but for the most part they work in favor of the carrier.

For the shipper, the biggest advantage is that as your volume grows, you automatically receive improved discount rates without renegotiation. This saves time and effort on your part.

For the carrier, the advantages are numerous. First, carriers have the same benefit that the shipper has in that they do not need to renegotiate as volume changes. In addition, volume tiers make tracking and auditing price points much more difficult, which again works in favor of the carrier. If you feel your discount levels are being misapplied, you will have a fairly difficult time proving it without doing a full audit of 52 weeks of shipping volume that can change every week, which is necessary to determine the average volume from which your discounts are applied. That level of complexity discourages shippers from performing an audit and encourages them to trust the carrier to apply the right discounts.

The most beneficial aspect of tier-based pricing for the carrier—and the most detrimental to the shipper—is the impact a temporary downturn in shipping volume will have on discount levels. Let's use an example to illustrate this impact. ABC Company normally ships about $50,000 worth of shipments per week, a $2.6 million annual run rate. At this volume level, ABC receives a discount of 68 percent for most expedited shipments. Last quarter was a bad one for ABC, and shipping levels dropped to an average of $10,000 per week for 12 weeks before business started to pick up again. The 12 weeks at lower rates have brought down the average weekly volume to $40,800, which only qualifies for a 58 percent discount level. Even if volumes quickly return to $50,000 after 12 weeks, another full 52 weeks would pass before the rolling average weekly volume reflected the change. To get to that average more quickly, you would need to spend more than $50,000 per week.

This discount drag is often overlooked in contract negotiations, to the benefit of the carrier. Unfortunately for some shippers, it appears that pricing tiers are here to stay. You may still be able to negotiate fixed discount rate contracts, but it is clear that tier based is currently the carrier default pricing model, and it is unclear how much longer carriers will provide any fixed discount levels. If you are negotiating a tier-based discount program, consider the following:

- *The shorter the better.* The Big Two usually start negotiations with a proposal based on 52-week rolling averages. Based on the previous example, you can see that calculating averages based on that time period can have a major downside for the shipper. You can negotiate shorter rolling average periods; we have seen carriers agree to terms as short as 13 weeks. The shorter the period, the more quickly your business will resume appropriate discount levels after a business downturn. A word of caution here: If having consistent discount levels that change infrequently is as important to you as lower costs, then "the shorter the better" might not be true. After all, the shorter the term for averaging, the greater the impact minor changes in volume will have on your discount levels.
- *Get an exclusion.* You can ask the carrier for language that prevents major changes in discount due to temporary downturns. For example, if there is one month or one quarter that obviously does not fit your shipping pattern, the carrier should be willing to factor it out of rolling weekly averages.
- *Say no to averages.* Rather than using a rolling weekly average, ask the carrier to price out weekly shipments based on actual weekly volume. You will still receive lower discount levels when volumes go down, but the recovery period will be one week, rather than up to 52. Again, a note of caution

here: If you are concerned about pricing volatility, this strategy may not be your best bet.

STRATEGIES BEYOND NEGOTIATIONS

Using strategic sourcing to stimulate competition and negotiate price points can have a major impact on your overall spend for small package shipping, in some cases reducing costs by 30 percent or more. Beyond negotiations there are several other strategies you can use to further reduce costs and ensure that the effort you put into strategic sourcing will benefit your company for years to come. Carriers are happy to help implement some of these strategies, but in other cases you will be on your own.

Mode Optimization

The term *mode optimization* refers to utilizing the service type that best fits your transit time requirements, based on the destination of the package. Many shippers do not realize that depending on the zone, they can downgrade their service level and still get packages to their destination within the necessary time. For example, many shipments delivered via a standard next day service to zone 2 can get there the next day via ground. The only difference is that while the shipment will almost assuredly get there next day within that zone, the shipment is not *guaranteed* to be there next day.

Mode optimization pares out costs by starting with a much lower gross charge and discounting from there. For example, the 2011 FedEx tariff rate for a five-pound standard overnight shipment to zone 2 is $22.60. The ground charge for the same shipment type is $5.79, which is 74 percent lower!

Carriers are often glad to help identify mode optimization opportunities. They look for the zones that have overlap between services and come back to you with recommendations. Carriers even provide routing guides by ship-to zip code, so your shipping staff knows which service type to use for every zip code based on the rules you set up around mode optimization. Of course, if you are shipping time-sensitive materials and need a guaranteed delivery time, mode optimization should not be considered.

Zone Skipping

Shippers sending large volumes of packages to particular states or regions can also benefit from zone skipping. To illustrate a zone-skipping scenario, let us suppose you have a distribution center outside of Dallas, Texas that ships high volumes of product to the Northeast. Rather than having your carrier pick up at your Dallas warehouse, you fill a truck with product and ship it to a carrier hub in New Jersey. Based on the new starting location, the rated zone for shipments could change from zone 7 to zone 2—a much less expensive shipment type. Depending on the quantities shipped and service type requirements, the benefits of zone skipping can often outweigh the costs of utilizing a third-party carrier to ship product from your warehouse to a carrier hub.

While zone skipping has many added benefits, from a logistics standpoint it can add complexity to your supply chain. When considering zone skipping, make sure the volumes of business and the shipment costs warrant the change. For example, moving from an average zone of 3 to an average zone of 2 is not very beneficial, but going from a zone 6 origin to a zone 2 origin will be.

New Services

As with any product or service in your supply chain, you should always be reevaluating the marketplace for new products or services that fit your needs. Collaboration can lead to suppliers bringing new ideas or new products to you. These tactics are also important in a straightforward spend category such as small parcel. Always be on the lookout for something that can benefit your business.

For example, FedEx now offers a unique product called SmartPost. At the time of this writing, UPS does not offer an equivalent service. The FedEx SmartPost product is for businesses that make primarily residential deliveries (such as Internet retailers). It allows a business to package and ship a product via FedEx on a regular delivery schedule, but the package actually gets delivered via the United States Post Office (USPS). The service type is an innovative offering that is a partnership between USPS and FedEx, and gives FedEx the ability to offer a lower-priced option than ground shipping, with only a slightly reduced service time.

While this particular service type may not work for your business (especially if you primarily ship business-to-business), it points to the importance of knowing what products and services are available. Once you establish a relationship with your new carrier, make your sales representative aware that you are interested in finding out about new products and services they may offer.

Dual Carrier Strategy

As with many other categories of spend, cost savings sustainability can be an issue in the area of small-parcel services. Often, shippers build their methodology around the technology of one carrier or another, making change difficult. The longer one carrier receives all of your business, the better that carrier understands the ins and outs of your service level requirements and builds rapport with your internal team. As you become more dependent on one shipper and the company begins to recognize this, you will find it much less willing to discuss pricing concessions or even holding pricing steady, and year over year your cost per shipment will begin to escalate.

To counter this issue, many shippers choose to utilize a dual-carrier strategy, which segments your business and allows you to work with at least two carriers at a time, such as both of the Big Two, one of them and the postal service, or a combination of the Big Two and some local or regional carriers. The segmentation could be by service type—for example, using one carrier for ground and one for air shipments, or shipping local and time-insensitive shipments via postal service and the remainder via FedEx or UPS.

The dual-carrier strategy ensures you always have a carrot available to motivate suppliers and stimulate competition, keeping your carriers on their toes at all times. It also ensures you do not gravitate to one technology or business process that limits your choice of carriers down the line. Further, it gives you the ability to quickly adapt should service levels fall or pricing escalate.

 IN SUMMARY

Sourcing small-parcel spend is really not that difficult; however, it is much more time consuming than the standard process of sending out a document and asking for bids back. If you do not have the time or in-house expertise to analyze data, or do not know where your target discount levels should be, your best bet is to engage an outside third-party consultant, which typically has the tools and software to quickly analyze offers from multiple carriers as well as benchmark data from many other organizations, so it can set the right target discounts for you.

The key to sourcing small-parcel services is taking the time to do a full comparison of offers (after you calculate what they actually mean), as well as being able to unify your team to deliver a consistent positioning strategy, so your supplier becomes convinced that they could lose the business. Aggressively negotiating price points and developing logistical or other process improvements will ensure that the savings are significant and sustainable for years to come.

Making Sense of MRO Spend

THE MAINTENANCE, REPAIR, AND OPERATIONS (MRO) spend category is a catchall for the parts and supplies companies purchase in order to maintain, repair, and operate their facilities and equipment. Sourcing this portion of a budget can be a significant undertaking, particularly for those unfamiliar with the day-to-day operations of manufacturing facilities. What makes MRO a challenge also makes it an interesting category to source. The supplier community is diverse, pricing schemes can be complex, and purchases in many cases are nonrepeatable, meaning you do not often buy the same exact part over and over again on a regular basis. To add to these challenges, in most organizations the maintenance managers and other end users are accustomed to managing the category themselves and can be resistant to change.

This chapter provides an overview of the MRO industry and the types of products that fall into the category. We then review the goals of sourcing MRO, including increasing efficiencies, developing and implementing purchasing controls and, of course, reducing costs. Finally, we provide details about the challenges buyers face when sourcing MRO, and how to overcome each challenge.

■ AN INDUSTRY OVERVIEW

Picture a homeowner. Think of all the products he or she needs to purchase and use in order to keep a home in good condition. Cleaning supplies are needed to sanitize bathrooms. Lightbulbs need to be replaced occasionally to keep lamps lit. Batteries are a must to keep smoke detectors working and ensure safety measures are met. A vacuum cleaner may need replacement bags. A lawn mower may only run on gasoline. Other products are needed based on the change in seasons, such as salt, a shovel, and a snow blower. Various tools are also required for ad hoc repairs around the home. Just as homeowners must maintain and repair their homes, so too must companies maintain their facilities. However, for an organization, these types of purchases are made on a much larger scale.

In a business, MRO products span across multiple business units and the spend falls under the purview of many different stakeholders. Some supplies relate to the prevention of safety hazards. Others are associated with providing a comfortable working environment for employees. Another portion relates to making sure there is very little disruption to actual production. Examples of MRO supplies include:

- Electrical supplies and electronic components
- General industrial supplies
- Bearings and power transmission
- Fasteners
- Lubricants
- Filters
- Pipes, valves, and fittings (PVF)
- Motors
- Safety supplies
- Laboratory supplies and equipment
- Original equipment manufacturer's (OEM) machine parts

It is important to note that MRO means different things to different people. Some may add janitorial supplies or even office supplies into this category, others bundle in services or segregate out parts for capital equipment. The diverse commodities listed are indicative of the substantial size and scope of the MRO industry. Regardless of what you categorize as MRO, the ultimate need you are looking to satisfy remains the same: It is the stuff you buy to keep your plant running in a safe, efficient, and effective manner.

Adding to the complexity in defining the category is the diversity of the supply base. Thousands of suppliers exist in the marketplace; some provide a wide range of products and others are more niche or specialty players. On a high level, the market includes:

- *Manufacturers:* These include the companies that make motors, bearings, and electrical components. Examples might include WEG (for motors), Gates (for belts), and Philips (for lighting and other electrical supplies). In this industry, the manufacturers control the market, and often dictate pricing on a customer-by-customer (rather than distributor-by-distributor) basis. We go into detail on the impact of manufacturers on the industry later in this chapter.
- *Specialists:* These are distributors with a single focus, such as PVF, electrical supplies, or safety supplies. Specialists, such as Columbia Pipe and Fitting or Arbill, market their technical experience and ability to help customers not just by supplying parts, but identifying what parts a customer actually needs to perform a particular function or stay within compliance rules and regulations. Most offer engineering and design support as well.
- *Generalists:* These include distributors that provide a broad array of parts over a wide variety of categories. They may provide electrical supplies, fasteners, general industrial supplies, and safety supplies, all in one catalog. Examples of generalists include Fastenal, MSC, Grainger, and McMaster-Carr. Generalists focus on providing a one-stop shop, easy ordering, and value-added services, such as vendor-managed inventory or free next day shipping. Their focus is on ensuring that you have the part you need (any part) at the time you need it (any time).
- *Partnerships:* Partnerships can be fairly diverse in nature, but normally include a group of specialists (and sometimes manufacturers) in a particular industry that come together to compete on a regional or national level. In the category of electrical supplies, partnerships such as Vantage Group or Vanguard National Alliance have pooled, in some cases, hundreds of individual local companies together in a loose affiliation or even through the formation of a new company to compete with national (semi-)specialists such as Wesco Distribution. In the area of bearings and power transmission, national partnerships such as Precision Industries were developed to compete with the likes of Motion Industries, Applied Industrial Technologies, and Kaman.
- *Integrated supply:* Also known as outsourced storeroom management or consolidators, these companies take over the entire process

of purchasing MRO on your behalf. This includes ordering products, managing inventories, and paying for goods. Integrated suppliers cater to companies that want to focus on their core competencies and out-source the day-to-day activities of parts procurement to someone else. Companies utilizing integrated suppliers expect to see value in lever-aging the overall volume purchased by integrated suppliers to reduce their per-unit cost when purchasing parts, and benefit from processing one vendor invoice a month rather than hundreds or even thousands. Suppliers focused in this area include supplyFORCE and Storeroom Solutions, although generalists such as Fastenal or Barnes Group or specialists such as Motion Industries are also beginning to offer some level of integrated supply services.

■ *Retailers:* Purchases from home improvement stores such as Lowes, Home Depot, and Sears Hardware often fall under the MRO category as well. Retailers offer easy access to thousands of general items, but if you are looking for a part that is somewhat unique, or a specific manufacturer, you probably will not find it here. In addition, most retailers do not offer anything substantial in terms of corporate discount programs, so you pay premium (retail) rates when buying from one.

The industry is further segregated into local, regional, and national play-ers, with some overlap. For example, your local electric distributor could fall into several categories. It may stand on its own and serve your local plant, but it could also partner with other local distributors to offer programs nationally through an organization, such as Vantage Group, to accommodate companies looking for local service and consistent pricing across locations.

Also available are services and sales teams that work day-to-day at your facilities; they are as diverse as the suppliers in the industry. Sales representa-tives at national companies may be able to deliver service offerings, technology, and consolidation opportunities, with local companies providing engineering support and technical expertise. Some reps can be highly capable, and oth-ers fairly unqualified, unknowledgeable, or downright unprofessional—all within the same company, operating under the same contract and service level agreement.

As you begin to analyze your spend data, you should keep this diversity in mind. You may see that multiple suppliers are used for the same type of purchase, or even the same part, either within the same plant or across mul-tiple facilities. This may represent a consolidation opportunity, or there may be valid reasons for using multiple suppliers. Before diving into the actual spend analysis, let us lay out the objectives often targeted by buyers when sourcing MRO commodities.

OBJECTIVES WHEN SOURCING MRO

Generally speaking, MRO is classified in the tactical spend area; however, some aspects of it can also be considered leveraged or critical, or even a combination of all three. As such, there are many different strategies one can utilize to obtain savings in this area. Over the course of our work we identified seven primary objectives customers seek to achieve when sourcing MRO.

1. Uncovering savings opportunities by identifying competitive pricing through alternates.
2. Establishing a more streamlined ordering process and developing ordering controls.
3. Standardizing internal data.
4. Reducing inventory levels and lead times.
5. Maximizing equipment uptime.
6. Rationalizing the supply base.
7. Developing a solid relationship with the supply base.

The goals you lay out for your initiative, along with the market assessment, guide the sourcing strategy and your approach to supplier engagement. After company usage information is analyzed and research is performed, these goals will be slightly adjusted and enhanced as the sourcing strategies are developed and information is prepared to send along to suppliers.

Cost Reduction and Supplier Rationalization

Generating a positive impact on a company's bottom line is the idea at the forefront of all sourcing initiatives. Some goals fluctuate depending on the product or service being sourced; however, cost reduction is the one always present in the mix. The likelihood of achieving savings for MRO products is significantly high based on the number of options available to buyers in the marketplace. The sheer number of suppliers that offer MRO parts and supplies is leverage in itself when negotiating with incumbent suppliers. The spend analysis may indicate several suppliers employed by end users that deliver almost identical product and service offerings. Besides the low risk of supply loss, spend consolidation is another driving factor for cost savings. Narrowing the number of preferred suppliers used by an organization delivers better volume-pricing agreements and makes supplier management an easier process. Savings can also be achieved through transitioning from branded items to more generic items or standardizing with certain manufacturers.

Ordering Process Efficiencies

The majority of MRO products are considered tactical purchases. This means that the costs associated with acquiring an MRO product can be greater or equal to the cost of the product itself. Therefore, a streamlined, simple ordering process is worthwhile to establish through an integrated program with the selected supplier or an online portal in which technology drives down the cost of acquiring a product. Wherever possible, the program should make invoice reconciliation easy or unnecessary to further drive down the internal costs of processing hundreds, if not thousands, of individual invoices.

Part Number and Specification Standardization

Buyers may find, when performing their spend analysis, that their company's internal ordering system does not deliver reliable information. If several locations are ordering the same product, descriptions are likely to vary and data entry errors may also exist. The hardest part of the data collection phase for MRO spend is organizing the spend data and making it supplier-friendly. Years down the road, when you wish to revisit this spend category, you do not want to have to go through the same standardization process again. Cleaning up and standardizing internal data helps give visibility to the category and make sourcing a much more productive process. It also aids in the ordering process, making it easier to select the right part and ensuring suppliers do not have to guess about what you ordered.

Inventory Level and Lead Time Optimization

The nature of MRO requires that a multitude of stock-keeping units (SKUs) be kept on hand in case a machine breaks. After all, the cost for an individual part is not much compared to that of a production line going down, even for a few minutes. In these cases, waiting for the next supplier delivery or running out to the local hardware store is not an affordable option. That said, the cost of managing and fulfilling MRO stockrooms at multiple locations can easily result in a substantial amount of cash being tied up in on-hand inventory. There are ways to optimize inventory levels using value-added services from suppliers, such as vendor-managed inventory or consignment. The option of outsourcing your stockroom altogether also exists and should be explored during an MRO sourcing initiative. Lastly, reviewing current inventory and identifying obsolete or no-longer-needed parts that can be sold back to distributors, reducing carrying costs, and opening up warehouse space, is often included as part of the scope of work of an MRO cost reduction initiative.

Maximizing Equipment Uptime

Hand in hand with inventory levels and lead-time optimization is maximizing equipment uptime. Having the right parts readily available when machines go down is a major service level component that comes into play with any MRO supplier. However, maximizing equipment uptime also means buying the *right* parts to begin with. The execution of MRO purchases is often rife with the acquisition of poor quality parts, retrofitted equipment, incorrect deliveries, incorrect orders, and using the wrong types of parts for the application. The right supplier or group of suppliers can assist in troubleshooting and resolving all of these issues.

Long-Term Supplier Relationship Development

Suppliers in the MRO industry are familiar with periodic customer turnover, realizing that price often trumps customer service. While part of this perspective holds true, it is worthwhile to evaluate a supplier's overall service offering. After all, in order to achieve a portion of the cost savings available, process improvements need to be implemented. Also, certain MRO products are considered critical in nature and are not available through many suppliers. For these market baskets, a good supplier relationship is essential.

Overall, the goals and objectives for the category will lay the groundwork for the initiative. As suppliers are engaged, make them aware of each goal and collaborate with them to achieve each one most effectively. The one goal that requires the most patience is the standardization of part numbers. As you dive into data collection and spend analysis, you will realize how much effort is needed to accomplish this goal.

 DATA COLLECTION AND SPEND ANALYSIS

The first hurdle to jump in an MRO strategic sourcing initiative is organizing the data you have and identifying the data you want. Before diving right into the data collection phase, it is worthwhile for buyers to develop a high-level overview of the vendors already used across their organizations. The amount of MRO products purchased by a company is driven by three primary considerations:

1. *Equipment related to a company's end product.* Some equipment that needs to be maintained is specialized based on the industry in which a company operates. For example, a mining company that has a large fleet of trucks in the field every day needs to pay close attention to the parts purchased to keep the fleet well maintained. If a tire blows out on a truck, it is best not to have that particular truck out of commission for the rest of the day.

2. *The number of plants or locations.* Multiple locations translate into more facilities and equipment necessary to be maintained. More locations also means that more stakeholders are involved in the spend category, which likely results in a decentralized purchasing structure.

3. *A company's use of maintenance service agreements.* The manufacturer of the equipment or another maintenance service provider may maintain some pieces of equipment used within a company on a regular basis. Engineers within a company are able to perform standard repairs on certain equipment. However, agreements may be in place if a piece of equipment is highly specialized. The implementation of these types of agreements is based on the value of the equipment being used. These agreements also cover any liability issues that arise and include the parts and supplies needed to perform repairs and properly maintain equipment.

Stakeholder Involvement

Knowing the nature of your company, you probably already have a good idea of what to expect when looking at your data. If you have multiple locations, be prepared to engage multiple spend owners and standardize the data across all locations. The first step in the data collection process is to understand how many suppliers are utilized and where each one fits within the organization. With the high-level spend information in hand, it is a good idea for buyers to take the time to survey their organizations. Most likely, some preferred suppliers are currently being utilized and it will be useful to gather details regarding these relationships. Identify who the stakeholders are for each supplier and hold preliminary conversations with each individual to understand the role each supplier plays across departments.

Engaging stakeholders early on helps buyers as they sift through the data and develop the baseline. These conversations help determine the service levels required from a supplier. Make the spend owners aware of your aim to analyze the entire MRO spend category. It is likely that they will be able to provide insight right away as to which suppliers are worth considering and which commodities have recently been looked at. The data collection process and detailed spend analysis are critical steps in the MRO sourcing process. Not only will they reveal the scope of work for the initiative, they also give you a head start on your research and the process of identifying alternate suppliers.

As conversations continue with specific spend owners, ask them to provide the following deliverables if you are unable to collect them yourself:

- Current contracts or pricing agreements
- Online access (if available)
- Current supplier price sheets
- Existing specifications (if required)
- Current inventory details and vendor-managed inventory requirements
- Supplier contacts and names of other end users
- Product and service specifications

Supplier Interviews

In some cases, the supplier contact information is enough to get you started. Once you have received feedback from end users regarding suppliers, interview each supplier to gain its perspective on the current relationship. Explain that you are conducting an initiative to analyze the company's MRO spend category and you want to bring the supplier into the process to fully understand the relationship and the value-adds it provides. As mentioned, stakeholders can speak to this, but by asking the following questions of suppliers, you are taking a more objective approach.

- How long have you been a supplier for us?
- How would you rate us as a customer?
- What could we do better as a customer?
- What issues (quality, service, delivery, payment, other) have you encountered while working with us? How have issues been resolved?
- Who places orders? (This indicates how centralized or decentralized the ordering process is.)
- How are orders placed? (Online, via fax, phone, or other method)
- What are your lead times?
- What services do you provide us that might not be in the contract or on an invoice?

- What services do you offer that your competitors do not?
- Do you offer maintenance or repair service?
- How many branches do you have? Where are they located?
- How much stock do you keep in your warehouse?
- How long does it take you to get a part if it needs to be ordered?
- How are products delivered?
- What services do you provide that we do not take advantage of?
- Who do you see as your top competitors?
- Do you have online catalogs and online ordering?
- What are your payment terms?
- How do you receive payment (check, ACH, or other method)? Do you have a preference?
- What are your preferred contract terms (length of contract)?
- Are your prices subject to change based on raw material costs? If so, how quickly are market increases typically rolled out? Do you have a formula for rate increases?
- Do prices decrease when markets take a downturn?
- Do you have a contract or pricing agreement in place with us?
- Do you charge freight?
- How are freight charges calculated?
- What are current freight rates?
- Are there other regularly occurring surcharges or accessorial service fees? Please explain them.
- Is there anything else we should know that we did not discuss yet?
- What would be the best outcome of this project for your organization?

The answers to these questions are factored into your baseline assessment. Crucial information on the relationship, ordering process, value-added services, terms and financials, pricing, and other details are necessary to gather. Receiving these details from both parties enables you to fully understand the current working relationship. If new information is relayed by the supplier, make the stakeholders aware of this and confirm that any new information shared is, in fact, correct.

As you carry out conversations with suppliers, also request any usage reporting to supplement the internal data with which you plan to work. Reconciling this information ensures that you have captured all the spend for a particular supplier. If stakeholders are unable to provide some deliverables, suppliers can most likely fill in the gaps. The deliverables that suppliers are normally able to pass along and should have on record are:

- Detail of items purchased and volumes (usage reports)
- Existing contractual and pricing agreements
- Specification sheets and technical data for targeted items
- Discount or markup structure for noncontract and contract items
- Online access (if applicable)

Digging through the Data

In order to quantify and measure the results of the sourcing initiative, a spend analysis needs to be performed. This comprehensive analysis should objectively identify the historical purchasing patterns and reveal possible sourcing strategies that can be further developed and considered. The analysis needs to get to the line-item level (by product) of each order—the amount of work performed in this phase really depends on how sophisticated current ordering processes are. Some portion of MRO purchases are likely placed through purchase orders; however, more tactical, recurring purchases can be made through an online ordering portal on which corporate credit cards are used. If the majority of purchases are made online, supplier usage reporting is likely available and used to compile the data. In most cases, a combination of your company's internal records and supplier data can be used to create a master spreadsheet.

The MRO data collection process can be tedious. If the majority of suppliers are regional or local players, they may not have appropriately sophisticated reporting systems to provide a breakdown of sales by SKU. Therefore, internal records and actual invoices are needed to develop line-item detail. The goal is to capture enough information to properly identify the part and allow alternative suppliers to quote it. Typically this means identifying the manufacturer part number, the distributor part number, or both.

Manually entering these records can be difficult and time consuming. One option for cleansing your data is engaging an outside party. Typically, a fee is charged for each line item of data. However, the cost savings achieved through this process usually far outweigh the minimal charges that are assessed. Plus, the turnaround time is usually quicker than if you do the work yourself.

Conversely, if suppliers are national in scope or have developed robust reporting systems, much of the data you need to get started is readily available.

Many consider MRO parts and supplies to be at the bottom of the sourcing totem pole, which explains why record-keeping in this area can be rather poor. Manual record-keeping of data often results in unintentional data entry errors. If you have multiple facilities, you will need to assemble a uniform file that

TABLE 20.1 Unclear Data

Supplier Name	Customer Reference Number	Item Description	Manufacturer	MFR Part Number
Wesco Distribution	98743561	FUSE, TIME DELAY: 600 V, 20 A	BUSSMAN MANUFACTURING CO	FRS R 20

encompasses all items across locations. Standardizing data is another challenge of MRO sourcing.

Table 20.1 illustrates a sales record for a fuse. This record has poor line-item detail information, which makes it difficult for anyone to determine exactly what type of fuse it is. Further, the data is inconsistent with normal naming conventions for this particular manufacturer.

Table 20.2 is an example of how the data looks after standardization. You may need to create multiple line items if the baseline prices vary across locations. Typically, if a contract is in place, you can apply that pricing across all locations.

Notice the category listed in the table. Time delay fuses are categorized in the electrical supplies market basket along with other product lines that are considered electrical items. Once the data has been cleaned, you will then be able to easily identify the different market baskets that exist. Slowly but surely the scope of work becomes apparent.

An Example of Dealing with Poor Data

A company conducting an MRO sourcing process found that it dealt with approximately 10,000 SKUs in the internal purchase order and inventory systems. Prior to going to market for all of the MRO spend categories, this data

TABLE 20.2 Standardized Data

UNSPSC Code	UNSPSC Category	Normalized MFR Name	Normalized MFR Part Number	Cleansed Description	Incumbent Supplier Part Number	Incumbent Supplier Packaging UOM
39121604	Time delay fuses	COOPER BUSSMANN, INC	FRS-R-20	FUSE, TIME DELAY, 600 VAC, 20 A, DUAL ELEMENT, CLASS RK5	05171250832	Each

required normalization. Specific items were not identified properly and part numbers were recorded inconsistently—manufacturer part numbers were often considered supplier internal reference numbers and vice versa.

For this particular case, a third-party provider was engaged to cleanse the data in order to present suppliers with reliable information in the request for quote/request for proposal (RFP/RFQ) process. Each SKU was assigned a manufacturer part number and a full, detailed description, standardized by product type. The SKUs were coded in order for the data to be broken out for consistency with the company's purchase order and inventory systems. These SKUs included all MRO purchases across all incumbent suppliers. The cleansed dataset also included United Nations Standard Products and Services Code (UNSPSC) coding information, making each line item easier to identify and categorize.

The output received was used to go to market and was formatted to be supplier-friendly. Consistent usage information was provided along with a standardized way of looking at the data, allowing suppliers to put their best foot forward and ensuring that the resulting bids generated an apples-to-apples comparison of current specifications.

As mentioned, if you find that you do not have the resources to properly analyze the mountain of purchasing information that has been assembled from inconsistent records of entries, then consider hiring a third party to assist. Normalizing the spend data is one of the greatest obstacles to overcome when sourcing the MRO category, and it sometimes makes the most sense to use all the help you can get.

The Scope of Work: Developing Market Baskets

The end result of your spend analysis is a cleansed and clarified database of information. Ultimately, proper MRO sourcing requires a breakdown of purchases to the SKU level and well-defined specifications for each part purchased. The easiest and most common way to do this is to identify the manufacturer part number for each SKU. This can be done by an internal team, your suppliers, or a third party. Once this is accomplished, it is time to categorize the supplies into market baskets. There are many ways to develop market baskets, but to do it properly you first need to develop a preliminary sourcing strategy.

Preliminary Strategies: Identifying Baskets

There are several reasons why a strategy must be developed prior to creating market baskets, and they are best illustrated through examples. Let us suppose one of the primary objectives of the sourcing initiative is to obtain enhanced services, such as engineering support and technical expertise. You will want a supplier with local representation that can be a regular resource at your plant, inspecting equipment and providing advice. In this case your strategy is to develop very specific market baskets; for example, motors, electrical components, and fasteners. You will award the fasteners business to one supplier, electrical to another, and so on, with each supplier providing its own technical specialists.

On the other hand, if your focus is on reducing the amount of suppliers you need to manage, getting product in as fast as possible, making ordering and purchase order reconciliation easy, and giving maintenance managers and other plant personnel the easiest access to as many types of supplies as possible, you may want to broaden your market baskets so that electrical, PVF, fasteners, and other industrial supplies all fall within one basket, and plan to award all that business to a single supplier.

Regardless of the strategy, how you define these market baskets should be reflective of the supplies offered by particular suppliers. Even when casting a wide net, you still probably will not want to keep bearings and power transmission products in the same category as, say, paint or janitorial supplies. Some commodities just do not belong in the same basket.

Assigning Parts to a Basket

Once you have established a preliminary strategy and have determined your market baskets, begin separating frequently purchased items into the baskets based on the nature of the individual items and their purpose. The data may be comprised of an enormous array of products, from general items such as screws, cleaning supplies, and lubricants, to more sophisticated and unique items, such as ball bearings, specialized drill bits, and machine parts. Essentially, you are looking to link each item to the supply base best suited to provide that item.

Think back to the example of the homeowner. Cleaning supplies are needed as well as lightbulbs, batteries, and many other products to keep the equipment in a house up and running. The likelihood of one store having all the needed supplies is relatively low. If a store does carry all the items needed, the margins for certain products may be significantly higher due to their slow inventory turnover. For example, the hardware store is likely to carry batteries and light bulbs and other standard products. However, if you are looking for gasoline for your lawn mower, you should head to the gas station.

Using a preestablished coding system such as the North American Industry Classification System (NAICS) or UNSPSC (see Chapter 2 for more information on these classification systems), or your own internal coding system (if it is consistent), is the easiest way to segment products into market baskets. For example, you may buy hundreds of different types of V-belts, using many different suppliers. Fortunately, all V-belts fall under the UNSPSC code of 26111801—V-belts. For every type of belt, regardless of supplier, description, or specification, you can assign this code. Once you have coded all your data, you can categorize all belts into the same market basket. In this case, that basket would most likely be "Bearings and Power Transmission."

Regardless of how you code individual line items, it is important to make sure your methodology is consistent. There can be a tendency to base your categorizations not on the product purchased but rather the supplier utilized. You may find that at one time you purchased a valve from McMaster-Carr. However, this does not mean that all McMaster-Carr purchases should be included in a "Pipe, Valve, and Fitting" market basket.

Prioritizing Projects

Once you establish market baskets you are ready to transition into the sourcing phase of the project. It is important to note that the market baskets you develop will each become a separate sourcing initiative or project. That means that the research, bid process, negotiations, and contracting for each of these baskets will be independent of each other (perhaps with some overlap), with supplier selection criteria established on a market-basket basis. With this shift in mind, you may decide to prioritize sourcing efforts based on the spend volume within a particular basket, the criticality of a type of purchase, the bandwidth of your team, or other internal priorities. Conversely, you may decide that running all projects in parallel makes the most sense.

Keep in mind that the project management methodology you choose should be reflective of the realities of your organization and the profile of your spend. Change management can be difficult, so choose a methodology that shows results quickly and builds momentum within your organization. Otherwise stakeholders, end users, and other team members will lose steam and the efforts you put into data cleansing and categorization may not pay off.

 ## RESEARCH

The objective of the research phase is to cast a wide net into the marketplace and identify major players that could be considered potential business partners.

For each commodity or market basket, a preliminary market assessment needs to be carried out. The results of this phase serve as the input for the development of the sourcing strategy for each project. During this stage, the focus is on identifying qualified suppliers based on your organization's requirements.

Be on the lookout for suppliers that offer:

- Optimized ordering processes that will lead to lower transaction costs and process improvements
- Inventory management services
- A diverse set of manufacturers (the incumbent supplier may only have one manufacturer for a particular product line, whereas other suppliers offer multiple manufacturers to choose from, providing increased flexibility in ordering)

If supplies and parts for certain pieces of equipment are being sourced, gather information relating to the equipment currently being used. Does it make sense to trade in old equipment and invest in new equipment? This approach may deliver process improvements and more options with regard to the parts and supplies needed to maintain the equipment.

The option of working directly with manufacturers rather than distributors for certain parts is worth exploring. In some cases, certain thresholds in spend and annual quantities need to be reached in order to develop a direct agreement with a manufacturer. Regardless, this option should be considered. Be sure to carry out the following actions during the research phase in order to have enough information to develop a sourcing strategy.

- *Identify suppliers.* The suppliers identified should meet the requirements defined in the baseline analysis.
- *Understand supply chains.* You want to develop an understanding of where your distributors get their product.
- *Understand market conditions.* Review commodity indexes for each market basket. This information is available through subscriptions as well as the Bureau of Labor Statistics. Analyze whether the current moment is the best time to source.
- *Understand the factors of cost.* How is unit pricing determined? What materials are built into this?
- *Review available technologies.*
- *Review alternative processes.* Analyze the relative values of new equipment with cheaper parts versus old equipment with more expensive parts.

- *Review alternative products and services.* What alternative manufacturers are available through other suppliers? Are there generic items you could be using instead of branded items?

Uncovering savings opportunities for the MRO category may be as simple as researching the available commodity-index pricing or gathering recent industry news on a particular category. For instance, it is possible that price increases were just passed through by your lubricant provider; however, the oil supply may have recently increased, and there may have been a downward trend in pricing over the past year. Therefore, the sourcing strategy for this market basket may be as simple as asking the incumbent supplier to justify price increases.

Your research will vary depending on the market basket, but the overall theme is to gather enough information to fully understand the spend category and develop a final sourcing strategy. Regardless of what the market indicates for each category, regroup with your team to share your findings and discuss each one separately to draw up a go-to-market strategy.

 ## GOING TO MARKET

In Chapter 4, "The RFx Process," we described four sourcing strategies: tactical, leveraged, critical, and strategic. Most companies classify MRO products and services as tactical purchases. However, some MRO items can be very high cost, placing them in the leveraged classification, or heavily specification-oriented, in which case they would be considered critical purchases.

For example, the purchase of general industrial supplies, such as batteries, a hand tool, a can of paint, or a broom, are often made when a sudden need arises. These products are low cost and the time and effort to obtain them can often exceed the unit price of the item, making their purchase tactical in nature. An easy way to obtain these products would be through an online ordering portal that integrates with your purchase order or requisitioning system. In this market basket, an RFP is normally issued to gain pricing information as well as details on a supplier's capabilities to streamline the ordering process for tactical purchases.

However, certain lab supplies have quality control standards that need to be met and specifications that may correspond with unique laboratory equipment, which would place them in the critical classification. The typical approach for going to market for critical purchases is to issue an RFP with an exhibit detailing all the necessary specifications. The RFP should welcome alternatively products or processes that provide for cost savings, opening the category to competition and potentially transitioning the spend into the tactical classification.

As you can see, even within the category of MRO, your final sourcing strategy can differ greatly between projects or market baskets. If your goal is to optimize the process and the costs associated with MRO, a one-size-fits-all approach to sourcing will not be effective. In this chapter, we do not go into great detail on how to create an RFP for MRO items. Sourcing strategy, RFPs and the bid process in general are covered in great detail in other sections of this book, and that information can be applied to MRO. However, we do discuss what to expect from a pricing perspective when suppliers are invited to quote on MRO items.

How Pricing Works

In the world of MRO, in which many different types of products are purchased, often in fairly low quantities, working with distributors that provide large catalogs of items is rather commonplace. The distribution model makes sense—buying in bulk is not really an option, and opportunities to standardize on particular manufacturers are limited to their catalog or line card, which may cover only a small portion of your total MRO purchases.

With that information in mind, it is interesting to note that in many market baskets within the category of MRO (such as electrical supplies, bearings, and power transmission), manufacturers dictate pricing on a per-customer basis. The purchasing power of large distributors that warehouse and inventory bulk quantities of particular products secures only negligible discounts from manufacturers. What the manufacturing community really wants to capture is the volume and opportunity presented by a particular end customer, and it will offer higher incentives on the basis of capturing business from that customer only.

So what is the impact of a manufacturer-controlled marketplace on your MRO purchases? Why does it matter to you?

First, it means that every time you go to bid, the distributors with whom you are negotiating are approaching manufacturers on your behalf. In some cases the distributors represent different manufacturers and there is no overlap in who negotiates with whom, but in other cases all the distributors are going to the same manufacturers to request pricing.

Second, if they are not going direct to the manufacturers for special pricing agreements—SPAs, as they are known in the industry—they are simply guessing at what manufacturers will agree to once they are awarded the business. Their guess is often close, but it is rarely 100 percent accurate. To some extent, the distributor, depending on its negotiating skills, is either going to get charged more or less than anticipated by the manufacturer. This introduces a fair amount of uncertainty into the process, and prevents all parties from achieving optimal pricing.

As you can see, the manufacturer-controlled marketplace leads to much inefficiency in the quoting process, and it also limits your ability to get the most aggressive pricing from distributors. Before going into much detail on why that is the case, we must first discuss the types of price models found within the MRO category.

Net Pricing, Discounts, and Markups

Generally speaking there are three types of pricing schemes in the category of MRO. The first one is rather standard: net pricing. During the bid phase, you provide a list of commonly purchased items, and the suppliers quote pricing for those items. It is easy to compare net price bids among vendors and quantify the total cost. Unfortunately, many of your purchases in the MRO category are one-offs or once-a-year purchases—they are not repeatable or high volume on a per-item level, but are substantial when aggregated.

Because many purchases are nonrepeatable, suppliers offer one of two options when negotiating prices for items not outlined on your net price bid: a discount off of list price and a cost-plus-markup.

A discount off of list price reduces the price by a certain percentage from an established gross price. It is important to note, however, that different suppliers' discounts are reflective of different gross prices. For some, the discount will be off of their retail price or published online price. For others, the discount will come off of a standardized tariff of manufacturer suggested retail pricing, such as Trade Service.

Under a cost-plus arrangement, suppliers quote pricing that represents their cost plus a predefined markup. The basis for the "plus" portion of pricing can actually be reflective of the manufacturer utilized (more common in electrical supplies) or of the category (such as in the cases of bearings and power transmission). In either case, the markup can differ by manufacturer or by category, as illustrated in the following example:

Category	Pricing Strategy
Actuators	Cost + 13%
Bearings	Cost + 16%

It is interesting to note that the pricing scheme offered is often based on the type of MRO supplier being utilized. MRO specialists, such as Wesco or Motion Industries, are more likely to offer a cost-plus-pricing strategy for items for which a net price is not defined (with some exceptions). On the other hand, MRO generalists, such as Fastenal and Grainger, are more likely to offer a discount off of their retail pricing.

Knowing What to Negotiate

Now that we have reviewed the types of pricing strategies quoted by distributors, we can explain why the quoting process can be ineffective for companies looking to reduce costs. First, consider that manufacturers dictate pricing on a per-account basis, and there are times that distributors do not go through the trouble of requesting pricing, instead guessing where the manufacturer will come in. In doing so, the distributors may very well be adding additional cost to the price to ensure they do not bid a price lower than the manufacturers will agree to. Their hope is that if they add a little fat to the price, but can still obtain a lower price from the manufacturer, they can pocket the extra profit.

However, distributors may also decide to guess low—which can lead to even bigger issues for their customers. Since most companies focus their quoting efforts only on the net-priced items, distributors are much more willing to provide competitive prices on these products—even if that means they take a substantial loss. They understand that most MRO purchases are not repetitive, so operating at a loss on the particular items that the customer is focused on is not a concern to them; they can easily make up the loss with a much higher markup on products that were not quoted.

To counter distributors quoting a net price only to provide substantially higher markups on other items, your bid document needs to include a section for suppliers to quote their pricing strategy for items not listed in your bid sheet. Requiring suppliers to predefine their markup and discount strategies helps ensure that markups are consistent, but does not, in itself, guarantee that their quotes for noncontract items are priced as competitively as the net-priced items. To do this, you need suppliers to guarantee that their pricing strategy is the same for both net-priced and marked-up items as part of their RFP or bid responses. For example, a bid document might say, "Please provide your markup strategy for items not listed in the bid sheet. The pricing strategy must be reflective of prices quoted as net." You can even ask for examples in the bid sheet to ensure that their pricing achieves this condition.

Your strategy of requiring distributors to guarantee their pricing strategies remains the same for both net and noncontract items; you are essentially forcing them to go to manufacturers on your behalf rather than simply guessing what they can get from the manufacturers. Without the flexibility to increase margin on noncontract items, the risk of a wrong guess is too high.

Unfortunately, the game does not stop when the manufacturers get involved. As discussed earlier, when the distributors go back to the manufacturer, they will ask for an SPA on your behalf. But SPAs can focus on providing higher discounts on certain types of products or product categories, just as distributor pricing can. The distributor and the manufacturer working together can still aggressively price items for which you are asking a specific quote, and leave higher margins on the table for the manufacturer regarding items on which you are not focused. The higher price still provides for higher dollars allocated to the distributor markup, as well as additional incentives and rebates awarded to the distributor by the manufacturer at the end of the year. Even though their pricing strategies remain the same, the prices really are not as competitive.

So how does a buyer counter this confederacy of suppliers looking for their pound of flesh? To some extent you cannot. MRO is not like office supplies, where distributor volume, much more than individual customer volume, dictates the price a manufacturer offers. The nature of manufacturer-controlled pricing means that to get the best pricing, you have to bring the manufacturer into the discussion when you are sourcing. In areas where you do have substantial volumes, you can talk directly to manufacturers about the potential to standardize on their product lines, and negotiate with them to ensure all your purchases receive the same levels of discount. This can be done before, during, or after the distributor selection process, but keep in mind that certain distributors only work with certain manufacturers, so if you go to a manufacturer first, you are limiting the choice of supplier you can interface with on a day-to-day basis. Working directly with manufacturers also allows you to understand the SPA you are receiving, which helps validate and audit information given to you by distributors, such as how they determine their markups or when price increases go into effect.

Still, in areas where product volumes are not substantial, you should work to get the best net pricing, discounts, and markups you can and move on. Manufacturers will not offer SPAs directly on low-volume purchases, and in the MRO process, focusing on every single line item is an exercise in futility. After all, these are tactical purchases—the cost to negotiate one-offs can easily exceed the price of the products.

CONTRACTING

Once you make a final vendor selection, it is time to award the business and move to the contracting phase. When contracting for MRO, you need to be careful that the rules you established for pricing during the RFP stage are adhered to. This may seem like a simple statement, but making sure suppliers agree to their pricing strategies in writing is not always easy.

Every contract should have an addendum that details net price points. For MRO contracts, a second addendum should be included that details the pricing strategy for noncontract items, as well as a guarantee that the strategy remains the same for both net-priced and noncontract items. Distributors often shy away from offering this second addendum when providing a first-round contract draft. The agreement also needs to include terms for handling price changes. There was a time when you could lock in pricing for two years or more, but those days are, for the most part, gone. Pricing for raw materials, such as steel, copper, and oil, is too volatile for distributors to guarantee long-term pricing; these days suppliers are often unwilling to extend pricing further than six months. When drafting the terms for price changes, keep these points in mind:

- *Get backup:* Any price increase should come with a letter of proof from the manufacturer that indicates which product prices are going up and the date of the increase. Without a letter backing up the change, establish that the price increase will not be accepted.
- *Establish a baseline:* Let us suppose you started an RFP process in the beginning of July, and by mid-July, manufacturers issued a 10 percent increase. Nine times out of ten, distributors will quote you a pre-increase price, and shortly after the business is awarded, you will receive a 10 percent price increase letter. At that point, it becomes less clear whether you awarded the business to the right supplier—what if another distributor had factored that increase into their quote and they were only off by a 5 percent margin? To counter this, your contract should include an addendum or language that states that pricing is based on the most recent price change letters from each manufacturer, and price increases will only be accepted from letters dated after the contract start date.
- *Keep it incremental:* As mentioned previously, it is often difficult to get pricing locked in for periods greater than six months. When contracting, distributors clearly outline that prices will remain unchanged for six months, but what about after that? It is important to include language that price

changes can only occur in six-month increments, otherwise after the first six-month period expires, price changes can occur whenever a manufacturer issues an increase letter.

- *Get notice:* Along those same lines, six-month price increases need to come with an official notice of increase at least 30 days prior to the change. This notice should also include a new price sheet from the distributor. If your requisition or PO system has unit pricing loaded in, you need time to make updates—otherwise your POs will not reconcile to an invoice. This takes time and effort on your part, and you want to make sure you get the appropriate level of notice and are not left trying to figure out what a 7.5 percent increase on bearings and a 12 percent increase on sheaves means to you.

- *Make it measurable and meaningful:* From a service level standpoint there are hundreds of terms and conditions you can include in an MRO agreement, detailing vendor-managed inventory arrangements, consignment, lead times and freight, among others. Most customers consider it a best practice to include terms around continuous improvement, requiring distributors to guarantee cost savings or improvements in a variety of areas, including time to process an invoice, machine uptime, or inventory carrying costs. These types of contractual guarantees are all valid, but only if you, as the customer, take the lead in monitoring them. Asking a supplier to guarantee a reduction in the time it takes to process an invoice is a great idea, and the supplier will do it, but it will use generic baselines or industry standards that may not be valid within your organization. You should focus on helping the supplier customize its continuous improvement tracking initiatives within your organization. If you do not have the time to lead these efforts, including them in a contract is meaningless.

 ## IMPLEMENTATION, COMPLIANCE, AND CONTINUOUS IMPROVEMENT

As with most strategic sourcing projects, even once the contract is signed and plants are alerted of supplier changes, your work is not over. The main challenge after a new agreement has been implemented is obtaining the full buy-in of those spend owners who utilized different suppliers prior to the selection of the new vendor. With any sourcing initiative, internal biases always exist. Most plants are used to doing things their own way, and taking instructions from corporate on how to buy will be new to them. In order to ensure the new program gets off the ground and savings projections are sustainable, you need to implement it in a way that makes clear to individual locations what to buy from whom. The implementation also needs to make ordering and receiving as easy as possible, allow you the ability to perform objective technical assessments of new manufacturers, and enable the monitoring of compliance with the new program on a plant-by-plant basis.

Ease of Buying

When the rollout of an MRO program begins, new purchasing procedures need to be communicated throughout the organization. These could include methods as sophisticated as setting up a new ordering system or punchout catalog, or as simple as providing locations with a spreadsheet detailing who the new supplier is by part or category, along with sales contact information, such as name, e-mail, and phone number. On the supplier side, ensuring a proper rollout is also critical, particularly if multiple locations are involved. National reps need to notify their local branches of new rules and contractual obligations and coordinate site visits to the plants they are serving. The goal is to make buying parts from the right supplier as easy as possible, so that maintenance teams and other end users only need to be concerned with what to purchase, not from whom to purchase.

Technical Assessments

If end users perceive that a new part does not have the same features or does not last as long as the old part, they will revert to buying from the original supplier. One of the biggest hurdles with product change-outs is getting a true assessment of apples-to-apples functionality. That is why, from a technical standpoint, any product changes that occur as a result of the sourcing initiative should be reviewed and approved by either maintenance or engineering. Performance expectations should be set when there is a change in manufacturer, and clear testing guidelines need to be established to avoid subjective analysis. Once the analysis takes place, results need to be communicated company-wide and new part change-outs need to be mandated. At this stage, assigning a technical resource to answer end user questions and troubleshoot issues provides consistency and ensures new product standards are adhered to.

Tracking Compliance

The tendency to revert back to the old ways of doing things is natural. End users may experience hiccups during implementation that give them a bad impression of a supplier, may be unclear about the savings potential, or may just like their old suppliers better. Further, people leave the organization and new people come in who are unaware of the initiative or the opportunity with particular suppliers.

To ensure savings are realized and sustained, you need to track compliance at the plant level. Compliance tracking can be tedious work, but overall it is the best way to ensure the program is adhered to. There are two ways to track compliance: savings obtained and savings lost.

1. *Savings obtained*: Tracking savings obtained involves reviewing usage with the new suppliers on a regular basis, such as monthly or quarterly, comparing the prices to the baseline (precontract pricing), and quantifying the savings received through the new program. The results are then relayed back to the sites and to senior-level management. In doing so, sites that are not optimizing their savings potentials can be compared against the sites that are, and corrective actions can be taken where necessary.
2. *Savings lost:* Tracking savings lost requires a little more finesse than tracking savings obtained. Lost savings can only be determined by identifying cases in which end users bought from the wrong supplier and, using one of several methods, quantifying what purchasing from that supplier cost you. Chapter 8, "Implementation and Continuous Improvement," goes into great detail on the ways to track lost savings.

It is best to engage in compliance tracking on a regular basis, but it is most critical at the beginning of the initiative. Monthly or even weekly reviews ensure that the program is making progress and new suppliers are getting embedded in local facilities. Waiting three or six months to start tracking compliance only to realize sites have not implemented the program appropriately could lead to a rocky start with a new supplier and issues with senior-level management expecting to see bottom-line cost savings.

 ## IN SUMMARY

Sourcing MRO can seem a bit daunting at first glance. In a typical organization, the MRO spend category is highly decentralized and multiple spend owners exist with a wide set of specifications. The number of national, regional, and local players for MRO products and services only compounds the issues that arise with decentralization and multiple stakeholders.

To obtain savings, you must understand that a one-size-fits-all approach will not work for MRO sourcing. The category can contain tens or hundreds of individual projects, each with its own strategy and opportunities. Some require working with manufacturers, others with distributors, and still others with third parties such as integrators, brokers, data analysis firms, or manufacturer sales reps. In an MRO project, obtaining competitive pricing is the easy part. Ensuring that competitive net pricing translates to across-the-board, sustainable cost savings requires much communication and monitoring.

Still, pricing is only one small aspect of sourcing MRO. A good initiative rationalizes the supply base and reduces the amount of invoices processed, reduces inventory carrying costs, and improves equipment uptime. It is important to keep your eye on the silver linings, as this is one category where substantial savings opportunities exist.

CHAPTER TWENTY-ONE

Analyzing Shipping Costs

N CHAPTER 19, we discussed ways to reduce costs on small-package shipping and reviewed the discount structures available from FedEx and UPS. The discounts are off of a published tariff, and tariff rates change based on a combination of service type, weight, and distance (divided into zones). Additional fees are then assessed for fuel, dimensions beyond an established threshold, and enhanced services.

In this chapter we discuss analyzing less-than-load (LTL) freight costs. This shipping method has similarities to small-package shipping, but also some major differences. The chapter begins by detailing some introductory concepts related to shipping. If you are already familiar with the shipping industry, the differences between types of shipments and the cost structures of carriers, you may want to skip ahead to the section that details the baselining process.

 ## AN OVERVIEW OF FREIGHT COSTS

Before getting into the details of LTL shipping, it is important to understand the difference between LTL freight and truckload freight. Truckload freight includes shipments of products that fill an entire trailer and are going from a single origin point to a single destination. That truck is entirely dedicated to your shipment. Conversely, LTL freight includes shipments that do not fill an entire trailer. The shipment could be one pallet of product or ten, but overall it does not take up the full capacity of the truck and can therefore be shipped along with other products for other customers. With LTL shipments, there are often multiple origination and destination points, even though they are generally located in the same basic region. The difference between these two shipping methods provides two entirely different cost structures.

In the truckload scenario, you are essentially renting the whole truck and driver for a given period of time, so your cost structure is fairly simple—for the most part it is a cost from point to point with additional charges for fuel. Further, that truck is taking one direct route—from the pickup location to the drop-off location, without the need to stop and pick up or drop off other products for other customers.

The LTL cost structure, by comparison, is fairly complex. The nature of LTL includes smaller loads to more locations. Your shipment is going on a truck along with many other shipments, and potentially getting on-loaded and off-loaded at different carrier locations: first a local hub, then a regional hub or national distribution center, then back to a different local hub near the final destination point. This is similar to how a small-package shipment works with a carrier such as FedEx. Pricing, therefore, takes other factors into consideration beyond origin and destination, including shipment weight and freight classification (more on this later). Due to the complexity of developing individual price points for potentially thousands of combinations of origin, destination, weight, and class, the carriers choose instead to provide discounts off of an established tariff.

The differences in pricing between truckload and LTL freight provide for completely distinct methods of data collection, data analysis, and sourcing. In fact, the two markets are completely separate—for the most part, truckload carriers do not provide LTL services, and vice versa.

 ## THE CHALLENGES OF ANALYZING LTL COSTS

As mentioned previously, the LTL pricing structure is complex. Carriers provide a discount off of tariff rates, with fuel surcharges and other ancillary fees assessed separately. The complexities of LTL provide challenges to objectively evaluating the quantitative and qualitative differences between carriers.

The first and most significant challenge is to make sure you understand that higher discounts do not always equate to lower shipping costs. Much like how small parcel carriers use their own tariffs and have different list prices, different LTL carriers utilize different tariffs. Some use their own, such as Conway Freight and their CNWY-599 tariff; others use a universal tariff, such as CzarLite. Each tariff has its own gross price points for individual shipments, and gross pricing can differ greatly depending on the strengths and weaknesses of the carrier.

For instance, a regional carrier that focuses on shipping in New England may have its own rate base, and that tariff would include rates for shipments to destinations outside of New England, such as Ohio. However, because they do not normally ship to Ohio, their base tariff rate for these shipments will be much higher than those of a carrier that ships to Ohio regularly.

In this example, the New England carrier might provide a discount of 60 percent off of its tariff for Ohio shipments, and the carrier that focuses on Ohio might only provide a 50 percent discount off of its tariff. However, the 50 percent discount could result in an overall lower price for the shipment, because the starting point (before discount) was lower with the Ohio shipper. Differences in tariff rates can be normalized, which allows shippers to properly compare discounts between carriers. We discuss ways to normalize tariffs later in this chapter.

It is also important to understand that the price on the bottom of an invoice or a total freight charge does not just represent the base cost of the shipment, but also includes fuel surcharges and other ancillary fees. Fuel surcharge is demonstrated as a percentage, and the percentage is charged against the net rate of the shipment, not the gross rate. Carriers add a fuel surcharge to most shipments to compensate for the ever-fluctuating costs of diesel fuel. Because diesel fluctuates greatly month to month or even week to week, carriers set pricing against a tariff and then build in the assumption that if average diesel costs go beyond a certain level, additional fees will be assessed. This keeps your net costs low if diesel stays within a certain range, and allows the carrier to provide pricing that does not build in the potential of skyrocketing fuel costs.

Table 21.1 shows an example of a fuel surcharge schedule. As you can see from the table, as average diesel prices go up, the surcharge increases. Carriers' surcharge schedules can vary, particularly as prices rise. Some carriers may use $0.01 increments rather than $0.05, or a combination of both. Additionally, surcharges may escalate at a faster or slower rate than 0.1 percent, as shown in the example after the fuel price surpasses $1.35.

Ancillary fees are additional charges incurred for services beyond the standard pickup and delivery of product. Ancillary fees include services such as

TABLE 21.1 Example Fuel Surcharge Schedule

When the Fuel Index for Diesel Fuel Is:	Fuel Surcharge Will Be:
$1.16–$1.20	1.6%
$1.21–$1.25	1.7%
$1.26–$1.30	1.8%
$1.31–$1.35	1.9%
$1.36–$1.37	2.0%
$1.38–$1.39	2.1%
$1.40–$1.41	2.2%

residential delivery, after-hours or weekend delivery, shipping and handling of hazardous materials, and so on.

Both fuel surcharges and ancillary fees should be factored in to any shipping analysis. Specifically, the fees need to be broken out and quantified on their own merit, rather than being looked at as part of the overall net price paid. Later in the chapter, we identify how the net impact of these charges on their own helps in refining sourcing strategy, comparing proposals, and negotiating final price points.

Another charge that is important to be aware of is the minimum charge, which is the absolute lowest net price a carrier allows for a shipment. For example, let us suppose that the gross rate for a particular shipment is $200, and you have a discount of 65 percent. The shipment should cost you $90. However, if you have agreed to a minimum charge of $125 with your carrier, you will be charged a net rate of $125 for the shipment, which equates to a discount of 37.5 percent.

There are also qualitative differences you need to consider when evaluating costs and comparing carriers. A major qualitative difference between suppliers is transit time, which is the amount of time (normally expressed as a number of days) it takes for a carrier to get a product to its final destination once that product has been picked up. Transit times can vary, sometimes dramatically, between carriers. Noting these differences helps provide an objective evaluation of carriers during the sourcing process.

 ## DEVELOPING YOUR LANE ANALYSIS

There are three goals for a shipping cost analysis. First, you want to understand the current cost structures of each of the carriers you use, including discounts, minimum charges, ancillary fees, and fuel surcharges. Second, you want to develop an analysis that allows you to compare and contrast the differences between each of the carriers and come to some conclusion about which carrier or carriers are the most cost-competitive. Third, you want to create a document that is easily converted into a request for quote or request for proposal.

Because it is difficult to forecast future shipping requirements, the analysis is based on a historical record of shipments. The time period used should be as recent as possible, and should include no less than three months and as much as twelve months of historical information. The focus here should be collecting enough information to accurately convey annual requirements. For example, if three months of usage information annualized accurately demonstrates total shipments and spend for a full year (within a margin of 5 percent to 10 percent fluctuation), then that information is most likely adequate for your analysis. However, if your business is cyclical and shipments peak or dip at one or more points during the year, then a larger sample set is needed to demonstrate a true picture of your shipping requirements.

As always, the first step in the process is data collection, and it is at this stage that you need to determine the project scope. There are four types of shipments you can consider as part of the scope of an LTL project: outbound shipments, inbound shipments, intercompany shipments, and third-party shipments. Depending on your goals, you can include one or all of these shipment types into the initiative; the complexity of data collection, analysis, and project management increases with each additional shipment type, but your savings can also increase.

Outbound Shipments

Outbound shipments are shipments originating at one of your locations and going to one of your customers. Outbound shipments are typically the easiest to identify and analyze because the carriers were likely selected by an end user or purchasing agent within your organization. Because your company selected the carrier you are paying for the shipment, so spend data and invoices are available in your accounts payable department.

The one exception to this is outbound shipments for which the customer specified the carrier used. In some cases, customers ask for a specific carrier to be used for all of their deliveries. This common practice means one of two things. First, it could mean that the carrier is invoicing the customer directly. If this is the case, you would not be able to view any spend data regarding the shipment and you can consider it out of scope.

Second, it could be the case that even though the customer specified the carrier, you are being billed for the shipment. This is not a problem if you are passing along freight charges on your invoice to the customer. Even if the price the customer is paying is not competitive, if the customer has selected the carrier and agrees to pay the price, the shipment is out of scope. However, if you are providing free freight or rolling freight charges into a unit price, you may want to include these shipments in the scope of work and show the customer the cost savings opportunity. Either way, your final analysis should clearly illustrate which shipments are from customer-specified carriers, because your sourcing strategy for this group of shipments will be different than for shipments where you retain 100 percent of the control.

Inbound Shipments

An inbound shipment is a shipment of product coming from your suppliers into one of your facilities. If the suppliers do not have their own trucks, then product is getting shipped via common carrier. Either you or your supplier can select the carrier used to ship product, and freight terms are typically defined by the party that makes the selection. If the carrier is selected by your organization, the freight term is called *inbound collect*. This means that the supplier invoice will not include a charge for freight. Instead, because you selected the carrier, the freight bill comes directly to your organization—you maintain the carrier relationship and pay the carrier bills.

If you already have LTL shipments that are inbound collect, you want to include these shipments in the analysis you are developing. There are many economies of scale that come from having a shipper drop product off at your location and at the same time pick up outbound shipments when necessary. Carriers often give greater discounts if they get a portion of both the inbound and outbound business.

When the supplier selects the carrier used and freight is added to the invoice, the freight term is called *prepay and add*. Collecting shipment information and understanding the actual costs for these shipments can be somewhat more difficult than outbound shipments or inbound collect. That is because the charge listed at the bottom of the invoice is normally a single line item, with no detail of gross charges, net charges, fuel and ancillary surcharges, or other relevant information that is needed to get a true bearing on costs, such as point of origin, shipment weight, and so on. Additionally, that supplier may be using the freight and shipping charges as a profit center for its business and may be marking up its costs before passing them onto the customer. Because these costs are more difficult to track, they are often overlooked. However, there are ways to incorporate inbound prepay-and-add shipments into your analysis and sourcing activities, which we discuss in a later section of this chapter.

Intercompany Shipments

Intercompany or plant-to-plant shipments are shipments that move product or materials from one of your locations to another. Often these shipments are made up of excess inventories or work in process. Intercompany shipments are easy to identify, as the carrier invoices will be coming to one of your locations. However, while developing your data set you should be careful to identify these shipments as intercompany (rather than outbound or inbound). Carriers are looking for dedicated routes, and shipments made between plants on a regular basis can be motivating to the right carrier.

Third-Party Shipments

Third-party shipments neither originate nor terminate at one of your locations, yet you are responsible for the freight bill for these shipments. The most common example of a third-party shipment is a drop shipment, in which you send product, such as a spare part, directly from one of your suppliers to one of your customers. If you are arranging the shipment, the freight is normally charged collect and you are directly billed for the freight charges. Otherwise, the supplier of the spare part bills you for both the cost of the part and shipping. Third-party shipments are not always easy to identify, and depending on the nature of your business, can be fairly infrequent. Overall, third-party shipments have very similar characteristics to inbound collect shipments, only instead of the product coming to one of your facilities it is going to an offsite location. If you do have a large volume of third-party shipments you should be careful not to overlook them during the data collection process.

 ## COLLECTING THE NECESSARY DATA

As you may have surmised, different types of shipments have unique characteristics that require alternative methods of data collection. Outbound prepaid and inbound collect shipments may have data readily available on carrier invoices or shipment histories. On the other hand, data for inbound prepaid shipments may only be available from a raw material supplier. So what information is needed to create a thorough lane analysis?

Overall, the data you want to collect is the same data carriers use to price out individual shipments: lane (where the freight is coming from and going to), classification (a description of goods), and weight. Of course, you also want to capture costs, along with some unique identifiers and other details, to help you develop a thorough understanding of your shipment characteristics for your analysis.

Lane

Above all else, carriers need to understand where shipments originate and where they are shipped. The only relevant pieces of information for the carrier are origination zip code and destination zip code, but for your analysis you should also include address information (street, city, state) if it is available. To enhance this data and make it more useful for you, classify the shipment (outbound, inbound, intercompany, and so on) and add the customer name if the information is available.

Classification

Beyond the shipment's origination and termination, carriers need to understand the type of goods being shipped. The reason for this is simple: Some products are easier to ship than others. Shipments that are odd shapes and sizes, unable to be palletized, or take up a lot of room but do not weigh much are all undesirable shipments for a carrier. Conversely, dense, palletized boxes that easily fit on a truck, are not temperature-sensitive, do not leak, are not hazardous, and are easy to handle are more desirable.

The National Motor Freight Traffic Association (NMFTA) has developed a rating system known as the National Motor Freight Classification (NMFC) to help simplify shipment classification. NMFC assigns every type of goods into one of 18 classes, which are rated on a scale of 50 to 500. A product rating of class 50 is the least expensive class of shipment; a product rating of class 500 is the most expensive class of shipment. The rating system is based on a combination of shipment density, storability (the shape of the goods, which may require it to take up excessive storage space), handling (whether it is palletized for easy manipulation or requires special handling), and liability (the fragility and value of the product).

To simplify the effect classification has on pricing, carriers agree to provide an average classification for all shipments within a certain range. For example, for any shipments rated between 50 and 100, a carrier might agree to charge based on an average classification of 65. This averaged rating is known as an FAK rating, for *freight of all kinds.*

When developing your lane analysis, you should attempt to collect both the actual rating information as well as the FAK. Doing so helps you determine whether the current FAK is reasonable, or if a different FAK should be considered when negotiating with carriers. The NMFTA publishes a list of FAK ratings that you may use for comparison purposes for the products or services you are shipping.

Weight

The last piece of information carriers need in order to provide you with an accurate quote is the weight of the shipment. As mentioned previously, the denser the shipment, the more desirable it is to the carrier. That is because the heavier the shipment, the more it costs to transport, and therefore the more they can bill. Over the past few years there has been some controversy over using weight as a consideration when shipping LTL. After all, the shipper is essentially leasing space on a vehicle, so square footage is a more accurate representation of cost. However, trucks need fuel, and heavier trucks use fuel more quickly. In addition, trucks have a maximum capacity in terms of both weight and space, so both are limitations. While some carriers have developed alternative tariffs that are based on the amount of space a shipment takes up on a truck, to date, this new way of assessing freight charges has not yet caught on industry-wide.

Lane, classification, and weight are the three elements that carriers need in order to accurately price shipments; however, a thorough lane analysis includes other information as well. Date of shipment helps you gain an understanding of the frequency of shipments, including what days, weeks, or months have the highest shipping volumes. A bill of lading number helps you tie your analysis back to actual shipments in case you make a mistake or need to double check your data. Carrier name ties a shipment to a particular carrier. However, the most beneficial pieces of additional data you need in order to gain a thorough understanding of shipments are transit times and costs.

Transit Times

Transit time is the number of days involved for the shipment to get from its origin to its destination. Different carriers can have substantially different transit times. However, often transit time is overlooked or considered equal during freight shipment analysis and sourcing. If the time necessary for a shipment to get from origin to destination is not of much consequence to your organization, then you may not need this information, but overall it provides a good qualitative comparison of the differences between carriers.

Costs

The last and most crucial pieces of data you need for your assessment are costs. Costs include gross price, net price, and discount, along with a separate column for fuel surcharge dollar amount and percentage. Ancillary charges should also be noted in your analysis. If there are recurring ancillary charges that appear on a majority of shipments, you may want to create columns in your analysis spreadsheet specifically dedicated to these charges. If ancillaries are few and far between, you can add a column for the charge amount and another column for charge description. To enhance your cost data, you should also identify the tariff on which your pricing is based. As you aggregate and analyze this information, you will find that understanding which tariffs are used may help you identify a preferable tariff, hence a preferable carrier.

 ## WHERE TO GET THE DATA

If you already have shipping software, such as Banyan Technology's Carrier Connect or National Traffic Service's Freight Audit and Bill Payment software, it is a relatively easy task to pull reports that give you all the information covered thus far. However, if you do not, collecting this data internally can be a tedious, manual process, which is nevertheless worth the effort to achieve significant cost savings.

To aggregate outbound and inbound collect shipments using information already available to you, you need to gather and assess carrier invoices. A freight invoice normally includes information describing origin, destination (or consignee), goods transported, total number of pieces, FAK rating, weight of goods, gross cost, discount, net cost, additional charges, and terms of shipment (prepaid, collect, or other methods).

Depending on the carrier, freight invoices may or may not include tariff name, bill of lading number, NMFC number by product, and actual rated class of goods. Still, even if all the information listed previously is included on the invoice, you need to enhance it by adding shipment type (inbound, outbound, or other type) and other relevant details, such as transit times. The good news is that the process does not need to be a manual one. Carriers have all this information in their systems and can provide it to you upon request. Specifically, you should request a report that includes the following field headings:

- Shipment date
- Origin/Shipper company name

- Origin/Shipper street address
- Origin/Shipper city
- Origin/Shipper state
- Origin/Shipper zip
- Destination/Consignee company name
- Destination/Consignee street address
- Destination/Consignee city
- Destination/Consignee state
- Destination/Consignee zip
- Number of pieces
- Description of foods (if applicable)
- FAK
- NMFC number(s)
- Actual rate class
- Weight of goods
- Gross cost
- Discount amount
- Net cost
- Fuel surcharge amount
- Additional charges and charge description
- Terms of shipment (prepaid, collect, other)
- Tariff name
- Bill of lading number
- Transit time (or date of pickup and date of delivery)
- Shipment mileage

Once you collect this information from each of your carriers, it is valuable to further enhance it by adding shipment type (inbound, outbound, or other method) and carrier name, then combine the data across all carriers. This is the starting point for your lane analysis, but depending on the scope of your initiative, you may have more information to collect.

 ## AGGREGATING AN INBOUND PREPAID FREIGHT HISTORY

All the shipping information you have collected to this point has been relatively easy to identify, because your organization is paying the freight bill. The carriers show up in your accounts payable (AP) system, invoices are received and validated, and the dock schedules shipments and works with the carriers on a day-to-day basis. However, there could be a large segment of freight spend you have not captured yet—inbound shipments in which the provider of the goods being purchased pays the freight bill and passes along the cost of freight to you.

Adding these shipments, known as inbound prepaid, into the scope of an LTL shipping analysis and sourcing event is a good idea—these shipments often represent the highest shipping costs for your organization. There are two reasons for this. First, suppliers often use freight as an additional source of revenue, meaning they pass along the carrier charges to you at a markup. Suppliers do this successfully because many buyers focus on the cost of the product being purchased when evaluating proposals and quotes, wrongly assuming that freight is equal between suppliers and passed along at cost. However, freight costs between material suppliers can vary dramatically depending on where the supplier is located, whether they mark up freight, and if so, how much they mark it up.

The second reason inbound prepaid costs can be the most expensive is that your raw material supplier may not be examining them very closely. If freight costs are merely passed along to the customer, and the customer has not expressed a concern in current freight costs, suppliers do not have much motivation to ensure rates are as aggressive as possible. Further, if the supplier is treating freight as a source of revenue, the higher the freight cost, the higher the additional profit.

There are two types of inbound prepaid shipments. The first, and easiest for which to collect data, is prepay-and-add shipments. For this shipment type, the supplier of the raw material provides an invoice that shows the cost of the good being purchased, and a price is detailed at the bottom of the invoice for the freight. While it may take a little more work to add these shipments to your lane analysis, understanding the net cost of freight is relatively easy.

The second type of inbound prepaid shipments is for raw materials that have delivered pricing. A delivered price rolls the cost of freight to your location into the price of goods purchased. Looking at an invoice will not help you derive the freight charge, as you see only a cost of goods. Understanding the freight costs for these shipments entails a bit more work. However, the likelihood is that you will not run into much delivered pricing when collecting information for an LTL project because most delivered pricing is based on truckload quantities.

While these two forms of inbound prepaid shipments require different methods of data collection, both start from the same basic premise. Your organization may have hundreds, if not thousands, of suppliers that provide you with raw materials and other goods on a regular basis. Rather than trying to incorporate all of these suppliers (and all of their shipments) into your analysis from the beginning, utilize an incremental approach. For your initial analysis and sourcing event, employ the 80/20 rule once again and identify the top handful of suppliers of goods and review their invoices. From there, determine the freight terms. Is freight added at the bottom of the invoice, or is the pricing included in the delivered charge? Is freight free, or is it inbound collect (meaning you already pay for freight on a separate invoice)?

Separate the invoices from the suppliers that have the most frequent inbound prepaid shipments. Are there commonalities in the shipments from each supplier? Are they always the same product and quantity, going to and coming from the same locations, or are there differences in types of shipments? Look for shipping trends or groups of shipments that have similar characteristics and that recur on a regular basis. Further segregate these invoices along these lines to develop your inbound prepaid lane analysis.

The lane analysis for inbound prepaid shipments will be slightly different than the lane history for shipments that you currently pay for, because you are working off a set of invoices that primarily contain product information, not freight information. There are two ways to develop a lane analysis for inbound prepaid shipments: an easy way and a hard way. The easy way, coincidentally, is also the most thorough, but the availability of data is not always assured.

The easy way to develop an inbound prepaid assessment is to enlist the suppliers of goods to assist in data collection. Review the invoices you have collected and identify the suppliers. Are you on good terms with these suppliers? Would they be willing to assist you in your initiative? If so, you can provide them with a template similar to the one listed for internally paid shipments and ask them to populate the database with their shipments to your organization. Keep in mind that there is certain information the supplier will not provide, including gross price, discount, and tariff information, particularly if they are marking up freight charges. This is fine; there are other ways to determine discounts, which we discuss later.

Most product suppliers are willing to provide a shipment history, particularly if you are on good terms with them. However, if the supplier is not willing to work with you, you can always aggregate the information manually from the supplier invoices. The information available to pull from these invoices includes origin, destination, description of goods, and the net cost of the shipment. You may also be able to get the weight or number of pieces, or both, depending on the product being purchased. To further enhance the data, you can request information from your warehouse, dock, or plant managers. Review the recurring shipments with them, and ask for their assistance in providing rough estimates of weight and the number of pieces per shipment. Ask them if they happen to know the NMFC codes or actual rate class of the shipment. They may even know average shipment transit times.

The data you ultimately aggregate for inbound prepaid shipments will by no means be as thorough as the data for shipments that you currently pay for. However, we later discuss further enhancements that become available as the data is analyzed and carriers are brought into the process. The data already collected will give you at least a rough understanding of costs and provide a comparison of current pricing versus the market.

 ## EVALUATING AND ENHANCING THE LANE ANALYSIS

Once you have aggregated the shipping data collected for outbound, inbound, and any other in-scope shipments into one database, you are ready to develop the lane analysis, in which you want to accomplish three things:

1. Provide an assessment of current costs and a comparison of each incumbent carrier cost structure versus the others.
2. Develop a shipping profile that clearly demonstrates where product is coming from and going to.
3. Create a summary of shipments and service level requirements that can be used during a bid process.

The Cost Assessment: Normalizing the Tariff and Developing a Baseline

Comparing the cost structures of multiple carriers can be a difficult task. After all, the likelihood that there are many identical shipments in terms of starting point, destination, classification, and weight is low. Shipments are based on customer orders, and customers do not always order the same products in the same quantity. Even if they did, you may be using the same carrier for those shipments time after time, so comparing one carrier's net pricing to another is difficult. Additionally, if you have shipments going out of multiple locations, even if weights and classifications are the same, the starting point, and possibly the ending point, may have changed.

Since most LTL shipments have at least one small aspect that makes them unique, a comparison of net cost to net cost will not be helpful in determining which carriers are providing the best price. This leads us to the next option:

comparing discount structures. As we have previously discussed, comparing the discount of one carrier to another is only helpful if both carriers are using the same tariff. If one carrier is using an older tariff or one that provides for lower gross rates to the areas where you ship most, then they may provide a smaller discount but still be more competitive.

Further, even if tariffs are the same, carriers also need to be using the same FAK rating. For example, if Carrier A and Carrier B both price your shipments using the same tariff, but Carrier A uses an FAK of 75 and the Carrier B uses an FAK of 100, Carrier A could provide a much smaller discount but provide a better overall net price, because shipments rated at 100 are more expensive than those rated at 75.

In order to develop a true comparison, you need to normalize or standardize the tariff structure across all carriers. Normalizing the tariff means taking one standard tariff, and adding the gross shipment price for that tariff at a particular FAK rating to your analysis. Then, rather than comparing the actual gross to actual net price to determine discounts, compare the standard tariff price to the actual net price to come up with a normalized discount by carrier. The easiest way to understand the value of normalizing tariffs is through an example.

Let's say Pastore's Car Parts ships product out of their location in Willow Grove, Pennsylvania. The company uses multiple carriers, and over the last week it has sent two shipments to Baltimore, Maryland using two different carriers. The first carrier used was Carrier A, which offered a 45 percent discount off of the tariff rate. The second carrier was Carrier B, which offered a discount of 50 percent off of the tariff. Table 21.2 illustrates the shipments and price points.

In reviewing this example, it would appear that Carrier B provided a more competitive price because their shipment weighed less and they also offered a higher discount. Now, let's analyze the same shipment, but rather than using

TABLE 21.2 Shipments with Multiple Tariffs

Origin	Destination	Description	Shipment Weight	FAK	Carrier	Tariff	Gross Price	Net Price	Discount
Willow Grove, PA	Baltimore, MD	Car batteries	425	80	Carrier A	ATARIFF	$725.00	$398.75	45%
Willow Grove, PA	Baltimore, MD	Spare parts	250	80	Carrier B	BTARIFF	$500.00	$250.00	50%

the actual discount and tariff structures charged by each carrier, insert the gross price from a neutral or standardized rate base.

As you can see in Table 21.3, when standardizing tariff rates and evaluating the new gross pricing against the actual price paid, Carrier A actually offered a more competitive discount for the shipment. The reason why the shipment appeared to be more costly was simply because that shipment weighed more.

Applying the standard tariff gross pricing across all shipments and then determining the average discount by carrier can help you identify which carriers are providing the best rates. As we discuss later, this analysis also has benefits during the sourcing process, because once rates are standardized, evaluating carrier proposals becomes much more simplified. To finalize the baseline, take the total gross costs (based on the standard tariff) and the total net costs for each carrier, then determine the discount. You now have an objective comparison of pricing across multiple carriers.

You may also want to consider analyzing discounts at the plant level, or even an individual lane level, particularly if you utilize many different carriers for the same lanes. The difficult aspect of tariff normalization is determining which standard tariff to use. There are many ways to determine the most beneficial tariff for your analysis. First you should consider what tariffs the carrier base is already using. Is there some consistency across carriers, or are they all using their own tariff structure?

One thing you do not want to do is standardize on a carrier-specific tariff, such the FedEx freight or Con-Way tariff. For your current evaluation, it may be fine, but keep in mind two things. First, carrier-specific gross tariff prices are based on the carrier's own strengths and weaknesses. Some carriers are more competitive in some lanes and not well established in others, and their tariffs reflect that. A neutral rate base is a level playing field that averages out the strengths and weaknesses of all carriers in an objective way.

TABLE 21.3 Shipments with the Same Tariff

Origin	Destination	Description	Shipment Weight	FAK	Carrier	Tariff	Gross Price	Net Price	Discount
Willow Grove, PA	Baltimore, MD	Car batteries	425	80	Carrier A	Standard1	$743.75	$398.75	46%
Willow Grove, PA	Baltimore, MD	Spare parts	250	80	Carrier B	Standard1	$437.50	$250.00	43%

Second, if you decide to engage in a strategic sourcing initiative, carriers bid based on competitors' tariffs. However, because they have no control over tariff rates, which could go up or down without their knowledge, they add in extra cost to offset the risk.

Some of the most common examples of neutral rate bases include the CzarLite and Continental. Keep in mind that these tariffs are subscription-based, so if you are not paying for it directly, the carrier(s) or your third-party logistics firm will be incurring cost to use the rate base and likely passing that cost along to you.

Of course, your baseline is not finalized once you have analyzed discounts. The evaluation should also include other factors, such as fuel surcharge, minimum charges, and high volume ancillary fees. Further, transit times and other service level requirements need to be factored in to give you both a quantitative and a qualitative assessment of the differences between carriers.

Developing the Shipping Profile and Preparing Bid Documents

Now that your baseline is complete, it is time to further enhance your analysis by developing a shipping profile, which provides some context to your shipments, giving you and others a clear understanding of the characteristics of your freight. A proper shipment profile includes at least three distinct assessments: a summary of total shipments, an inbound/outbound analysis, and a regional shipment assessment.

1. *Summary of total shipments:* In the original baseline analysis, each shipment is treated as a unique row in a database. While line-item detail is helpful, summarizing the information allows you to easily identify most traveled lanes. Sum up each column of data individually for total weight, cost, and number of shipments for each unique lane of traffic (based on origin and destination zip codes and FAK) using a database program, such as Microsoft Access or a pivot table in a spreadsheet application such as Microsoft Excel. Now you can sort the new analysis by cost, by number of shipments, or by weight to see which lanes have the biggest impact on your organization.
2. *Inbound/outbound analysis:* An inbound/outbound analysis compares the destination of the most frequently traveled outbound shipments to the origin of the most frequently traveled inbound shipments. Identifying similarities between the origination point and the destination of certain products

is helpful in two ways. First, from a logistical standpoint, understanding commonalities between outbounds and inbounds may help you cut down shipping and receiving lead times and get product to your customers and from your suppliers faster. For example, if you have a carrier shipping product to a customer in Scranton, Pennsylvania and you also have a supplier shipping product out of Scranton, you can plan orders so the carrier picks up supplies and drops off finished product, all during the same run. This consolidates carriers used, eliminates duplicative scheduling, and gets product to your door faster, ultimately saving you money.

Second, certain carriers can provide very competitive rates for particular lanes of traffic. If you have a large quantity of shipments in a particular lane that is both going out of and coming into a certain location, carriers will want to see that information and make some decisions about how they can leverage their own economies of scale around those shipments.

3. *Regional shipment assessment:* By adding a couple of additional enhancements to the summary of total shipments, you can gain a broader perspective of your shipping characteristics. Sort the summary by number of shipments and add a column called *lane type*. Then categorize each lane as local, regional, or national. In most cases, you would classify any shipment that does not leave the state of origin as a local shipment. Regional shipments are any that go only to a bordering state or stay within a particular region, such as New England or the Southwest. A national shipment is one that goes outside of that particular region.

  Breaking out shipments into local, regional, and national categories helps during the bid analysis and implementation process. During the bid analysis process, you will be able to determine which suppliers are most competitive for particular categories of shipments by creating a pivot table demonstrating total costs by category. If all your shipments are local or regional in nature, you might find that using a national carrier does not make much sense. Conversely, if most of your shipments are cross-country, asking a regional carrier to participate in a bid may not produce tangible results. Once you move on to implementation, you can use this information to develop routing guides for each facility that will allow it to easily identify the optimal carrier for each shipment.

Developing a shipping profile helps you develop a thorough understanding of your shipments, but its usefulness extends beyond the informative. Ultimately, the shipping profile helps you develop your sourcing strategy, and is easily transitioned into a bid document that carriers can use in preparing proposals.

LTL Cost Savings Opportunities

Once your shipping profile is finalized and converted into a bid document, you are ready to go to market. The sourcing process for LTL shipping services is similar to sourcing for other project areas, and this chapter is not intended to go into great detail on the LTL sourcing process. However, during the bid process there are some aspects you want to keep in mind.

As always, the process starts with market research and supplier identification. As we have discussed, requiring each supplier to bid off the same tariff makes analyzing responses much more efficient. Along with tariff standardization, suppliers should be asked to provide their estimated transit times for your most frequented lanes of traffic. This allows you to compare not just costs, but service levels, and give you the opportunity to determine what transit times are acceptable for your shipments.

Once you compile the bids and begin evaluating next steps, keep in mind that you want to balance having too many cooks in the kitchen against keeping all your eggs in one basket. Many shippers make the mistake of either utilizing too many carriers or single sourcing their LTL requirement. Both of these tactics should be avoided for multiple reasons. The foremost reasons all involve risk. Using a single carrier can be more expensive, but also opens you up to risks such as carrier bankruptcy, strike, rate changes, and so on. Having too many carriers can also increase your risk because you do not have large volumes with carriers, and are no longer a preferred customer. Additionally, using a combination of regional and national carriers based on their individual strengths and weaknesses in specific lanes normally *optimizes* shipping costs. However, cherry-picking the best carrier for every shipment is an inefficient use of time, and is too difficult to manage. Because of this, it is important to develop guidelines. Once you have selected carriers, you can develop routing guides for each of your plants to help them determine which carriers should be used for each shipment. The routing guide can be a simple spreadsheet, or even a map of the United States indicating the best shipper choice by state.

During implementation, it is time to go back to customers that specified that certain carriers be used for their shipments. Continuing to use their carriers for their shipments is always an option, but presenting them with savings opportunities available through a transition to your new preferred carriers may motivate them to change their positions, which has the added benefit of making your loading docks more efficient and driving more volume to the preferred carriers. If they are not willing to switch carriers, ask them to transition to an inbound collect shipment type, so that your accounts payable team no longer has to manage payments to a carrier that is not your first choice.

There are many other cost savings opportunities in the field of LTL. Utilizing a third-party logistics (3PL) firm or other strategic sourcing consulting firm allows you to combine your volume with many other shippers and thereby leverage improved rates. Shipping optimization tools, such as Banyan or Red Prairie software, simplify the carrier selection process, as they allow shippers to see which amongst their select group of carriers can provide the lowest cost or fastest transit time for each particular shipment. In addition, most optimization tools automatically update if there are changes to tariffs or if carriers are providing temporary incentives on particular lanes, so your information remains current.

 IN SUMMARY

LTL shipping is an area in which strategic sourcing and implementation of best practices, such as optimization tools, can have a major impact on bottom-line costs. However, you will also find huge challenges in collecting and aggregating data to demonstrate savings and building a business case for change.

Developing a clear baseline is the key to building the internal consensus needed to make changes. Further, a clear baseline analysis and shipment profile can easily be converted into a bid document and analysis tool to compare carrier proposals. As with most categories of spend, the more detailed the information you can provide to the supply base, the more competitive the bids will be, as the additional costs of unknown factors get parsed out.

Optimizing freight costs may require outside help. Universal tariffs come with subscription fees, optimization software needs to be licensed, and third-party logistics firms require compensation. However, the benefits provided by these tools and resources can far outweigh their initial investment costs as they help you build your business case and implement a sustainable, long-term cost savings program.

CHAPTER TWENTY-TWO

Sourcing Services

E VER SINCE STRATEGIC SOURCING WAS DEVELOPED, there has been great debate as to the effectiveness of this process when sourcing services. Many argue that purchasing intangibles is too complex, services are too customized, and suppliers too diverse to adhere to the guidelines of strategic sourcing. The phrase "but we are different . . ." often arises when speaking to end users about oversight or involvement from an external group, such as purchasing or finance.

Fundamental strategic sourcing principles can be utilized to create competition, evaluate offers, and negotiate contracts for services, regardless of the targeted purchase. While the obstacles and challenges you face when sourcing services may be different from those of sourcing products, in the end you can see the same effectiveness of results from the efforts put forth. Conversely, some challenges that you encounter with sourcing services are also very similar to those you might experience while sourcing goods, such as gathering pertinent spend data, clarifying the scope of work, and overcoming internal or external political issues.

Services are vital to any business because they provide crucial operational functions that your own business may not have the resources or knowledge to perform internally. For a medium-sized business, this can encompass dozens of essential services that are needed across a wide range of departments, from operations and facilities to finance and marketing. These can include, but are not limited to:

- *Facilities services:* Facilities services cover a wide range of functions to keep fixed assets, such as equipment or buildings, operating in an efficient and proper manner. Facilities services include everything from cleaning and security services to IT equipment maintenance. Fixed assets can represent a large capital investment; it is crucial that the services that support these investments are diligently sourced.
- *Marketing services:* Marketing and advertising services can range from full service marketing-campaign management to specialty and niche marketing services. Broadly speaking, these services include media buying, public relations, online identity management, writing, design, and production.
- *Financial services:* Financial services provide essential business functions, either as a stand-alone business unit or as an extension of other resources. Financial services may include accounting and auditing, risk management, fiduciary services such as banking or credit card processing, and other essential functions.
- *Administrative services:* Administrative services provide functional support in areas such as human resources in the form of staffing services or outsourced customer service. In an office environment, administrative services can also include courier or other shipping services, document management services, and payroll processing.
- *Information technology (IT) services:* IT services can include equipment servicing for copiers and computer hardware, troubleshooting and help desk services, and consulting services required for needs identification and new software and hardware implementations.

Based on this sample listing, it is easy to see that the category of services is rather diverse in nature. This chapter demonstrates that even with such a broad scope, there are commonalities between types of services that can be effectively addressed when developing a cost-savings strategy and applying strategic sourcing principles. As you will see, the tried-and-true total cost management (TCM) principles that fixed-asset-heavy companies rely on come into play much more than when sourcing products. For example, consider the total business impact of a failed, ineffective marketing services contract. The cost of lost customers and diminished business development can be much more costly in the end than a little extra legwork during the service sourcing process.

The chapter also makes distinctions regarding how the process of sourcing services is different from that of sourcing products, while walking through each step in the process. Lastly, the chapter provides case studies that demonstrate successful services-based strategic sourcing engagements.

 ## USING SPEND ANALYSIS TO SOURCE SERVICES

The sourcing of services starts where all other sourcing initiatives begin: with the spend analysis. Since the goal, as always, is cost savings, your goal is to identify services that have the highest cost for your organization, and therefore the biggest impact on the bottom line. Review the cost centers that are of critical importance to your company. Then, look for services that cross multiple cost centers or departments. What common services are utilized by more than one department? Remember, you are analyzing the total spend of services, not necessarily the total spend of one supplier.

If your company has multiple locations, examine the services that are contracted at each location and whether you are using the same supplier at all of them. It is common to see a large, multiple-location organization use several different suppliers for the same service. You will see later on in the process that by leveraging those various locations into one agreement you can escalate your savings opportunities. Not only will this provide cost reduction but it can make compliance and supplier management easier.

Once you have identified the proper spend and service categories to analyze, you want to focus on baselining this information, which should encompass the following elements:

- *The type and scope of service.* Ask yourself what category the targeted service fits into so you are able to gather accurate and comparable market data when the time comes. Detail the scope of work and how this work is performed.
- *The cost and pricing structure of the service.* Some services may be priced at an hourly labor rate for work performed, while others may include a detailed and complex, or even obscure, pricing structure. While you are baselining spend you may find that a vendor may just charge a catch-all price with no cost detail or breakout, especially if no formal contract exists.
- *External and internal influences on the service.* Later in this chapter we show how external forces, from political and economic considerations to labor union relations, can have a significant impact on your services. Make sure

that you gather any necessary data that describes this impact. For example, if a key internal decision maker has an aversion to a particular supplier, this needs to be addressed during the sourcing process.

This information provides a solid starting point and ensures an apples-to-apples comparison. The baseline data for services can be retrieved from contracts, purchase orders, invoices, quotes, and forecasts. Internal usage reports, as well as supplier-provided usage reports, also provide a good level of detail. Depending on the availability of information, plan on collecting at least 6 months of data and up to 12 if your business is cyclical. As you gather this documentation and review it, enter it into a spreadsheet or document to summarize it for ease of access and understanding.

Not only do you want to analyze the current spend as indicated but, as you move through the first few steps of the sourcing process, you want to determine what areas, if any, you would like to improve. Obviously you want to save money, so you want to reduce costs, but also consider the relationship with suppliers and the level of service you are receiving. Are there areas in which you are receiving subpar service, or no service at all? All of this becomes relevant as you define the scope of work.

Before you can jump into sourcing any kind of service, it is imperative that you identify the key decision makers. This includes anyone who has a financial or operational stake in the process, and has the ability to make decisions and make them stick. Keep in mind that it is worthwhile to identify these individuals within your organization as well as on the supplier side. You do not want to hit a major speed bump in the middle of the process when you find out that a vital participant was left out in the beginning and now that person wants to throw his or her weight around and change the direction of the whole project.

 DEFINING THE SCOPE OF WORK

As in other sourcing activities, the most important aspect of sourcing services is the preparatory work involved. You need to understand the scope of work in order to understand the spend and what further information is necessary to collect from suppliers. You will benefit most from reaching out to end users to gather details on the services being provided. End users are able to provide the greatest and most accurate information about the detail of the services, as well as an honest evaluation of the quality of services. End-user interviews can clarify what areas are not being satisfied and can provide insight into the areas that are most important to those who have direct contact with suppliers and their services.

Start by identifying which end users are key players in the initiative. If you are working with copier maintenance services, for example, pinpoint the individuals who use the equipment and work directly with the current supplier the most. If you are examining a department with 50-plus employees, you may find that speaking to all of them is an inefficient approach. Someone who does not have much interaction with this area of spend will not be able to provide insight into how well the services are being performed. Make sure those with whom you speak have a relevant stake in the outcome of the process.

The end user interview should answer the following questions:

- What are the services being performed?
- What is the frequency with which they are being performed?
- What does the current supplier do well?
- What does the current supplier do poorly?
- What is not being done that you would like to see the supplier add to its services?
- What is the process for reporting and addressing performance issues?
- How are the services managed? For example, how would one request services outside of the standard schedule, if they are needed?

Of course, other questions should be added, based on the specific category of servicing being sourced.

Along with speaking with end users, supplier interviews are another way to clarify or validate the scope of work and allow you to get a more complete picture of the services being performed. You need to ask suppliers to confirm that the services noted in the agreement are actually being performed as indicated. Also find out if they are providing any other services that are not being charged for, or that are not included in the contract. Find out suppliers' opinions of the customer and how good they believe the relationship is. This will benefit you by helping determine how the relationship can be improved or whether your company is not taking full advantage of the services available to them. Some other areas that are useful to explore during supplier interviews are:

- Who is a supplier's main point of contact at the company, if there is one?
- How efficient is the order and request process?

- How do they differ from the competition?
- How many branches and locations do they have and where are they located?
- How does their pricing fluctuate—are there annual increases or are prices based on the market?

Again, depending on the type of services they provide, you may find it prudent to get more granular information from suppliers.

Contracts and service agreements are also pertinent to discover the services that are being performed, or at least those that should be performed, as per the contract. Important points to pay attention to in contracts and service agreements include the type of services, including the frequency at which they are performed, and the service level that has been agreed upon. Take note of payment terms and termination clauses that might exist, as this will become important if you decide to move to a new supplier.

Additional services that may not be included in the base cost are also important to note. For example, most janitorial service companies include most general, daily cleaning in a base cost, but some services, such as power washing and floor stripping, may cost extra. Review what is included in the base cost other than services, such as equipment needed to complete the services, necessary supplies, and any other ancillary charges. Service schedules as documented in the agreement are also important to keep in mind when sourcing the service. As the customer, you want to thoroughly evaluate the schedule to determine whether it is appropriately satisfying your needs.

An Assessment of Wants versus Needs

There are multiple parties that affect the final form of the scope-of-work document for services, from internal decision makers to the incumbent supplier. As you finalize the scope of work, be sure to make an assessment of what is actually needed versus what is perceived to be needed—in other words, what is wanted. Over a period of time with one supplier, services and amendments may have been added or removed that may have caused the service to vary from its fundamental goal, thereby accumulating additional costs. These value-adds may or may not be necessary or beneficial, but should not be taken for granted.

To identify what is a want versus what is a need in a service spend category, begin by creating a list of each service task, fee, or product that is incurred within the scope of work. With the primary goal of the service in mind, ask the following questions of each service task:

- *Is this critical to achieve the goal of the service?* Be sure that the service you are sourcing has a clearly defined objective and that the vendors involved are proven experts at achieving it.
- *Is the service task performed throughout the organization designed or oriented toward one particular group?* For example, the accounting department requests automatic air fresheners as part of the janitorial service and the supplier decides to implement this across the entire organization. This has now become a company-wide cost increase based on a small request on the part of just a few people.
- *Can this be performed internally?* First, take a look at your own payroll. Evaluate the ability of your internal workforce or potential new positions to perform any of the tasks that have been sourced to the service. Is the service you are sourcing an extension of an existing department, or is the service a completely unique task that cannot be performed internally? If, for example, you find yourself paying a graphics design services retainer of $100,000 per year, hiring a full-time graphic designer for $80,000 starts to make sense.
- *What is the service's role and importance as a revenue generator?* Make sure that the goal of the service you are sourcing is clearly defined, as this resides at the heart of a wants-versus-needs assessment. Marketing activities directly generate leads, new business, and revenue. heating, ventilation, and air-conditioning (HVAC) maintenance is an operational expense. This will help prioritize contingency and budget cuts when they become necessary. Cutting back on the marketing budget during a recession is a common (although ill-advised) practice, but shutting the heat off due to a broken piece of HVAC equipment in January is not an option, unless all your employees are penguins.
- *What is being oversold and underutilized?* Suppliers often tout a shiny new reporting system, inventory management tool, or service that can help your organization reduce costs. These "enhanced" services can end up carrying on for decades if they are never really closely examined. The truth is, if a service is being performed, somewhere there is an associated cost. Even if it does not appear as a line item on an invoice, it is factored into the cost of doing business. Keeping this in mind, negotiate lower costs with a supplier by offering to forgo some of these de facto services.
- *What can be combined or consolidated?* While this is not always a case of want versus need, sometimes it can be. For example, end users in an

organization may *want* an individual printer in each office because it is seen as more convenient and even a sign of status. What is *needed* is really just an ability to print documents. One central networked printer for a group of offices in this case eliminates printer maintenance and print management costs.

To answer these questions objectively, conduct a survey across a wide and diverse group of individuals from within and outside of your organization. Look at companies in your peer group and compare how they prioritize and evaluate their services. You will be surprised at how many services you can identify that are unnecessary and can be cut out of the scope. Remember that the 401(k), now the overwhelmingly dominant retirement plan for companies, was at first considered a dastardly alternative to the then-standard pension plan. Now, pension plans are seen as bureaucratic overhead and a troublesome relic to maintain, while 401(k) plans, in which the burden of management has been shifted to a third party and employees, have become the standard solution for retirement savings.

Service Specifics

The following service-specific risk factors are frequently encountered when sourcing service-related categories. Take these into account as you begin to build a scope of work. Services often involve a deeper level of integration into a company's operations and therefore can act as barriers for change, sometimes even with cost savings available. Taking these extra considerations into account ensures that your service-sourcing labor, once implemented, can bear the fruit of long-lasting and sustainable savings.

Materials Escalation

Service contracts are often tied to a market index. This provides the supplier with built-in periodical revenue growth and is presented to customers as a reasonable way to keep up with ever-increasing material costs. This increase is usually applied annually on the contract anniversary date. The Producer Price Index (PPI) is one of the most common measures, but the index used for this purpose can be anything from an oil futures index to the Consumer Price Index.

Your first priority with regard to a market index escalation should be to eliminate it altogether. Citing evidence of a long-term downward forecast in the cost of the material in question can serve as a negotiation point. You can, however, use that same market intelligence to work the indexing to your advantage.

Suppliers occasionally include wording that allows for a materials cost decrease or increase depending on the index. If you are willing to take a calculated risk, a decreasing materials index can actually lower your costs.

For example, an elevator maintenance supplier may base its annual materials cost adjustment on the annual metal products PPI increase or 5 percent, whichever is greater. In this "whichever is greater" scenario, you are essentially at the mercy of the market. The fixed percentage here acts as a minimum, so you can expect at least the 5 percent increase annually. Under this scenario, you will be stuck with a significant escalation in your service costs if a sharp increase in the referenced index occurs. In another example, an elevator maintenance supplier bases its annual materials cost adjustment on the annual metal products PPI increase, or 5 percent, whichever is *less*. This scenario is more tolerable, as the maximum allowable annual increase is 5 percent.

If you decide that an indexed materials cost increase is reasonable, be aware of the market risks to which you are exposing yourself. Research the historical changes of the index in question. Read financial journals, publications, and other media to get an idea of how the index has behaved historically under the economic conditions similar to those at the time of the execution of your request for proposal (RFP) process. Market data, such as the PPI, can be found on the United States Bureau of Labor Statistics's website.

Union Relations and Labor Escalation

Services can often include an added labor dimension that carries additional risk and exposure to hidden costs. Labor unions may already directly perform the service you are sourcing or they may be heavily involved in the supportive and administrative functions of the service. If a labor union already exists within your organization, you can avoid labor disputes by sourcing a union labor service provider. If you can prove that a union service provider cannot provide comparable service, a nonunion service provider can be sourced and coexist with your organization's local union. However, to ensure smooth implementation, always discuss the services needed and the options available with the union representatives at your organization. Avoid the consequences of any labor unrest by making sure that the company can continue to perform the tasks during a strike or work stoppage, even if it means the owner of the company is vacuuming the floors at your business.

Along those same lines, minimize exposure to increases in labor wages and labor unrest if the service providers you are sourcing are unionized. An increase in labor costs is often cited—more frequently than the increase in the cost of materials previously mentioned—as the rationale for a supplier's increase request. Become familiar with the union involved in the service you are sourcing by reviewing the union contract and historical wage increases.

Input Product Inclusion

Including input materials (e.g., cleaning supplies for janitorial or filters for HVAC) as part of your service contract increases buying power for the service provider. In turn, this increases your leverage and can reduce overall costs. For example, we would be willing to bet that Trane, one of the largest heating, HVAC companies in the United States, gets a better deal on air filters than any organization it serves could ever possibly achieve.

Service Brokers

Bundled facilities management services can reduce the payroll and other administrative costs associated with managing a large number of services and their respective contracts. Companies that provide these services are sometimes referred to as service brokers. These providers contract with all types of small and specialty service providers to create a complete services management offering under one name and provide a one-stop shop for everything from janitorial services to electricians. Contract management and payment is simplified for the buyer into one supplier.

The simplicity and significant reduction in administrative costs with this setup seems like a no-brainer, but there are downsides to super-centralizing your service contracts. Service brokers have just as much of an obligation to satisfy their subcontractors as they do to satisfy you. Account representatives and customer service can find that they have their hands full trying to cater to two separate customer bases with different goals. More importantly, since the service broker is taking a piece of the pie from his subcontractors, cost savings just may not be achievable. Carefully evaluate the total value of your individual contracts, consider any possible reduction in administrative costs or payroll, and proceed with caution.

Warranties

A warranty policy should also be part of any service contract that involves equipment. Be sure to check the warranty associated with the purchase of new equipment. Make sure that your service provider is certified to service manufacturer warranties of the equipment in question. If a new piece of equipment is purchased to replace equipment that is currently under a service contract, make sure that there is a policy in place to allow for a reduction in the fee associated with this equipment while it is under warranty.

Maintenance Agreements

One of the most common types of services found across multiple categories of indirect spend is an equipment maintenance or preventive maintenance (PM) agreement. Before any maintenance contract is sourced, a thorough evaluation of the equipment to be serviced should take place. Create a list of each piece of equipment in question. Gather as much information about each piece of equipment as you can. Document everything from the make, model, and serial number to the age of the equipment. Some equipment may require the inspection of an expert, such as an engineer, to be thoroughly understood. If you cannot fully document the service requirements of the equipment internally, do additional research or hire the right help by finding an expert in your professional network. Taking a thorough inventory of your equipment ensures that when the time comes to develop your RFP, the prospective suppliers are bidding accurately.

If the equipment is old and needs constant upkeep, a PM program can be cost effective. If the equipment is brand new or relatively new and needs few or no repairs for a number of years, you should ask for a time-and-materials contract.

A time-and-materials maintenance contract can sometimes seem like the special sandwich at the local burger joint that you can still order, but that is not advertised and not listed on the menu. A standard PM contract is usually offered by a sales representative upon the purchase of brand new equipment. This is especially common with medical equipment maintenance, such as a magnetic resonance imaging (MRI) machine. Instead of paying for preventive maintenance on equipment that will most likely work properly for a number of years, a time-and-materials contract only obligates you to pay for parts and labor hours worked when a piece of equipment needs to be repaired.

 DOING YOUR MARKET RESEARCH

After you have identified exactly the services to be performed, defined your current and future scope of work, and developed equipment inventories where necessary, you can begin to research the market to gain a better understanding of the supply base. Keep in mind the service-specific risks and possibilities outlined previously when you begin your market research. Not only do you want to start developing a supplier list for the bidding process, but this also serves as a discovery phase in which you can educate yourself on all of the aspects of the service and the information necessary to accomplish the goals of the initiative. Take the time to ask suppliers questions, and make sure to fully utilize your incumbent supplier to provide information on the processes involved with its services.

The first step in the research process is supplier identification. Start by searching the Internet for companies that perform the services in the region(s) in which you require service. By conducting one-on-one interviews, you can determine whether the suppliers are initially able to fulfill the bid requirements. You need to qualify suppliers by asking the following questions:

- Can they fulfill the scope of work requirements?
- Can they cover all of the locations in the service area?
- Can they support your technical needs as well as service specifications?
- What drives competitiveness in this industry?
- Are they able to satisfy the basic terms and conditions required by your company?

Try to collect as much information as possible during this process. Most suppliers welcome sharing information about what they do, especially if they perceive the possibility of gaining business from it.

Do not limit yourself by the size of companies; if they claim to have the ability to do the job, it is worth giving them a chance to bid. Small companies can often provide service enhancements with less overhead, making their pricing attractive. Not only do you not want to automatically disqualify smaller suppliers, you also do not want to neglect the incumbent in the sourcing process. Even if your goal is to transition away from the incumbent, it can still be useful when leveraging pricing and processes.

Be sure to collect the basic data from all qualified suppliers. This includes contact information, brief company history, points of qualification, and any other information that might be useful in the sourcing steps to come. Also make sure that you identify value-added elements that the supplier might possess. These include services that could provide benefits beyond the scope of work currently being performed. For example, although a janitorial company would provide cleaning services, it may also be able to provide paper goods and other toiletries at a discounted price. In this situation it has leverage with its suppliers since it purchases this same pool of goods on a regular basis and most likely at higher volumes than you would. It is important to take advantage of value-adds like this, or at least consider them, when comparing suppliers.

SERVICE-SOURCING STRATEGIES AND THE SERVICES RFP

Once you have researched the market, it is time to develop a sourcing strategy. A key component to developing your strategy is determining whether or not the scope should be consolidated or further broken down into separate market baskets before approaching suppliers. For example, courier services can span throughout your organization, ranging from basic document delivery to money-related deliveries and more. You may find that certain suppliers have a market niche and it is more cost-efficient to source the different scopes of work from more than one supplier. Then again, you may find one supplier that has the ability to manage all of the services. In general, your focus should be on supplier rationalization—not consolidation. Consolidation typically means reducing the number of suppliers for a particular service; supplier rationalization entails picking the right amount of suppliers to satisfy your requirements.

If you are sourcing maintenance services for equipment, you may decide to build your strategy around equipment maintenance insurance (EMI), which is an outsourcing program that removes the inefficiencies of managing equipment maintenance by consolidating all maintenance contracts into one insurance policy. An insurance provider converts all contracts with incumbent suppliers into a grouping of time and materials contracts. It then calculates the predicted time and materials costs for each given piece of equipment over a given period of time, based on historical actuarial data. This lower expected cost becomes your monthly premium. Additionally, the administrative costs associated with managing each contract are reduced.

As you can see, limiting your strategy to emulating the way business is done now is not always the best way to approach suppliers, as alternatives to the current scope of work exist. In services procurement, this is often the case.

Beyond scope of work, be sure that you have a thorough understanding of the pricing models available for the service you are sourcing. Services have a widely varying set of pricing structures. Some service providers develop a base cost that covers a majority of the work performed and then provide a separate rate structure for extra services.

The best way to determine pricing models is to review your current pricing structure. Not only will this aid you with baselining the data but it helps with comparing alternate suppliers' bids. Ask yourself, why are the rates structured in this way? Do other suppliers structure pricing differently? One very important aspect of understanding not only what the pricing is but also how it is developed is that it helps you during the bidding process. This further ensures you can answer supplier follow-up questions and confirm an apples-to-apples cost comparison.

A service RFP should put emphasis on ensuring that the cost associated with the scope of services and work performed can be easily broken out and analyzed. Include the following attributes into a service RFP:

- A scope of work that is measurable against the spend allocated to it. In a maintenance contract, one way to achieve this is by organizing the RFP by pieces of equipment. In this way, a repair done to a specific printer can be calculated against the cost of the printer. A printer maintenance call that costs $400 on a $300 printer should be a red flag to factor into considering a preventive maintenance program.

- An a la carte listing of additional services and extras available that are not in the regular scope of work should be included. This may sound strange, but consider a facilities manager requesting window washing to be performed one day, despite knowing that this service is not in the contract. Including this list of extras protects against a heavy premium or a blank-check price from the supplier.

- Performance standards that are measurable and intertwined with the defined scope of work. Include discounts or rebates for nonperformance before any other disciplinary action. This approach has two benefits. First, suppliers will be the most motivated to correct their performance; nothing motivates like money. Second, if the infractions are tolerable here and there, some small cost savings can actually be achieved without any major overall service impact.

- Standard RFP information such as desired contract terms, references, service locations, and other information previously discussed as vital to sourcing via RFP.

- Servicer definitions that outline who is to perform the work. For example, if you are sourcing accounting services and you expect a CPA to perform the work, be sure that this is expressed. This protects against suppliers utilizing less-than-qualified personnel in an effort to cut costs. Other professional designations and certifications, labor union information, and personnel restrictions should also be included.

Now that you have gathered the data and a good understanding of how the suppliers create their pricing, you can begin to develop the RFP. Service RFPs can range from very basic requests for information to highly organized and complex documents. The most important thing to remember when writing the RFP is that you cover all of the key points that you would like to see in the responses.

 ## CASE STUDIES

As previously mentioned, services require special attention and a customized sourcing process based on the type of service. The following real-world case studies illustrate how utilizing strategic-sourcing methodologies, combined with a customized sourcing strategy, can provide meaningful savings for the organization undertaking the initiative.

Case Study 1: Elevator Maintenance

A large commercial facility spent approximately $1.3 million per year on elevator preventive maintenance across the entire campus. Over 100 elevators and three escalators were covered under preventive maintenance, which provided for a first- and second-shift mechanic to perform PM duties Monday through Friday, and one mechanic on Saturdays. The monthly preventive maintenance fee before the sourcing event totaled just under $100,000, not including overtime and other additional charges incurred.

To begin the sourcing project, the scope of work within the context of the PM agreements was evaluated. Invoices, service reports, and the full contract were reviewed to determine where charges were being incurred. The sourcing lead reviewed invoices and callback reports provided by the elevator contractor to identify which services frequently incurred overtime or callback charges. The goal was to determine which charges could potentially be included in the scope of a new preventive maintenance agreement. These charges were categorized into five spend groups, representing about $150,000 in annual spend: testing, escalator repairs, holiday charges, misuse and abuse repairs, and miscellaneous callbacks.

Testing included all safety testing which may have been necessary under city and state standards and regulations.

Escalator maintenance and repair was covered under the agreement, but the company was arranging for PM service and repairs to be performed during the weekend to avoid disruptions during busy weekdays. Under the local union agreement, escalator repairs require one helper and one mechanic. Since the agreement provided for only one mechanic on Saturdays, an additional helper was routinely called in for weekend escalator repairs, thereby incurring overtime charges for the helper.

Holiday and standby charges were incurred as a result of the union holidays. When the company required maintenance coverage from the elevator maintenance provider on such holidays, the rates for these maintenance personnel were billed at double time.

Misuse and abuse repairs were related to repairs needed as a result of misuse or abuse to the elevators.

Miscellaneous off-hour callbacks were for service callbacks during off-hours and for miscellaneous tasks completed by elevator mechanics that did not fall under the PM scope. For example, a mechanic was called upon to install a new handrail in an elevator as an aesthetic feature.

These callback charges were analyzed for savings opportunities one at a time, starting with the safety testing. Since safety testing was being performed during off-hours to minimize service disruptions, a small hourly weekend shift was added in which to perform all of the annual testing. In this case the testing would occur under the monthly PM cost, not as an overtime billing. The same situation occurred with escalator maintenance: It was already included in the contract, and a simple operational hours shift eliminated overtime costs incurred by doing the work on weekends.

To eliminate the holiday standby charges, a mechanic was simply eliminated from service during the elevator mechanic union's holidays. In the case of a busy retail facility this can be difficult; however, for nonemergency or nonessential facilities, a day of one elevator being out of service usually has little or no impact on daily business operations.

Miscellaneous off-hour service calls are difficult to eliminate since accidents and one-offs are a normal part of everyday operations. In this case, an independent elevator expert provided a system of custom performance standards and stringent maintenance requirements so that the elevator contractor was measurably accountable for any work. This helped further reduce the chances that a breakdown would occur during off hours.

Beyond operational shifts and adding to the scope of the PM agreement, pricing was also reviewed, and three types of discounts commonly available with elevator maintenance companies were negotiated into the contract. In this case, the discounts were identified simply by asking the supplier what the customer could do in order to obtain better pricing. Maintenance service providers reduce fees for a contract term that is mutually beneficial. In this case, a 3 percent discount was achieved for an extended contract term, along with a 1 percent discount for prepayment and a 9 percent volume discount, based on the addition of elevators, which were previously covered by a separate provider, into the coverage of the contract.

Lastly, the labor rates that apply to overtime and callbacks should they happen were reduced based on market rates gathered through a request for information (RFI).

All in all, the company saved over $160,000 a year without transitioning to a new vendor, or even going to market with a full-blown RFP process. Instead, savings were obtained by identifying gaps in the current process, asking the incumbent supplier what was important to them, and identifying market rates for overtime through an RFI. The process also improved the relationship between the supplier and customer, because both benefited through the new program.

Case Study 2: Janitorial Services

As part of a company-wide effort to achieve cost savings, a corporation reviewed its in-office janitorial services spend within a particular region. The goal of the initiative was to standardize the scope of work and consolidate to one preferred supplier across all locations.

The company has over 100 office locations throughout three states, which were using multiple vendors, from local mom-and-pop shops to national service providers. Each office was responsible for employing a janitorial service at its own discretion, and subsequently there were a wide range of services being performed across the region. In other words, the process was very decentralized.

Upon review of the information at the individual office level, the company found that while many offices had unique requirements, most were receiving similar services on a consistent basis. In addition to the various scopes of work being performed, cost structures ranged from service only, to a blended rate for service and supplies, to service with supplies added as an additional charge. Some offices had formal written agreements and others did not; some had termination clauses and others did not.

Solution Phase One: Data Collection and Cleansing

In order to analyze the full scope of data, the company had to collect all contracts and survey each office for a better understanding of individual needs pertaining to the services and scopes of work at each office. Each office completed a short survey detailing the following:

- Level of service currently received
- Types of services performed
- Frequency of services
- Satisfaction rating on overall service (including identifying the tasks that the suppliers did well and the ones that they did not do well)
- Processes in place for performance measurement
- Included supplies, if any

This information was then compiled and compared to determine a baseline scope of work and service level at each office. Contracts were also collected and the information analyzed to determine the terms of each agreement, including pricing, terms, and conditions such as termination clauses, annual price increases, and, most importantly, the agreed-upon scope of work that would be performed for the price.

Solution Phase Two: Standardization

Once all of the various contracts and scopes of work were collected the company reviewed the range of services provided to determine which were universal and which were more unique to a particular office type. A standardized scope of work was developed that included universal tasks to be performed on a weekly, monthly, and annual basis. In addition to these standard tasks, an a la carte list was developed for services to be performed on an as-needed basis. One important step in analyzing the various services was to assess which services were required versus those services that were merely desired. Required services are more likely to be included in the typical task list, while desired services, such as carpet shampooing, may be more suited for the a la carte list to be provided per request. Including one-off tasks in the weekly service rate would raise costs unnecessarily. Finally, the company assigned a frequency of service (one time per week, three times per week, or five times per week) to each location.

Solution Phase Three: Sourcing for Savings

Once a standard scope of work was developed the company went to bid. Working with the supply base, the sourcing lead chose 5 locations (out of more than 100) that most closely represented the average office size and scope. Suppliers toured these facilities, which negated the need to visit all 100 locations, and gave suppliers a comfort level that the initiative was a serious one.

Janitorial service providers generally construct their base costs using the frequency of services, cleaning space square footage, and scope of work. Using the various baseline details per office, the company was able to establish a standard pricing schedule that could be applied across the board. Another advantage to sourcing over 100 locations together was the ability to leverage the total spend. Pricing and scorecards were evaluated and a vendor was selected that could meet the needs of over 95 percent of the facilities.

Final Solution Phase: Implementation

When implementing a new service solution across multiple locations, commitment from the supplier and from the end user's management team is vital. To accomplish this, the team leading the sourcing effort worked closely with the individual offices to confirm and assist in giving notice to current suppliers, coordinating supplier meetings to review the individual offices, and ensure that the new supplier started service when specified. The company was committed to aligning the corporate goal of cost savings and standardization on a divisional level and worked closely with the end users to highlight this objective. Vendor support on a regional basis was also pertinent to a successful transition.

Challenges that were faced included ensuring that most of the required tasks were included in the standardized scope of work. End user resistance was also a challenge as some of the offices had been using the same vendors for long periods of time and had developed positive relations with them. Disrupting this relationship in any sourcing initiative proves to be challenging.

In the end the company was able to achieve an annual savings of approximately 30 percent through negotiations with the supplier base, while standardizing the scope of services and consolidating the supplier to a single source, and savings were implemented quickly in a decentralized environment by developing and following a thorough implementation plan and enlisting high-level corporate sponsorship to support and mandate the initiative.

Case Study 3: Advertising

A company's primary objective is to generate revenue, and one of the largest spend areas that directly impacts a company's revenue stream is advertising. An advertiser's goals are to retain current customers, attract new ones, and spur organizational growth. These goals are not easily achievable. A comprehensive marketing plan must first be developed to provide direction in launching an advertising campaign. This plan takes into account multiple aspects including but definitely not limited to:

- Annual revenues
- Target audience and demographics
- Line of business (industry)
- Number of years in business and industry
- Competitive landscape
- Internal personnel and in-house capabilities

The main challenges for marketing managers are figuring out how much money to allocate to the advertising budget and whom to engage to assist in managing and spending that budget. A wide variety of services are carried out to launch an advertising campaign. Typically, a creative team is responsible for the creation of advertisements and a campaign's message. A production and design team is also assembled to bring the campaign to life through filming, recordings, and photographs. Media buying and planning is another service that is often considered the most important component of the advertising process. Campaigns can be developed and the actual advertisement may be flawless; however, if you are unable to place your ad in front of the target audience, the campaign can fall flat. Media placements vary, from television and radio broadcast buys on both the national and local levels, to bus shelter ads at a popular bus stop corner. Other media outlets besides television, radio stations, and outdoor ads include newspapers, magazines, and the most complex, the Internet. Account management is another portion of an advertiser's budget that covers miscellaneous services.

A particular customer was utilizing a full-service advertising firm that delivered a wide range of services and specialized in the customer's industry. These services, of course, translated into a variety of service and commission fees incurred by the customer, which included:

- An account management service fee billed monthly for miscellaneous, day-to-day activities performed. This fee was incurred for time spent on preparing reports, attending client meetings, monitoring the competitive landscape, and so on.
- Service fees billed for ad hoc jobs in which the firm's team members tracked their hours and an hourly rate was applied. Each job required a strategic planning aspect along with creative direction, production, media planning and placement, research, and other services.
- A markup applied to production services and materials. For example, the agency used outside resources to shoot and edit a television commercial.

- Commission fees for the firm's efforts related to the planning, placement, and continuous monitoring of the customer's media buy schedule. A commission rate based on the media's gross costs was billed.
- Travel and out-of-pocket expenses. The firm passed through certain expenses with no markup. These charges were associated with travel accommodations, shipping charges, messenger services, and so on.

The services provided by the agency of record could be delivered by a number of other parties present in the marketplace, from generalists, such as the company's existing agency, to specialists, such as media-buying firms. The customer analyzed each of these buckets of spend and found that the majority of costs were in the placement of actual media buys—TV ads, radio ads, and so on. Media-buying firms that specialize in the optimization of media schedules and have strong relationships with media outlets were engaged to better understand the advantages they offer. In the discussions with the media buyers, the customer found that unbundling, a popular industry term for breaking out the media-buying function from the creative, is a trend that has existed for quite some time. Some advantages of this sourcing strategy are:

- More accountability
- Additional tools that allow for better research capabilities
- Greater leverage
  - Media-buying firms have a wide range of clients and are able to leverage volume across all clients with national and local station representatives.
  - More volume allows delivery of more value-adds.
- Lower commission fees
- Greater exposure
- Advanced reporting features

The media buyer engaged by the customer audited existing cost structures and found better rates were available and credits were due. The company interviewed several companies that were references provided by media buyers. They described, based on real-world experience, how their media buyers worked with their creative agencies to produce the optimal results. Based on these discussions, the customer determined that the incumbent firm could still carry out all other functions, but would be expected to collaborate with the selected media buying firm to deliver a successful advertising campaign.

Marketing managers and other individuals tied to this spend category are often reluctant to examine other opportunities and consider the possibility of disrupting current relationships with vendors that deliver highly valuable services. However, although a customer's media buy schedule has several factors rolled into it, generally speaking, it is a commodity, and particular firms with volume behind them get access to the best rates.

In this case, the customer decided to unbundle services, utilizing the creative agency in the areas in which it was strongest and a media buyer to place ads using its leveraged buying power in the marketplace. When selecting a media-buying firm and separating the media-buying portion of a budget from the creative, communication among all parties is essential. There are ongoing debates as to whether or not advertising services should be separated out to more specialty firms. The risks involved in doing so are typically outweighed by the benefits that a company can realize.

 ## IN SUMMARY

Conducting projects to source services requires the same basic resources and knowledge as sourcing any other areas of spend. The difference lies mainly in how well you understand the scope of work, the goal of the service, the total cost impact, and the value of the supplier. While you will encounter end users with their own objectives (and objections) in almost every area of spend, the level to which they are involved changes depending on the level of human interaction. For example, when dealing with office supply vendors, the end user is buying pens and pencils and working with the sales representative on a weekly or perhaps monthly basis. When sourcing something like janitorial services, the end users connect with the people in the process on a daily or weekly basis and at a different, more personal level. With each service you source, you will find a different level of interaction between the suppliers and end users, some much more involved than others.

When managing intangibles such as services, you need to stay connected with the needs of the end users while maintaining the company's perspective on generating cost savings and maintaining quality service levels. A well-defined scope of work is a vital tool for doing so. The end users and suppliers need to develop a clear understanding of the work that is being completed or should be completed. This allows everyone involved to track any errors, accuracies, and changes.

A precise scope of work also helps streamline operations across multiple locations within your organization. A streamlined approach to operations allows for better controls, which help you to overcome any disputes with end users. All in all, as in any area of sourcing, you will benefit by remaining focused on cost reduction, service level improvements, and refined supply chain management.

About the Authors

 JOE PAYNE, DIRECTOR OF STRATEGIC SOURCING

As Director of Strategic Sourcing for Source One Management Services, Joe works with midmarket and Fortune 1000 companies to reduce procurement costs utilizing a set of strategic sourcing processes that he has perfected over time. Joe manages and leads a team of consultants, including project managers and analysts, who oversee projects from start to finish, including auditing spend; researching process changes; interviewing suppliers; planning, executing, and finalizing negotiation of new contracts; implementing changes; and monitoring new client/supplier relationships. Joe is personally responsible for delivering over a hundred million dollars' worth of hard-dollar savings to Source One's clients.

During his career with Source One, Joe has developed insight into the challenges that organizations face when undertaking initiatives to reduce costs in the area of indirect spend. While reviewing the consulting market and existing printed publications, he identified a gap in this critical component of business and created the idea for this book.

Joe is a long-standing contributor to the Strategic Sourceror blog and leads discussion groups and brainstorming sessions at various training seminars and networking events. Prior to joining Source One, Joe worked as an analyst for Accenture.

Joe holds a Bachelor of Science degree in operations and information management from the University of Scranton.

WILLIAM R. DORN JR., DIRECTOR OF OPERATIONS

As Director of Operations for Source One Management Services, William manages the organization's daily activities, including the human resources, information technology, Web development, research and development, marketing, and finance departments. Additionally, he leads the sourcing initiatives of highly technical spend categories.

William created and manages the development of www.WhyAbe.com, the world's only free electronic-sourcing tools website. He also is the developer, administrator, and frequent contributor to the Strategic Sourceror blog. William is also a guest speaker and presenter at various international trade events and conferences.

William joined Source One in 2003 as director of management information services before moving into the more encompassing role of director of operations. Immediately prior to joining Source One, William spent a year consulting with a start-up firm, Fortera, in which his primary roles were to assist the United States Department of Defense in developing best practices in the acquisition of commercial-off-the-shelf (COTS) software, and also acted as project manager for the American Institute of Certified Public Accountants' (AICPA) transition of paper-based CPA exams to electronically administered exams. William started his career as a draftsperson, designing industrial compressor components for Compressor Products International (formerly a Division of Goodrich and then EnPro Industries). His career evolved over the course of almost a decade through various positions including mechanical engineer, manufacturing supervisor, quality assurance manager and, ultimately, as process engineer supporting multiple locations on a corporate level. As a process engineer, William specialized in the implementation of manufacturing ERP systems and utilized his Six Sigma background to define and implement cost reduction programs in all aspects of business, from order entry to manufacturing to product shipment.

William holds a Bachelor of Science degree in information technology and an Associate of Arts degree in electronics and engineering, and is a certified Six Sigma Black Belt.

About the Contributors

 ## DAVID PASTORE

As a project manager at Source One Management Services, David leverages his experience in the marketplace to help his clients stay at the forefront of technological evolution, maintain clean and optimized networks, and negotiate contracts that save the client money while maximizing their agility in today's dynamic business environment. David consults with clients in a variety of industries to identify their unique requirements and develop a strategic plan. Supported by his team of analysts, his projects are undertaken with a holistic perspective of the client's infrastructure and plan, and are designed to ensure the client reaches its financial and operational objectives.

Prior to joining Source One, David worked as an analyst for Paragon Computer Professionals. He holds a Bachelor of Science degree in management information systems from Lock Haven University of Pennsylvania

 ## KATHLEEN DALY

As a senior project analyst for Source One Management Services, Kathleen works closely with internal resources to execute sourcing strategies and identify process improvements and cost reduction opportunities in various spend categories. Kathleen's main responsibilities are the development and implementation of best-in-class agreements for Source One clients through extensive research, detailed spend analysis, supplier negotiations, and change management. Her sourcing efforts have delivered savings in several categories, particularly marketing services, office supplies, and facilities management services.

Kathleen holds a Bachelor of Science degree in marketing with a concentration in management from the University of Scranton. Kathleen also contributes to the Strategic Sourceror blog where she connects her sourcing experiences with current events.

JENNIFER ULRICH

As an analyst at Source One Management Services, Jennifer collaborates with internal resources, suppliers, and customers to streamline operations, reduce costs, and create value. Jennifer has delivered significant hard-dollar savings in multiple categories including janitorial services, office supplies, courier services and MRO. Jennifer dedicates her time to nurturing supplier and end-user relationships, working on strategic sourcing projects, and ensuring the success of those projects through the proper implementation processes.

Jennifer is a regular contributor to the Strategic Sourceror blog and has a Bachelor of Science degree in marketing and a Master of Business Administration from the University of Phoenix.

SCOTT DECKER

Scott Decker is a senior project analyst at Source One Management Services specializing in facilities, services, and capital spend strategic sourcing. Prior to joining Source One, Scott was with Hilton and Pyramid Hotels as a buyer, as well as purchasing director for the prestigious New York Athletic Club. Scott brings expertise in sourcing through his experience managing capital renovation projects and sourcing a wide range of facility operational services. Scott holds a Bachelor of Science degree in hotel, restaurant, and institutional management from Pennsylvania State University.

Index